A HISTORY OF JEWISH LITERATURE
VOLUME III

A VOLUME IN THE
CWRU PRESS TRANSLATIONS

Israel Zinberg's *History of Jewish Literature*

Vol. I	*Part One:*	The Arabic-Spanish Period
Vol. II	*Part Two:*	French and German Jewry in the Early Middle Ages
	Part Three:	The Jewish Community of Medieval Italy
Vol. III	*Part Four:*	The Struggle of Mysticism and Tradition Against Philosophical Rationalism
Vol. IV	*Part Five:*	Italian Jewry in the Renaissance Era
Vol. V	*Part Six:*	The Jewish Center of Culture in the Ottoman Empire
Vol. VI	*Part Seven:*	The German-Polish Cultural Center
Vol. VII	*Part Eight:*	Old Yiddish Literature from Its Origins to the Haskalah Period
Vol. VIII	*Part Nine:*	The Berlin Haskalah
Vol. IX	*Part Ten:*	Hasidism and Enlightenment (1780–1820)
Vol. X	*Part Eleven:*	The Science of Judaism and Galician Haskalah
Vol. XI	*Part Twelve:*	The Haskalah Movement in Russia
Vol. XII	*Part Thirteen:*	Haskalah at Its Zenith (published posthumously, 1966)

An Analytic Index to the *History of Jewish Literature* will appear in Volume XII.

Israel Zinberg

A HISTORY OF
JEWISH
LITERATURE

TRANSLATED AND EDITED BY BERNARD MARTIN

*The Struggle of Mysticism and Tradition
Against Philosophical Rationalism*

THE PRESS OF
CASE WESTERN RESERVE UNIVERSITY
CLEVELAND & LONDON
1973

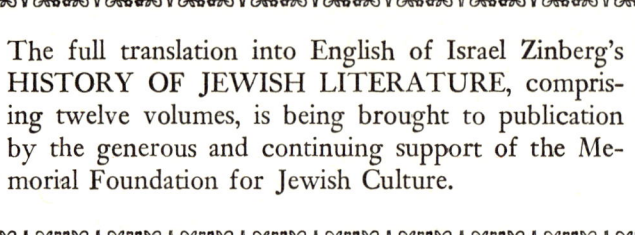

The full translation into English of Israel Zinberg's HISTORY OF JEWISH LITERATURE, comprising twelve volumes, is being brought to publication by the generous and continuing support of the Memorial Foundation for Jewish Culture.

Copyright © 1973 by the Press of Case Western Reserve University.
All rights reserved.
Printed in the United States of America.

Library of Congress Cataloging in Publication Data

Zinberg, Israel, 1873–1938.
   A history of Jewish literature.
   Translation of Di geshikhte fun der literatur bay Yidn.
   Includes bibliographical references.
   CONTENTS: v. 1. The Arabic-Spanish period.—v. 2. French and German Jewry in the early Middle Ages. The Jewish community of medieval Italy.—v. 3. The struggle of mysticism and tradition against philosophical rationalism.
   1. Jewish literature—History and criticism. I. Title.
PJ5008.Z5313   809'.889'24   72-183310
ISBN 0-8295-0241-6 (v. 3)

Contents

A Note on Israel Zinberg / xi

Acknowledgments / xiii

Transliteration of Hebrew Terms / xv

Abbreviations / xvii

PART IV: THE STRUGGLE OF MYSTICISM AND TRADITION AGAINST PHILOSOPHICAL RATIONALISM

BOOK ONE

Chapter One: THE MYSTICS OF PROVENCE / 3

Two views of the world—The rationalist God concept and religious enthusiasm—Peacemakers and compromisers—Shemtov ben Joseph Falaquera and his *Iggeret Ha-Vikkuah*—His didactic narrative *Ha-Mevakkesh*—The unsatisfied "seekers"—Isaac Ibn Latif—The ways leading to mysticism—The source of the mystical tendencies—The doctrine of "emanations" and *sefirot*—The "fathers" of the Kabbalah in Provence—Isaac the Blind and the Midrash *Ha-Bahir*—Azriel and his *Perush Eser Sefirot*—The incomprehensible *Ayin* and its emanations—The Kabbalist Isaac ben Jacob Ha-Kohen and his *Maamar Al Ha-Atzilut Ha-Semolit*—The "left *sefirot*" and the ten classes of warfare and wickedness—The protest against rationalism—Jacob bar Sheshet's *Shaar Ha-Shamayim*

Chapter Two: NAHMANIDES AND HIS FOLLOWERS / 21

The Kabbalist school of Gerona—Nahmanides as Talmudist—Nahmanides and Maimonides—Nahmanides' optimism; the world as miracle—Nahmanides as religious poet, Kabbalist, and Bible exegete—Nahmanides' disputation with Pablo Christiani and his move to Palestine—Abraham Abulafia as a person and as a "seeker"—The "mystery of the letters"—The substitution of the name for the thing—The confusion of *being* and *thinking*—Abulafia's dreams concerning the advent of the Messiah—His disciples—Joseph Gikatilla—Abulafia's propaganda in Rome—His "prophetic" books and their style—Ink and blood—The mystic against the rabbis—The "revelation" of the *Zohar*

Chapter Three: THE ZOHAR / 41

Moses de Leon and the *Zohar*—The various elements of the *Zohar*—The *Zohar* and Jewish mysticism—The doctrine of the *Ein Sof*—The ten *sefirot* and the "contraction" of the *Ein Sof*—Androgyny in Jewish mysticism—The unity of thinking and being—The ethical element in the Kabbalah—The role of the person in the *Zohar*—The concept of the "high man" (*Adam Ilaah*)—The correspondence between the upper and lower worlds—"The *tzaddik* is the foundation of the world"—The mysteries hidden in the prayers—The doctrine of the soul—The creatures and their prototypes—The Temple of Love

Chapter Four: THE RENEWAL OF THE STRUGGLE AGAINST RATIONALISM / 55

The *Zohar* on the rabbis and philosophers—Platonism and Aristotelianism—The distinction between allegories and symbols—The antagonism of the Kabbalists toward Aristotelian rationalism—The beginning of the struggle—Solomon Petit—The Jewish court aristocracy as champions of rationalism—The "philosophizing" preachers—Levi ben Abraham of Villefranche and his astrological views—The "decree" of heaven as pretext for apostasy—The appearance of Abba Mari of Montpellier; his letter to Rabbi Solomon ben Adret—Rabbi Solomon ben Adret's attitude toward philosophy—Abba Mari's *Minhat Kenaot*—Rabbi Solomon ben Adret and Levi of Villefranche—The ban of the rabbis of Barcelona—Jacob ben Machir and the followers of the Tibbons—The bitter struggle

Chapter Five: RABBI MEIR OF ROTHENBURG, RABBI ASHER BEN YEHIEL, AND RABBI SOLOMON BEN ADRET / 79

The tragic situation of the Jews in Germany—The Rindfleisch massacres—Rabbi Meir of Rothenburg as Talmudist and religious

Contents

poet—Rabbi Isaac ben Moses and his *Or Zarua*—Rabbi Asher ben Yeḥiel—His "Testament"—His flight to Provence—Rabbi Asher ben Yeḥiel and Rabbi Solomon ben Adret—The ban of Rabbi Solomon ben Adret—The rationalists and their *Aderabah*—The struggle centered around Maimonides—The champions of freedom of thought—Menaḥem Meiri as a man and as a scholar—Yedaiah Ha-Penini and his *Ketav Ha-Hitnatzlut*—The bitter end—The Provençal communities in exile—Joseph ben Solomon Ibn Yaḥya and his elegy—Yedaiah Ha-Penini as poet; his *Beḥinat Olam*

Chapter Six: ISAAC ALBALAG AND THE DOCTRINE OF THE "DOUBLE TRUTH" / 99

Isaac Albalag and his *Tikkun Deot Ha-Pilosofim*—Albalag as a thinker—Albalag's views on the creation of the world and the divine will—The "natural order" and the "Torah order"—Belief and persuasion—The idea of the "double truth" in Christian theology and in Albalag—Albalag as a personality

Chapter Seven: ISAAC IBN PULGAR AND JOSEPH IBN KASPI / 109

The apostate Abner of Burgos and his essay denying free will—Ibn Pulgar and his *Ezer Ha-Dat*—On five types of opponents—Two "classes" among the Jews—Joseph Ibn Kaspi and his attitude toward Maimonides—His *Sefer Ha-Sod* and the polemic against it—Ibn Kaspi as "truth-seeker," litterateur, and Bible exegete—His "Testament"

Chapter Eight: MOSES NARBONI AND GERSONIDES / 125

Perpignan as a center of free thought—Moses Narboni as a freethinker—His commentary to Maimonides' *Guide for the Perplexed*—Gersonides the encyclopedic scholar—Gersonides as an Aristotelian—Differences of opinion between Gersonides and Aristotle—Gersonides' views on immortality—Gersonides as rationalist and as Bible exegete

BOOK TWO: 1348–1492

Chapter One: THE CULTURAL DECLINE OF SPANISH AND PROVENÇAL JEWRY / 143

Maimonides' *Guide for the Perplexed* and Gersonides' *Milḥamot Adonai*—The terrors of the Black Plague—The rabbis and leaders of the era and their conservative tendencies—Rabbi Yom-tov Lipmann Mühlhausen and his *Sefer Ha-Nitzahon*—The cultural decline of Spanish and Provençal Jewry—Isaac Israeli, Immanuel Bonfils, Estori Parhi, and Shemtov Ibn Ardutial—Jacob ben Asher and his *Arbaah Turim*—Bahya ben Asher and the strengthening of mystical tendencies—The eclectics—David Ibn Bilia—Meir Aldabi and his *Shevilei Emunah*—Aldabi's battle against the "philosophizers"—The legend that Maimonides became an ardent Kabbalist

Chapter Two: THE CLERICAL REACTION IN SPAIN AND THE LITERATURE OF POLEMICS AGAINST CHRISTIANS / 165

The clerical reaction in Spain—Court Jews—The moral decline of the Jewish aristocracy—Solomon Alami's *Iggeret Ha-Musar*—Jew-hatred on the part of the Christian populace—The economic foundations of this hatred—The struggle for the crown of Spain and the consequent sufferings of the Jews—The persecutions of the Jews and anti-Jewish agitation—Polemic literature—The disputations of Moses de Tordesillas and Shemtov Ibn Shaprut—The agitation of the Catholic clergy—The massacre in Seville—The Marranos and the informer-apostates

Chapter Three: LAMPOONS IN RELIGIOUS DISPUTATIONS; JOSHUA LORKI AND PROFIAT DURAN / 179

Lampoons and tracts as weapons—Solomon Bonafed as poet and polemicist—Joshua Lorki and the apostate Paul of Burgos—Lorki's letter—The Marrano Profiat Duran and the drama of his life—Duran's *Al Tehi Ka-Avotecha* and *Kelimmat Ha-Goyyim*—The introduction to his *Maaseh Efod* and its cultural-historical significance—Three tendencies among the Jewish intelligentsia of the era

Chapter Four: HASDAI CRESCAS AND HIS ERA / 195

The intensification of mystical tendencies after the massacre at Seville—The Kabbalist and miracle-worker Moses Botarel—Abraham of Granada and his *Berit Menuhah*—The battle against rationalist philosophy on three fronts—The rabbis Menahem Ibn Zerah and Isaac bar Sheshet—The mystic Shemtov ben Shemtov and his *Sefer Ha-Emunot*—Back from Maimonides to Jehudah

Halevi—Hasdai Crescas as scholar and polemicist—Crescas as a thinker; his way and his system—The boundaries between the realms of religion and philosophy—Criticism of Aristotle's system and of Greek philosophy—Crescas on Maimonides' thirteen principles—Crescas' views on the extent of the world and on God's attributes—Not knowledge but love is the fundamental quality of God's nature—Divine knowledge and human freedom—The purpose of "the work of creation"—Crescas' attitude toward the Kabbalah and rationalism—"Thou shalt love the Lord" as basic principle of action and creation—The creation of the world as necessity—The infinity of the universe

Chapter Five: SIMEON DURAN AND JOSEPH ALBO / 227

The significance of Ḥasdai Crescas—The epigones—Philosophically educated theologians—Rabbi Simeon bar Tzemaḥ Duran and his work—Duran as dogmatist—His views on the advent of the Messiah—Duran as champion of Judaism—What is "heresy"?—Joseph Albo and his *Ikkarim*—The influence of his predecessors—The significance of Albo's work—The consolation offered by Albo

Chapter Six: PREACHERS AND DEFENDERS OF THE FAITH / 241

Persecutions by the Catholic Church—The Jewish preachers and apologists—Ḥayyim Ibn Musa's *Magen Va-Romaḥ*—Isaac Nathan's Bible concordance—Joseph ben Shemtov as preacher and polemicist—His philosophic work, *Kevod Elohim*—Joseph ben Shemtov as disciple of Ḥasdai Crescas—His attitude toward Aristotle and the question of immortality—His controversy with Maimonides and Gersonides—Only the Torah provides immortality—Laws of nature and religious laws—Joseph ben Shemtov against the "philosophizers"—The closed circle—Abraham Bibago's *Derech Emunah*—Ethical-philosophical preaching and Isaac Arama, its most eminent representative—Arama as preacher—His tract against the rationalists, *Ḥazut Kashah*—His struggle against the "plague of philosophy"

Chapter Seven: KABBALISTS AND SATIRISTS / 261

The anonymous Kabbalist—The *Sefer Ha-Kanah* and *Sefer Ha-Peliah* and their mystical style—The Kabbalah as highest authority—The "secrets of the Talmud"—The battle against the

Contents

pleasures of this world—Indignation at the rabbis—The struggle for a "long-lost thing"—The last appearance of the Maimunists—Shemtov ben Joseph as compromiser between the "two lights"—The satire *Alilot Devarim*—The rationalist author—The literary value of *Alilot Devarim*—The last Jewish poet in Andalusia, Saadiah Ibn Danan—Ibn Danan as author of love poems—Ibn Danan as Maimunist and polemicist

Chapter Eight: DON ISAAC ABRAVANEL / 281

The great expulsion—The sufferings of the exiles—Echoes of the catastrophe in Hebrew literature—The apostates among the intelligentsia and the court Jews—Joseph Yaabetz and his *Or Ha-Hayyim*—Isaac Abravanel—Abravanel as Bible exegete and harbinger of the coming "redemption"—Conclusion

Bibliographical Notes / 291

Glossary of Hebrew Terms / 307

Index / 313

A Note on Israel Zinberg

DR. ISRAEL ZINBERG is widely regarded as one of the foremost historians of Jewish literature. Born in Russia in 1873 and educated at various universities in Germany and Switzerland, he devoted more than twenty years to the writing, in Yiddish, of his monumental *Die Geshichte fun der Literatur bei Yidn* (History of Jewish Literature). This work, published in eight volumes in Vilna, 1929–1937, is a comprehensive and authoritative study of Jewish literary creativity in Europe from its beginnings in tenth-century Spain to the end of the Haskalah period in nineteenth-century Russia. Based on a meticulous study of all the relevant primary source material and provided with full documentation, Zinberg's history is a notable exemplar of the tradition of modern Jewish scholarship known as *die Wissenschaft des Judentums* (the Science of Judaism).

In addition to his *magnum opus*, Zinberg, who earned his living as a chemical engineer, wrote numerous other valuable monographs and articles on Jewish history and literature in Russian, Hebrew, and Yiddish. In 1938, during the Stalinist purges, he was arrested by the Soviet police and sentenced to exile in Siberia. He died in a concentration camp hospital in Vladivostok in that same year.

The reader who wishes a fuller introduction is invited to consult the Translator's Introduction to Volume I of Zinberg's *History of Jewish Literature*.

Acknowledgments

The generous support of the Memorial Foundation for Jewish Culture, New York City, and of Mr. Leonard Ratner and the Ratner Family, Cleveland, is gratefully acknowledged by publisher and translator alike. Without this generosity it would not have been possible for Israel Zinberg's monumental work to reach the new audience that it is hoped a translation into English will afford. The editor and translator wishes to express his appreciation to his friend Dr. Arthur J. Lelyveld, Rabbi of the Fairmount Temple of Cleveland and President (1966–1972) of the American Jewish Congress, for his aid in securing a grant from the Memorial Foundation for Jewish Culture for the publication of this work. He also desires to acknowledge his gratitude to the staff of the Press of Case Western Reserve University for their kind helpfulness at every stage in the publication of this work.

Transliteration of Hebrew Terms

א is not transliterated	ו = v (where not a vowel)	ל = l	פ = f
		מ = m	צ = tz
ב = b	ז = z	נ = n	ק = k
ב = v	ח = ḥ	ס = s	ר = r
ג ,ג = g	ט = t	ע is not transliterated	שׁ = sh
ד ,ד = d	י = y		שׂ = s
ה = h	כ = k	פ = p	ת ,ת = t
	כ = ch		

ָ = a ֱ = e
ַ = a ִ = i
ֹ ,וֹ = o ֵ = ei
ֻ ,וּ = u ֶ = e
short ָ = o ׂ = o
יֵ = ei ֲ = a

vocal *sheva* = e

silent *sheva* is not transliterated

Abbreviations

JQR	*Jewish Quarterly Review*
JQR, n.s.	*Jewish Quarterly Review*, new series
MGWJ	*Monatsschrift für die Geschichte und Wissenschaft des Judentums*
PAAJR	*Proceedings of the American Academy for Jewish Research*
REJ	*Revue des Études Juives*
ZHB	*Zeitschrift für hebräische Bibliographie*

BOOK ONE

CHAPTER ONE

The Mystics of Provence

THE controversy between the disciples of Maimonides and their adversaries that erupted in Provence in 1232 was stilled at the end of the decade. The pyres on which not only Maimonides' *Sefer Ha-Madda* and *Guide for the Perplexed* but entire cartloads of tractates of the Talmud were burned appalled both sides. The controversy, however, did not end with a definitive peace but merely with a temporary armistice that could change at any moment into a new and bitter struggle. Nor was this possibility something dependent on anyone's malevolence; no deliberate "stirrers of conflict" were at work here. The potentiality for renewed conflict was inherent in objective factors, in the profound contradiction between the two ideologies which dominated Jewish intellectual circles of the age.

Maimonides, with his lucid and keen intellect, believed it possible to bring the elemental chaos of human feelings, conceptions, and impressions under the control of strict, firmly established principles. He attempted to categorize the living, ongoing processes of human consciousness in schematic, logical laws and generalizations. Being the great systematizer and seeker of the plain meaning that he was, he wished to derive from the complex and variegated texture of life the simple essence, the clear, commonsense principle. But in the then rudimentary state of such branches of knowledge as general cultural history, psychology, and the investigation of man's conscious and unconscious feelings and perceptions, this one-sided rationalism was, in fact, incapable of illuminating the chaos of human instincts, passions, purposes, and expressions of will. "Common sense," the critical thinking which sought to explain everything and govern everything, was, given the condition of the natural sciences at that time, actually able to illuminate only a very small segment of man's emotions and actions. The obscure depths of man's soul, of the unconscious, ongoing life process, remained sealed to it. Philosophical rationalism, however, refused to recognize this. Common sense, according to the rationalist view, is the sole commander and ruler. It can and must understand everything, for everything is under its dominion, and what the mind does not grasp simply does not exist. It is not surprising that Maimonides' rationalist concept of God could not satisfy men of passionate feeling for whom faith was a requirement of the heart, not a problem of the intellect. To these deeply religious natures, with their rich and varied inner experiences, the intellectualist theories of Maimonides' philosophic-religious system, with their logical demonstration of the utility of the various commandments of the Torah, were far too cold and arid.

To be sure, various attempts were made at that time to effect a compromise between these antithetical tendencies. But these compromises could not succeed, for they were incapable of providing what was most required—an organically integral world view that would unite thought and feeling and satisfy the demands both of the inquiring mind and the longing heart. Especially interesting in this respect is the literary activity of Shemtov ben Joseph Falaquera (born c. 1225, died after 1290), one of the most learned writers of the thirteenth century. A man of encyclopedic knowledge, thoroughly familiar with Greek-Arabic philosophy, Falaquera composed a series of works[1] on philosophy and psychology, wrote a commentary to Maimonides' *Guide for the Perplexed*,[2] and rendered into Hebrew the substance of Solomon Ibn Gabirol's philosophical work *Mekor Hayyim*. An ardent admirer of the two

---

1. The list of the works that he wrote up to the time he was in his forties is given at the beginning of his *Ha-Mevakkesh*.
2. This commentary is entitled *Moreh Ha-Moreh* and was published by Biseliches in 1837. Falaquera here provides an excellent, genuinely scientific, translation of many difficult passages in Maimonides' *Guide* which, in his view, Samuel Ibn Tibbon had not rendered correctly. At the end of his book (pp. 148–58) Falaquera offers some very significant philological remarks on Ibn Tibbon's philosophical terminology.

great rationalists, Maimonides and Averroes,[3] Falaquera while still in his youth wrote his *Iggeret Ha-Vikkuaḥ*,[4] in which an adherent of rationalist philosophy (*ḥochmah*) carries on a debate with a *ḥasid* or pietist. The work endeavors to show that philosophy and Torah are twin sisters who can and must live together in concord and peace.

The author, however, was too keen-sighted to fail finally to recognize that one cannot resolve sharp contradictions and effect a reconciliation or compromise between radically divergent world views through apologetic disputations. He properly appreciated the dissatisfaction that many of his contemporaries painfully experienced, their restless drive to seek the right way of life leading to the hidden truth. This problem is clearly reflected in Falaquera's didactic narrative *Ha-Mevakkesh*, which he completed in the fall of 1263. In form this work belongs to those unique literary products, beloved by the Arabs, of which it is difficult to decide whether they are philosophical or belletristic. A classic example of the genre is provided by the Arabic thinker Abu Bakr Ibn Tufail[5] in his masterly philosophical novel *Ḥai Ibn Yaktan*, which was translated into numerous European languages. The hero of this work is a unique kind of Robinson Crusoe. When still an infant, he is cast away on a lonely island, is there brought up by a gazelle, and all alone, by virtue of his indefatigable drive for truth, attains the highest levels of knowledge of the world and God. When, in his old age, he becomes familiar with men and their petty claims and notions, he concludes that only in solitude, in withdrawal from the ordinary world, in constant striving toward the heights, and in searching for the eternal and non-ephemeral, lies man's supreme goal. Ibn Tufail's novel was extremely popular among the Jews of Spain. At the end of the thirteenth century it was translated into Hebrew (*Iggeret Ḥai Ben Mekitz*), and Moses Narboni wrote a commentary on it. There is no doubt that the versatile and cultured Falaquera was quite familiar with this Arabic work, the influence of which is discernible in the literary form of his *Ha-Mevakkesh*.

---

3. On Falaquera's attitude toward Averroes see the introduction to his *Moreh Ha-Moreh*. When Solomon Petit began his battle against Maimonides, Falaquera wrote an open letter in which he appears as an ardent adherent of the latter's philosophy; the letter is published in *Minḥat Kenaot* (Pressburg, 1838), as well as in *Iggerot Kenaot*.
4. First published in Constantinople (1570), and later in Prague (1610). We have employed Jellinek's edition of 1875.
5. Born in Cadiz, Andalusia, in 1100, died in Morocco in 1185.

"Before everything else, acquire wisdom! Reason is the essence of man; nothing beside it has any value whatever." With this our author begins his credo. He relates how, in his youth, he devoted much attention to poetry and wrote numerous songs. When he grew older, however, he became convinced that poetry is merely an idle pastime. "I divorced the goddess of song and fell in love with wisdom; to the daughter of knowledge I betrothed myself forever." The largest part of *Ha-Mevakkesh* itself is, nevertheless, written in poetic *makama* style. To be sure, the poems woven into the rhymed prose bear witness that their author did indeed "divorce" the goddess of song—but it may also be doubted that he was ever connected with her.

The hero of the narrative is the eternal "seeker"[6] who wishes to explore the various ways in which men look for true happiness and the ultimate degree of perfection. Which way is the best, the *right* way? The "seeker" goes first to the man of wealth, who perceives the foundation of man's happiness and power in gold. Unsatisfied, he proceeds further and comes to the proud possessor of physical strength, who sees the essence of life in might and struggle. "Know," says the strong man,

that the whole world is based only on struggle. In the weak and fearful resides a base soul. The beauty and grandeur of man's spirit disclose themselves in courageous battle alone. Only that which strives toward victory really exists and lives; the weak and lowly must go under. Triumph—in this is life, and in humility and lowliness, death. And since every creature strives for life, it does not wish to beg but to obtain everything through struggle.[7]

From the strong man the "seeker" turns to the great artist, from him to the famous physician, from the physician to the simple *ḥasid*, or pious man, who wishes to know nothing of wisdom but only of moral virtues. Then he goes to the philologist, and from him to the poet.[8] With each of these he spends months and years and still remains discontented. "He became convinced," the author notes, "that these ways do not lead to genuine happiness. They are merely fore-stages which can only bring one to the road of supreme happiness—which is knowledge."[9]

6. On the affinity between Falaquera's "seeker" and a narrative of Al-Ghazali's, see *Hebräische Bibliographie*, X, 86.
7. *Ha-Mevakkesh*, p. 26 (Amsterdam edition, 1772).
8. The views which the author expresses on the significance and value of poetry (*Ha-Mevakkesh*, pp. 56–62) have a definite historical interest.
9. *Ibid.*, p. 64.

The Didactic Narrative Ha-Mevakkesh

And our hero sets out to wander further. He comes to the pious believer who gives him to understand that "one should not enter into speculative investigations or rely on human reason but on the sacred Torah, in which there are divine mysteries that reason cannot attain."[10] The hero, in whose person the author himself speaks, responds to the orthodox believer angrily and contemptuously: "Foolishness has clogged your heart, deafened your ears, and blinded your eyes."[11]

From the believer the "seeker" goes to the scholar, the keen Talmudist who is also proficient in the natural sciences. An admirer of the *Guide for the Perplexed*, the scholar declares in the spirit of Maimonides that it is not worthwhile to waste one's time on dialectic and disputation and that, to acquaint oneself with the Oral Law, "it is sufficient at present" to study Alfasi, Maimonides' *Mishneh Torah*, and his commentary on the Mishnah.[12] "Do not like many others, who sit entire nights over one point of law, and when one asks them about it in the morning, babble and know not what to answer." Thoroughly to understand the Torah, the scholar insists, one must become familiar with all the other sciences. The "seeker" follows the scholar's advice. The succeeding thirty pages (72–102), which describe how our hero becomes acquainted with specialists in the various scientific disciplines, have a certain cultural-historical interest. We find here, in a clear form, a general overview of the state of all the major sciences of that age.[13]

10. *Ibid.*, p. 66.
11. *Ibid.*, p. 70.
12. *Ibid.*, p. 72.
13. Another scholar of the thirteenth century, Joseph Ibn Aknin of Barcelona (not to be confused with Maimonides' favorite pupil of the same name), the author of a work on measures and weights in the Bible and Talmud, gives in the twenty-seventh chapter of his Arabic work *Tab al-Nufus* (The Medicine of the Soul) a complete program of the education prevalent in that era. He divides the sciences in precisely the same way as Falaquera. Ibn Aknin lists the following disciplines: logic, mathematics, geometry, optics, astronomy, physics, mineralogy, botany, zoology, psychology, and metaphysics. This chapter is reprinted in M. Güdemann's *Das jüdische Unterrichtswesen während des spanisch-arabischen Periode* (Vienna, 1873), pp. 140–43. A greatly abbreviated version, translated into Hebrew by S. Eppenstein, is found in *Sefer Ha-Yovel Le-Naḥum Sokolow* (Warsaw, 1904). A list of the sciences of that time is also provided by a contemporary of Falaquera's, Isaac Ibn Sahulah, the author of *Meshal Ha-Kadmoni* (first edition, p. 9), and by Abraham Ibn Ezra in his *Yesod Mora* (pp. 11, 16), as well as in his Commentary to the Pentateuch (Exodus, Chapters 3, 31). All of them group the sciences according to the order which the Arabic philosophers, especially Al-Farabi, introduced.

The "seeker," we are told, undertakes a diligent study of the various sciences with the foremost scholars, but finally reaches the conviction that all these "merely wander around the king's palace, but none has penetrated into it and seen the king himself."[14] Then he decides to turn to the man of greatest perfection who fathoms with his acute mind the most hidden depths, to him "who is called in Greek 'philosopher.'" Here, however, the author abruptly breaks off his narrative. He simply mentions incidentally that the "seeker" spends three whole years with the philosopher. But it remains unclear whether our hero finally discovers what he had so tirelessly sought or whether he is still wandering over the world looking for the truth of life.

The attentive reader must acknowledge that a cold, dry wind blows through Falaquera's narrative. But the learned author is not to blame for this. The fault lies rather in the whole system and world of ideas in which this disciple of Maimonides lived and for which he fought. It is quite understandable that in the rationalist atmosphere, where everything appeared so plain and clear, everything was weighed in the scales of logic, and in regard to everything its rational purpose and practical utility were sought, the number of unsatisfied "seekers" with longing souls, who looked for a solution to the tangled and insoluble enigmas of life, had to increase. And it was not among the rationalist philosophers of Falaquera's school that they could find what they sought.

Extremely interesting in this respect is Falaquera's contemporary, Isaac ben Abraham Ibn Latif (c. 1228–c. 1290), a man of broad philosophical learning with a noble, sensitive spirit. In moving and tender words, he tells of his own life-drama[15]—how he knocked on all doors, wandered over all paths, searched everywhere for the pure truth, sought after God's living word. He relates how he came to the philosophers and found smug, self-satisfied men, proudly certain that they possessed the truth, that all their theories and ideas were based on firm foundations. I became convinced, declares Ibn Latif, that they live in error. Their entire structure hangs in thin air. They think that the truth is with them and that their thought has attained the way to eternal light, but they grope in darkness like blind men. "Hidden from them is the living source; they still wander outside and cannot find the entrance into the sanctuary. . . ."[16]

14. *Ha-Mevakkesh*, p. 102.
15. In *Tzurat Ha-Olam*, Chapter 5; also at the beginning of his *Iggeret Ha-Teshuvah*.
16. *Tzurat Ha-Olam*, p. 9.

Ibn Latif could not accept Maimonides' view that everything Aristotle taught about the order of the terrestrial, sublunar world and nature is pure truth and that only a fool will refuse to assent to it. I am certainly in danger, he remarks ironically,[17] of being declared an ignoramus and ill-informed. Nevertheless, I venture publicly to express my doubts and to point out that neither in Aristotle's physics nor in Ptolemy's astronomical system is everything true. I find that what they say of the spheres, cycles, and planets, as well as their doctrine on the nature of matter and form, are full of contradictions and unproven assumptions. "Do you not see," he calls out, "that all their attempts to demonstrate logically the existence of the spheres and of the First Cause remain ungrounded?"[18] Discontented, his heart filled with doubt, Ibn Latif prays: "My God, O God of Abraham, show Thy grace to me, Thy servant, that I may have the privilege of seeking out Thy deep mysteries, the great secrets of the Torah and of prophecy."[19]

Falaquera's hero in *Ha-Mevakkesh* calls the simple believer "a fool" because he refuses to acknowledge common sense as the highest authority in matters of faith. The believer, however, is unmoved. The genuinely religious person does not require the confirmation of philosophy to demonstrate to him that there is a God in the world and that the teaching of the Torah is true and right. For the true believer there is a greater authority, that of the tradition which testifies that the Torah is from heaven and that God revealed Himself to His people on Mount Sinai. The medieval rationalist endeavored to investigate the idea of God, to understand the greatness of God by way of intellectual inquiry; the medieval believer, however, felt God with his entire soul and carried Him in the depths of his heart. And there, where the individual experienced in himself, in his limited "I," his kinship with the divine and eternal, religious feeling flared up with mystical ardor. Faith became a mystery, filled with divine wonders. Most of the restless "seekers" of the thirteenth century, therefore, found peace and contentment not in the realm of rationalist metaphysics but among the mystics, with their passion and flaming feeling which refused to recognize the rigorous laws of logic and impetuously broke through to the heights, to the heavenly spheres. Rationalism wished to be the sole ruler of cultural life, but the mentality of the Middle Ages was not suited to this, and the rebellion soon broke out. Indeed, in the thir-

---

17. *Ibid.*, p. 6.
18. *Ibid.*, p. 8.
19. *Ibid.*, pp. 9–10.

teenth century, just when Maimonidean rationalism was marching triumphantly through Spain and Provence, its bitter adversary, the "Torah of the heart," the mysterious Kabbalah, came to the foreground of Jewish cultural life.

We have noted in the second volume how certain mystical ideas and tendencies migrated from Babylonia to Italy, and from there to the banks of the Rhine. We have seen how these ideas were for a long time cultivated only in limited circles, but at the end of the twelfth century entered the broader arena of Jewish life. They began to dominate the minds of German Jewry and also crossed the Pyrenees and engaged the interest of the Jewish intelligentsia of Spain. In the greatest Spanish Jewish poet and thinker of the eleventh century, Solomon Ibn Gabirol, the doctrine of emanation, according to which the world was created through powers which stream out of divinity, already played a highly significant role. There is no doubt that Ibn Gabirol's philosophy was elaborated under the influence of Arabic thinkers who became familiar with the ideas of the neo-Platonists Philo and Plotinus, through Syrian scientific literature. The emanation doctrine was already systematically worked out among these Arabic thinkers. The first significant Arab philosopher, Al-Kindi, participated in the Arabic translation of the philosophical work *Teologia*, in which there is a description of how, out of the eternal source of light, the "intelligible world" or the "heavenly man" emanated. From the "intelligible world" radiated a new emanation of light—the "universal soul of the heavenly world."[20] Already in Ibn Gabirol's times, the author of *Ma'ani al-Nafs* (Reflections on the Soul)[21] endeavored to combine the emanation doctrine with the ten *sefirot* of the *Sefer Yetzirah*. In *Ma'ani al-Nafs* the first emanation is called *Hochmah* (Wisdom), as well as *Shechinah* (Indwelling Divine Presence) and *Kavod* (Glory).[22]

In Ibn Gabirol the flame of mystical fervor was integrally combined with unshakable faith in the power of knowledge and inquiry. An inspired lyricist, the poet of great *Weltschmerz* was persuaded that on the wings of free speculative thought man

20. See A. Harkavy, *Hadashim Gam Yeshanim*, X, 17; S. Munk, *Mélanges de philosophie juive et arabe* (Paris, 1859), pp. 252–56, 290.
21. It was long believed that this work was written by the famous author of *Hovot Ha-Levavot*, Bahya Ibn Pakuda. A Hebrew translation, *Sefer Torat Ha-Nefesh*, was published by Isaac Broydé (Paris, 1896). The notion that *Ma'ani al-Nafs* was composed by Bahya was decisively refuted in A. Borisov's article "Pseudo-Bahja" in the Leningrad *Bulletin de l'académie des sciences de l'URSS, classe des humanités*, 1929, pp. 775–97.
22. See Harkavy, *op. cit.*, X, 18; A. Guttmann, *MGWJ*, 1897, p. 451.

The "Fathers" of the Kabbalah in Provence

could rise to the heavens and there assuage his thirst for the source of truth. The ideas of this brilliantly endowed neo-Platonist, however, found very slight response among the Jewish intelligentsia. Another system of ideas dominated Jewish intellectual circles of that era: Aristotelian rationalism. This quickly gained primacy over Jewish cultural life in Spain, and Ibn Gabirol's *Mekor Hayyim* and its doctrine were forgotten. But not for long. In the high tower of Aristotelianism the air was free and bright but cold and frosty, and many searching and longing souls left it, unsatisfied. The neo-Platonist star rose once more. The mysterious depths of the Kabbalah, the "hidden wisdom," again called and attracted men.

It is interesting that popular legendry associates the birth of mystical tendencies in Spain and Provence with the name of the scholar who first came forth with a protest against Maimonides' rationalism. An ancient legend relates that the prophet Elijah appeared to the pious scholar Rabbi David and revealed hidden secrets to him. These secrets were transmitted by Rabbi David to his only son Abraham, the author of the *Hassagot*, a set of critical notes to Maimonides' *Mishneh Torah*.[23] Rabbi Abraham ben David (Ravad II) was in fact a Kabbalist. He wrote a commentary on the *Sefer Yetzirah* in which he speaks at length of the divine power inherent in the letters of the Hebrew alphabet.[24] The same legend relates that Rabbi Abraham ben David transmitted the mysteries revealed by the prophet Elijah to his son Rabbi Isaac the Blind. The life of Rabbi Isaac, who is considered by many the "father" of the Kabbalah, is veiled in a web of fantastic legends. What has been definitely established is only that he, too, wrote a commentary on the *Sefer Yetzirah* and devoted much attention to the doctrine of transmigration of souls.[25] It is possible that Rabbi Isaac is the author of the well-known mystical Midrash entitled *Sefer Ha-Bahir*[26] (also known as *Midrash Rabbi Nehunyah*

---

23. See *Matzref Le-Hochmah*, p. 66 (Warsaw edition); Graetz, *Divrei Yemei Yisrael*, IV, 357.
24. *Matzref Le-Hochmah*, p. 51, where these words of Rabbi Abraham are quoted: "The Hebrew letters are not like the letters of other languages, for they are alive."
25. One legend relates that before Isaac became blind he could at once tell from the face of any man whether his soul was a new one or one transmigrated from another person who had lived earlier (Commentary on the Torah by Rabbi Menahem Recanati, *Parashah Va-Yeshev*).
26. It appears extremely dubious to us, however, that this work was composed by one person, especially a scholar of Provence. Evidence to the contrary is given by the Kabbalist of the thirteenth century, Isaac Kohen, of whom the philosopher Isaac Albalag and the Kabbalist

ben Ha-Kanah) in which is presented for the first time, in a clear and systematic form, the doctrine of the emanated *sefirot*. In this work the *sefirot* are portrayed as the primordial elements of *maaseh bereshit* (the creation of the world), as the first emanation of the divine existence. The *sefirot* together comprise the entire cosmos; they are called *Kol*—the "whole" of the world.[27] But not all the *sefirot* are of the same degree. The most important are the first three, *Keter Elyon* (Exalted Crown), *Hochmah* (Wisdom), and *Binah* (Understanding); these are regarded as having radiated from themselves the other seven, out of which the material world was formed.[28]

Isaac the Blind's mystical doctrine was elaborated by his two

---

Shemtov ben Shemtov speak with reverence. Isaac Kohen relates that the *Sefer Ha-Bahir* was composed in Palestine, whence it was obtained by the German Kabbalists; from Germany it passed over to the Kabbalists of Provence, but not in complete form. Shemtov ben Shemtov reports Isaac Kohen's account of the matter in his *Sefer Ha-Emunot* (Part VIII, Ch. 9). See also Gershom Scholem's interesting article "Zur Frage der Entstehung der Kabbala," in *Korrespondenzblatt*, 1929, p. 6. Scholem writes: "Hier [in *Sefer Ha-Bahir*] liegt in der Tat ein Jalkut mystischer Dicta aus ganz verschiedenen Zeiten und Quellen vor."

27. *Sefer Ha-Bahir*, Ch. 15: "And I called it by the name *Kol*, for everything is dependent on it, everything comes forth from it, everything requires it, everything looks and waits for it, and from thence do the souls come." This idea is already expressed very clearly by Solomon Ibn Gabirol, as well as by Moses Ibn Ezra in his poem *Be-Shem El Asher Amar*.

28. *Sefer Ha-Bahir*, Chapters 50–51. It has been conjectured that the author of the *Sefer Ha-Bahir* employed the work entitled *Masechet Atzilut*, written by a mystic of the twelfth century, Jacob Nazir (see Jellinek, *Auswahl Kabbalisticher Mystik* [Leipzig, 1853], p. 6), in which the doctrine of the four different worlds is already to be found: "The Holy One, blessed be He, created four worlds corresponding to the four letters of His name, and these are the world of *Atzilut* (emanation), the world of *Beriah* (creation), the world of *Yetzirah* (formation), and *Asiah* (action)." This work also already mentions the "mystery of contraction or concentration" (*sod ha-tzimtzum*). *Masechet Atzilut* is reprinted at the end of *Midrash Aggadat Bereshit* (Lublin edition, pp. 112–20) and in Jellinek, *op. cit.*, pp. 1–8.

[A later note by Zinberg]: The well-known scholar of Kabbalah, Gershom Scholem, notes in *Tarbitz*, III, 47, the influence of Abraham bar Ḥiyya's work on certain parts of the *Sefer Ha-Bahir*. Scholem also shows that previous scholars of the Kabbalah were in error when they believed that *Masechet Atzilut* was written as early as the twelfth century. Through a thorough analysis of the evolution through which the idea of the four worlds of emanation, creation, formation, and action passed in Jewish mysticism, Scholem demonstrates that *Masechet Atzilut* was written no earlier than the fourteenth century.

disciples from Gerona, Ezra and Azriel, especially the latter.[29] Of Ezra we know merely that he wrote a commentary on the Song of Songs which is frequently mentioned by the medieval Kabbalists. About his friend Azriel (1160–1238) we have somewhat more information. A man of philosophical education, Azriel endeavors, in his brief commentary on the ten *sefirot*,[30] to explain the foundations of Kabbalist doctrine in philosophical terminology. He proceeds from the basic principle on which both Jewish and Arabic thinkers sharply insisted: that no positive qualities can be attributed to divinity—"neither will, nor intention, nor thoughts, nor words, nor deeds."[31] The concept of God excludes any notion whatever of change and alteration, for God is beyond every limit. Hence, human thought cannot attain to Him at all, and the philosophers who assert that our idea of God can only be negative, i.e., that we can merely know what God is *not* and speak only of the qualities and attributes He does *not* possess, are indeed correct. Here, in the philosophical-theological world view of the Kabbalist Azriel, already appears the unique dialectical way of thinking with which the whole of Jewish mysticism, with its neo-Platonist coloration, is permeated. The great No and the great Yes, the negative and the positive, are not two separate and distinct worlds, for one gives birth to the other and is transformed into its opposite.

Taking this view, Azriel sets forth the theoretical principle that became the foundation of the whole later Kabbalah. God, the universal Yes-sayer, the primordial source of everything that is, is the great, incomprehensible, and hidden Nothing (*Ayin*), the boundless, indivisible, and unitary Infinite (*Ein Sof*), who contains in Himself the whole cosmos with all its creatures; no entity exists or can exist outside Him. Here Azriel has occasion to ex-

---

29. Zunz (*Gottesdienstliche Vorträge*, second edition, p. 417) and Landauer (*Literaturblatt des Orients*, 1854, p. 196) wish to show that Ezra and Azriel were one and the same person. This, however, is not so. The poet Meshullam Dapiera, who lived at that time, speaks of two distinct mystics (see *Moreh Mekom Ha-Moreh*, p. 12). Another contemporary, an anonymous poet, notes: "And Ezra and Azriel were a help to me" (*Otzar Nehmad*, II, 85). A mystic of the second half of the thirteenth century also speaks of two different Kabbalists, Ezra and Azriel (see Jellinek's *Philosophie und Kabbala*, p. 2). Gershom Scholem has also found in an old manuscript an indication that Azriel was Ezra's son-in-law (see *Kiryat Sefer*, VI, 26).
30. *Perush Eser Sefirot*, printed together with Meir Ibn Gabbai's *Derech Emunah*, Berlin, 1850. See also Jellinek, *Beiträge zur Geschichte der Kabbala*.
31. *Perush Eser Sefirot*, 4.

plain and resolve numerous contradictions and difficulties—and this also in a dialectical manner: how from nothing (*ayin*) something (*yesh*) is born, how from the infinite the finite and limited come, how from that which is beyond time the temporal and the becoming are formed. If no creature can exist outside the *Ein Sof*, how explain the emergence of the world? For if we say that the world was created at a certain moment, at that moment a change had to occur in God and His will, for He passed from rest to work and from being a non-creator became a creator. But in the *Ein Sof* no change can occur. It is also extremely difficult to understand the relationship of the infinite "nothing" to the "something," to the real world. Divinity, as eternally existing and infinite power, is the superlative degree of absolutely indivisible and unitary spirituality; how, then, can it be the source of the material world which consists of so many different elements? And how can one explain the fact that, regarding the infinite and incomprehensible God, such human, corporeal expressions as God's hand, God's voice, God's wrath, and the like are employed in the holy books and in the Torah itself? All these difficulties and contradictions Azriel attempts to resolve through his doctrine of emanation (*atzilut*). Between the infinite and the finite, between divinity and the universe, there is an intermediate link, a transitional stage—the *sefirot* or emanations. These are God's reflection but not God Himself; and it is these and their garment that must be understood by all the expressions that speak of God's qualities and attributes in the sacred books.

The problem of *maaseh bereshit*, the creation of the world, receives in Azriel's system unique forms. Potentially the whole universe exists from eternity in the womb of the *Ein Sof*, and the "work of creation" consists only in the fact that the world, which formerly existed merely *in potentia*, became, through the free divine will, an actual phenomenon. One cannot speak, Azriel insists, of world *creation*. To create "something from nothing" is logically impossible, for outside the *Ein Sof* nothing from which the world could be created can exist. It is, therefore, not correct to say that God "creates"; one must say, rather, that He *emanates* everything out of Himself. As the sun radiates light and warmth out of itself and is at the same time in no way diminished thereby, so the *Ein Sof* emanates from Himself the basic elements of the cosmos, the ten *sefirot*, and remains absolutely unchanged and undiminished in power.[32]

32. The distinction between creation and emanation is underscored a number of times by Azriel in the following words: "All creation,

Azriel and His *Perush Eser Sefirot*

These ten *sefirot* are in Azriel's *Perush Eser Sefirot* divided into three groups. The first consists of *Rum Maalah* (Exalted Height), *Hochmah* (Wisdom), and *Binah* (Understanding or Intelligence). This is the intellectual or intelligible world, the *olam ha-sechel*. The next three *sefirot*—*Hesed* (Lovingkindness), *Tiferet* (Beauty), and *Pahad* (Awe)—are the moral-spiritual world, the *olam ha-nefesh* (world of the soul). And the last four—*Netzah* (Eternity), *Yesod* (Foundation), *Hod* (Majesty), and *Tzaddik* (Righteousness)—are the material world, the *olam ha-guf* (world of the body).[33] To the combination of all ten *sefirot* into one Azriel gives the name *Kavod* or Glory ("Know that all the *sefirot* are called His *Kavod*"), a term which, as we have noted, figured prominently in the work of the German mystics, Jehudah Hasid and Eleazar of Worms.

But it is not in this alone that an affinity between the author of the *Perush Eser Sefirot* and the German mystics of his generation appears. Like the latter, Azriel also wrote a commentary to the prayers and, just as do the authors of the *Sefer Hasidim*, he seeks profound, hidden mysteries in them. He is also highly indignant at those who endeavor to obtain, in a utilitarian-rationalist way, "reasons for the commandments" and to demonstrate intellectually the practical usefulness of each individual law of the Torah. In typically mystic fashion, he perceives in the commandments cosmic phenomena of incalculable significance. Every commandment influences the divine emanation. A fervent prayer, exalted with *kavvanah* (devotion or intention), is a ray of light which rises from below to meet the divine emanation flowing from above. Prayer is the mediating agency which links the material world with the source of life, the *Ein Sof*.

In Azriel's *Perush Eser Sefirot* we note how the Jewish mystics attempted to resolve the inconsistency implicit in affirming that the *Ayin*, the absolute, indivisible, and unitary spirituality, is the source of the variegated material world. But still another contradiction associated with the profound enigma of the universe required resolution. God is conceived as entirely good; He is the source of light; He is the "whole" (*Kol*) of the universe; everything exists only in Him, and outside of Him nothing can be. But how, then, are the forces of wickedness and hatred, the dark powers that rule the world, to be explained? God is the God of justice—and yet the world is steeped in blood and filth, the

---

when something is taken away from it, is diminished . . . the power of emanation, when something is taken away from it, is not diminished."
33. *Perush Eser Sefirot*, 3b.

Temple is in ruins, the *Shechinah* is in exile, and the power of wickedness, the kingdom of Edom, dominates the earth.

This contradiction, the problem of the struggle between good and evil in the world, had to engage the attention of the Jewish mystics, and we shall see what an important place is occupied in the later books of the Kabbalah by the *kelipot* (shells), the *sitra aḥara* (other or "demonic" side), and the "prince of Edom." But a younger contemporary of Rabbi Azriel, Isaac ben Jacob Ha-Kohen, already concerned himself with this problem in a treatise entitled *Maamar Al Ha-Atzilut Ha-Semolit*.[34] Isaac Ha-Kohen, who was born in Spain but lived for a long time in Provence, points out first of all that the ideas he expresses in his treatise are derived from certain "elders in the kingdom of Germany," then from a Kabbalist work of Jehudah Ḥasid of Regensburg, and mainly from a *kuntras* or notebook which the sages of the Kabbalah showed him in the Provençal city of Arles. This *kuntras*, Isaac further relates, was brought from Palestine by "a great and pious scholar" of Damascus. It must be borne in mind that precisely in the Near East, from which the major sources of which Isaac made use derive, teachings about magic and demonology flourished. There also the dualistic Persian doctrine of the "two powers," of the luminous kingdom of good and the dark kingdom of evil, found a powerful resonance.

Isaac Ha-Kohen tells us in his treatise that corresponding to the ten "holy *sefirot*" are ten "left *sefirot*," which are the "ten classes of strife" (*eser kitot ha-tigrah*). The first three classes "had no endurance and were blotted out from the world"; it is of these, Isaac explains, that the ancient legend that "God built worlds and destroyed them" tells. The remaining seven *kitot ha-mekatregin* (classes of the accusers), with all their hosts, carry on perpetual warfare with the angels of light and holiness. This is the kingdom of Samael, the "great serpent," and under Samael's banner is the "prince of Esau," who carries on constant war with Jacob. Isaac considers it necessary to note several times that Samael, with all his armies and "hosts of accusers," also derives from the one

---

34. First published by Scholem in *Maddaei Ha-Yahadut*, II, 244–64. Supplements to Isaac ben Jacob Ha-Kohen's *Maamar Al Ha-Atzilut Ha-Semolit* were published by Jacob Moses Toledano in *Ha-Tzofeh Le-Ḥochmat Yisrael* (1929), pp. 261–67. Scholem discusses at length another work of Isaac Ha-Kohen's, a commentary on Ezekiel's chariot, in his work *Le-Ḥeker Kabbalat Rabbi Yitzḥak ben Yaakov Ha-Kohen* (in *Tarbitz*, II–III). He notes the syncretistic character of Isaac's mystical outlook, in which various and often contradictory elements of Gnosticism and neo-Platonism are interwoven.

Jacob bar Sheshet's Shaar Ha-Shamayim

source, the source that is all good, for there is no other. To be sure, he indicates that the "classes of the accusers" do not derive directly from the third emanation, the *atzilat ha-teshuvah* (emanation of repentance or return), for between them there is a barrier (*masach mavdil*). This is the power which streams out of the third emanation and bears the name Mesuchiel. Nevertheless, Isaac must finally conclude that the existence of the "barrier" cannot alter the situation and it must be admitted that the kingdom of wickedness also stems from the good source.[35] The later Kabbalists, as we shall see, attempted to resolve this contradiction in a dialectical manner. Isaac, however, does not enter into profound speculations; he declares frankly, "Our knowledge does not attain to this deeply hidden mystery, for it is sealed." He also gives the reader the pious advice: "Be silent and do not entertain impure thoughts; seek not what is too wonderful for you and inquire not into what is veiled before you."

It is interesting that precisely at that time a voice protesting sharply against the "philosophizers," who glory in their human reason and believe that the intellect is the only sure guide in matters of faith, was raised from within the mystical circles. "For our great sin," laments Azriel's contemporary and fellow townsman Jacob bar Sheshet, in his treatise *Shaar Ha-Shamayim*[36] which he composed in 1246,

breakers down of the fence [*portzei geder*] have appeared among us Jews, men who spin falsehood in their hearts and distort the truth. They falsify our Torah and blaspheme God. They fabricate the notion that our holy commandments serve only common, practical goals: some of them are hygienic principles calculated to preserve health, others regulate social-economic life, still others, political life and the order of the state. . . . They have likened the God of Jacob to the foreign gods. . . . They blunder in the crooked paths of Greek philosophy. They wish to seek out everything through logical theories and they remain groping in the darkness, become ever more confused, and cannot find a way out. They have forsaken the living source. They have cast off the yoke of Torah. Each of them relies on his own understanding. . . . Arrogantly they declare that the world is eternal, and that when our teacher Moses wrote, "In the beginning God created," he intended thereby only to deceive the multitude. They assert that God's providence does not rule the earth or man's life, that the

---

35. *Maddaei Ha-Yahadut*, II, 259.
36. First published in *Otzar Nehmad*, III, 153–65. *Shaar Ha-Shamayim* is written in rhymed prose. The date is indicated in the following phrase: "and 1178 years of the exile have already passed" (*ibid.*, p. 163).

righteous receive no reward and the wicked no punishment. All this have the wicked of the people devised. One must only sharpen the mind, for thought alone is immortal; it alone remains after man's death.[37]

Jacob bar Sheshet also speaks with great indignation of the rationalist view of the significance of prayers and petitions. Like all the other mystics, Jacob sees in prayer the profoundest mystery. Furthermore, he expresses an idea that testifies to his fine insight and the fact that he appreciated the importance of mass psychology and recognized it as a factor of great moral significance. He writes:

I would have valued the prayers very highly even if they were merely a convention, a matter of agreement, which has come down to us as a tradition from our fathers, for in that tradition, in what has been accepted by the will and consent of the whole community, the moral power of every people inheres. And the individual who rebels against the tradition of the community, who withdraws from the way of life of the people and casts off the tradition which he absorbed with his mother's milk, destroys his spiritual world with his own hands.[38]

Jacob bar Sheshet cannot pardon the rationalists who think that the entire value of the prayers consists merely in the fact that they purify man's thought and awaken in him the remembrance of God. They therefore consider praying aloud great foolishness and a desecration of God's name. That poor and needy people rise from sleep at night and with weeping and tears beseech God is to be explained, according to them, only by the fact that the multitude is foolish and ignorant. How, they argue, can one address Him who is hidden and incomprehensible with weeping and petitions, crying, "Answer us! Rise up and aid us!"? What sense has our constant repetition, "Blessed art Thou, O God"? Does God need our blessings and our praises?[39]

Our author considers such an attitude toward prayer the greatest sin. "The name of him who denies the holy prayers," Jacob declares,

will be blotted out of the memory of the people. He who recognizes only reason declares war not against us but against our teacher Moses and all the later prophets to whom God revealed himself. He carries

---

37. *Ibid.*, pp. 163–64.
38. *Ibid.*, p. 165.
39. *Ibid.*, p. 164.

Jacob bar Sheshet's Shaar Ha-Shamayim

on war with the sages of the Mishnah, with the men of the Talmud, and with all of our great and chosen ones.[40]

And he cries out passionately: "Woe to those with hard hearts and impure thoughts, who blunder in crooked ways and scrabble in the dark! Woe to those who follow foreign scholars, allow themselves to be led astray in their false paths, and forsake the sure ways of the sacred Torah!"[41]

40. *Ibid.*, p. 165.
41. In the theoretical part of *Shaar Ha-Shamayim* is discernible above all the influence of the *Sefer Yetzirah* and of Solomon Ibn Gabirol's doctrine of God's will. While among other Kabbalists of that time the first divine emanation bears various names (in *Masechet Atzilut* it is called *Keter;* in *Sefer Ha-Bahir, Keter Elyon;* in *Perush Eser Sefirot, Rum Maalah*), Jacob bar Sheshet calls it by the same name as Ibn Gabirol: *Ratzon* (Will). It is possible that we have here, in addition, the influence of Jacob's contemporary Isaac Ibn Latif, who also calls the first emanation *Ḥefetz* (Will or Desire). See his *Tzurat Ha-Olam*, p. 16.

CHAPTER TWO

Nahmanides and His Followers

FROM the Kabbalist school of Gerona, to which Azriel and Jacob bar Sheshet belonged, also came the celebrated figure who, with his great reputation and authority, was especially instrumental in causing mystical ideas, in the course of a rather brief period, to attract the attention of broad Jewish circles in Spain and Provence. This was Rabbi Moses ben Nahman, better known as Nahmanides or Ramban,[1] whom we have already encountered in considering the first controversy involving Maimonides and his works.

Nahmanides was born in Gerona in 1194. A man with a sensitive, deeply believing soul, endowed with brilliant capacities, he acquired renown for his investigations in the realm of Talmudic scholarship while still a youth. With his keen mind and remarkable dialectical skill, he quickly obtained an honored place among the foremost Tosafists. In Nahmanides' youthful works his characteristically conservative tendencies are quite clearly noticeable. He has the utmost reverence for the *Rishonim*, the earlier Talmudic authorities; he cannot praise their wisdom sufficiently, and every word of theirs is sacred to him. "He who learns Torah from the 'ancients,' " Nahmanides declares, "is like one who drinks old wine." It is therefore

---

1. Some scholars believe that Nahmanides is to be identified with the Jewish scholar who figures in Christian documents under the name Bonastruc de Porta.

no accident that in his first important work, *Milḥamot Adonai*, Nahmanides champions the "ancient" Alfasi and defends him against the sharp strictures of Zeraḥyah Ha-Levi, the author of *Ha-Maor*. Only when it is obvious to him that one of the *Rishonim* has in fact been mistaken does he confess it openly and defend himself by saying: "I do not wish to be like an ape walking around with a book in his hand."

A physician by profession, Nahmanides was familiar with the natural sciences and philosophy of his time. Nevertheless, Hillel of Verona and Zeraḥyah Ḥen[2] were not in error when they declared that Nahmanides was no great expert in philosophical matters. A man with a profoundly religious nature and permeated with mystical feeling, he found the cold, logical theories and principles of Aristotelian philosophy alien and uncongenial. In his *Shaar Ha-Gemul*[3] he refers ironically to the *ḥachmei ha-meḥkar* (philosophers) who dare to speak so expansively of God's wondrous works and assume a critical attitude to what we have by way of tradition from our holy ancestors, when the structure of their own body, not to speak of man's soul, is a sealed mystery to them. With all his reverence for the famous author of the *Mishneh Torah*, Nahmanides could nevertheless not pardon Maimonides for the rationalistic ideas so prominent in his *Guide for the Perplexed*. Maimonides had taken considerable pains to explain rationally the miracles related in the Torah. For Nahmanides, however, the miraculous was the most *common* thing. For him the whole world was one great miracle, a marvelous revelation of God's boundless power. He who does not believe that in certain moments of our life miracle rules our actions, he who refuses to understand that not everything can be explained naturalistically and that the mechanical laws of nature do not regulate all things, Nahmanides declares, ought not to take part in studying the Torah which Moses our teacher has given us.

Maimonides and Nahmanides represent two different worlds. Maimonides attempts to prove that the Jewish religion is, above all, the reflection of divine wisdom and is constructed on the solid foundations of logic and reason. All the principles and premises of Judaism can therefore be explained rationally. Indeed, according to Maimonides, therein lies its grandeur and power. For Nahmanides, however, Judaism is primarily a revelation of the profound divine mystery which man's reason cannot grasp but

2. See Vol. II of our *History*, pp. 191–200.
3. The last chapter of his *Torat Ha-Adam*, in which the laws and customs connected with the proper treatment of a corpse are presented. We have utilized the Constantinople edition of 1518.

for which his soul yearns in passionate rapture. Grasped by an intense faith in God's graciousness and in the endless glory of His wonders, Nahmanides, with the delighted eyes of a simple child, looked astonishedly at the world surrounding him in which everything is so beautiful and all things bear the stamp of divine love and wisdom.

At a time when most of the contemporary Christian mystics regarded the "sinful" world with contempt and scorn, and followed the road of asceticism and solitude, Nahmanides considered all aspects of life precious and sacred. In the terrestrial world, too, in every pulsation of life, the mystic of Gerona glimpsed the hidden secret of unfathomable divine wisdom.

Characteristic in this respect is Nahmanides' little work *Iggeret Ha-Kodesh*,[4] in which the matter of sexual relationships between man and wife is treated. The rationalist Maimonides, who considered only the spiritual phenomena bearing the impress of man's speculative thought as worthy and important, looked contemptuously on the physical aspects of human life that are associated with passion and desire. In man's erotic instincts Maimonides perceives something shameful and bestial, as well as the most serious obstacle on the way to perfection. This view is sharply attacked by Nahmanides in his *Iggeret Ha-Kodesh*. "The author of the *Guide*," he declares, "allows himself to be led astray by Aristotle and believes with him that there is something shameful in sexual intercourse; the Greek philosopher was greatly in error."[5] Where the metaphysician Maimonides saw merely the low and beastly, the dialectical thinker Nahmanides discerned the holy radiance of creative power, the profound mystery of immortal life. With his powerful faith in the infinite wisdom and grace of God's creation, Nahmanides could not regard man's erotic instincts and sexual life as shameful or unworthy, for the desires that lie in the nature of man are also bound up with the great divine goal, and that which is marked by divine providence cannot be evil and unclean.

The enthusiastic exegete of the Torah, in which family life figures so importantly, could not possibly view sexual union as sinful, but enveloped it in the same mantle of sacredness as the purely spiritual phenomena of life. The conjugal life of man and wife is, for Nahmanides, a holy mystery. "Above the couch of man and wife," he affirms, "hovers the divine Presence." In sexual intercourse, in the will to create new life and renew the human

---

4. We have employed the old Constantinople edition of 1590.
5. *Iggeret Ha-Kodesh*, Chapter 2.

race, Nahmanides was persuaded, lies the secret that reveals God's glory and greatness.[6]

It is readily understandable that a man of such strong feeling as Nahmanides of necessity became interested in the "esoteric wisdom,"[7] which his teachers, Jehudah ben Yakar and Azriel, the author of *Perush Eser Sefirot*, imparted to him. There is no doubt that Nahmanides was also familiar with the works of the German mystics. Eleazar of Worms, the author of *Rokeah*, is quoted by him in his famous letter to the French rabbis, and there is even a popular legend to the effect that Eleazar, with the aid of "combinations of letters," flew on a cloud to Spain to acquaint Nahmanides with the mysteries of the Kabbalah.[8]

Like Isaac the Blind, Nahmanides devoted considerable attention to the doctrine of transmigration of the soul which played such a significant role in the later Kabbalah. We have observed in the first volume of our work, speaking of Maimonides and Jehudah Halevi, how these two philosophers, with their diametrically opposed views of the world, regarded the problem of the human personality and its development. Jehudah Halevi sees in the tradition of the fathers the commanding power that dominates the moral consciousness of the individual and serves as the guide of all his action and behavior. The great national religious-cultural forces that are assembled and live in the garment of tradition are, in Halevi's view, hallowed through the course of many generations; they become the "categorical imperative" in the heart and consciousness of the individual which liberates him from doubt and gives him the firm assurance that so must things be, so ought to be done and not otherwise. The individual, Halevi is

6. Again (*ibid.*): "Sexual union is holy and pure. . . . Let no man dare to say there is anything disgraceful or ugly in it. . . . God created everything as His wisdom decreed, and He created nothing in which there is disgrace or ugliness. . . . When sexual union is for the sake of God there is nothing purer than it. . . . When a man unites with his wife in holiness and purity, the *Shechinah* [God's indwelling presence] is with them." A significant part of *Iggeret Ha-Kodesh* (Chapters 3–6) was employed almost verbatim in the well-known ethical work *Menorat Ha-Maor* (sections 181–86).
7. On Nahmanides' commentary to the *Sefer Yetzirah*, see Gershom Scholem's article, "Perakim Mi-Toledot Safrut Ha-Kabbalah," in *Kiryat Sefer*, VI, 385–400.
8. See *Maddaei Ha-Yahadut*, II (1927), 254; Steinschneider-Malter, *Safrut Yisrael*, p. 155. On the basis of this legend, it is indicated in *Kore Ha-Dorot* and other sources that Nahmanides studied the Kabbalah with Eleazar. (See also Joseph Sambari in Neubauer's *Seder Hachamim Ve-Korot Ha-Yamim*, I, 125.) The legend is very colorfully presented in *Maaseh Nissim*, No. 7.

convinced, draws his moral and spiritual powers from the cultural treasures of the people, which they have inherited from their fathers. Maimonides, however, sees the highest degree of man's spiritual perfection in speculative thought; and the bearer of thought is not the community but the individual. Not the legacy and tradition of past generations, but the proud, free thought of the singled-out individual who stands above the multitude—this is what raises the human personality to the supreme level and endows it with immortality. The problem of the immortality of the soul is entirely separated by the rationalists of Maimonides' school from the community. The privilege of immortality is enjoyed only by that person who can delve into philosophical problems and whose acute thinking attains to the heights of the "active intellect."

Quite different is the attitude of the mystics to the question of the immortality of the soul. The mystery of man's spiritual life, of his soul, exercised a magical attraction for the mystics who preceded Naḥmanides. Eleazar of Worms wrote a special work, *Ḥochmat Ha-Nefesh*,[9] on it. His contemporary and friend, the poet Samuel ben Kalonymos, carried on a correspondence with him on the subject, and in a lovely poem expresses the longing of the soul for the mysterious and super-terrestrial. The poem begins: "On the couch, in deep sleep, the soul leaves the body. Like a dove she flies to the heavens and perceives in holy stillness the hidden mysteries. She does not wish to leave the celestial heights, but the commandment is stern and she must return to her dark prison. She wakes from her sleep but can no longer forget the heavenly dream!" "My soul," declares another mystic of that era, Isaiah bar Joseph, in one of his poems, "pants like a hart for the spring of living waters and aspires to God in the heavens. Oh, when will she fly like a bird to her Creator in His heavenly sanctuaries? She thirsts and yearns for eternal light, to bow before Him, the God of eternal life."

The immortality of the soul is, among these mystics, strictly connected with the community. They regard the individual's soul as a link in the long chain of the generations that are united through the tradition and spiritual heritage of the fathers. It is understandable that, holding this view, our mystics gave so much attention to the belief in metempsychosis or transmigration of souls. Naḥmanides, as well as the later Kabbalists, was convinced that the soul, after separating from the body, does not return immediately to its source but is first transferred into another

9. First published in Lemberg in 1876.

mortal and once again traverses a human life path in the terrestrial world. But not only does a man's soul live on after his death. Being a reflection of the eternal source of light, it lives from eternity, from before the "work of creation." This thought is beautifully reflected in the first verse of Naḥmanides' well known prayer "Merosh Mekadmei Olamim": "From the beginning of all eternities, I [the soul] have been kept in His hidden treasures. From the incomprehensible [*Ayin*] He brought me forth, and at the end of days I shall be summoned back before the King."[10]

Along with Jehudah Ḥasid and Eleazar of Worms, Naḥmanides also believed in the tremendous power hidden in the "combination of letters." In every letter of every name of God lies a special secret. Through "combining" these letters, the "pious of the generations" can perform the greatest miracles—"kill and revive, uproot and tear down, build and plant, make waste and destroy."

Naḥmanides believed that the mysteries of the "wisdom which is hidden from the eyes of all and is broader than the sea" ought not to be revealed to the masses. Nevertheless, he himself frequently mentions these mysteries, even if only by way of allusion. In his well-known sermon *Torat Adonai Temimah* he asserts that "the entire Torah from 'In the beginning' to 'before the eyes of all Israel' consists only of 'names.'" The same is true of the prophetic books. In Ezekiel, for example, in the section on "the chariot," or in the chapter in which the "valley of dry bones" is treated, one can obtain through "combinations of letters" a "name" such that one may revive the dead with it.[11]

The same idea is expressed by Naḥmanides in the introduction to his commentary on the Torah, which he completed in the last years of his life after he had been compelled by order of the government to leave his home and had settled in Palestine. Naḥmanides was already a man of seventy when the king of Aragon demanded that he, as chief rabbi of the country, accede to the wish of the apostate Pablo Christiani and hold a public disputation with the latter on matters of faith. The disputation was attended by the king, along with his courtiers and many prominent members of the clergy.[12] Naḥmanides won the debate,

10. We quote from Geiger's *Melo Chofnajim*, pp. 39–41, where this prayer is given in its entirety.
11. *Torat Adonai Temimah*, pp. 30–31.
12. Naḥmanides himself wrote an account of the disputation (printed in *Milḥemet Ḥovah* [Constantinople, 1710]; reprinted separately in 1929). Fritz (Yitzḥak) Baer, in his article "The Disputations of Yeḥiel of

thus greatly enraging the priests, who accused him of having blasphemed the Christian religion. The court ruled that the rabbi must immediately leave the country.[13] Driven from his home, Nahmanides set out for Palestine.[14] In 1267 he settled in Acco, which soon became an important cultural center since his great reputation attracted numerous students. He died shortly after completing his commentary on the Torah (1270).

Through Nahmanides and his vast authority, a strong interest in the "hidden wisdom" began to develop in broad Jewish circles. There is also a certain connection between Nahmanides' name and his move to Palestine in his old age and the sudden appearance of the greatest and most revered of Kabbalist works, the *Zohar*, in the collecting and editing of which his two ardent followers, Abraham Abulafia[15] and Moses de Leon, undoubtedly participated.

Abraham ben Samuel Abulafia, born in Saragossa in 1240, is a distinctively medieval figure. A richly gifted man with a dreaming, poetic nature, he also possessed a bizarre Oriental imagination which often passed over into pathological emotion and enthusiasm. It is therefore not surprising that throughout his life he was an indefatigable seeker after the supernatural and the miraculous. At the age of eighteen he was orphaned, and about two years later set out on a long and difficult journey to the Near East to seek the legendary river Sambatyon, in order to visit the "Ten Lost Tribes" believed to be living on its other side. He arrived, however, only at the port of Acco and from there had to turn back because of the great war "which broke out between Esau and Ishmael,"[16] i.e., between the Crusaders and the Mongols.

Paris and Nahmanides" (Hebrew), *Tarbitz*, II (1931), 172–87, presents a critical examination of Nahmanides' "disputation" and comes to the conclusion that this account, as well as the Latin reports of the disputation that have been preserved, is "not a faithful and accurate account but a propaganda piece."

13. David Kahana endeavors to show (*Ha-Shiloah*, XXXII, 266) that it was not Nahmanides who was sentenced to banishment but another rabbi of Gerona. It is difficult to agree with Kahana's arguments.
14. The letters which Nahmanides sent from Palestine to his relatives, and in which he describes the conditions prevalent there at that time, have a significant cultural-historical interest (they were reprinted together with the account of the disputation, *Vikkuah*, in 1929). Travelling over the sea, Nahmanides composed a "prayer of the sea" (*Tefillat Ha-Yam*) which begins with the words "O God, great, mighty and fearful" (published in Nathan Hannover's *Shaarei Tziyyon*).
15. Abulafia writes of Nahmanides in his *Hayyei Ha-Nefesh*, "Rabbi Moses ben Nahman, who enlightened the eyes of the exile."
16. So Abulafia relates in his biographical notice published in Jellinek's *Bet Ha-Midrash*, III, xl–xlii.

Abulafia traveled for a time through Greece and Italy, and settled in the city of Capua to study philosophy with Hillel of Verona. "I devoted myself to philosophy wholeheartedly," he relates; "day and night I meditated on it. I studied through the *Guide for the Perplexed* several times." Later he even gave lectures on Maimonides' philosophical works.[17] His enthusiasm for Maimonides was so strong that he sang of him in religious poems, and his poem "Eshtasheah Bimshol Kadmon"[18] ends with the eulogy: "Those who read the Torah of Moses ben Amram with the doctrine of Moses ben Maimon are saved." Soon, however, he became dissatisfied with philosophical studies. For his longing soul, the rational, logical theories of Aristotle's system were too cold and arid, and he relates how "the overly clever philosophizers" who boast "that only they have attained the real truth" became repugnant to him.

Abulafia again became a restless "seeker." He delved into the theoretical Kabbalah, which for the first time provided adequate material to his feverish imagination. However, he quickly became discontented with it as well. Its arguments and theories about the emanations and the ten *sefirot* also smacked excessively, in his view, of cold philosophical schemes. Abulafia found that the mystical doctrine of the *sefirot* did not resolve the great enigma of the world, did not reveal the profound mystery of how worlds are created out of the womb of eternal chaos, and did not show man how he, too, can participate in this tremendous process of creating and giving birth. The *hachmei ha-sefirot* (the sages of the *sefirot*), says Abulafia, are indeed close to the right way, but they have not found "the shortest way."

Abulafia very acutely underscores the weak side of the doctrine of the *sefirot*. The sages of the Kabbalah are themselves not clear what the nature of the *sefirot* really is—whether they are to be considered separate existences, independent powers and "intelligences," or merely "vessels" and instruments of creation. "You must know," Abulafia writes[19] to an acquaintance named Jehudah Shalmon,

17. *Ibid.*, p. xli.
18. Printed in the collection *Shirim U-Zemirot Ve-Tishbahot* (Constantinople, 1545), No. 12. Even later, when Abulafia became an ardent mystic, he remained a devoted disciple of Maimonides and saw in his *Guide for the Perplexed* profound mysteries which he discusses in a special work, *Hayyei Ha-Nefesh*.
19. The letter was published by Jellinek in *Ginzei Hochmat Ha-Kabbalah*, I, 13–28.

The "Secret of the Letters"

that the men of the Kabbalah, as convinced monotheists, reject the doctrine of the Trinity. They themselves, however, exchange the tri-unity for a ten-unity with their *sefirot* doctrine. The Christians believe that God reveals himself in three forms and yet remains one, and some of the Kabbalists maintain that divinity consists of ten *sefirot* which are all combined in the divine oneness.[20]

With moving simplicity Abulafia recounts further in the same letter how he has always sought the "point of truth," and thrown himself from one science to another, but all these lead to "the self-praise of wisdom," not to that for which his soul longs: prophetic ecstasy and the beauty of prophetic revelation.[21]

Only at the age of thirty-one, when he returned to Spain, Abulafia relates,[22] did he finally discover what he had so relentlessly sought. In Barcelona he immersed himself in the *Sefer Yetzirah* and its commentaries, and it was the exponents of this work, especially the German commentators, and foremost among them Eleazar of Worms, who opened his eyes:

> God's spirit awakened in me, the holy spirit touched my soul, and I saw wondrous miracles, tremendous visions. . . . And grieved was my heart that I had not, for so long a time, found the proper person to point out the right way to me, and I blundered for fifteen years, groped in the dark like a blind man, pursued seductive shadows, until God had mercy on me and enlightened my eyes.

We note that, according to Abulafia's own account, the *Sefer Yetzirah* and its German interpreters "enlightened his eyes." A considerable influence was also exercised on him by the Kabbalist books *Bahir* and *Pirkei Rabbi Ishmael*,[23] as well as Abraham Ibn Ezra's *Sefer Ha-Shem*, on which he wrote a commentary.[24] He steeped himself in the mysteries of the "practical Kabbalah" with its *gematriot* and *tzerufei otiot* or "combinations of letters." Abulafia was convinced that the Hebrew language with its alphabet is in no way comparable to other languages. The latter are merely products of social development; each is an organic growth

20. *Ibid.*, p. 19.
21. *Ibid.*, p. 18.
22. Jellinek, *Bet Ha-Midrash*, III, xlii.
23. Abulafia himself notes this in his "Sheva Netivot" (published by Jellinek in his *Philosophie und Kabbala*, p. 21).
24. Abraham Ibn Ezra was inclined towards mysticism but antagonistic to those who believed that miracles can be performed through "combination of letters." In his *Sefer Ha-Shem* he declares: "Those who say that they can perform great deeds with God's name do not know the name."

created by a particular society.²⁵ Hebrew, however, transcends time; it has existed eternally, even before the "work of creation." This view of the language of the Bible was widespread in the Middle Ages. It was expressed by many of the great Jewish scholars of that era, among them Solomon Ibn Gabirol in his *Anak* and Jehudah Halevi in his *Kuzari*. Abraham Ibn Ezra also insists: "And the wisdom of the language of Torah and Scripture is unique; of all languages it is pre-eminent.... And I saw that the holy tongue is the chief language."²⁶ Even Maimonides was convinced that Arabic is merely slightly corrupted Hebrew.²⁷ Jehudah Ibn Matkah explains in his *Midrash Ha-Hochmah* that the holy language is the source of all others. Immanuel of Rome also held the same view.²⁸ Only Zerahyah Hen expressed "heretical" ideas with regard to this question. It is therefore not surprising that the mystic Abulafia considered the words of the Bible eternal "ideas," and the letters of the alphabet symbols of eternal creative powers. The world itself was created through words (*memrot*), through the "combinations" of Hebrew letters and names. It is these combinations (*tzerufim*) that are the *sefirot* through which God brought the universe into being. Letters, words, and names thus obtain a special significance. They are no longer merely signs by which man designates the phenomena and objects of the world about him; they themselves are the fundamental elements of being, the universal "ideas" that preceded "the work of creation," and the whole real world, everything that exists, is merely their reflected image.²⁹

We cannot here dwell on the question to what extent this view of the Jewish mystics derives from the influence of the ancient

---

25. See Jellinek, *Philosophie und Kabbala*, p. x.
26. *Safah Berurah*, 1a, 4b.
27. *Iggerot Ha-Rambam*, II, 27b.
28. *MGWJ*, 1885, p. 244.
29. This view is maintained by Abulafia not only in his religious-mystical works but also in his purely philological works, such as *Sod Darchei Ha-Nikkud Ve-Havarat Ha-Tenuah* (see *Hebräische Bibliographie*, IV, 76–77). In very similar fashion the *Zohar* portrays the creation of the world: according to the form or image of each *word*, God created the corresponding object. See *Zohar*, II, "Parashah Terumah," 161a: "'In the beginning God created the heavens and the earth'; He looked at this word and created the heavens. It is written in the Torah, 'And God said, Let there be light'; He looked at this word and created the light. And so it was with each word." It is also important to note that Abulafia's contemporaries, the brothers Jacob and Isaac Kohen, wrote special treatments of the mysteries that are concealed in the letters and in the "vowel points and their form" (see *Maddaei Ha-Yahadut*, II, 201–19, 265–68).

The Confusion of Being *and* Thinking

Greek thinkers Pythagoras and Plato. We must, however, stress how historically unjustified are those who endeavor to show that we have to do here with ideas that are especially characteristic of the mystics but absolutely foreign to the rationalist, scientific, sober world view of the Peripatetics, the disciples of Aristotle. It is precisely in Aristotle's philosophy that the confusion of the *word* with the *thing* and the substitution of *thinking* for *being* appear most clearly. We must bear in mind that for man only that exists, in general, which he receives through sense perception and which he denotes with a word, or to which he gives a name. As long as a thing has no name and is not designated by a word, it does not exist for man and has not penetrated his consciousness. There is a profound significance in the ancient Biblical account (Genesis 2:19) of how God, immediately after creating all the beasts of the earth and the birds of the heavens, led them before Adam so that he might give them *names:* "And whatever Adam called every living creature, that was the name thereof." In this connection, it is also interesting that in ancient times the belief prevailed among the Jews that, after a person's death, his name continues to exist but not his soul.[30] "In the beginning was the word." But not only does God create the universe with the word; man also creates his world with the aid of the word.[31] The profound Russian scholar A. A. Potebnya writes:

Between the word and the thought of the thing in question there was such a close connection that, with a change in the word, it always seemed that the thing also was changed. . . . Both in speech and in poetry there are very clear indications that among all the Indo-European peoples the conviction was widespread that the word is the thought itself, that the word is the living truth, wisdom, the source of poetry. Like wisdom and poetry, the word was regarded as the chief foundation of human nature. The word is the thing itself. This idea is reflected not only in the affinity between the terms that denote "word" and "thing" but also in the widespread belief that the words are identical with the true substance of the phenomena.[32]

Given such a close relationship between the word and the nature of the thing, a relationship that accompanies man like a shadow through the entire course of his difficult and painful road of cultural evolution, it is quite understandable that human

30. See Max Weber, *Das antike Judentum,* pp. 154, 236.
31. One must bear in mind that not words alone but letters as well are not merely inanimate signs, for they, too, were originally images and symbols of living creatures and real objects.
32. In his *Misl I Yazik* (Thought and Language), fourth edition (1922), pp. 142–43.

thought finally came to the conclusion that where there is a concept, there must also be a corresponding entity. We speak of "justice," "truth," "beauty." These must then have a substance; something which is the bearer of these concepts must exist. Socrates was certain that every word, every name, in its origin expressed the essence or nature of some entity. His disciple, Plato, went even further in embodying abstract conceptions. To him it was clear that first in the order of being and existence are the concepts, the forms, the "ideas" of things, not the things themselves. The "beautiful" exists not only in beautiful things, and the "good" lives not only in good persons; the "beautiful" and the "good" as universal concepts are the true essences. Not only do they have their independent life, but they are in fact the only possible realities, the only real and actual existents. What we perceive with our senses is merely the accidental, the pale and transient reflection of true reality. The general logical concept which man obtains as the result and sum of real, individual phenomena is completely separated from the particular; it receives an independent, universal existence and becomes the bearer of the only important, true, and valuable essence. In the word, in the abstraction, one begins to see the chief substance and content of the thing, its prototype and pattern, its creative idea.

All this, however, is characteristic not only of Plato's doctrine. On the contrary, the tendency to seek the true essence in the word, to see in the concept independent existence, the only real and universally valid existence, appears in considerably larger measure in Aristotle's system—in his doctrine of general and particular ideas, and in his distinction between the essential and the accidental, between the potential and the actual, between form and matter. Precisely in the classical metaphysician Aristotle, who lacked the poetic intuition and inspired feeling of his master, did Plato's universal "ideas," which were saturated with radiance and beauty (and were the source of dialectical movement and constant development, obtaining their consummate expression after extensive metamorphoses in the nineteenth century in the brilliant system of Hegel), become frozen into metaphysically lifeless, arid, abstract concepts. It was in Aristotle that the final confusion of thinking and being, and the substitution of the concept for the thing occurred. The concrete perception of the thinking person was considered a foreign, merely "potential" quality of an absolutely independent reality which he must further reflect on and investigate. This literally idolatrous view of the word, this metaphysical dialectic about the connection between the one and the many, this mingling of the forms of *thinking* with the forms of *being* and the objective with the subjective elements of our perceptions and ideas, are highly characteristic of Aristotelian modes of thought. And it was this error and this confusion which, because of Aristotle's immense authority, dominated medieval European thought.[33] These assumed particularly crude forms in Christian scholasticism, which owes to them the fact that it wandered so long lost in the forest of metaphysical argumentation and dialectic.[34]

This chaos, this confusion of concept with actual being, attains its highest degree in Abraham Abulafia. Not only does he see hidden in the word, in the name, singular creative powers;[35] he is also convinced that, under certain circumstances, one can utilize these concealed powers and, with their aid, bridge the gulf between the finite and the infinite, the ephemeral and the eternal. With the help of ingenious *gematriot* and combination of the letters of the divine "names" in the Torah, Abulafia is persuaded, one can unveil the profoundest secrets and perform the greatest miracles. The entire text of the Bible is transformed by him into symbols and mysterious signs, whose real meaning can be discovered only through *gematria, notarikon,* and *temurah.*[36] "Only with the aid of *ḥochmat ha-shemot* [the science of names]," declares Abulafia, "can man attain the supreme degree of perfection."[37] Not every mortal, however, enjoys the privilege of fathom-

33. It suffices to note the controversy between the Nominalists and Realists in the Christian philosophy of the Middle Ages.
34. A brilliant analysis of this weak aspect of Aristotle's system is given by Albert Lange in his *Geschichte des Materialismus.*
35. It is characteristic of Abulafia that he underscores the fact that in the Bible the first six days of the week have no special names; they are simply called the first day, the second day, etc. Only the holy Sabbath has its own name. "Hence the Sabbath day is the most complete antithesis of the weekdays." See Abulafia's *Ḥayyei Ha-Nefesh,* Part I, Chapter 4. We quote from the manuscript in the first Firkovich collection, No. 185.
36. *Gematria* is the substitution of one Hebrew word for another whose letters, when considered as numbers, add up to the same number as the letters of the other word, e.g., *Yose* instead of *Elohim* (both of these add up to the number 86). *Notarikon* is treatment of the letters of a certain word as the initial letters of other words; e.g., *mayyim* becomes *Meherah yavo mashiaḥ* (The Messiah will soon come). *Temurah* is rearrangement of the order of the letters of a word, e.g., from the word *yismaḥ* (he will rejoice) one forms the word *mashiaḥ* (Messiah).
37. *Sefer Ḥayyei Olam Ha-Ba Ve-Hu Perush Shem Ha-Meforash,* 35a. This work of Abulafia has not been published. We have utilized a parchment manuscript in the Harkavy Collection of the library of the Society for the Dissemination of Enlightenment Among Jews.

ing the "hidden things of the Torah" (*sitrei ha-Torah*). Abulafia believes that only the elect few, the morally unblemished who have been "refined like gold through severe trials," are endowed with the great gift; only they are capable of performing miracles with the help of the mysteries concealed in the Torah.[38] But they also can employ their wondrous power only to a definite end: to exalt God's name and to praise His great deeds.[39] Hence, Abulafia attacks the "fools," the "masters of the name" (*baalei ha-shemot*) of his time, who imagine that it is possible to exploit the power of "combination of letters" for purely personal and selfish purposes.[40] He also provides precise prescriptions on how the chosen few must conduct themselves in order to obtain the required state of "cleaving to the divine" (*devekut*) and "spiritualization" or separation from corporeality (*hitpashtut ha-gashmiut*).[41] In this condition, Abulafia asserts, a man, through long repetition of "names" and combination of their letters in various orders, can merit becoming "one with open eyes," for whom all the divine secrets of the Torah are revealed and the most mysterious enigmas of life are disclosed.

The ardent mystic Abulafia believed that he had succeeded in fathoming the profound mysteries, in tearing away the veil of the eternally concealed riddle of life. He was persuaded that the holy spirit rested upon him, that the spirit of the prophets had awakened in him, that he was the man "with open eyes." "The Creator of all the worlds," he asserts, "revealed Himself to me. He disclosed to me His great secret, and informed me about the end of the exile, the time when the redemption will begin."[42] He was certain that the dawn of the day of redemption had already arrived, for the great "shepherd," the redeemer who had been so long awaited, had already appeared—and that the redeemer was none other than himself, Abraham Abulafia! "God the Creator of the heavens," declares Abulafia,

has heard the cry of Jacob's children and sent a messenger to His people, and the messenger is named Zechariah.[43] For His persecuted

38. *Hayyei Ha-Nefesh*, Part I, Chapter 1.
39. *Sefer Hayyei Olam Ha-Ba* (manuscript), 4a.
40. Ibid., 31a.
41. These prescriptions are strongly reminiscent of the conduct of the Yordei Merkavah, when they wished to attain the supreme level of ecstasy. The passage containing these prescriptions in *Sefer Hayyei Olam Ha-Ba* is very characteristic of medieval mysticism in general.
42. Jellinek, *Auswahl Kabbalistischer Mystik*, p. 18.
43. Abulafia at times calls himself Zechariah, at other times Raziel, for both names add up in *gematria* to the same total as the name Abraham,

Abulafia's Disciples

people, which every nation has reviled and oppressed, the day of joyous tidings has arrived. Now the messenger Zechariah comes, descending on a light-winged cloud dripping dew. . . .[44]

The fiery preaching of the dreamy mystic made a considerable impression. Enthusiastic pupils who eagerly imbibed every word of the "messenger" soon appeared. In the narrow circle of Abulafia's disciples, the foremost place was occupied by a young man of philosophical learning named Joseph ben Abraham Gikatilla who became renowned for his mystical writings.[45] This favorite pupil of Abulafia's came to mysticism, as did his teacher, only after being disappointed by philosophy. "I perceived," Gikatilla laments,

how dark and crooked are the paths on which my people wander. I saw persons who deny providence and wish to show that man's fate depends entirely on the spheres and planets. Relying on the authority of Aristotle, they completely reject the idea of man's freedom of will and power of choice. They refuse to take any account of whether man feels God in his heart. They insist that everything occurs according to the order of the iron laws that govern nature, and that God is not the ruler and guide of the world. They do not believe that the Torah is from heaven or that the universe was created at a definite moment. They believe in the eternity of the universe and that everything has been in motion throughout all time, according to precise laws in which no alteration can occur. On this basis they deny all miracles and wonders, for these would contradict such laws. They refuse to recognize that belief in miracles is the foundation of our Torah and reject it. Thus they deny the entire Torah.[46]

Gikatilla's yearning eyes saw surrounding him nothing but wonders. His powerful imagination sought only the extraordinary, and with all the ardor of his soul he devoted himself to the mystical

---

namely, 248. On occasion he also calls himself Berachyahu, which is equivalent in *gematria* to the name Abram.
44. From Abulafia's *Sefer Ha-Ot* (published in the Graetz *Jubelschrift*, *Ateret Tzevi*, Part II, pp. 65–85), p. 75.
45. Gikatilla notes in the introduction to his *Ginnat Egoz* that he was born at Medinaceli, Old Castile. In the library of the Asiatic Museum in Leningrad there is a manuscript of *Ginnat Egoz* which was completed in 1561. In the introduction there is an indication (missing in the printed edition) that Gikatilla was born in 1248 and wrote this work at the age of twenty-six.
46. *Ginnat Egoz*, Part I, 13a. Maimonides also noted the contradiction between the belief in miracles and Aristotle's doctrine of the eternity of the universe in his *Guide for the Perplexed*, II:25: "The belief in the eternity of the universe . . . fundamentally contradicts the [Jewish] religion and denies all miracles."

world with its hidden and unfathomed depths. In these depths, he realized, great dangers lurk. "Burning and destructive is the flame of the secret wisdom," declares Gikatilla, "but better to be consumed in this pure golden flame than to grope in the darkness like beasts of the forest."[47]

Like his teacher Abulafia, Joseph Gikatilla steeped himself in the secrets of *gematriot*, and it was to these that he devoted his major work, *Ginnat Egoz*.[48] The word *Ginnat* is in fact formed from the first letters of *gematria, notarikon,* and *temurah*;[49] and the word *egoz* (nut), the author explains, is the symbol of the "hidden wisdom."[50]

Gikatilla became renowned as a leading Kabbalist. Legend relates that he performed great marvels and was therefore called Joseph Baal Nes, "Joseph the miracle-worker." Abraham Abulafia also testifies that his disciple was "wondrously successful and God was with him."[51]

Abulafia, however, was not content with his small circle of followers. He wanted the entire world to recognize his "mission," and therefore left his disciples and set out for Italy. In Urbino in 1279 he wrote his first "prophetic" book, *Sefer Ha-Yashar*, and after it quickly followed scores of Kabbalist works in which genuinely inspired pages, filled with powerful feeling and rich in poetic imagery, are mingled, without any order, with bizarre incantations, strange "names," and a chaos of incomprehensible words and allusions.[52]

In his *Sefer Ha-Ot* Abulafia writes: "And God said to the messenger Zechariah: 'Lift up your voice, take your pen in hand, and

---

47. *Ginnat Egoz*, 3a (the Hanau edition).
48. First published in Hanau in 1615.
49. The author discusses at length these three major foundations of the practical Kabbalah at the end of the second part of his work (64).
50. *Ginnat Egoz* consists of three parts. In the first, God's "names" are discussed; in the second, "combinations of letters" and the foundation of the "sacred" numbers—3, 7, and 10; in the third, the Hebrew vowels, which are here considered as symbols and emblems (e.g., the *ḥolem, shurek,* and *ḥirek* are allusions to the "upper" world, the "middle" world, and the "lower" world). Gikatilla also composed numerous other works on the Kabbalah. One of these was translated into Latin by a Christian scholar, Riccius. The translation was published in 1516 and was utilized by the celebrated Johannes von Reuchlin in his *De Arte Cabalistica*.
51. Jellinek, *Bet Ha-Midrash*, III, xli.
52. Abulafia himself indicates (Jellinek, *Philosophie und Kabbala*, p. 23) that he composed 26 books of Kabbalah and 22 books of prophecy. Most of these were lost. Part of Abulafia's literary legacy was published by Jellinek.

Ink and Blood

let all know God's word.' And God was with him, and Zechariah wrote down everything that God commanded him."[53] This mystic, whose soul was carried into the whirlwind of fantastic dreams, wrote not only with his hand but with his heart's blood. "What is born in the heart is brought into the world with fiery script and flaming pen. . . . Fearful and terrible is the power of the pen. The ink is blood, God's name is in it, and every drop of the liquid waters the earth, fertilizes the wasteland."

This image of inanimate pages vivified through pen and ink and fructified with the blood of the heart and nerves is frequently repeated by Abulafia. In *Sefer Ha-Ot* he writes: "Thus God said to me:

> Here is your soul, and her name is blood, and the spirit that lives in you is called ink. . . . When I heard of the great difference between my soul and my spirit, I was filled with delight. . . . Then I understood that my soul bears the color belonging to its nature. It is red like blood, and my spirit is also as it should be—black like ink. And great was the struggle in my heart between blood and ink. . . . And ink overcame blood, and the Sabbath overcame the weekday.[54]

Abulafia's prophetic books, however, did not find any response. The people refused to acknowledge the new "prophet." His brethren stubbornly turned away from the "messenger." Those to whom he was sent, those whom he wished to liberate, were unwilling to recognize him and greeted him with scorn and laughter. The last hour, he believed, had come. All must be awakened from the sleep of darkness and the slumber of ignorance. The day of redemption for the chosen people was arriving, but no one awakened, no one wanted to recognize what was happening![55]

But Abulafia did not despair. If his own people would not listen, he would tell the whole world of his mission and proclaim the truth revealed to him. He would announce to all peoples the tidings: the day of redemption approaches, and soon God's glory will be revealed before all. To influence the Christian world and attract its attention, he combined the doctrine of the ten *sefirot* with the doctrine of the Trinity. "God's name," declared Abulafia, "manifests the essence of unity in three-fold form. But the trinity is the complete unity."[56]

53. P. 67.
54. Graetz *Jubelschrift, Ateret Tzevi*, p. 81.
55. *Ibid.*, p. 79.
56. It must, however, be noted that Abulafia regarded Jesus with hostility and contempt. Landauer (*Literaturblatt des Orients*, 1845, p. 590)

In 1280 Abulafia traveled to Rome, motivated by the fantastic notion of demonstrating his divine mission to the head of all Christendom, Pope Nicholas III. Miraculously the dreamer managed to escape death and left Rome after spending a month in prison.[57] He then went to Sicily and in Palermo preached fiery sermons about his "mission." His propagandist activity distressed the rabbis and the leaders of the Jewish community. They inquired of the greatest Spanish scholar of that period, Rabbi Solomon ben Adret, what attitude they should adopt toward the "prophetic" preachings of this mystic. Solomon ben Adret was strongly opposed to Abulafia and perceived in his activity a serious threat to the Jewish community. He therefore immediately wrote to the Jews of Sicily, advising that they guard themselves against this "false messiah," this "vile man," this "terrible liar and seducer."[58] On receiving this reply, the Sicilian Jews began an intense persecution of Abulafia. One of his disciples laments that they put the "prophet" in prison and took away his entire fortune; even his books passed into the hands of the "robbers."

These persecutions only confirmed Abulafia's belief that he was, indeed, "God's messenger" who must suffer for the sins of the world:

God sent His people the redeemer who would heal their wounds and reveal to their sages and scholars His holy name. The sages of Israel, however, are very sick. They are afflicted with diseases whose like are not even mentioned among the curses written down in the Torah of Moses, the man of God. . . . And they rose, these who deny true wisdom, these afflicted with deathly sicknesses; they blasphemed God and His anointed with impudent words. . . . God's wrath has therefore flared up against the rebellious people who deny Him. He sent His reprover to them, but they met him with scorn, pursued him from city to city, from land to land.[59]

Embittered by the persecutions which he suffered, Abulafia poured out his hatred and indignation on his opponents, the "scholars of the Talmud" and rabbis. On the small, isolated island of Comino, near Malta, to which he had to flee from his enemies,

---

quotes the following passage from Abulafia: "I, Raziel the son of Samuel, know the blessing and the curse; I know the unclean bastard; I know Jesus and Mohammed."

57. A fantastic account of how he was saved from being burned at the stake is given by Abulafia in his *Sefer Ha-Edut* (the account is published in *MGWJ*, 1887, p. 558).
58. Solomon ben Adret, *Responsa*, No. 548.
59. *Sefer Ha-Ot*, p. 78.

The "Revelation" of the Zohar

Abulafia in 1288 wrote his "prophetic" work *Sefer Ha-Ot*, from which we quoted earlier. This is the first Hebrew book in which the Talmudists and rabbis are spoken of with such open hostility.

> And God, in those days, said to Zechariah: Write this book, reveal in it the way of the scholars of Israel—how they glory in everything that is most hateful to Me. They say: What need have we to think of God? What good will remembering Him do? Of what use will it be for us to consider and count His holy "names"? Better to count our gold and silver. This will certainly be useful to us and our friends.[60]

Abulafia speaks with the same hatred in his other work, *Imrei Shefer*, of the "majority of the scholars of the Talmud," calling them "fools who will have no correction, for they consider themselves great sages." This group is very certain that their learning "is greater than all other wisdoms." He, Abulafia, however, knows that "the distinction between the Talmudist and one who has fathomed the secret of the Ineffable Name is no smaller than the distinction between the Jewish Talmudist and the gentile scholar."[61]

Imrei Shefer was written by Abulafia in the year 1290. What subsequently happened to him is unknown. He suddenly disappears, and his later life is veiled in mystery.

At just that time an event occurred which is of the greatest consequence not only for Jewish mysticism but for the further development of all of Judaic culture. A great work, a treasury of the whole Jewish mystical world of ideas, the greatest and most brilliant memorial of the Kabbalah and mystical creativity produced in many generations, suddenly appeared. This monumental work made its appearance wrapped in mystery and wreathed in miraculous legends. It was not a book, but a revelation. And it was revealed not to a common mortal but to the godly Tanna Rabbi Simeon bar Yohai. Full of splendor was the revelation; hence, the wondrous book bears the title *Zohar* (Splendor).

---

60. *Ibid.*
61. See Jellinek, *Philosophie und Kabbala*, pp. 35 ff., where the first three chapters of Abulafia's *Imrei Shefer* are reprinted.

CHAPTER THREE

The Zohar

NEAR the end of the 1280's Moses ben Shemtov de Leon[1] of the Spanish city of Guadalajara, a composer of many rather ordinary Kabbalist books, began to disseminate numerous copies of a work entitled *Midrash Ha-Zohar*, which until then was completely unknown. De Leon declared that this work had been written through the holy spirit by the second-century Tanna Simeon bar Yoḥai during the time he had lived hidden in a cave, and that his disciples had later completed it. The ancient manuscript was alleged to have been found by Naḥmanides when he was in Palestine. Naḥmanides sent it to some relatives in Catalonia whence, according to de Leon, it came into his hands.

1. It is interesting to note that Moses de Leon was, like Abraham Abulafia, an ardent follower of Maimonides in his youth. In the manuscript collection belonging to Baron Günzburg there was a copy of the *Guide for the Perplexed* at the end of which the copyist noted that he had written the manuscript for Moses de Leon and completed it in the year 1264. At the beginning and end of this manuscript there are poems praising Maimonides and his *Guide*. When Moses de Leon died has not been determined. On this question, see G. Scholem's article in *Maddaei Ha-Yahadut*, I (1926), 16–29.

The Zohar

The question of the real origin of the *Zohar*, which was immensely revered by Jews for centuries, is to the present day not entirely resolved. In the Haskalah period the hostility of the *maskilim*, or "enlightened," toward mysticism in general and Hasidism in particular strongly hindered the objective, scientific investigation of this question. Even such a great scholar of the Haskalah era as the historian Heinrich Graetz[2] brands the *Zohar* a "book of lies" which the "falsifier" and "charlatan" Moses de Leon wrote for the sake of financial gain.

There is no doubt that it was not Moses de Leon, a mediocre writer with a prosaic, bland style, who was the author of this extraordinary work, in which naive, infantile notions and bizarre superstitions are so uniquely interwoven with a profoundly philosophic and imaginative world view, borne on the wings of great inspiration and embodied in colorful, Oriental, genuinely poetic, imagery and symbolism.[3] It is also clear that the *Zohar* is

2. Graetz approaches the problem of the *Zohar* not as a scholar but as a polemicist. The following are a few quotations from his "scientific" polemic against the Kabbalah and the *Zohar*, which he despised so intensely. "Discord is the mother of this sinister creation" (*Geschichte der Juden*, VII, 74). "He [Nahmanides] promoted the Kabbalah greatly by clothing it with his authority and thereby contributed his share to the obscuration and degeneration of Judaism" (*ibid.*, p. 56). "These four Kabbalists of first rank. . . . Isaac Ibn Latif, Abraham Abulafia, Joseph Gikatilla and Moses de Leon . . . obscured the spiritual light which scholars from Saadia to Maimonides had brought into Judaism with the darkness of a barbaric chaos, and instead of a purified God-faith proclaimed fantastic, indeed blasphemous, chimeras and delusions. The benightedness of the succeeding centuries in the Jewish world is mainly their work . . . and the injuries which they inflicted on Judaism are still discernible to the present day" (*ibid.*, p. 220).
3. In recent times the distinguished scholar of Kabbalah, G. Scholem, has especially concerned himself with the question of the authorship of the *Zohar*. See his previously mentioned article, as well as *Kiryat Sefer*, VI, 109. Of interest in connection with the still-unresolved problem of the origin of the *Zohar* are the following points noted by Scholem: Isaac Ibn Sahulah quotes in his *Meshal Ha-Kadmoni*, which appeared in 1281 (hence, five years before Moses de Leon's first work), the *Midrash Ha-Ne'elam* (see *Tarbitz*, III, 181–83). Scholem also points out that the thirteenth-century version of the *Midrash Ha-Ne'elam* differs in many details from the later version. Scholem further notes that "in any case the *Zohar* was already in existence at the time the *Sefer Ha-Rimmon* and the *Mishkan Ha-Edut* of Moses de Leon, as well as the works of Gikatilla on the *sefirot* and the 'reasons for the commandments,' were written" (*Tarbitz*, III, 42). Almost all the Kabbalists of the beginning of the fourteenth century, he also points out, make considerable use of the *Zohar* but still do not know of the *Raya Mehemna* and *Tikkunei Zohar*; hence, these sections were composed considerably later than the other basic parts of the *Zohar* (*ibid.*, pp. 55, 58).

The Zohar *and Jewish Mysticism*

not a unitary work written by one pen and created from one mold. Some of its parts, such as the *Sifra Di-Tzeniuta*, the *Idra Rabba*, and the *Idra Zutta*, are apparently very old, and their birthplace is certainly the area where Jewish mysticism was born, the Near East.[4] It is also possible that these mystical notebooks were actually connected by folk tradition with the popular name of Rabbi Simeon bar Yohai, the beloved hero of numerous mystical compositions.[5] Whether these notebooks were in fact transmitted from the Near East to Spain through Nahmanides or through other hands is naturally difficult to determine and also not very important. There is, further, no doubt that many pages of the *Zohar*, as Landauer[6] established in his day, were written by Abraham Abulafia. Moses de Leon was probably merely the editor, who reworked and again redacted the collected material. At the present time, however, it is difficult to obtain a clear picture of de Leon's editorial work, for the printed text of the *Zohar* is very different from that which he issued in his time. In later generations many passages were eliminated and new ones inserted. The *Zohar*, indeed, is the great "catchall" in which all the mystical elements that found a literary echo in the Jewish world from the time of the Essenes and Gnostics through later centuries are assembled.

In the *Zohar*'s world view the *Ilat Ha-Ilot*, the absolute and only primordial cause, transcends all conceptualization and explanation. The original creative power, the *Zohar* teaches, is the *Ein Sof*, the unconditionally infinite and indivisible Unity. To express its essence through any name or term is impossible, for it is beyond human understanding. God is the universal negation, the boundless No or Nothing (*Ayin*). We do not know and comprehend, and it is not possible to fathom, His nature.[7]

In the *Ein Sof*, the absolute unity which transcends every form, all the infinite potentialities of the most varied creative powers, as well as all the innumerable forms of being and becoming, are concealed. The connecting link between the hidden Infinite and limited being is the ten *sefirot* or *middot* (attributes), the first revelation of the Creator. These *sefirot*, which are merely different

---

4. A. Franck, in his *La Kabbale*, especially stresses the influence of Parseeism on the *Zohar* (pp. 200–288, in Jellinek's German translation).
5. E.g., *Tefillot Rabbi Simeon ben Yohai, Nistarot Rabbi Simeon ben Yohai, Mechilta De-Rabbi Simeon ben Yohai*.
6. In *Literaturblatt des Orients*, 1845, pp. 178 ff. Landauer, however, committed the error of thinking that Abraham Abulafia was the author of the entire *Zohar*. S. Bernfeld also fell into the same error; see his *Daat Elohim*, p. 378.
7. *Zohar*, III, 288b (we paraphrase from the Mantua edition, reprinted in Amsterdam in 1728).

reflections of the one light that emanates out of the "Cause of Causes," are in their totality still not the *complete* image of the Absolute-Infinite or *Ein Sof*. They are merely a reflection of His concentrated light (*tzimtzum*), for only in this form can the Infinite reveal Himself. In Solomon Ibn Gabirol's philosophy the entire universe, with all its phenomena, consists of the union of matter (*yesod*) and form (*tzurah*) in all possible relationships and degrees. According to Ibn Gabirol's view, *yesod* or matter is the passive element, which receives influence; *tzurah* or form is the active element, which exercises influence. The same fundamental idea is stressed in the *Zohar*. Everything that is consists of the union of these two elements, the active "masculine" and the passive "feminine."[8] Through their union arise not only the material phenomena but also the spiritual world and all spiritual representations. These elements, with all the phenomena deriving from them, constitute the entire universe in the form of an infinite chain which obtains, with every new link, ever cruder forms, and becomes always more corporeal the greater the separation between itself and the source of light and life—the Creator of everything that exists.

The first and highest emanation of the *Ein Sof* is called in the *Zohar* "Crown" (*Keter* or *Kitra Ilaah*), "White Head" (*Resha Hivvra*), or "First or Simple Point" (*Nekudah Rishonah* or *Nekudah Peshita*). "When the most hidden of all the hidden

---

8. *Zohar*, III, 290a. "Nothing could exist," the *Zohar* further declares, "until the Eternal revealed His form—the form which is the embodiment of the masculine and the feminine" (III, 292). This idea of androgyny or double sexuality, of the emanation of the essence of both elements, the masculine and the feminine, from the "Cause of Causes," which occupies a central position in the *Zohar* is also encountered in Abraham Abulafia and in virtually all the older mystics. According to Abulafia, the three most profound and exalted world enigmas are the *sitrei bereshit* (secrets of creation), the *sitrei merkavah* (secrets of the chariot or throne), and the *sitrei arayot* (secrets of sexual union). See the preface to Abulafia's *Hayyei Olam Ha-Ba*. In the same work Abulafia notes that the mystery of the masculine and feminine is hidden in the *Shem Ha-Meforash* (Ineffable Name). The idea of divine double sexuality, which numerous Gnostics expressed, is raised by Abulafia to a complete system. It is also frequently found among the sages of the Talmud: "Everything which the Holy One, blessed be He, created in His world, He created male and female" (*Baba Batra*, 74b). "In the creation of man out of the 'dust of the earth,' the word 'dust' signifies the masculine element and the word 'earth' signifies the feminine element." It may also be noted that the idea of divine double sexuality occupies an important place in the thought of several Greek philosophers (Xenocrates and others), as well as among the Stoics.

The Doctrine of Androgyny in Jewish Mysticism

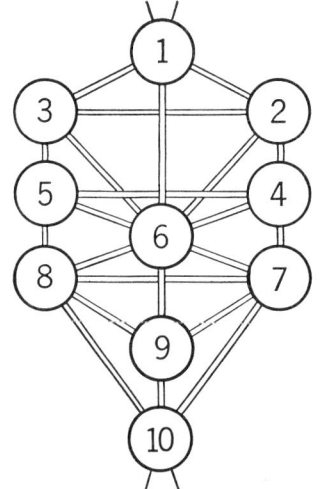

1. Keter
2. Hochmah
3. Binah
4. Gedulah
5. Gevurah
6. Tiferet
7. Netzah
8. Hod
9. Yesod
10. Malchut

GENERAL SCHEMA OF THE *SEFIROT*

wished to reveal Himself, He first of all created a point."⁹ This primal divine emanation is the source from which the infinite light flows, but it still has no image or form. Out of *Keter*, in which all the other *sefirot* are potentially present, emanates the second *sefirah*, *Hochmah* (Wisdom), which also bears the name *Abba* (Father), because it is the "father" of the active, fertilizing element of all being. Along with *Hochmah* there emanates from *Keter* the "feminine" *sefirah* known as *Binah* (Understanding or Intelligence), which is also called the Primordial Mother (*Imma Ilaah*). These two *sefirot*, the first bearers of masculinity and femininity, are the source of everything that is. They are the antipodes or extremes, the two sharpest opponents (thesis and antithesis), which are blended together in a harmonious whole in their common source, *Keter*,¹⁰ together with which they form the first triad embracing the highest, purely spiritual, world, the *olam ha-sechel* or the *olam ha-muskal* (intelligible world). These first three *sefirot* form, according to the *Zohar*, a complete unity. That which in the ordinary world is divided into three separate ele-

---

9. *Zohar*, I, 2a. The name *Nekudah Rishonah* is also given to the first emanation by Isaac Ibn Latif in his *Shaar Ha-Shamayim*, which he composed in 1244.
10. According to the commentators on the *Zohar*, the two *sefirot* called *Hochmah* and *Binah* are not united directly in *Keter* but in its reflection, which is named *Da'at*. *Da'at* is not considered a separate *sefirah*. On this, see Moses Cordovero's *Or Ne'erav*, Part VI, Chapter 1. See also his *Pardes Rimmonim*, Part III, Chapter 8.

ments—the thinker, the thought, and the phenomenon thought about—are united in the divine into a single whole; they are one and the same. The *Zohar* here expresses the idea that centuries later occupied such a prominent place in German Idealistic philosophy, the doctrine of the complete identity of thinking and being, of the ideal and the real (*Identität des Denkens und Seins, des Idealen und Realen*).

After the first three *sefirot* comes the second triad, which comprehends the moral world, the *olam ha-nefesh* (world of the soul), whose corporeal symbol is the heart. From the divine thought two *sefirot* emanate: the masculine *Gedulah* (Greatness) and the feminine *Gevurah* (Power), both of which are united in the third *sefirah*, *Tiferet* (Beauty). Beauty, the *Zohar* teaches in the *Idra Zutta*, is the supreme revelation of moral perfection in life; it is like the sun which, with its rays, illuminates everything on earth and without which all things would be steeped in darkness.

The third triad embraces the real, natural world (*olam ha-teva* or *olam ha-murgash*). The masculine and feminine *sefirot*, *Netzah* (Eternity) and *Hod* (Majesty), are blended together in their unifying principle, *Yesod* (Foundation). The tenth *sefirah*, *Malchut* (Kingdom or Sovereignty), is the link that unites the three triads of *sefirot*, the *olam ha-atzilut* or "world of emanation" with the three real worlds, where the *sefirot* first obtain the possibility of revealing themselves in concrete, limited forms. These three worlds are called in the *Zohar*: (1) *olam ha-beriah*, the world of active-creative ideas, (2) *olam ha-yetzirah*, the world of created forms, and (3) *olam ha-asiah*, the world of creative matter, or the world of action and creation.[11]

11. In the old manuscripts of the *Zohar* the ten *sefirot* are also portrayed in the form of a tree. The masculine *sefirot*, all of which are on the right, are called the right side; the feminine, the left side; and the synthesizing or uniting *sefirot*, which are in the center, are called the middle column. For a more detailed discussion, see Cordovero's *Pardes Rimmonim*, Parts VII–VIII. The *Zohar* also distinguishes the *sefirot* according to their colors. Already in Solomon Ibn Gabirol's *Tikkun Middot Ha-Nefesh* we find allusions to color mysticism, e.g., when he speaks of various spiritual qualities as colored. The same theme is touched on by the Kabbalist Azriel in his *Perush Eser Sefirot*, but it is only in the *Zohar* that it is first systematically developed. There each *sefirah* has its own color. The first *sefirah*, "White Head," is also called the dazzling white light. The *sefirah* called *Din* (Justice) is blood-red. The *sefirah* named *Tiferet* (Beauty) is purple. The *sefirah* called *Malchut* (Kingdom) has the hue of sapphire and glistens with all kinds of colors. Moses Cordovero devotes a special section of his major work, *Pardes Rimmonim*, to this matter; the section is entitled "The Gate of Colors." He returns to the same subject in his other work, *Or Ne'erav*, Part IV, Chapter 4.

The Concept of the "High Man" (Adam Ilaah)

When we pass over into the real world, one of the most characteristic motifs in the *Zohar* at once appears very clearly—the *ethical*, which occupies a much more important place than the purely philosophical. The entire work, constructed so unsystematically and strangely, is unified by one intense desire which pulsates in each of its pages. This is the restless striving of the believing and loving heart to unveil the enigma of life, which is so filled with evil and terror, to fathom and grasp the moral essence that lies hidden in the mystery of the universe.

We have observed that in the Arabic translation of the ancient work *Teologia*, which was erroneously ascribed to Aristotle, the first divine emanation bears the name "the high man."[12] This abstract concept, in which the influence of Philo's doctrine of the "heavenly man" and of Plato's theory of "ideas" is discernible, is incorporated in the *Zohar* in altogether unique forms. "The earthly world," the *Zohar* teaches, "is created precisely after the pattern of the upper world; everything that exists above has its reflection on earth, and everything is one."[13] The unification or combination of the ten *sefirot* through which the *Ein Sof* reveals itself bears in the *Zohar* the name *Adam Kadmon* or *Adam Ilaah*, i.e., the pattern, the prototype, the "idea" of man. This abstract metaphysical concept, however, here receives concrete, human, ethical forms. The image of man, the *Zohar* maintains, is the pattern of everything that exists in the heavens and on the earth. Indeed, it is because of this that God created man after His image; no form and no thing could exist as long as man's image was still lacking, for it bears in itself all other images and everything that exists does so only by virtue of it. If it were not, there would be no world.

Since the *Zohar* proceeds from the assumption that nothing in the world is destroyed[14] and everything is "united in God" (*hakol bo*), it concludes that it must deny the well-known principle that the world is created *ex nihilo* (*Me-Ayin*). In the view of the *Zohar*, by the *Ayin* (Nothing), from which the world is created, must be understood the *Ein Sof*, the highest creative power, which is, for us, the absolutely negative, the infinite, incomprehensible "Nothingness."

The presently existing world, however, declares the *Zohar*, is not the first world that God created. Before this world many others

---

12. See Harkavy, *Ḥadashim Gam Yeshanim*, X, 17; Munk, *Mélanges de philosophie juive et arabe*, p. 258.
13. *Zohar*, II, 20a.
14. According to the *Zohar*, II, 100a, "nothing in the world is entirely lost, not even the breath issuing from man's mouth; like every other phenomenon, it also has its definite purpose."

existed.[15] "Why," asks the *Zohar*, "were all the earlier worlds destroyed? — Because man was still not created. As long as man's image did not exist, the worlds could have no endurance. They were all destroyed until man's image appeared."[16] "Man," the *Zohar* further affirms, "is simultaneously the highest level and also the essence of all creatures. . . . As soon as man was created, everything was complete—both the heavenly world and the earthly world; for everything is connected with man, who contains in himself all phenomena and all forms and images."[17]

In the view of the *Zohar*, man not only occupies the central place in the nature of reality; he also unifies in himself *what is* with *what ought to be*. He is the criterion of all values, the incarnation of the absolutely spiritual and the absolutely moral, i.e., the truly divine. Man's significance consists not only in that he bears the image of God and that God's stamp is impressed on his spirit; divinity itself is also revealed only through man, by means of his striving and acting. In short, man is incarnate divinity, the revelation of the Absolute-Infinite in limited, concrete forms. Thus the sharpest antitheses are brought together in a dialectical manner in the *Zohar*: the infinite with the limited, the universal, concealed "No" with the concrete "Yes." Man, the *Zohar* teaches, is the representative of divinity on earth. He is the *Shechinta Tataah*, the earthly *Shechinah*, with which the Creator entered into an eternal covenant.[18] He is the measure and bearer of all values, "and when the world was already created, nothing could have any endurance until God decided to create man, who observes His Torah; and for his sake the world endures."[19] The terrestrial world is merely a reflection of the heavenly, ideal world. Yet this heavenly world can reveal its activity only as a result of the stimulus it receives from below through man, who is the major link uniting the two worlds. The earthly world, according to the *Zohar*, is dependent on the celestial, and the celestial operates according to the same order as the earthly.[20]

One is reminded of the well-known Talmudic statement: "I saw a world turned upside down" (*Pesaḥim* 50a). The *Zohar*,

15. *Zohar*, III, 61. The same idea was expressed by the sages of the Talmud. The following passage is interesting: "Rabbi Abbahu said: God created worlds and destroyed them until He created the present one and said: this one pleases me; the others did not please me" (*Bereshit Rabbah*, III:7).
16. *Zohar*, III, 135.
17. *Ibid.*, II, 48b, 74a.
18. *Ibid.*, I, 56a.
19. *Ibid.*, II, 161a.
20. *Ibid.*, III, 40b.

considering man the center of the universe, knows of no separation between this world and the other; the heavens come down to earth and the whole universe is transformed into a heavenly kingdom. Stressed with utmost sharpness in the *Zohar* is the profound ethical idea that without the active will of man even God's blessing cannot prevail. "No influence comes down from above unless it is preceded by a stimulus from below," declares the *Zohar*. Two streams of light flow toward each other. Toward the celestial light streaming from above on all creatures rise luminous rays from below. Man does not passively accept God's grace and favor as the decree of an external will but himself influences the upper spheres. The human heart and will are the key that unlocks the gates of God's grace. "There is never any stirring of the attribute of mercy from above without a stirring of the heart below." The enthusiasm of the heart, the feeling of love, is the supreme dynamic power in the universe. "Love," says the *Zohar*, "is the profound mystery of God's unity and wholeness; it is the link connecting the highest with the lower levels. It raises all that lives to the celestial heights, where everything is forged together in one wholeness."[21]

Even less than Solomon Ibn Gabirol's *Mekor Hayyim* does the *Zohar* recognize any sharp distinction between spirit and matter. Matter or corporeality is also spirit, but in a cruder form, less permeated with the rays streaming out of the source of light and life, the *Ilat Ha-Ilot* or Cause of Causes. In the Kabbalist view, the material elements, the *kelipot* or shells, are not inanimate; in them also God's spirit, though to a lesser degree, lives. "God," teaches the *Zohar*,[22] "is the beginning and the end of all levels in the work of creation; all bear His stamp." The *kelipot* also carry God's seal; they, too, are permeated with His rays. Everything is one unity; in everything God's spirit breathes; all levels of creation strive and yearn toward each other in order to unite with what is higher and more luminous. The inanimate streams to what lives and breathes, and everything that has the breath of life in itself draws toward man, whose soul is immortal. Everything in the world is permeated with God's light and strives toward this light; and men are the *tzinorot* or channels through which the divine light flows. Man is the agent through whom God's spirit and grace are carried over from the *sefirot* into the real, terrestrial world. And the entire purpose and goal of the "work of creation" is to reveal the spirituality of the human personality, to draw it closer

21. *Ibid.*, II, 216a ("Parashah Va-Yakhel").
22. *Ibid.*, I, 21a.

to the "idea" of *Adam Ha-Kadmon* (Primordial Man) who is the foundation of God's creativity, the beginning and end of the "work of creation."

Through every sin and transgression which man commits, the divine light is diminished and God's radiance obscured. The commandments must be fulfilled not only because the Torah has ordained them or because to do so is useful for man, but because thereby man influences the "upper worlds," magnifies the holy and the exalted on the earth. Man's deeds, in the view of the *Zohar*, bear a high ethical stamp. It is for this reason that the *tzaddik*, the pious and godfearing man, occupies such an important place in the Kabbalah. "*Tzaddik yesod olam*" (the pious man is the foundation of the world), says the *Zohar*. On him the world rests, and even an angel is not comparable to him.[23] "The *tzaddik*," further declares the *Zohar*, "is the guiltless sacrifice who atones for the sins of the world."[24] But every ordinary mortal also fulfills a great task with his pious life, with the good deeds and commandments he performs, for each soul is designated to participate in *tikkun ha-olam* (the improvement or perfection of the world).

In Maimonides' view one can serve God only with the mind, through sharpening one's thought and through arduous striving to comprehend as much as possible of the nature of God and the greatness of His deeds. But only the elect few can serve God in this intellectual way. The plain man has no possibility of drawing near to God. His prayer, which is filled with praises and images taken from pictorial language, smacks of anthropomorphism, and this, in Maimonides' opinion, is "blasphemy." The Kabbalah, however, which appeals more to the heart than to the mind and believes that God must be felt in every tremor of the soul, insists on the great psychological significance of collective prayer, the enthusiasm and spiritual exaltation that man experiences when he pours out his heart before God. Prayer, says the *Zohar*, raises man to the loftiest levels, brings him close to God, awakens God's grace and transforms it from potentiality into actuality. A fervent

23. *Ibid.*, III, 68b.
24. This idea is already to be found among the older Kabbalists. In *Sefer Ha-Bahir*, e.g., we read (Chapter 44): "There is one pillar reaching from the earth to the heavens and its name is *tzaddik* [the pious or righteous man] . . . when there are *tzaddikim* in the world this pillar is strengthened, but if there are not it is weakened. The *tzaddik* bears the burden of the world, as it is written, 'the *tzaddik* is the foundation of the world,' and if he is weak the world cannot endure. Therefore, even if there is only one *tzaddik* in the world, it endures, as it is said, 'the *tzaddik* is the foundation of the world.'"

prayer that brings the soul into ecstasy and lets it pass over into transport and negation of being "makes the worlds tremble." It reaches to the "heavenly soul," to the source of femininity and maternity, to the "Mother" of the world, the *sefirah* called *Binah*. The *sod ha-tefillah* (mystery of prayer) has an especially important place in the *Zohar*. Every word in prayer lives its individual life, is filled with profound significance, purifies and elevates the soul to the source of light and beauty. And not only the chosen few but the entire people of Israel can be sanctified and come close to God with the aid of prayer.

Considering the cosmic function that the human personality performs, according to the *Zohar*, it is natural that this great Kabbalist work devotes much attention to the question of the nature of the human soul. Solomon Ibn Gabirol in his *Keter Malchut* assigns souls the most honored of places, beneath the Throne of Glory itself. So also the *Zohar*; in its view, the source of man's soul is the "Soul of the World" (*Keter Elyon*), in whose womb all souls have rested throughout eternity, even before "the work of creation."[25] "When God decided to create the world," we read in the *Zohar*, "the image of the world revealed itself, as it were, before His eyes. And He created all the souls that would be embodied in all future generations in the children of men; and all of them appeared precisely in the forms they would later take on in the terrestrial world."[26] "Man's soul is the image and pattern of universal being, the highest level of its perfection."[27] The *Zohar* compares the soul, in a poetic image, to the light of the eye. "Before everything else," we read in *Tikkunei Zohar*, "God created the soul. It is written in the Torah, 'And the earth was waste and void and the spirit of God hovered over the face of the waters.' Everything was waste because man's eye was still closed. As soon as his eye opened, God at once said, 'Let there be light,' and there was light."[28]

Just as the *sefirot* form three triads, so the soul, which is the reflection of the *sefirot*, consists of three elements: *neshamah*, *ruaḥ*, and *nefesh*. The highest level is *neshamah*; this unites man with the *olam ha-sechel* (the intelligible world). *Ruaḥ* is the moral nature

---

25. The doctrine of the eternal preexistence of souls was undoubtedly taken over by the Jewish mystics from the neo-Platonists. On this, see M. Joel's *Die Religionsphilosophie des Sohars*, pp. 332, 348.
26. *Zohar*, II, 96b ("Parashah Mishpatim").
27. *Ibid.*, II, 141b.
28. *Tikkunei Zohar*, Gate 70, p. 362 (we quote according to the Brody edition, 1883). The comparison of the human soul with light is also to be found in Solomon Ibn Gabirol.

of man, which links him with the symbol of moral beauty, the *sefirah* called *Tiferet* (Beauty). The third part, *nefesh*, is the lowest level that binds man to the material world, the *olam ha-asiah*.[29] "And all three parts are one; they are united in a single wholeness." This triadic nature of man's soul and its association with the body is picturesquely compared by the *Zohar* to the flame of a candle:

If one looks at the flame of a burning candle, he observes two parts, a clear white and a dark blue. The upper part, the clear white, ascends upward; the dark part is in the middle and appears to be the foundation of the white. Both parts, however, are so closely united that they form one flame. But the dark is connected with the burning material beneath it. The same is true of man's soul. The life force in man is similar to the dark blue flame which draws its nourishment from the burning materials it surrounds. And just as these materials are burned up by the blue flame, so the life force consumes the fluids of man's body. The moral powers of man, *ruaḥ*, are like the clear white part of the flame, which constantly strives upward; but as long as the candle burns, the clear flame is connected with it. The highest part of man's soul, *neshamah*, is like the uppermost part of the flame, which the human eye cannot see because it actually manages to separate itself from the flame and ascend to the heights.[30]

But the *Zohar* is not content with speaking of these three elements of man's spirit. With its idealistic outlook, it stresses another symbolic motif. "All the phenomena of the world," we read, "all the creatures which have already been or which have been appointed to come into being at some future time must first of all disclose themselves before the Creator in their true structures or forms."[31] The *idea*, the image, of the creature exists before the

29. *Zohar*, II, 142b ("Parashah Terumah"). When a pious man dies, the *Zohar* teaches, the noblest part of his spirit, *neshamah*, rises at once to the Throne of Glory on high. The second part, *ruaḥ*, ascends to Paradise, and the third, *nefesh*, which is the lowest part, remains below in the body. But when a sinful man dies, his *neshamah* encounters great hindrances on its way to the Throne of Glory. His *ruaḥ* also has no possibility of coming to Paradise, and his *nefesh* can find no rest on earth. This doctrine of the three levels of the human soul was very widespread in the Middle Ages. Christian scholasticism speaks of three kinds of independent spiritual powers in every person: (1) *anima vegetabila*, (2) *anima sensitiva*, and (3) *anima rationalis*. The first is possessed by men and beasts in common with plants. The second is to be found in men and beasts alone. The third, which is immortal, is found only in men.
30. *Zohar*, I, 51a, 83b.
31. *Ibid.*, III, 61b.

The Temple of Love

creature itself comes into the world. So, says the *Zohar*, it is with man also:

> At the moment when the body is united with the soul, God sends down to earth the person's image [*deyokna*] which carries the divine stamp. It is this image that stands by at the moment of conjugal union between man and wife. If the eye could see, it would observe this image standing at their heads. It has a human face, and the child that is to be born will carry its form. . . . This form meets us when we are born into the world, grows along with us, and accompanies us when we depart from the world.[32]

"This form," the *Zohar* adds, "is a celestial phenomenon."

Man's soul, which is a reflection of the divine *sefirot*, the *Zohar* affirms, is in constant connection with these *sefirot*, and the bond between them is never severed. The fact that it comes down to the lower world and unites with an earthly body is for the soul, in the view of the *Zohar*, not a sad descent but, on the contrary, an exalted privilege. It is this that gives it the possibility of fulfilling its great task—to participate in the "work of creation," to raise everything with which it comes into contact to a higher level, to illuminate it with a divine light, and afterwards, itself radiant and permeated with light, to be united with the eternal source of light. But only when the soul has fulfilled its mission does it return at once to the eternal source. If it has not completed it, it is condemned to transmigration; it must again unite with an earthly body and wander further in the lower world:

> And the children of men do not know the ways of the Holy One, blessed be He. They do not know how every day judgment is exercised over man. They do not know how souls come to judgment before they descend to the earthly world and afterwards, when they return from this world. Men do not know how many transmigrations souls have to undergo, how many naked souls wander lost in the world and are not allowed into the palace of the King of the universe. Men do not know how many worlds are destroyed and how many hidden mysteries occur at the destruction of each world. They do not know and do not see how many souls are hurled like stones thrown from the hollow of a sling. . . .[33]

The righteous and purified soul, however, the *Zohar* insists, raises itself freely and without hindrance into the upper worlds

---

32. *Ibid.*, III, 104 ("Parashah Emor").
33. *Ibid.*, II, 99b, "Parashah Mishpatim" (quoted according to the Sulzbach second edition, p. 163).

The Zohar

"where, in one of the hidden corners of the highest celestial spheres, there is a palace called the Temple of Love."[34] There the deepest mysteries occur. There all the souls that are loved by the heavenly King gather. There God Himself and all the holy souls rest, and the Master of the universe unites with them "in a kiss of love."

34. *Zohar*, II, 97b ("Parashah Mishpatim"); I, 168a ("Parashah Be-Shalaḥ").

CHAPTER FOUR

The Renewal of the Struggle Against Rationalism

SHORTLY after Landauer[1] pointed it out, other investigators[2] also stressed the fact that in the *Zohar* a definite hostility to rabbinic or Talmudic Judaism is discernible. In the *Zohar*, as these scholars noted, the Mishnah is compared to a hard stone and to a maidservant who aspires to displace her mistress.[3] Elsewhere the *Zohar* accuses the Mishnah of having obscured the light of the Torah and charges that it became the grave of Moses and that no one at present knows where his grave is.[4]

To encounter in certain passages of the *Zohar* such an inimical attitude toward rabbinic Judaism should occasion no surprise. For we know that Abraham Abulafia—who, for personal reasons, hated the "crude scholars" who desire, in his view, to know of nothing besides arid *pilpul* or hairsplitting and consider this more important than all the sciences—had a definite relationship to the *Zohar*. It would be erroneous, however, to think that this animus is present throughout the entire *Zohar*. It must not be overlooked that great attention is devoted in it to every particular of the religious cult; observance of the commandments and laws of the Torah is, for its authors, of transcendent importance. For this reason alone the *Zohar* could not be hostile to the greatest collection of the Oral Law, the Talmud, in which every detail of the

1. *Literaturblatt des Orients*, 1845, pp. 422, 570.
2. For example, Graetz, *Geschichte der Juden*, VII, Beilage 12.
3. *Tikkunei Zohar*, Chapter 27. In another place the Mishnah is called the young manservant's concubine.
4. *Zohar*, II, 27.

six hundred thirteen commandments is so lovingly and carefully explored. Indeed, the *Zohar* is filled with passages in which the immense value and importance of studying the Mishnah and Gemara is explicitly stressed.[5] In that era the Kabbalah still did not think of any struggle against Rabbinism and the Talmud; it sought only to imbue these with its spirit, to clothe them in its mystical enthusiasm.

Quite different, however, was the attitude of the Kabbalah to religious philosophy in its Aristotelian garb. To be sure, the Kabbalah, at that time, was still not a principal opponent of philosophy. We have noted that one of its "fathers," Azriel, sought to ground the theoretical Kabbalah on a philosophical basis in his *Perush Eser Sefirot*. Isaac Ibn Latif was similarly concerned, and for the imaginative Abraham Abulafia, those who studied philosophy were far more acceptable than the arrogant Talmudic scholars.[6] The philosophic ideas which obtained a response among the Jewish mystics were, however, neo-Platonic ideas, permeated with the religious enthusiasm of Philo and Solomon Ibn Gabirol and the poetic inspiration of the "divine" Plato. This was not an abstract philosophy, wrapped in a royal mantle of free speculative thought, but an intimate texture of ideas created through the ecstasy of profound religious experience and striving for the hidden divine light that would illumine and revive the longing soul. Such yearning for the mystically hidden was, as we have already suggested, in a certain sense a protest against Aristotelian rationalism, which began increasingly to dominate the minds of the enlightened Jews of that period in Spain and Provence. The mystics could hardly be satisfied with the logical arguments whereby the rationalists sought to demonstrate that the Torah of Moses is entirely congruent with Aristotle's ideas. Should all this be true, ironically notes the editor of the *Zohar*, Moses de Leon, a question arises: What need was there for the revelation on Mount Sinai with all its thunder and lightning, if it tells us only what Aristotle taught very calmly and without clamor?[7] De Leon thinks that, by always talking of peace between the Torah of Moses and Aristotle, the Jewish Aristotelians wish only to dazzle men's eyes so that they may more easily, and without suspicion, smuggle in the philosophical ideas of their Greek master.

5. Numerous quotations to this effect are given by M. Joel in his *Die Religionsphilosophie des Sohars*, pp. 69–70.
6. In his introduction to *Imrei Shefer*, published by Jellinek in his *Philosophie und Kabbala*, pp. 33–38.
7. *Avkat Rochel*. The second part of this work is actually a large fragment of Moses de Leon's *Nefesh Ha-Ḥochmah*.

The Distinction Between Allegories and Symbols

The rationalistically-minded followers of Maimonides recognized in all the stories of the Torah only abstract allegories and considered the positive and negative commandments from a purely utilitarian point of view. For the mystics, however, here was a wondrous world of profound symbols and divine mysteries. Even in the plain narratives of the Bible the *Zohar* perceived hidden mysteries, "secrets of secrets." It strongly berates those who believe that the Torah intends only to relate simple tales and common events in the life of various men and nations. These stories are merely the outer covering under which exalted mysteries are concealed. They are only the garment for the body in which the "soul of souls" (*nishmata de-nishmata*) is hidden. That this soul of souls might be revealed for the *olam ha-shafal* (lower world) and that we, with our human eyes, might recognize its glory, it had to put on corporeal dress.[8]

But it would be a great mistake to think, as some scholars do, that the *Zohar*, like the rationalists, considers the narratives of the Bible merely parables and allusions. The authors of the *Zohar* are certain that these deal with actual events.[9] But all phenomena are no more than a symbolic reflection of yonder being. Everything that exists in this world is merely a pale reflection of the "ideas" and real images, which are the only true essences, the sole bearers of actual being. This highest reality, the ideal prototype of all creatures and events, is the *nishmata de-nishmata* which only the keen-sighted eyes of the righteous and true servants of the heavenly King, whose souls were present at Mount Sinai at the time of the giving of the Torah, can discern. Where the rationalists perceived only abstract allegories, the *Zohar* saw profound symbols filled with real and multifaceted content.[10]

No less divergent is the attitude of the Kabbalists, on the one hand, and the rationalists, on the other, in regard to the matter of fulfilling the commandments of the Torah. "He who violates any

---

8. *Zohar*, III, 152a.
9. This is already emphasized by one of the first commentators on the *Zohar*, Menahem Recanati, when he expounds in a purely mystical way the narrative of Adam's expulsion from the Garden of Eden. He adds: "Know and understand that even though we have explained this entire section by way of mystery [*al derech ha-sod*] the tree of life and the tree of knowledge, the rivers, the cherubim, and the flaming sword were all real."
10. The great distinction between the Kabbalists and the rationalists in interpreting the allusions which they found in the narratives of the Bible was already noted by the well-known fifteenth-century preacher Isaac Arama. See his *Akedat Yitzhak*, Chapter 7, pp. 54–55; *Hazut Kashah*, Chapters 11–12.

commandment," the *Zohar* teaches, "thereby creates a defect in the upper worlds." For the Kabbalists observing the prescriptions of the Torah is not only a mark of piety and reverence for God, and not merely a pedagogic instrument; it is also a *creative act* of vast importance in the entire "work of creation," for it is an act of *ethical* significance. It is a triumph of light over darkness, a raising of common matter to the level of spirituality, a drawing close to the *Ilat Ha-Ilot* (Cause of Causes), the source of light and wisdom.

The ardent Kabbalah and rationalist Aristotelianism were two different worlds, two inimical worlds, and the profound contradictions between them necessarily produced an obdurate struggle. It is therefore quite understandable that just at the end of the thirteenth century, when the *Zohar* was completed and first appeared publicly, a bitter struggle against the rationalist followers of Maimonides again erupted in Spain and Provence. Associated with the mystics in this struggle were the *hachmei ha-Talmud* (Talmudic scholars), the rabbis, against whom Abraham Abulafia had polemicized. The first portent of this conflict was the appearance of the fanatical mystic Solomon ben Samuel Petit (the Little).

Solomon Petit was a native of northern France but lived in Palestine, in the city of Acco. There, together with several other orthodox zealots, he began to propagandize against Maimonides' *Guide for the Perplexed*. In the lands of the East, however, the authority of the author of the *Mishneh Torah* was immense. Maimonides was the "great eagle," and whoever dared insult him was regarded as a blasphemer desecrating the honor of the Torah itself. The head of Oriental Jewry, the Nasi Yishai ben Hezekiah ben Yishai of Damascus, proceeded against Petit with an admonition that he would excommunicate anyone who dared "calumniate Maimonides' *Guide for the Perplexed*."[11] Petit, however, was one of those stubborn fanatics who are not intimidated by threats. He departed for Europe, travelled through France and Germany, and in these countries collected depositions from many rabbis to the effect that the *Guide* was a dangerously heretical book and must be put away forever in a *genizah*.[12] On his return journey to Palestine, Petit stopped in Rome to agitate against Maimonides' works. Here, however, he had no success; the followers of Maimonides residing there attacked him very sharply. The prominent scholar Hillel of Verona also assailed him, and Petit had to leave

---

11. *Kerem Ḥemed*, III, 169; *Iggerot Kenaot*, 21.
12. *Ibid.*

Italy at once. On returning to Acco, he and his followers issued a proclamation to the effect that, on the authority of the rabbis of France and Germany, it was forbidden to read Maimonides' "heretical" works. At that time, apparently, some fanatical opponents of Maimonides rubbed out on the philosopher's tombstone in Tiberias the inscription "Moses, the chosen of the human species" and wrote instead "Moses, the son of Maimon, the excommunicated and the heretic." The energetic propaganda of the anti-Maimunists greatly disturbed all the rabbis of the Near East. The exilarch of Mosul, David ben Daniel, in 1288 excommunicated Solomon Petit and his adherents, and warned further that he would excommunicate everyone, "whether it be a man or a woman, who would utter false rumors about Rabbi Moses ben Maimon and his works" or who would apply to the external political authorities to proscribe any of these works.[13] After him the Nasi of Damascus also issued a ban.[14] They were joined by the most prominent leaders of the Spanish community,[15] the head of the Talmudic academy of Babylonia, Samuel ben Daniel Kohen,[16] and many others. Maimonides' grandson, David ben Abraham, also came to Acco to fight against Petit and his followers.[17]

What subsequently happened to Solomon Petit has not been determined. We know only that both parties applied to the foremost rabbinic authority in Spain at that time, Rabbi Solomon ben Adret, to effect a compromise,[18] and after this Petit's name is nowhere mentioned. Soon thereafter, however, in Spain as well as in Provence, a strong anti-rationalist movement began. And Rabbi Solomon ben Adret, who at the time of Petit's attack was the arbitrator and compromiser, was, in this new struggle, one of the most active leaders against the rationalists.

We have noted that the greater the influence of the Kabbalah grew in Jewish circles, the stronger dissatisfaction with the Aristotelian school became. After Maimonides' death, a definite spiritual decline occurred in this school. Rationalist ideas became a thing of fashion and came into the hands of semi-educated dilettantes. These dilettantes haughtily decked themselves in a philo-

13. J. Kobak, *Sefer Ginzei Nistarot*, III, 121–22.
14. This ban was published in *Kerem Hemed*, III, 179–83. Here the date indicated is 1286, but this is certainly a scribal error. It should be 1288. On this see Graetz, *Geschichte der Juden*, VIII, Beilage 8; Vogelstein and Rieger, *Geschichte der Juden in Rom*, I, 405.
15. *Iggerot Kenaot*, 22.
16. *Sefer Ginzei Nistarot*, III, 24.
17. See the second letter of Hillel of Verona to Maestro Gajo (*Hemdah Genuzah*, p. 21).
18. See Rabbi Solomon's letter in *Letterbode*, IV, 128.

sophic, freethinking cloak. Religious-philosophical questions were turned into philosophical playthings and pastimes. Interpretation of the Biblical text allegorically became extremely popular. Allegories were spouted even from the pulpits of synagogues, without taking any account of the religious sentiments of the pious listeners.

The spread of the rationalist mood among the Jewish intelligentsia was greatly aided by Jacob Anatoli's *Malmad Ha-Talmidim*. This work enjoyed widespread popularity among the "philosophizing" circles of Spain and southern France. It was frequently read on Sabbath afternoons before large assemblies,[19] and Anatoli's rationalistic interpretations of the Bible were considered the ideal pattern.[20]

Even Heinrich Graetz, who presents an overly one-sided portrait of the struggle between the followers of Maimonides and their opponents, is compelled to admit that the "correlating methods" which Maimonides employed to combine the Aristotelian world view with the Biblical were extremely inappropriate. "To make peace between these two antithetical world views," says Graetz,

Maimonides had to sacrifice not only certain particulars of the Jewish religion but also the plain meaning of the Biblical text, and even more of the Talmudic *Aggadah*. His followers and disciples, however, could no longer be content with these sacrifices. Step by step, with logical, commonsense arguments, they also gradually disturbed a great deal in the Jewish faith that Maimonides had left untouched.[21]

It must, however, be noted here that Maimonides' following consisted of very diverse elements. Among them were doubtless men of acute and original mentality who were attracted to him by his free speculative thought, his indefatigable striving for knowledge, and the courage with which he endeavored to consider critically all religious and poetic ideas from a purely rational

---

19. According to the letter of Solomon ben Isaac of Lunel in the Parma manuscript of *Minḥat Kenaot* (see Renan-Neubauer, *Les Rabbins français*, p. 668, and especially *Letterbode*, IV, 124).
20. See *Minḥat Kenaot*, Letters 22, 68, and especially 9, in which Rabbi Solomon ben Adret, speaking of Anatoli, whom he calls "the old king" (*ha-melech ha-zaken*), says bitterly: "He expresses in his work opinions that are as bitter as gall and wormwood. We have heard that his work is considered by many the loveliest crown and ornament, that men refresh themselves with his words, words in which we see only error and confusion" (*Minḥat Kenaot*, 44).
21. Graetz, *Geschichte der Juden*, VII, 354–55.

standpoint. But these were in the minority and did not hold the dominant place. The leaders among the Maimunists were men of an altogether different stripe. In the Spanish kingdoms (Castile, Aragon, Catalonia), and also in part in Provence, there was a rather considerable class of "court" and "finance" Jews. These Jewish grandees had a great deal of intercourse with the non-Jewish cultural world, chiefly with the Christian nobility, and this influenced their way of life. Their outlook was doubtless broader and more liberal than that of the rest of the Jewish community, but it had the disadvantage of being diffuse and without deep roots. The Jewish aristocracy certainly possessed a degree of culture, but it was the kind of superficial half-culture generally characteristic of the representatives of the so-called larger world and of the high nobility. Wealthy, aristocratic young Jews were eager to enjoy all the pleasures of life but were hindered at every step by the numerous "thou shalt nots" of the Torah, by the severities and prohibitions Judaism had inherited from the past. It was not at the dictation of free speculative thought that these youths yearned to liberate themselves from religious restrictions, but out of the desire to enjoy unhindered everything their hearts and unrestrained imagination wished. Their rationalistic rhetoric and contemptuous attitude toward the "superstition" of the "multitude" were merely the cloak with which they covered their own emptiness and lack of principle.

Hence, it is not surprising that Maimonides' prosaic allegorical interpretations of various narratives in the Bible took on, among his and Jacob Anatoli's followers, extremely bizarre and, at times, infantile and absurd forms.[22] In fact the entire Bible was transformed by these men into an allegorical commentary on Aristotle's philosophy. Rabbi Solomon ben Adret is not far from the truth when he complains that among the rationalists the whole Torah became nothing more than parable and allegory.[23] Abraham and Sarah, Lot and his wife, are merely allusions to the distinction between "form" and "matter." Isaac and Rebecca are references to the "active intellect" and the understanding soul; Amalek is the "evil inclination"; the war of the four kings against five related in the Book of Genesis is an allegorical portrait of how the four basic elements struggle against the five senses. Even the greatest

22. Of the influence of Christian theologians in this connection, we have spoken in the second volume of our work. Simeon An-Duran also notes this in his summons (see the Zunz Jubilee Volume *Tiferet Sevah*, p. 151: "Those who portray the Torah and its commandments according to the way of the Christians have come into the gates").
23. Rabbi Solomon ben Adret, *Responsa*, No. 416.

The Renewal of the Struggle Against Rationalism

of the prophets, Moses, who spoke with God "mouth to mouth," is no more than an allegory. The daughter of Pharaoh, Amram and Jochebed, Moses' wife Zipporah and their sons, Jethro and his other daughters—all these are merely parables that depict allegorically the struggle of man's spiritual powers when they strive after "divine wisdom."[24]

Even stranger forms of Maimonides' rationalism were adopted among his followers in that era. The philosopher himself had endeavored to present persuasive reasons for the commandments of the Torah, to explain the usefulness of each precept and statute, to show that ethics is built on purely utilitarian foundations and that its motive power is purposefulness. This view especially contributed to the destruction of the religious sentiment in the hearts of his adherents. If all the commandments have a purely rational, utilitarian purpose, the important thing is simply to *understand* this purpose with the mind and, once this is achieved, it is quite superfluous to fulfill the commandment itself. Those commandments, moreover, whose usefulness it was difficult to demonstrate rationally were declared "superstition" and "foolishness." The men who took this view also regarded the miracles related in the Torah with contempt and scorn.[25] Characteristic of these rationalists and their attitude toward Jewish ritual is the question one of them publicly put before his opponents at a gathering in a synagogue: "Give me to understand why Moses forbade us to eat pork. Is it because it is injurious to health? But the physicians have not found any harmfulness whatever in it!"[26] Such ideas, which, of course, necessarily repelled every orthodox Jew, were expressed not only in scientific inquiries and in conversations in narrow circles; they were also carried into the street, proclaimed at public gatherings, at banquets and wedding feasts, even from pulpits in synagogues.[27] In the place of customary sermons on morality and proper conduct, philosophic discourses were given in which the attempt was made to interpret verses from the Bible in a dialectical and hairsplitting way by means of quotations from Aristotle and other Greek thinkers.[28]

---

24. See *Minḥat Kenaot*, 31, 41, 46, 48, 72, 89, 133, 153, etc.; Rabbi Solomon ben Adret, *Responsa*, Nos. 416–17; Simeon An-Duran's summons in the Zunz Jubilee Volume, pp. 159–60.
25. See *Minḥat Kenaot*, 41, 46, 133, 153, etc.; Rabbi Solomon ben Adret, *Responsa*, Nos. 414, 416, 417.
26. *Iggerot Kenaot*, 152–53.
27. See *Minḥat Kenaot*, 94, 134, 175.
28. *Ibid.*, 20, 31, 41, 58, 153.

Levi ben Abraham of Villefranche

The most prominent of such preachers at that time was Levi ben Abraham ben Ḥayyim[29] of Villefranche, near Perpignan. Levi was descended from a cultured family of Languedoc, his father being a well-trained Talmudist and religious poet.[30] Because of an unhappy romance,[31] Levi as a young man had to leave home and settled in Montpellier, where he became friendly with the well-known scholar Moses Ibn Tibbon. He lived in great poverty[32] and earned a scant livelihood by giving lessons in languages and natural science.[33] Levi's favorite occupation was philosophy. Of non-Jewish thinkers, he most admired Aristotle and his Arabic commentator Averroes,[34] and of the Jewish philosophers Maimonides, whom he calls "the illuminating star of Israel, the crown of all sages." Properly to understand Maimonides' *Guide for the Perplexed*, Levi believed, one must first obtain some knowledge of the other sciences. To this end he composed in 1276 a work in which he presents, in the form of a poem, a general overview of all branches of knowledge.[35] This work is entitled *Battei Ha-Nefesh Veha-Leḥashim* and consists of 1,846 verses in which the author sets forth the elements of the major sciences—philosophy, logic, and physics—as well as a discussion of the basic problems of ethics. Each verse ends with the syllable *rim*. Because the verses were written in extremely obscure and difficult language, the author himself indited a commentary to almost every single one.[36] Since in this work Levi gave only a general overview, he

---

29. For a detailed discussion of him see A. Geiger, *He-Ḥalutz*, II, 12–28, and *Otzar Neḥmad*, II, 94–97; S. Sachs, *Kerem Ḥemed*, VIII, 195–99; Carmoly, *La France israelite*, pp. 46, 54; Renan-Neubauer, *Les Rabbins français*, pp. 628–47 (where the contents of his works are given); and Zunz, *Zur Geschichte und Literatur*, pp. 471–72. The year in which Levi ben Abraham was born is not known. In any case, he was born no earlier than the late 1240's, for in his work *Battei Ha-Nefesh*, which he composed in 1276, he notes that he is still "young in years."
30. Zunz, *Literaturgeschichte*, p. 481.
31. Carmoly, *La France israelite*, p. 487.
32. Levi ben Abraham complains of his hard life in the introduction to his *Battei Ha-Nefesh*, as well as in the first chapter of the work.
33. *Minḥat Kenaot*, 48.
34. In the introduction to his *Battei Ha-Nefesh* Levi ben Abraham writes: "And the books of Aristotle are better and more satisfactory than the books of anyone else, and the commentaries of Averroes are superior to all other commentaries."
35. On the influence of Jacob Anatoli on Rabbi Levi, see Leo Baeck, *MGWJ*, 1900, pp. 159 ff.
36. The work has remained in manuscript. Only the introduction has been published (in *Otzar Ha-Safrut*, III, Part Six, pp. 19–23) and several verses (in *Literaturblatt des Orients*, 1848, pp. 553, 568). We have

later wrote a large scientific work in two parts, entitled *Livyat Ḥen*. The first part deals with the sciences—mathematics, geometry, astrology, physics, and metaphysics; the second is concerned mainly with religious-philosophical problems.[37]

Rabbi Levi ben Abraham was a man of comprehensive knowledge but lacked an integral world view. In his mind Aristotle's philosophic doctrine was mingled together with vastly different ideas and conceptions. A great admirer of Maimonides, Levi still believed firmly in astrology[38] and considered it the profoundest science, despite the fact that Maimonides himself was its most determined opponent. To be sure, in this respect Levi probably manifests not so much his own lack of system as his fidelity to Aristotle's system, for the latter clearly contains certain astrological elements. In Aristotle's view, the stars are living creatures, "spheres" endowed with wisdom, which are at a far higher level than ordinary mortals. These heavenly spheres actually govern the universe. According to Aristotle's philosophy, divinity has no intercourse with the terrestrial world; everything that occurs in the lower world is merely the result of the spheres and their powers, which operate with strict regularity. This led to the conclusion that man's actions, his character and fate, depend on the situation of the stars and planets at any given moment. Such a view necessarily implied complete fatalism, the conviction that "there is no wisdom and no understanding," that everything is predetermined and that man's will is powerless. Characteristic of this view is a question which a contemporary[39] of Rabbi Levi ben Abraham put before Rabbi Isaac Ibn Latif:

Hippocrates and Galen composed numerous medical works which investigate the properties of various medicinal herbs and drugs, explain what kind of remedy must be employed in one disease and what in another. Ptolemy and his disciples, however, describe in their works the effects of the spheres and how each individual planet exercises influence on a definite area. According to the demonstrations

employed an old copy of the entire work which is contained in the first Firkovich Collection, No. 464.
37. Rabbi Levi's religious-philosophical views are discussed by Leo Baeck in the article cited above.
38. When Rabbi Levi complains in his *Battei Ha-Nefesh Veha-Leḥashim* of his bitter fate, he insists that it is the planets that have persecuted him and given him no rest.
39. Todros Abulafia, who later became an ardent follower of the Kabbalah and composed the well-known Kabbalist work *Otzar Ha-Kavod*. Abulafia (died 1298) also wrote numerous poems. His *diwan*, *Gan Ha-Meshalim Veha-Ḥiddot*, was published in 1932 by D. Yellin.

of these scholars, everything that occurs here in the lower world is the result of the powers that the planets and constellations disclose following definite laws. How, then, can the physicians with their remedies be of help? How can they avert what the celestial spheres have decreed?[40]

Rabbi Levi ben Abraham was such an ardent devotee of astrology that he saw in the whole Torah only astrological mysteries, which he attempted to explicate in a rationalistic-allegorical manner. While the sages of the Talmud saw in the twelve planets an allusion to the twelve tribes of Israel, the author of *Livyat Hen* saw in the twelve tribes an allusion to the twelve planets. The *Urim* and *Tummim* were, according to Levi's explanation, the astrological instrument known as the astrolabe. The entire sanctuary with all its vessels, the *efod* and *hoshen*, were also astrological implements whose function is to work on the stars and planets and to disclose their secrets, secrets still hidden in the womb of the future.[41]

These rationalist-allegorical subtleties and theories were very widespread in Jewish intellectual circles. They became a thing of fashion, and even half-educated young people, wealthy dilettantes, and courtiers, who paid very slight attention to scientific matters, draped themselves in the philosopher's toga, played skeptic and freethinker, mocked the old customs and the "fanatical" multitude that was so ready to believe all kinds of follies and old wives' tales. "Young people," complains Rabbi Solomon ben Adret, "come with questions: why do the foolish Jews make fringes on their garments, affix *mezuzot* to their doors, and put *tefillin* on their heads? Has it not long since been shown that all these customs have no sense whatever?"[42]

"Crude young men," laments another writer of that period, "leap about. They come together in the streets and market places and prate of learned matters in order to show ignoramuses and women that they are knowledgeable."[43] "The danger is great," warns Crescas Vidal of Marseilles, "that through these philosophizing young people the whole earth will be covered with heresy and the Torah become a mockery and scorn."

---

40. *Kovetz Al Yad*, I, 51. Here Ibn Latif's answer is also printed. Interesting as well are the ideas which the ardent disciple of Maimonides, the talented author of the satire *Alilot Devarim*, expressed on this matter (see *Otzar Nehmad*, V, 207).
41. *Kerem Hemed*, VIII, 125-239; *Minhat Kenaot*, 104, 106, 153.
42. *Minhat Kenaot*, 94.
43. Joseph Ibn Kaspi, *Hatzotzerot Kesef*, p. 104.

The Renewal of the Struggle Against Rationalism

What these men feared was at least partially realized. The critical and detached attitude to matters of faith prevalent in the educated circles led to some very melancholy results. The incidence of conversion to Christianity began to increase greatly. It was, after all, "unreasonable" to suffer trials and afflictions for the sake of a faith that has no independent value. To defend their defection from the community and the heritage of their fathers on moral grounds, men became fatalists and pointed out that all is decreed by heaven, that man's fate and action are determined by the stars and spheres, and against their decree the human will is powerless. Some of the apostate fatalists, e.g., Abner of Burgos (1270–1346), afterward became fierce enemies of Judaism and persecuted their erstwhile brethren. It is therefore not surprising that the orthodox circles became increasingly apprehensive about the survival of Judaism and began to consider means of protecting the faith from the "heretical" ideas of the freethinking rationalists.

Once again, as seventy years before, a struggle against the rationalists broke out. This time also the struggle first began in Montpellier, the major Jewish community in Languedoc. As Solomon ben Abraham of Montpellier had done earlier, so now another ardent fanatic with a powerful, militant nature came forward. This was Abba Mari ben Moses Ha-Yarḥi, who also bore the Provençal name Don Astruc de Lunel.[44] Abba Mari had a certain knowledge of philosophy, and revered Maimonides and his *Guide*.[45] Aristotle, for him, was "the God-seeker among the nations of the world" who followed the same path "as Abraham our father in his time" and, with his own mind, arrived at the concept of a single, infinite deity free of all corporeality.[46] But since Aristotle was unfamiliar with the revelation of God's Torah, Abba Mari insists, he could not attain with his own reason to the two foundations of the Jewish faith: the creation of the world *ex nihilo* through God's free will, and divine providence.

The Jewish rationalists, complains Abba Mari, in attempting to interpret the meaning of the Torah according to Aristotle's system deny the heritage of their fathers and undermine the foundations of Judaism. They reject the most important principles—the divinely revealed character of the Torah, the creation of the world,

---

44. He was born around the year 1250. For a discussion of him, see Gross, "Notice sur Abba Mari de Lunel," *REJ*, IV, 200.
45. See his introduction to *Minḥat Kenaot*, Chapter 6, and also his *Sefer Ha-Yareaḥ*, Chapters 8–10 (pp. 127–28).
46. *Minḥat Kenaot*, 15.

and God's providence. Such people ought to be excluded from the camp of Israel.[47] "I declare relentless war," this zealot cried,

> against all who undermine the foundations of the religion and lay waste the fertile fields of the faith. As long as I live, I shall, with all my forces, with the power of my word and pen, wage an implacable struggle against those who wish to make ideas imported from the outside rule over our sacred Torah. I will go courageously on my way. The wild cries of the enraged beasts will not frighten me, nor the sharp claws of the predatory birds. I will not return my sword to its sheath until I shall have purified God's holy temple.[48]

Abba Mari himself, however, was not sufficiently known in the Jewish communities, and his attack would not have made any special impression. He therefore applied to the renowned rabbi of Barcelona, Solomon ben Adret, who was highly regarded not only by the Jewish communities but by the government as well,[49] and requested the latter's aid in his "holy war." Rabbi Solomon was a great scholar. A disciple of Nahmanides and Jonah Gerondi, he raised the eminence of the rabbinate in Spain to the highest level. Jews applied to him from the farthest lands with questions on religious and legal matters. For his decisions and decrees the greatest reverence prevailed throughout the Jewish world.[50] The keen dialectic of the Tosafists, which Nahmanides popularized in Spain, attained its peak in him. His *novellae* to many Talmudic tractates are a monument not only of scholarship but also of dialectical skill. The remarkable acuteness of his analytic mind is also demonstrated in his work on the laws of *issur ve-hetter* (what is prohibited and permitted), *Torat Ha-Bayyit*.[51]

47. *Ibid.* Abba Mari notes three major motifs in Aristotle's system, as interpreted by Averroes' school, which are utterly at variance with the foundations of Judaism: (1) that the world is eternal; (2) that it is not God who is the guide of the world but rather the spheres which influence its order; and (3) that there is no individual immortality of the soul, and consequently the doctrine of reward and punishment is refuted.
48. Introduction to his *Sefer Ha-Yareah* (*Minhat Kenaot*, 122).
49. See Jean Régné, *Catalogue des actes de Jaime I, Pedro III, et Alfonso III, rois d'Aragon, concernant les Juifs*, 1056, 1181, 1597.
50. Rabbi Solomon ben Adret's *responsa* (over three thousand of them) were published in seven volumes.
51. This work was criticized by Solomon's townsman Rabbi Aharon Ha-Levi, in his *Bedek Ha-Bayyit*. Solomon promptly replied in his *Mishmeret Ha-Bayyit*. For details see I. H. Weiss, *Dor Dor Ve-Doreshav*, V, Chapter 3. On Rabbi Aharon, see Renan-Neubauer, *Les Rabbins français*, pp. 523–28. Like his teacher Nahmanides, Rabbi

The Renewal of the Struggle Against Rationalism

Under the influence of his teacher Naḥmanides, Solomon ben Adret became very fond of the Kabbalah. Along with this, however, he also had a certain knowledge of the "external wisdoms" or secular sciences. To his opponents he proudly declares: "You think that the sciences are foreign to me, but you are mistaken. I am also proficient in them and know how to appreciate them."[52] He has the greatest respect for Maimonides, often quotes his *Guide for the Perplexed*, and not infrequently introduces arguments from the natural sciences into his legal *responsa*. He considers it necessary, however, constantly to insist that philosophical wisdom and the divinely revealed Torah are two diametrically different entities that cannot be united. Philosophy and the natural sciences, Solomon points out, concern themselves exclusively with rational arguments and firmly established laws. In these realms relentless necessity, the iron chain of causes and effects, prevails. Here, in the domain of strict regularity, there is no place for miracles and wonders that are contrary to the established laws of nature and the principles of logic. But the faith that was given through revelation is the disclosure of divine marvel. Faith is inconceivable without miracles. Here the mechanical, automatic laws of nature have no dominion. One cannot, says Solomon, demonstrate through logical theories or in an experimental fashion the truth of the miracles described in the Torah—how, for example, water can be made to flow from a rock with a staff. We believe firmly in all the miracles of the Torah, but the rationalists cannot explain these with logical arguments. "They consider themselves wise in their own eyes and regard us as dumb animals."[53]

It was to Rabbi Solomon ben Adret, as we have already observed, that both parties applied at the time of Solomon Petit's attack with the request that he seek to effect a compromise. Now, in the year 1303, Abba Mari challenged him, as a great scholar in Israel, to "gird up his loins" and attack "those who cut down the plants." Abba Mari complains in his first letter to Solomon ben Adret,

Filled with pride and arrogance is our present generation. Presumptuously it criticizes its counselors and guides. . . . Many pursue follies[54]

Solomon ben Adret also carried on polemics with various adversaries of the Jewish faith. He responded to the attack of the Dominican monk Raymund Martini against Judaism, and issued forth even more sharply against a Moslem freethinker named Aḥmad Ibn Ḥazm. His polemic against Ibn Ḥazm was published by Perles in 1863.

52. See his letter to Isaac de Lattes (*Minḥat Kenaot*, 97).
53. *Minḥat Kenaot*, 40; Rabbi Solomon ben Adret, *Responsa*, No. 414.
54. In his monograph in German on Rabbi Solomon ben Adret, Perles

and abandon the most important principles. They break God's covenant, adopt alien doctrines, and destroy the treasures of our Torah. They give blasphemous sermons from the pulpit. Their only occupations are physics and logic. Averroes' works and an essay of Aristotle are more precious to them than anything else. They think only of astrology, of the position of the stars and the condition of the planets.[55]

In his second letter to Solomon ben Adret, Abba Mari insists that he is not at all opposed to Greek-Arabic philosophy and the natural sciences, and that he knows how to appreciate them. It is only that he perceives a dangerous threat in the rationalists' desire to subordinate the Torah to philosophy and to have man's mind rule over the divine revelation. Those who allow themselves to express such heretical ideas, indignantly exclaims Abba Mari, "are deserving of being uprooted, destroyed, and burned."[56] He therefore requests Rabbi Solomon to issue forth with excommunication and curse against all who venture to interpret the Torah in an allegorical fashion.

In his reply Solomon declares that he is in complete agreement with Abba Mari, but that since he is quite distant from Provence and not personally acquainted with the conditions prevailing there he considers it improper to be the first to come forth against the heretics of Montpellier. He therefore proposes that Abba Mari organize all who are prepared to fight for the sake of God's name and then consult with him on how to proceed further against the freethinking rationalists.[57] At the same time Solomon turned to one of his friends in Provence, Don Crescas Vidal of Perpignan,

---

translates this passage erroneously, reading the Hebrew word *tefillot* (prayers) instead of *tefelot* (follies).
55. *Minḥat Kenaot*, 20.
56. *Ibid.*, Letter 5. All the letters, proclamations, and summonses related to this religious struggle were collected by Abba Mari into a work entitled *Minḥat Kenaot* at the wish of Rabbi Solomon ben Adret (*op. cit.*, pp. 138, 140). This collection has a somewhat one-sided character, since Abba Mari did not deem it desirable to include all the letters of his adversaries. Nevertheless, *Minḥat Kenaot* has a definite cultural-historical value, inasmuch as it provides a clear picture of the ideological struggle which was carried on so obdurately in Spain and Provence at the beginning of the fourteenth century. The manuscript from which Mordecai Biseliches published *Minḥat Kenaot* for the first time in 1838 consisted of only 104 letters. In other copies the number of letters is larger. Neubauer published from an old Parma manuscript all the letters lacking in Biseliches' edition (*Letterbode*, IV-VI).
57. *Minḥat Kenaot*, 21-22.

and asked him to familiarize him with the cultural conditions in southern France.[58] Don Crescas expressed his complete agreement with Abba Mari and, for his part, proposed to Solomon that he issue a decree to the effect that no young man be allowed to study philosophy or the natural sciences before attaining the age of thirty.[59]

Several of Abba Mari's followers also informed Solomon ben Adret that the foremost of the rationalists, Rabbi Levi, was staying at the home of the well-known philanthropist Solomon Sulami in Perpignan. Sulami, whom Solomon ben Adret knew quite well, was a scholar in Talmudic literature, and the orthodox rabbi of Barcelona was deeply distressed at the report that so pernicious a heretic as Rabbi Levi should have been welcomed in the house of this worthy man. "The teachings of such a heretic," Rabbi Solomon declared,

are far more dangerous than the attacks we suffer from those who believe otherwise than we. These assail only certain principles of our faith, but Levi and his followers deny the whole religion and reject everything. God is my witness that I am much more fond of a Moslem than of such heretics who presume to turn our patriarchs into mere parables and philosophical allegories. By making symbols and allusions out of everything, they undermine the foundations of the Torah, for in this way one can declare all the commandments and laws mere allegories that have no practical significance. Thus they give the most effective weapon into the hands of our Christian adversaries who also argue that the laws and commandments of the Torah are merely allusions and symbols. These persons [Levi and his followers], however, go even further. Not only do they undermine the foundations of the Jewish faith; they deny all religions. And when the peoples among whom we live become aware of this, they will certainly at once take the severest measures against us.[60]

Rabbi Solomon ben Adret therefore dispatched a very indignant letter[61] to Solomon Sulami berating him for harboring a heretic such as Rabbi Levi in his home. Just at that time a misfortune occurred in Sulami's family; his young daughter died. In this event the pious father saw a punishment for his "sin," and poor old Rabbi Levi was compelled to leave his house.[62]

58. *Ibid.*, 44–45.
59. *Ibid.*, 48.
60. *Ibid.*, 51–52.
61. *Ibid.*, Letter 15.
62. *Ibid.*, p. 55.

The Ban of the Rabbis of Barcelona

To satisfy Abba Mari and his followers, Solomon ben Adret finally decided to accept Don Crescas Vidal's proposal. Abba Mari received from Barcelona a writ signed and sealed by Rabbi Solomon, fourteen other rabbis, and representatives of the community as well. In this writ the study of philosophy and other sciences before the age of thirty is placed under a ban and curse. Only those who are past this age and already quite proficient in the Talmud and its commentaries are permitted to look into the "books of the Greeks," i.e., scientific books of secular content.[63] However, the cautious and prudent Rabbi Solomon ordered Abba Mari to read the document publicly in the synagogue of Perpignan only after ascertaining that the most prominent leaders of the community sympathized with its content.[64]

It became clear, however, that not all the leaders of the community in Montpellier agreed with Abba Mari. At that time there lived in Montpellier a very respected member of the Tibbon family, Samuel Ibn Tibbon's grandson, Jacob ben Machir,[65] a prominent physician and astronomer who soon afterward became dean of the medical faculty at Montpellier. He was a man of comprehensive knowledge. His original astronomical works, for instance his well-known *Reva Yisrael* (on the quadrant and astrolable), as well as his Latin translations, occupy an honored place in the history of astronomy in the Middle Ages. His works are quoted with respect by such scientists as Copernicus, Reinhold, and Claudius.[66] In order to disseminate scientific knowledge in Jewish circles, he translated numerous philosophical and scientific works from Arabic into Hebrew, among them Euclid's *Elements*.

When Jacob ben Machir read the proclamation of the rabbis of Barcelona, he requested Abba Mari not to publish it.[67] But Abba Mari refused, and on the next Sabbath in the summer of 1304 the document was read before the congregation in the synagogue. Thereupon Jacob, together with his relative Jehudah ben Moses Tibbon, immediately issued forth with a sharp protest against the "zealots" who wished to suppress freedom of inquiry and knowledge. The Tibbons succeeded in attracting to their side many

63. *Ibid.*, Letter 20.
64. *Ibid.*, beginning of Letter 21.
65. His Provençal name was Don Profiat Tibbon. Among Latin authors he is called Profatius Judeaus. Jacob was born in Marseilles around 1236 and died after 1312.
66. See S. Sachs in *Kerem Ḥemed*, VIII, 196; Renan-Neubauer, *Les Rabbins français*, pp. 603–23; Steinschneider, *Hebräischen Übersetzungen*, pp. 505, 607, 976.
67. *Minḥat Kenaot*, Letter 21.

The Renewal of the Struggle Against Rationalism

prominent members of the community,⁶⁸ and thus two parties were formed and a bitter controversy broke out between the followers of Abba Mari and the Tibbons.⁶⁹

The party opposing Abba Mari, which was headed by Jacob ben Machir and Samuel ben Reuben of Béziers, addressed itself first to the foremost leader of the orthodox group, Rabbi Solomon ben Adret, dispatching a long letter⁷⁰ to him in which they endeavored to show that Judaism had never been hostile to secular culture or education. In Biblical times King Solomon was proficient in all the sciences. The men of the Mishnah and Talmud also had great knowledge in various branches of science. It is further pointed out in the letter that the prohibition against studying the sciences before the age of thirty will result in future generations remaining without knowledge, for if one does not study in his youth he will be ignorant throughout his life. The authors therefore request Rabbi Solomon ben Adret and his followers "to return the sword to its sheath" and not spread controversy in the house of Jacob.

Among those who subscribed to this letter was an old friend and admirer of Rabbi Solomon ben Adret, Solomon ben Isaac of Lunel. Rabbi Solomon ben Adret replied to him in a special and very interesting letter in which the writer's personality is reflected most clearly. He declares categorically that he cannot fulfill the request "to return the sword to its sheath," for there is no question here of personal motives. He is fighting for the honor of the Torah, and where the faith is in jeopardy "I remain firmly on the watch and no danger can frighten me."⁷¹

At the same time, apparently, Rabbi Solomon ben Adret dispatched to Montpellier his brief letter⁷² sharply attacking Jacob Anatoli and the latter's *Malmad Ha-Talmidim*. This "old king,"⁷³

---

68. *Ibid.*, Letters 21–24.
69. Certain personal motives also contributed to this ideological controversy. The followers of Rabbi Solomon ben Adret and Abba Mari attacked with some extremely sharp expressions Jacob Anatoli, the author of *Malmad Ha-Talmidim*, and his father-in-law Samuel Ibn Tibbon, the freethinker and translator of Maimonides' *Guide*. The Tibbons of Montpellier regarded this as an insult to their entire family.
70. *Minḥat Kenaot*, Letter 24. Rabbi Solomon ben Adret replied to both of his major opponents, Jacob ben Machir and Samuel of Béziers, together (his letter is published in *Letterbode*, IV, 130). Samuel ben Reuben promptly withdrew from the party of the Tibbons and regretted the fact that he had given his signature to the letter mentioned above (see *Minḥat Kenaot*, 89–93).
71. *Minḥat Kenaot*, Letter 30.
72. *Ibid.*, Letter 9.
73. Both Neubauer and Gross are in error in believing that by *ha-melech*

complains Rabbi Solomon, rules over many of our people; he is the ornament of their hearts, the crown of their heads. But his book is not the staff of support but the staff of strife.[74] We have, therefore, with the consent of our sages and the heads of the community, driven this book out of our land, for its pages are full of ideas bitter as gall and wormwood. We have heard that among you this work is very beloved and highly esteemed, that you interpret all the weekly readings from the Torah according to Anatoli's commentary. We, however, find in it no order, but only darkness and confusion.

Solomon ben Isaac's reply[75] to Rabbi Solomon ben Adret's letter is characteristic. He addresses him with deep respect, calling him "angel of God, father of Torah, father of wisdom, father of piety." Nevertheless, he reproaches him for having allowed himself to be led astray by the "false Ahitophel" (i.e., Abba Mari) and for having attacked the Provençal communities so angrily. We have heard, he writes, that you even complained of us to the French rabbis, those grim enemies of philosophy and science, who wish to know of nothing but study of Torah. You insult us in your letter, declare us heretics and worshippers of all kinds of idols and idolatries. Your sharp attacks on the author of *Malmad Ha-Talmidim*, Solomon of Lunel further writes, have greatly enraged everyone here, especially his relatives and grandsons. In protest, every Sabbath from midday until the afternoon service, they read the words of *Malmad Ha-Talmidim*, and most of the members of the community listen attentively. It was calm and quiet in our camp, but you, in following the intriguer, have disturbed the peace and incited brother against brother.

At the same time the Tibbons' party sent a letter to the rabbis and heads of the community of Barcelona.[76] What sense has your ban? they asked. Is it right that, because of a few "breakers down of the fence" who follow false paths, thousands of innocent persons should suffer? Do you wish for this reason to close the

---

    ha-zaken (the old king), Rabbi Solomon ben Adret means Samuel Ibn Tibbon.

74. The word *malmad* means the staff or bar of the yoke in which oxen are harnessed together.
75. This letter is missing from *Minhat Kenaot*. Abba Mari did not have it at hand ("The reply that Rabbi Solomon of Lunel wrote was not available to me" [*Ibid.*, 78]). The letter was published by Neubauer in *Letterbode*, IV, 123–25.
76. Published by Neubauer in *Letterbode*, IV, 169–73. Under the document are the signatures of Isaac bar Abraham bar Jacob of Avignon, Solomon bar Moses bar Mordecai, Jehudah bar Moses bar Isaac, Solomon bar Joseph of Marseilles, Saul bar Solomon, and many others.

sources of knowledge to the young? Because of one foolish drunkard, is it forbidden to enjoy wine? Can the light of knowledge be a danger for our Torah? No one among us believes this except a few blind fanatics who, out of petty zealotry, cannot pardon educated men their wisdom and knowledge. How can these obscurantists understand what is good and what evil? You have permitted yourselves to be led astray by one from whom even his own family and near ones have turned away because he has calumniated and carried gossip about his community. You regard our rabbis and sages as worthless men and come to us from a foreign country with your bans and excommunications. Do not forget, however, that much earlier, before you came forth with your ban, the exilarch, the Nasi of Damascus, issued a command that no one should dare forbid study of the books of Maimonides, especially his *Guide for the Perplexed*. But is it possible to study this profound work without extensive knowledge of philosophy and the natural sciences? How can it be required that a man blindly follow the accepted customs, fulfill the commandments and precepts, and not be permitted to explain them logically? By what right can one place chains on man's free thought so that he should not be able to seek out the profound wisdom of the Creator's acts and works? Therefore, know that we in our community, in agreement with our sages, have determined, with an oath and a grievous ban, that no one shall presume to prohibit the study of any work whatsoever of Maimonides or of other scientific works."[77] "More than once," the Tibbons proudly add,

have controversies and quarrels on this question occurred, and each time all the decrees of those who fought against truth and science have become dust and ashes. The works which they persecuted, the works of knowledge and culture, were in no way diminished in brilliance, and they will illuminate the path for coming generations as well.

Rabbi Solomon ben Adret promptly replied to Solomon of Lunel[78] and, together with the rabbis of Barcelona,[79] also sent a letter to the leaders of the community in Montpellier.[80] First of all, he protests against the charge that he has allowed himself to be led astray by one who, out of personal motives, did not inform

77. *Letterbode*, IV, 172.
78. *Ibid.*, pp. 125–31.
79. *Ibid.*, X, 53–57.
80. Exclusive of Rabbi Solomon ben Adret, nine rabbis signed this letter, but among them were only four who also signed the document with the ban.

him correctly and gave him false information. "No," declares Rabbi Solomon, "you are mistaken. Not a single individual but entire communities, hundreds of honorable men, applied to me, and this not in secret but openly, with their full signatures. . . . For three years now they have been urging me not to be silent but to step forth with weapon in hand."[81]

"You take it amiss," Rabbi Solomon ben Adret further writes,

that we, men of a foreign place, presume to intervene in your affairs, give you our opinions, and frighten you with excommunications and bans. But you are mistaken. The writ we sent you is merely a notice that *we*, in order to protect our children from the plague of heresy, have taken the decision that from this day on among *us*, in *our* land, no one may study philosophy and the natural sciences until the age of thirty. This applies only to *our* children, not yours. We do not command *you*, we only propose that you accept the same decision among yourselves, but you are free to do as you think best.

Rabbi Solomon ben Adret was also strongly offended by the contemptuous tone in which Solomon ben Isaac speaks in his letter about the rabbis of France. "No," declares Rabbi Solomon, "I did not write to them, for their children are beyond danger. There is no reason to fear that there, for the sake of Greek philosophy, they will forget the sacred Torah and push it away into a hidden corner." Solomon, however, indignantly asks: Why the scorn with which you permit yourself to speak of the scholars of France? I bow reverently before these righteous men who have produced such great figures as Rashi and Rabbenu Tam and have spent their whole lives with great dedication in the tent of Torah. From my youth on I have had the profoundest reverence for the rabbis of France and Germany, and my hope is that my end might be like theirs. May I enjoy the privilege in the "world of truth" (the next world) of having my soul rest with theirs. Rabbi Solomon further writes: You champion the honor of Maimonides and his works. But who of us ever dared attack this great scholar? We all consider him our master and benefit from his teaching. You have deemed it necessary to send me the decree of the Nasi of Damascus. But you must know that I myself have been involved in this matter. At that time both sides turned to me, the Nasi and the rabbis of Acco, on the one side, and Solomon Petit's followers, on the other; and with God's help I made peace between the two parties.[82] Solomon ben Adret adds: I have the greatest respect for

81. *Letterbode*, IV, 126.
82. *Ibid.*, p. 128.

The Renewal of the Struggle Against Rationalism

Maimonides. His name is highly esteemed and revered in our academies. I am also bound in warm friendship to his grandsons. But did not Maimonides himself constantly insist that he wrote his *Guide* only for select individuals, for those who have great knowledge in all branches of Judaism? You, however, violate his will by putting his work into the hands of young people who have as yet no firmly settled views, and to these such a book must bring only harm and no benefit whatever. At the end of his letter Solomon again insists that he had to come forward because many communities requested him to do so, and he could not stand idly by when God's Torah was in jeopardy.

It was not, however, in Montpellier alone that the writ of Rabbi Solomon ben Adret and the other rabbis of Barcelona produced a split in the community and the formation of two hostile parties. The same thing happened in Barcelona itself. Of this we learn from the packet of letters published by Neubauer[83] which are rich in interesting details clearly characterizing the internal life of the Spanish communities of that era.[84]

One of the fourteen rabbis who subscribed to the proclamation that no one is to study philosophy before the age of thirty, Machir bar Sheshet, complains in his letter to the Provençal communities that in Barcelona "base men," led by one Samuel bar Benveniste, came forward. They had the impudence to blaspheme and mock the name of "the light of the exile" Rashi, and at a public gathering sharply attacked several rabbis and honorable men who subscribed to the excommunication. When the heads of the community warned this leader of the "stirrers of conflict" that they would place him under the ban, he quickly applied for aid to the government and managed to obtain a letter of protection from the queen of Castile. And when the leaders of the community of Montpellier decided to excommunicate this "wicked man," he again obtained a letter from the queen to the lord of Montpellier with a command that the latter strictly forbid the Jewish community to undertake any kind of punishment against him.[85]

---

83. *Ibid.*, pp. 160–73; V, 53–58.
84. One of these letters, which Rabbi Solomon ben Adret sent to Avignon (*Letterbode*, V, 57–58), was apparently written several years later, for Solomon here expresses his regret that the community of Avignon has also been afflicted with the plague of controversy and conflict, whereas it ought to be the fortress of all Jewry, for Avignon is the capital city of the pope. Since the pope's exile in Avignon began in 1308 and Solomon died in 1310, this letter was written sometime during the intervening period.
85. *Letterbode*, IV, 163.

The Bitter Struggle

The Provençal communities (Lunel, Béziers, and Montpellier) promptly reacted to Machir bar Sheshet's letter. They decreed that the "breaker of the fence" Samuel bar Benveniste should, as punishment for his grievous sin, "go into exile," travelling on foot from Barcelona to Lunel, and on the entire way be lashed in every city before the local rabbi. The "sinners and rebels" who, together with Benveniste, had blasphemed Rashi's name and impugned the honor of respected men of the community were to be put under the ban for a month's time. In the course of this period, they were to be flogged every Monday and Thursday and sit in the synagogue on the mourner's bench, separated from all as outcasts by a distance of four cubits.

In the meantime the controversy flared ever higher. Both sides carried on extensive propaganda and distributed proclamations to various communities.[86] From Argentiers, Lunel, Avignon, Perpignan, and other cities, Rabbi Solomon ben Adret received letters assuring him that he would be aided in his "controversy for the sake of heaven." In Narbonne Abba Mari's party found powerful support in the head of the large community residing there, the Nasi Kalonymos bar Todros.[87] A special emissary, Jacob ben Jehudah, in the winter of 1304 travelled around for propaganda purposes among the Provençal communities in the name of Abba Mari's party.[88] Rabbi Solomon ben Adret, taking into consideration the intense opposition of the Tibbons and their party, determined for the time being to abstain from further measures and to publish the absolute prohibition against studying philosophy and the natural sciences only when no less than twenty communities should assent to it.

At the same time Abba Mari's party received an accession of strong support in the person of the famous Talmudic scholar Rabbi Asher ben Yehiel, who had just arrived in Spain from Germany. To the latter country we must now turn our attention.

---

86. As at the time of the first controversy, so now the rationalists and their adversaries employed the weaponry of lampoons and epigrams. One such lampoon from Abba Mari's party, written in verse, was published by Isaac Last in *Asarah Kelei Kesef*, II (1903), 143-44.
87. *Minhat Kenaot*, 121, 141.
88. Stylistically typical is Jacob ben Jehudah's letter to Rabbi Solomon ben Adret (*Minhat Kenaot*, Letter 53). It is written in such high-flown rhetoric that it is literally impossible to make sense of the sea of assonant words and Oriental ornamentation.

CHAPTER FIVE

Rabbi Meir of Rothenburg, Rabbi Asher ben Yeḥiel, and Rabbi Solomon ben Adret

IN the course of the thirteenth century the condition of the Jews in Germany became increasingly intolerable. Even in the first half of the century, when Frederick II was still alive, numerous Jewish communities suffered greatly from the surrounding populace which persecuted them with relentless hatred, and thousands of Jews perished at its hands. The situation became even worse after Frederick's death, when the quarrel among his heirs began and the struggle for the imperial crown broke out (1254–73). The "law of the fist" dominated the land, and everyone did as he pleased. In this chaotic political situation the defenseless Jews suffered more than all others. The Catholic Church, for its part, exploited the unsettled times to oppress the hated "blasphemers of Christ" all the more severely. At the Church Council in Mainz (1259), all the restrictions that had been enacted against the Jews at previous councils were renewed and intensified. Horrible "blood libels," resulting in the killing of many innocent victims, became ever more frequent. The kings and princes continued to increase the special taxes imposed on Jews, while at the same time constantly diminishing their rights in commerce and trade.

The economic position of the Jews became ever more difficult, and the persecutions became so unbearable that in 1286 many Jewish families decided to leave Germany. Rumors were noised abroad that somewhere, not far from Palestine, the Messiah had already appeared and that the redemption was at hand. In the cities of the Rhine groups of Jewish emigrants ready to set out for the Orient assembled. But the measure of suffering was still not filled, and the troubles of the Jews increased after the death of the Emperor Rudolph (1291), when civil war again erupted and two pretenders battled for the imperial crown. A half-crazed knight named Rindfleisch organized bands of marauders. Like a fierce storm they swept over all of Bavaria and Austria in the summer of 1298 and drowned the Jewish populace in blood.[1] Over one hundred forty Jewish communities perished through fire and sword, among them the ancient community of Nuremberg where, among the 628 victims, the famous Talmudic scholar Rabbi Mordechai ben Hillel, whose *Sefer Mordechai* in later generations occupied one of the most honored places among the great collections of legal decisions, died together with his whole family.[2] With monstrous cruelty Rindfleisch's bands annihilated tens of thousands of Jewish victims. In the Nuremberg Memorial Book we read these terrifying lines: "May God remember, like the souls of Abraham, Isaac and Jacob, the souls of all the communities that were killed and stoned and burned and strangled and slaughtered and drowned and broken on the wheel and hanged and buried alive for the unification of God's name."[3]

Under such terrible conditions there could naturally be no possibility of normal cultural development. In this respect the tragic life of the greatest Talmudic scholar produced by German Jewry in the thirteenth century, the Tosafist Rabbi Meir ben Baruch (known as Maharam of Rothenburg), is not untypical. Rabbi Meir, who was born in 1215 and died in 1293, was the only scholar after Rabbenu Gershom and Rashi upon whom later generations conferred the title "the light of the exile."[4] In the year 1286 he headed one of the groups that was about to set out for Palestine.

---

1. For details of the Rindfleisch massacres, see *Quellen zur Geschichte der Juden*, III, 29–58, 66, 164–215.
2. For a discussion of Mordechai and his work, see S. Kohn, *Mordechai ben Hillel*, and I. H. Weiss, *Dor Dor Ve-Doreshav*, V, 79–82. An elegy on his death appears in *Quellen zur Geschichte der Juden*, III, 173.
3. The longing for revenge expressed in many of the laments and supplications composed at the time of the massacres of 1298 is quite understandable. The *paytan* Tamar ben Menahem, in one of his laments, calls down fire and brimstone on the murderers and begs God to destroy them like Sodom and Gomorrah. See *Kovetz Al Yad*, III, 15.
4. For details of his tragic life see S. Back, *Rabbi Meir ben Baruch aus Rothenburg: Sein Leben und sein Wirken, seine Schicksale und Schriften* (1895), and J. Wellescz, "Meir ben Baruch de Rothenbourg," *REJ*, Vols. 58–60.

Rabbi Meir of Rothenburg

The departure of the spiritual leader of the entire Jewish population of Germany would naturally have encouraged the emigration of Jews from the country. This, however, was considered extremely undesirable from the point of view of the emperor's financial interests. The Jews were, after all, the emperor's *Kammerknechte* (*servi camerae*), who paid very substantial taxes to the treasury of their lord and proprietor. Rabbi Meir was therefore arrested at the order of the emperor and imprisoned in the fortress of Enzisheim. The Jewish community offered a large ransom for the aged scholar, but Meir was opposed to being ransomed, out of fear that the government would employ this method more frequently to extort ever larger sums from the Jews. The rabbi was fated not to see the outside world again; he was held in prison until he died in 1293. Even after his death the authorities, out of their desire for revenge, refused to surrender his body to the Jewish community. Only fourteen years later did a wealthy Jew of Frankfurt, Zusskind Wimpfen, succeed in purchasing Rabbi Meir's remains for a very large sum and bringing them to burial in the cemetery at Worms.

Most of the works Rabbi Meir of Rothenburg wrote were lost,[5] but those that have survived reflect quite clearly not only his acute mind and considerable literary talent, but also the backwardness and one-sidedness of the spiritual and intellectual world in which the Jews, ruthlessly persecuted and oppressed, lived at that time in Germany. Rabbi Meir had in him a spark of the true poet, but he was too occupied with "words of Torah" to devote himself to "words of song." Only when he learned that the sacred books had been burned on the pyre in 1242 was the Tosafist transformed into the poet. In a lovely elegy entitled "Sha'eli Serufah"[6] he gave expression to his profound sorrow:

> Ask, is it well, O thou consumed of fire,
> With those that mourn for thee,
> That yearn to tread thy courts, that sore desire
> Thy sanctuary;

---

5. For the titles of his works, see Weiss, *Dor Dor Ve-Doreshav*, V, 74–76, and Renan-Neubauer, *Les Rabbins français*, pp. 458–61.
6. This elegy is modeled after Jehudah Halevi's Ode to Zion, *Tziyyon Ha-Lo Tishali*. Both are traditionally read in the synagogue on the Ninth of Av, together with other elegies and laments. Rabbi Meir also composed several other religious poems; on this, see L. Zunz, *Die synagogale Poesie des Mittelalters*, p. 310, and *Die Literaturgeschichte der synagogalen Poesie*, pp. 357–62.

That, panting for thy land's sweet dust, are grieved,
And sorrow in their souls,
And by the flames of wasting fire bereaved,
Mourn for thy scrolls;

That grope in shadow of unbroken night,
Waiting the day to see
Which o'er them yet shall cast a radiance bright,
And over thee?

Ask of the welfare of the man of woe,
With breaking heart, in vain
Lamenting ever for thine overthrow,
And for thy pain;

Of him that crieth as the jackals cry,
As owls their moaning make,
Proclaiming bitter wailing far and nigh;
Yea, for thy sake.

And thou revealed amid a heavenly fire,
By earthly fire consumed,
Saw how the foe unscorched escaped the pyre
Thy flames illumed!

How long shalt thou that art at ease abide
In peace, unknown to woe,
While o'er my flowers, humbled from their pride,
Thy nettles grow?

Thou sittest high exalted, lofty foe!
To judge the sons of God;
And with the judgments stern dost bring them low
Beneath thy rod.

Yea, more, to burn the Law thou durst decree—
God's word to banish hence:
Then blest be he who shall award to thee
Thy recompense! . . .[7]

It was not as a religious poet that Rabbi Meir of Rothenburg acquired renown but as a Talmudist and legal authority. His

7. The complete text of Rabbi Meir's elegy is given in *Kinot Le-Tishah Be-Av*. For comments and explanations, see Baneth, *MGWJ*, 1929, pp. 295–303. [The translation here given is by Nina Salaman. —B. M.]

novellae and *responsa* testify to his very lucid and logical mind. But this brilliant leader of German Jewry was also humbly subservient to the "tradition of the fathers," to all the innumerable restrictions and severe customs which the benighted and melancholy Jewish communities of the Middle Ages produced. "It is forbidden"—this is the chief slogan and guide of Rabbi Meir as a legal decisor. The extent to which he was a pedantic *maḥmir* (one who makes the law more strict) may be illustrated by several examples. In winter, no matter how cold it may be, one may not, according to Rabbi Meir, heat an oven on the Sabbath, even through the agency of a non-Jew. To prevent any violation of the Talmudic prohibition against carrying any object on the Sabbath, he ruled that Sabbath garments should be sewn without pockets. The keen Tosafist also allowed himself to enter into a deep discussion whether it is permissible on the Sabbath for children to eat little cakes with letters inscribed on them. By eating the cake the child, after all, "rubs out" the letters and this, as is known, is a serious transgression. Rabbi Meir decided that such cakes may be given only to suckling infants, and that only when there is no alternative. Many such strict decisions by Rabbi Meir were diligently collected by his naive disciple, Rabbi Samson ben Zadok,[8] who preserved them for future generations.

We note how, in the bloody century of persecution and degradation, Jewish thought became ever more timorous and restricted and its world ever narrower and more isolated. The German Jew was frequently compelled to sacrifice everything for the sake of his sacred Torah, the heritage of his fathers. Hence, he observed every punctilio of this heritage with utmost devotion. He had no desire to enter into inquiries whether all these things were absolutely necessary and important. Every custom, everything received as a legacy from previous generations, was beloved and precious. Isolated from the external world by an iron wall of cruelty and hatred, the Jews of Germany felt themselves like "sheep surrounded by wolves." Hence, they were so obdurately concerned only with restraints and fences, with separating themselves all the more from the hostile external world, with surrounding themselves with ever new restrictions, one harsher than the other.

One of the most eminent rabbis of that time, Rabbi Isaac ben Moses of Vienna,[9] a disciple of Rabbi Eleazar of Worms, the

---

8. In his well-known *Tashbetz* (Nos. 38, 51, and many others).
9. In point of fact he spent only his last years in Vienna. See H. Tykocinski, *MGWJ*, 1911, pp. 478–500.

author of *Rokeaḥ*, tells of this very frankly. In his famous book of laws, *Or Zarua*,¹⁰ he has occasion to point to a law about which Rashi was a *mekil* (one who adopts a lenient interpretation) and immediately adds:

> Rashi decided this way only for his own generation when the Torah was exalted, when great sages for whom all the laws were clear, lived. Then men could depend on them. But now, in our orphaned generation, when knowledge of the Torah is, by reason of our many sins, so small and the wells of wisdom are dried up, blessed are those scholars who do not rely on their own wisdom, who are afraid to be lenient and hold fast to the principle that it is better to forbid than to permit.¹¹

The pious disciples of Rabbi Meir of Rothenburg assembled with great diligence all the restrictions and harsh customs of the time and lovingly wrote them down for future generations so that none might be forgotten. Ever greater and more multi-branched grew the vast collections of laws and commandments, statutes and customs.

The outstanding disciple of Rabbi Meir, as well as the most respected Talmudic authority of that age, was Rabbi Asher ben Yeḥiel, better known as Rosh (or Asheri). Born in the middle of the thirteenth century (he died in Toledo in 1327), Asher as a child witnessed a terrible massacre in his community in 1264 and saved his life only, as it were, through a miracle. Hence, it is hardly surprising that the darkness and dread of that fearful era is so strongly reflected in his well-known book of ethical instruction, *Sefer Ha-Hanhagah* (also called *Sefer Oreḥot Ḥayyim*), which he wrote in the form of a "testament" for his children.¹²

10. In the introduction to the *Or Zarua*, in which the author deals with "combinations of letters" and *notarikon*, the influence of the Kabbalist doctrine of his teacher, Eleazar of Worms, is especially discernible. This work contains numerous interesting details of significance for the cultural history and folklore of the Jewish communities of Germany and Bohemia in the Middle Ages. Himself born in Bohemia, Isaac led a wanderer's existence. In the course of his life he lived in various cities in Germany, Austria, and France, and thus had occasion to become familiar with the customs and ways of life of their Jewish communities.
11. *Or Zarua*, I, 119, end of No. 416.
12. When a Christian professor of the eighteenth century became familiar with the ethical principles of the rabbi of the thirteenth century, he wrote in astonishment, "Kaum hätte man in den damaligen Zeiten solche Sittenlehren von Christen erwarten sollen, als dieser Jude seinen Glaubensgenossen hier vorgeschrieben und hinterlassen hat" (Hirt, *Bibliothek Theol.*, V, 43; quoted by Zunz, *Zur Geschichte und Literatur*, p. 123).

"Beware that you do not rejoice in your heart"; "One may not laugh or be merry"—statements such as these are here frequently reiterated. "See to it for the sake of God's name that you remove yourself from pride," Rabbi Asher admonishes. "Make yourself lowly as the dust of the earth that is trodden by all."

After the death of Rabbi Meir of Rothenburg, Rabbi Asher became the universally recognized spiritual leader of German Jewry. His *yeshivah* or Talmudic academy attracted hundreds of young men not only from the German lands but also from Bohemia and Russia. Jews applied to him with religious inquiries from the farthest countries. His collection[13] of Talmudic laws and statutes became one of the fundamental works on which the whole later rabbinic legal literature was constructed.

A typical representative of the medieval German ghetto, Rabbi Asher was an orthodox zealot who refused to acknowledge any wisdom whatever besides the "wisdom of the Talmud." He had an attitude of utter contempt for all secular sciences. "Your worldly wisdoms are not known to me," he proudly declared to the Jews of Spain, "and I thank and praise God who has kept me from them, for they may lead a man away from the fear of God and His Torah." Especially hateful to him was philosophy; whenever he mentions it he immediately quotes the verse from Proverbs, "All who come to her will not return." Like Rabbi Solomon ben Adret, he also insisted that there can be no compromise between philosophy and faith, for they follow divergent paths. Philosophy bases itself on logical assumptions and arguments of reason; faith, however, is founded on sacred tradition.[14]

At the beginning of the fourteenth century Rabbi Asher had to leave Germany. The government cast its eye on him and, recalling the tragic end of his teacher, he fled in the summer of 1303 to Savoy.[15] But there again he did not feel completely secure, since the Duke of Savoy was a vassal of the German emperor. He therefore went to southern France.[16] In Provence he first encountered a

13. The list of all the decisions in this collection (which was assembled by Rabbi Asher's son, Rabbi Jacob) is printed in most editions of the Talmud under the title *Piskei Ha-Rosh*.
14. *Sheelot U-Teshuvot Ha-Rosh*, No. 55, 9b.
15. See *Iggerot Shadal*, p. 680; *Avnei Zikkaron*, p. 8. There is a legend to the effect that Rabbi Asher's flight from Germany was connected with the negotiations that were being carried on at that time with the government on the matter of ransoming the body of the deceased Rabbi Meir of Rothenburg (see Neubauer, *Seder Ha-Ḥachamim*, I, 143).
16. Rabbi Asher tells of all the hardships he endured in his letter to one of the followers of Abba Mari (see *Minḥat Kenaot*, Letter 52).

liberal intellectual environment, with cultivated Jews who had, besides their Jewish heritage, extensive knowledge of philosophy and natural science. "There [in Provence]," relates Rabbi Asher,

> I saw an extremely beautiful land, and the people appeared to me very fine and honorable. . . . I soon realized, however, that I was mistaken. I had believed all of them to be pure white and they turned out to be black. Only a few did I find there who remained faithful to God and His sacred Torah. But even these have not the courage to stand firm against the general stream of wickedness. All, great and small, study natural science and have entirely forsaken the Torah. They do not cross its threshold and have broken its restraints.[17]

Hence, when Rabbi Asher visited Montpellier, he greeted Abba Mari very warmly as a "fearless champion who, with great courage, girded up his loins and, weapon in hand, attacked the breakers-down of the fence."[18] Nevertheless, Rabbi Asher at first displayed considerable caution. He warned that the controversy might cause a serious conflict and, in order to make peace between the contending parties, proposed a conference of representatives of both sides at which Rabbi Solomon ben Adret should serve as arbitrator. Apparently, however, he quickly renounced this proposal and placed himself entirely on the side of Abba Mari after going from Provence to Spain in 1305, spending some time in Barcelona with Solomon ben Adret, and being elected by the community of Toledo as its chief rabbi at Solomon's suggestion. It is somehow symbolic that precisely at that time a German rabbi who wished to know nothing of "external wisdoms," i.e., the sciences, and even in the realm of Talmudic scholarship recognized only the authority of the Franco-German codifiers and decisors,[19] was chosen to head one of the oldest and most prominent Spanish communities.

This event gave added courage and strength to the orthodox party, and Rabbi Solomon ben Adret finally decided to take stern measures. On the "Sabbath of Vision" (July 31, 1305) in the great synagogue of Barcelona, a proclamation of thirty-six rabbis was read strictly prohibiting anyone for fifty years, under a ban and curse, from studying the natural sciences (except medicine, which is essential for practical life) or reading any books dealing with Greek philosophy, whether in Hebrew or in any other language, until he reaches the age of twenty-five, "in order not to bring men

---

17. *Minḥat Kenaot*, 101.
18. *Ibid.*, 109.
19. See *Sheelot U-Teshuvot Ha-Rosh*, Nos. 20–21.

to temptation and not lead them away from the paths of Torah." The ban applied also to those instructing young people under the age of twenty-five in these forbidden studies.[20]

The rabbis of Barcelona circulated their ban, sealed with their signatures, to all the communities of Spain and Provence. To it they added a lengthy explanation setting forth the reasons which motivated them to take such severe action. The rationalists are here charged with numerous grievous sins: they falsify the Torah, give godless sermons from the pulpits, violate the commandments, and deny that the Law of Moses was divinely revealed.[21]

In a separate proclamation the rabbis of Barcelona fiercely assailed those who permit themselves to expound the Torah in an allegorical-philosophical fashion. Such sinful men, they declared, must be separated from the camp of Israel. Their sin must not be forgotten until they die, and the fires of hell are prepared for them. Their books must be banned and burned, so that no memory of them survives.[22]

Rabbi Asher ben Yehiel was extremely pleased with this decision and immediately added his signature to the ban of the rabbis of Barcelona. He considered it necessary, however, to emphasize that, in his opinion, the secular sciences ought to be forbidden both to young and old, for it is explicitly stated in the Bible, "And thou shalt meditate on it [the Torah] day and night." Since the Torah must be studied day and night, it follows that one may be concerned with the sciences only in those few moments that belong neither to the day nor the night, i.e., only at the time of twilight.[23]

Among the rationalists the ban created tremendous excitement and indignation. Their leaders, with the Tibbons at their head, at once issued a counter-ban. In the documents that have come down to us it bears the name *Aderabah* (On the Contrary). This *Aderabah* ban applied to (1) those who prevent their children, no matter of what age, from studying natural science and philosophy; (2) those who dare impugn the honor of Maimonides and his work; and (3) all who allow themselves to calumniate any writer who sincerely expresses his philosophical views.[24]

The ideological controversy became so intense that the *mitnagdim* or opponents, i.e., the freethinkers, deemed it proper to apply for aid in their struggle to the governmental authority. They re-

---

20. *Sheelot U-Teshuvot Rabbi Shelomoh ben Adret*, No. 415.
21. *Ibid.*, No. 416.
22. *Ibid.*, No. 417.
23. *Minhat Kenaot*, 178.
24. *Ibid.*, 150.

quested the "lord" of Montpellier not to allow the orthodox in that city to publish their ban against those who fight for science and enlightenment.[25] The mayor of Montpellier gladly consented, publicly explaining the motives that impelled him to aid the freethinkers: If the Jews are not permitted to study philosophy and are forbidden to employ the allegorical method in Bible exegesis, "every possibility that Christianity will be accepted by any of them will thereby be precluded."[26]

To demonstrate openly their contempt for the ban and proclamations of the rabbis of Barcelona, the Tibbons and their followers in Montpellier assembled on the Sabbath in the synagogues, preached rationalistic sermons, and read aloud Anatoli's *Malmad Ha-Talmidim* and similar works.[27] Bearing in mind the fact that Solomon Petit had been unsuccessful in his day because he had specifically attacked Maimonides, for whose memory Jews in all the lands of the East had the profoundest respect, the Tibbons and their party endeavored to show that their opponents aimed their ban above all at the writings of the great philosopher.[28] The Tibbons regarded this as the best means of discrediting their opponents at the bar of public opinion, for they realized how highly Maimonides was revered in the Spanish and Provençal communities. The orthodox also understood this quite well and therefore employed all measures to refute the charge.[29] Rabbi Solomon ben Adret himself immediately issued a public declaration on the matter:

In order to blind the eyes of men, they [our opponents] give out false rumors to the effect that I have blasphemed Maimonides and his writings. . . . They devise slanders and accuse me of being an enemy of Maimonides. Let them not only with their mouths praise the great scholar, but show that they really follow his ways. Let them be like him in true fear of God and in fulfilling all the commandments and precepts.[30]

25. Abba Mari's disciple, Simeon ben Joseph An-Duran, who also participated in the controversy, complains of this to Rabbi Solomon ben Adret (see *REJ*, XXIX, 224).
26. *Minhat Kenaot*, 142.
27. See An-Duran's letter to Rabbi Solomon ben Adret (*REJ*, XXIX, 222).
28. *Minhat Kenaot*, 143, 150.
29. *Ibid.*, Letters 82, 84–86. See also the previously mentioned letter of An-Duran to Rabbi Solomon ben Adret, as well as Solomon ben Adret's letter to Solomon bar Isaac of Montpellier (*Letterbode*, IV, 125–31).
30. *Minhat Kenaot*, 166.

Rabbi Solomon ben Adret and his followers were justified when they insisted that their struggle was not at all like the "first controversy" initiated by Solomon of Montpellier, and that they had no intention of waging war against Maimonides' works.[31] In fact, their struggle went much further. To be sure, they always maintained that they were not opposed on principle to secular knowledge; they wished merely that young Jews should devote themselves to the natural sciences and philosophy only after first having obtained an adequate degree of Talmudic knowledge. But it was clear that what was involved here was nothing less than a revolution in the entire system of education—a closing to future generations of all paths leading to secular knowledge and free inquiry. This would necessarily result in Spanish Jewry enclosing itself within the narrow confines of the Halachah, like its brethren in Germany and France. Jacob ben Machir rightly noted this in his letter to Rabbi Solomon ben Adret,[32] declaring that the prohibition against studying the secular sciences before the age of twenty-five must necessarily bring it about that the next generation would be permanently without knowledge, for whoever does not study in his youth will remain ignorant his whole life through. This was also quickly realized by many who were opposed on principle to the rationalists and their activity. They understood at once that what was at issue here was the question of freedom of thought and knowledge, and they issued forth decisively against the ban of the Barcelona rabbis and Abba Mari's propaganda activity.

The first to attack the party of Rabbi Solomon ben Adret and Abba Mari was the noted Provençal scholar of that era Menahem ben Solomon Meiri.[33] An ardent disciple of Maimonides, he made use of the philosopher's method of inquiry, and his well-known commentary to the Talmud, *Bet Ha-Behirah*, is distinguished by its organized structure and lucid, simple language. Completely foreign to him were the dialectical subtleties of the Franco-German school, and his style is free of all the rhetorical flourishes and

---

31. "By what right," Simeon An-Duran angrily demands, "do you make us responsible for the sins committed by those men at the time of the first controversy? How do you have the gall to confuse us with those who undertook to attack Moses, the man of God? We bow before him and follow his ways" (Zunz Jubilee Volume *Tiferet Sevah*, II, 153).
32. *Minhat Kenaot*, 24.
33. His Provençal name was Don Vidal Solomon. Born in Perpignan in 1249, he died in 1306. For details about him, see Renan-Neubauer, *Les Rabbins français*, pp. 528–47.

ornamentation which were then so fashionable. With his keen critical-historical sense, Meiri realized that to achieve an adequate understanding and proper estimate of the laws and statutes which the authors of the Talmud had established, one must, first of all, ascertain just when each of the Tannaim and Amoraim lived. To this end, he placed before his commentary to *Pirkei Avot*[34] a literary-historical "introduction" (*petiḥah*) in which he provides, in strict chronological order, a general overview of how the Oral Law developed from the first Tannaim on to his own time.[35] It is, in fact, no rhetorical exaggeration when the poet Jehudah Ibn Zabara declares enthusiastically, "Great beyond measure are the commentaries on the Mishnah and Gemara; some are too brief, others fearfully long, without limit and bound; until Menaḥem Meiri appeared and created his *Bet Ha-Beḥirah*."[36]

Meiri was a categorical opponent of the rationalists and their allegorical manner of explaining the reasons for the commandments of the Torah. But he saw in the orthodox party a definite threat to free inquiry and knowledge, and when Abba Mari requested him to add his signature to the ban of the Barcelona rabbis, he responded with a sharp protest. "With great pleasure," he writes in his open letter,

I learned that you came forth against the rationalist preachers. I had hoped that through you this very unfortunate phenomenon would finally come to an end. . . . For it is truly disgraceful to see how men without knowledge presume to preach from the pulpit, distort the plain meaning of the Torah, and confuse minds with bizarre notions that have no basis either in the Bible or Talmud. But suddenly I received the sad news that you, together with Rabbi Solomon ben Adret, had issued a ban against secular knowledge and declared war against the bearers of science and education. You say publicly that since secular knowledge has spread among us in Provence, heresy has been strengthened in the land and men have begun to forget God. . . .[37]

34. Reprinted in Vienna in 1854 by Z. Stern, who also provides in it a biography of Meiri.
35. For a discussion of the significance of this work, see Weiss, *Dor Dor Ve-Doreshav*, V, 89–91.
36. Meiri's "introduction" was later employed by his countryman, Isaac ben Jacob Lattes, in his valuable historical chronicle *Shaarei Tziyyon*, which goes up to the year 1372. *Shaarei Tziyyon* was published, with numerous notes, by S. Buber in 1885. For a discussion of Lattes, see Renan-Neubauer, *Les Écrivains juifs français*, pp. 692–982.
37. Regrettably, this letter has not come down to us in full. Abba Mari mentions it in *Minḥat Kenaot* (No. 93), but does not provide the text. The content of this interesting document is known to us only from

Yedaiah Ha-Penini and His Ketav Ha-Hitnatzlut

Meiri further writes:

You attack the "external wisdoms." Do you not yourselves understand that one cannot dispense with the sciences, that it is ridiculous to prohibit important and useful works merely because some idea expressed in them may be misunderstood and because there are those who might draw false conclusions from it? Do you not realize that the scientific investigators and thinkers are the pride of the nation? You desire to make the whole people stupid and ignorant. You wish that Israel, which even in ancient times was renowned as a "wise and understanding people," should obtain the reputation of a backward and barbarized multitude. Foolish people commit follies. Well, then, punish them, let them understand that they are in error and follow a false path. But do you really believe that the erroneous and improper steps of some fools can bring the entire existence of our religion into jeopardy? If some who study philosophy commit errors, draw incorrect conclusions and stray from the right way, must one therefore declare war against philosophical investigation and thinking in general? Were the gates of the *Pardes*[38] locked because Elisha ben Abuyah became an apostate after entering them?

Contemporaneously with Meiri another prominent representative of Provençal Jewry came forth—Yedaiah Ha-Penini[39] (the son of Abraham Bedersi), who later became quite famous as a poet. Thanks to the literary environment in which Yedaiah grew up, he very early manifested a love for poetry, and at the age of fifteen composed his well-known prayer "Bakashat Ha-Memim," which consists of a thousand words, each of which begins with the Hebrew letter *mem*. Abraham Bedersi was so enchanted by

---

Simeon An-Duran's reply to Meiri's letter, in which numerous passages from the latter are quoted. An-Duran's reply was published by D. Kaufmann in the Zunz Jubilee Volume *Tiferet Sevah*, II, 142–74. For biographical details about An-Duran, see Renan-Neubauer, *Les Rabbins français*, pp. 695–700.

38. *Pardes* really means orchard or pleasure garden, but in the Talmud the term is used symbolically as the name for the realm of esoteric wisdom. According to a Talmudic legend four Tannaim "entered the *Pardes*" but only one of them, Rabbi Akiba, returned in peace and unharmed. Another, Elisha ben Abuyah, became a heretic and an unbeliever and "cut down the plants" (i.e., abandoned his faith).

39. Born in the city of Béziers. There is no agreement on the date of his birth. According to some scholars, he was born sometime between 1275 and 1280; others suggest between 1255 and 1260. His Provençal name was En Bonet, a translation of his second Hebrew name Tuvyah, with which he signed his youthful work *Ohev Nashim*. For a discussion of his life and work, see *Les Écrivains juifs français*, pp. 359–402. It is conjectured that Yedaiah collected all of his father's poems into one *diwan* (*ibid.*, p. 398).

Yedaiah's poetic debut that he celebrated the beauty of his prayer in a poem in which he asserts that his son "strikes fire with his golden verses that are beyond all price." "Bakashat Ha-Memim," however, is only an artificial piece, with numerous rhetorical flourishes but very little poetic inspiration. The influence of his father's watery rhetoric is also noticeable in Yedaiah's second work, which he composed at the age of eighteen, the poem *Ohev Nashim* (it also bears another title, *Tziltzal Kenafayim*).[40] The gallant young poet here attacks the "enemy of women," Jehudah ben Shabbetai, and his poem *Minhat Yehudah* (see Volume One, Chapter Eight), and champions the cause of the offended daughters of Eve. Yedaiah relates how, in a land of good-for-nothings, the men decided to drive away their wives, and tells the events that ensued. There are some witty passages in the work, and some quite lovely songs are also interspersed in it. But the entire piece is extremely diffuse and tedious, and the narrative is literally drowned in a sea of rhetoric, so that the reader loses the patience to hear the "lover of women" out to the end.

Much more interesting is another of Yedaiah's works, written at approximately the same time, his didactic essay *Sefer Ha-Pardes*.[41] Here he appears as a thoughtful, serious, and intellectually curious young man, who presents us with his view of the world, his estimate of science, morality, and the like. Yedaiah ingeniously weaves his maxims and thoughts together with parables and fables. Of particular interest is the last chapter, in which rhetoric and poetry are discussed. The significance of the poetic art, the author insists, is immense. "Without poetry, there can be no religion. It is the foundation of every faith; it softens man's heart and strengthens his belief." "A true poet does not hasten to publish his work, for what pleases him immediately after he has written it may later appear to him petty and vain." "Beware of arousing the poet's hostility, for his falsehood will be more readily believed than your truth."

From his youth on Yedaiah diligently studied Greek-Arabic philosophy, treated speculative questions in his writings, and wrote commentaries and supplements to the works of Avicenna,

40. Published by A. Neubauer in the Zunz Jubilee Volume *Tiferet Sevah*, II, 1-19. The poems that are woven into this work were published, with critical notes and explanations, by S. Sachs in *Kovetz Al Yad*, IX (1893).
41. First published in Constantinople in 1515; reprinted by Joseph Luzzatto in *Otzar Ha-Safrut*, III, Part Four. Several fragments which are lacking in these editions were published by L. Dukes in *Ha-Levanon*, V (1868). See also *Les Écrivains juifs français*, pp. 366-68.

Yedaiah Ha-Penini and His Ketav Ha-Ḥitnatzlut

Averroes, Al-Farabi, and others.[42] His favorite thinkers, however, were Abraham Ibn Ezra and Maimonides. These two, especially the latter, were for him the incarnation of the highest degree of human knowledge. Hence, it is hardly surprising that as soon as he learned of the ban of the rabbis of Barcelona, he addressed a letter of protest, *Ketav Ha-Hitnatzlut*,[43] to Rabbi Solomon ben Adret, a letter which created a considerable sensation in its day.

Following the fashion of that era, Yedaiah, at the beginning of his letter, addresses flowery Oriental compliments to Rabbi Solomon, calling him "the prince of God," the "pillar of light of his generation," "the well of righteousness and justice," etc. After all these eulogies, however, the poet expresses very openly and strongly his feeling of anger and indignation: Where has it ever been heard that entire communities in which are so many worthy and pious men, rich in knowledge and good deeds, should be declared nests of sin and blasphemy, and these men themselves considered bands of debauched and vile sinners? You, he charges, have made us a mockery and scorn in all the dispersions of Israel, and all this because among us were a few men who were not sufficiently prudent and whose entire fault consists in the fact that, in their public appearances, they disclosed to the people what it is more desirable to keep secret.[44]

Yedaiah himself belonged to the right wing of Maimonides' followers, who employed the rationalist-allegorical method of their teacher quite cautiously. It therefore seemed to him that the other rationalists of Provence also went no further than he. Hence he insists that he is in perfect agreement with Rabbi Solomon ben Adret that those who declare the historical personalities of the Bible merely allegorical symbols, and the commandments and laws simply moral maxims, are deniers of the root principle of Judaism and undermine the foundations of the faith.[45] We, however, asserts Yedaiah, remain loyal to the teaching of Maimonides, who never permitted himself to express such heretical ideas. In interpreting the stories and legends of the Bible and Talmud, Maimonides made use of the allegorical method only when it was a question of maintaining the God concept free of corporeality and

---

42. On this see Steinschneider, *Hebräischen Übersetzungen*, pp. 110 and 186; and *Les Écrivains juifs français*, pp. 375-98.
43. Printed in the *Responsa* of Rabbi Solomon ben Adret, No. 418. It was published separately by S. Bloch in 1809, and reprinted in Warsaw in 1881.
44. *Ketav Ha-Hitnatzlut*, pp. 21-24 (according to the Warsaw edition of 1881).
45. *Ibid.*, p. 39.

material forms and images. With his explanations of the "reasons for the commandments," Maimonides strengthened and deepened their value.[46] For—Yedaiah insists—philosophical enlightenment confirms faith; it preserves its purity and does not allow its springs to be muddied by superstition.[47] But you—Yedaiah addresses Rabbi Solomon ben Adret and his followers—have declared war against philosophy and free inquiry. Your effort, however, is in vain. Philosophical thought made itself at home among the Jews already in the time of Saadiah Gaon, blossomed in the generation of Abraham Ibn Ezra, and reached its acme when the star of Moses ben Maimon arose—he whose name is honored not only among the Jews but among the sages of the peoples of the world.[48]

You are revered among us, Yedaiah declares at the end of his letter; we take high account of your rabbinic authority. But, know this—we cannot and will not surrender scientific inquiry. It is our breath, our life, and even if Joshua should appear and attempt to stop the sun of culture and enlightenment, no one would follow him, for our great teacher Maimonides has left us another Torah as a legacy. We shall not part with it, but will faithfully transmit it to future generations.[49]

In actuality, the two sides could not find a common language that would have enabled them to come together and discuss the issues dividing them. Even the calm and sedate Yedaiah Ha-Penini refused to take note of certain phenomena in his environment whose reality simply could not be denied, and in which the orthodox rabbis perceived the most serious threat to the survival of Judaism. The controversy would have become even more intense, but suddenly an external power intervened. Altogether unexpectedly, French Jewry was struck by catastrophe. The avaricious king of France, Philip the Fair, issued a decree in July 1306 that the Jews were to be expelled from the country. The community of Montpellier, the major center of the controversy, was dispersed. Abba Mari went into exile, roamed about in Arles and afterward in Perpignan, and soon disappeared completely from the stage.[50] His follower Simeon ben Joseph An-Duran moved to Aix, where in a tender elegy he lamented the destruction of the Provençal communities.[51] Menahem Meiri died in the

46. *Ibid.*, pp. 37–39, 68–69.
47. *Ibid.*, pp. 27, 49–50.
48. *Ibid.*, p. 70.
49. *Ibid.*, p. 75.
50. His two elegies on the death of Meiri and Rabbi Solomon ben Adret were published in *Letterbode*, V, 73–79.
51. The elegy was published by D. Kaufmann in *REJ*, XXIX, 225–28.

same year, and about four years later the aged Rabbi Solomon ben Adret also died.

Solomon's disciple, Joseph ben Solomon Ibn Yahya,[52] mourned his teacher's death in an elegy which, because of its unique meter, became a pattern and prototype for all the later so-called echo poems. Ibn Yahya's elegy is constructed according to the principles of Arabic meter. All its verses end with the same syllable, *rim*, and in the closing word of each verse the last syllables of the preceding word are repeated. The poem thus conveys the impression of a kind of echo, as if to the elegiac sounds of the lament all of nature responded with a sorrowful echo. Thanks to Ibn Yahya's lovely elegy, this extremely complex metrical form obtained great popularity, and many later poets attempted to write similar poems. We therefore present here, in prose translation, a few verses of the first Hebrew "echo" poem:[53]

On the peaks of Gilead and Lebanon arise, O goddess of song! Let your weeping break forth from the Mount of Avarim, and let the cry of lamentation resound in all corners.

Turn to Noph and Tahpanhes. Over the tents of Samaria proclaim to all the children of exile: Fallen is the pride and splendor of the Torah; its crown is cast into the grave.

Wherever you turn, arouse sobbing and lamentation. Weep like a virgin in sorrow, girt in sackcloth.

Shave your heads like the eagle, you poets.[54] Change your joyous songs into bitter weeping.

Let cries of lamentation choke the sounds of drums and trumpets; let the ostriches with their sobbing voices deafen not solitary forests and islands but noisy cities and towns.

Let God's holy servants tremble in terror. The Levites' song must be made dumb. Wrap yourselves in beggar's garments, you nobles and princes; in sackcloth and cloaks of mourning clothe yourselves, you great and rich.

Cast away the diamonds and garlands from your heads and deck yourselves with dust and ashes. With prickly thorns cover the splendid portals which glistened with colorful hangings.

Forget the blooming gardens, you carefree maidens; forsake, you bridegrooms, your lovely chambers.

On the dark day on which our protector and guardian fell, and the sheep remained solitary and forsaken; snuffed out is the brilliance

52. The Yahya family produced a whole series of significant personalities, of whom we shall have occasion to speak later.
53. The poem was first published in Gedaliah Ibn Yahya's *Shalshelet Ha-Kabbalah*. It was reprinted, with a corrected text, by D. Kaufmann, in *ZHB*, I, 24–25.
54. Among the peoples of the Orient shaving the head was a sign of mourning.

of the unforgettable Solomon who with his light illuminated our tortuous way.

Of all the major participants in the bitter *Kulturkampf* Yedaiah Ha-Penini alone not only did not depart from the scene shortly after the expulsion of the Jews from France, but manifested his full creative power only later. Indeed, under the influence of the recently experienced catastrophe, he produced a work which made him famous in subsequent generations. The melancholy and pessimistic outlook that now dominated his spirit was expressed in his didactic poem *Behinat Olam*, which soon became one of the most popular works among Jewish readers. Numerous commentaries were written on it,[55] and it was also translated into many European languages[56] and published in a large number of editions.[57]

The difference between the poem *Ohev Nashim*, written by the eighteen-year-old Yedaiah, and the creativity of the mature poet of *Behinat Olam* is vast. In this work, too, the poet in places exaggerates and overwrites. Here also his style is very artificial. The reader is wearied by the excessive richness and assonance of words and syllables, and by the effects which the poet too frequently endeavors to attain through plays on words. But he gladly pardons these relatively minor rhetorical defects, enchanted by the lovely pictorial language and dazzled by the rich colors. Philosophic thought and the profoundest questions of life are forged together in the flame of poetic inspiration and appear in vivid images and verses filled with noble sorrow and bitter pain.

In content and poetic value, *Behinat Olam* really consists of two separate parts. The first and most important occupies the first twelve chapters; the second, the last five. In exalted, passionate language the poet portrays in the first chapters the magnificence of the human spirit, which he regards as the reflection of God in the terrestrial world. Proud and mighty is the flight of man's thought into the boundless distances. It embraces all worlds, soars freely over all the depths and heights—yet it must crawl powerlessly in the dust of the earth, shackled by the chains of profaneness and bodily infirmity. The most precious diamond, the poet declares, is the target of blind accident; the "divine son" must grope in darkness and languish in dust. Man is endowed with

---

55. Of the older commentators, the most important are Jacob Ibn Haviv, Joseph Frances, and Yomtov Heller; of the modern, Y. D. Frank-Kamenetzki.
56. Latin, German (eight times), French (twice), Italian, English, and Polish.
57. S. Wiener in his *Kehillat Mosheh* lists over seventy editions.

deathless, omnipotent thought; nevertheless, his fate is to rot and disappear. But he is not only a plaything for the cold and cruel laws of nature; he himself disgraces his immortal greatness and frivolously exchanges it for the petty pleasures of this world. The monarch of free thought is a slave to low desires. The tragic contradictions of man's life are portrayed by the poet in these moving images:[58]

An infinitely wide, deeper than abysses, wildly turbulent sea is the world;
And time—a tottering bridge built over it.
It is suspended on lines rotten and ephemeral from the beginning;
And this is the way that leads to eternal bliss,
To the glory and splendor of the divine light . . .
Wide as a man's span is this bridge, without railings and support,
And you, son of man, are compelled your whole life through
Ceaselessly to traverse the narrow passageway.
See how narrow is the way; you cannot turn aside to the right or to the left—
And do you still dream of power, greatness, and brilliance?
Look, on the right, on the left, death and dissolution await you—
And has your heart not yet lost its courage?
Can you still proudly raise your arm?
Do you rely on your wealth gotten through labor,
Obtained with the might of your bow?
In it do you hope to find protection
Against the great storm of the sea that covers you with its waves?
Try to oppose the wild anger of the ocean,
Conquer its chariots with their powerful riders!
Let yourself be led astray by the web of your dreams,
Only touch the foaming cup of arrogance and pride—
At once your steps totter on the narrow passage,
Already you are lost and fall into the depths.
And you will descend from abyss to abyss, and no one will save you,
No one will call out, "Oh, turn back."

In powerful verses the poet expresses his pain and indignation over the nothingness of the world, "this spring of rottenness and corruption," over the senseless play of blind fate which deals kindly with the petty and base, and treats the best and noblest of men like stepchildren. "The peel is cared for and preserved, and

---

58. Beḥinat Olam, Chapter 8.

the kernel is trodden underfoot." "The cedars of Lebanon are burned, and the prickly thorns live and endure."[59]

In vivid imagery Yedaiah portrays the vanity of the world, "this dark cave which is the dumping place for all kinds of refuse and rotten things." And man, "the impotent fly, with cut-down wings, must struggle in the dirty cage which, like a grain of sand, has lost its way amidst the countless stars."[60] "And I, miserable and suffering, have been sent here to be the target of every merciless trouble and storm. . . . When I consider my bitter fate, when I understand what a vain, dazzling plaything my whole life is, I can no longer find consolation anywhere."

Yedaiah Ha-Penini, the fervent admirer of the author of the *Guide for the Perplexed*, does, however, attempt to find consolation—in Maimonides' world of ideas. To perfect one's understanding, to immerse oneself in the grandeur of the idea of God—this is the highest end for man on earth, and no power in the world can break man's will when he strives toward this exalted goal.[61]

In lovely images the poet portrays how man's soul, the heavenly bird enclosed in the bodily cage, longs for the heights and is drawn to the source of light and knowledge. The tremendous power of this source, Yedaiah insists, is attested both by those who strive for it and those who run away from it, "as one can recognize the power of the sun's rays not only from the eagerness with which the eagle strives toward the heights with his mighty wings, but also from the dread with which the bat hides itself so that the rays will not strike its darkened eyes."[62]

To taste of the tree of knowledge, declares the poet, is to unite with the tree of life, the tree of eternal life. As in his *Ketav Ha-Hitnatzlut* to Rabbi Solomon ben Adret, so here also Yedaiah insists that wisdom and knowledge are inextricably bound up with the Torah, "the wondrous stroke of lightning which God revealed to the world." And the poet who so greatly admired Maimonides concludes his work with the following lines:

The end of the matter is this: Whether your heart turns to the right or left, hold fast to that in which he who was the last among the great scholars in time but the first in importance, our teacher Rabbi Moses ben Maimon, may his memory be for a blessing, to whom none of the sages of Israel after the close of the Talmud can be compared, believed. Then, I am confident, you will be rich in knowledge and wisdom, and in all their chambers revere God's might and greatness.

59. *Ibid.*, Chapters 10–11. These two chapters were translated into German by Moses Mendelssohn.
60. *Ibid.*, Chapter 12.
61. *Ibid.*, Chapter 16.
62. *Ibid.*, Chapter 13.

CHAPTER SIX

Isaac Albalag and the Doctrine of the "Double Truth"

WE have observed how deeply persuaded Yedaiah Ha-Penini was that faith and philosophy live together in perfect concord and are not at all inconsistent with one another. Dissenting from this view, however, were not only such pious and orthodox scholars as Rabbi Solomon ben Adret and Rabbi Asher ben Yeḥiel, but even many among the convinced Aristotelians. In this respect Yedaiah Ha-Penini's contemporary, Isaac Albalag, the translator of, and commentator on, Averroes and Al-Ghazali, is of particular interest.

Of Albalag himself we know virtually nothing. It has not even been established where he lived, whether in northern Spain or in Provence.[1] It is also not definitely known when he wrote his works. In his still-unpublished[2] major work, *Tikkun Deot Ha-Pilosofim*, there is, to be sure, a date indicating when it was composed. This date, however, is not correctly given by various

1. We believe that Albalag came from Spain, because in one place he speaks of three "true Kabbalists" who lived "in *our* land." All three of these were from Old Castile—from the cities of Burgos, Segovia, and Toledo.
2. Only the first and least interesting part of Albalag's work was published by H. Auerbach, *Albalag und seine Übersetzung des Maḳaẓid Al-Gazzalis* (Breslau, 1907).

scholars. J. H. Schorr, who published[3] numerous fragments of Albalag's work, points out that in the Paris manuscript the year 1292 is noted, and in another manuscript the year 1294. These dates are also given by Heinrich Graetz and other scholars. Apparently, however, Schorr was mistaken, for such a reliable and competent authority as Solomon Munk reports[4] that in the Paris manuscript the date 1334 is given (fol. 145), and the same year is also indicated in the manuscript we have employed,[5] as well as in another which Steinschneider mentions.[6]

Isaac Albalag was a thoroughgoing Aristotelian and expressed such heretical ideas (for that time) that they elicited profound indignation in orthodox circles. He was denounced as a "vile man, heretic, sinner and apostate,"[7] a "denier of the root principle,"[8] and even a "frivolous, evil, corrupt fool."[9] The pious Moses Rieti, in his poem *Mikdash Meat*,[10] bars the gates of heaven to him.

"One must not close the gates of inquiry," says Albalag, "because of the fact that man with his weak mind cannot, in any case, attain all the mysteries and profundities of the hidden truth, but one must faithfully follow Aristotle's command: to analyze everything according to one's understanding and freely express one's view."

Albalag set as his goal to demonstrate the falsity and groundlessness of the notion that philosophy undermines the foundations of faith. To this end he reworked into Hebrew, and wrote a large commentary on, the well-known work of the Arabic thinker Al-Ghazali, *Makazid al-Falasifa* (Tendencies of the Philosophers).[11] In his introduction Albalag attempts to show that both

3. In *He-Ḥalutz*, IV, VI, VII.
4. *ZHB*, XII, 154.
5. We have utilized the manuscript of Albalag's work which was originally contained in the library of the Jewish scholar Tzevi Katzenelbogen in Vilna (see the correspondence from Vilna in *Literaturblatt des Orients*, 1845, No. 14) and is now in the Friedland Collection of the Asiatic Museum in Leningrad.
6. In his *Hebräischen Übersetzungen*, p. 299.
7. See Shemtov ben Shemtov, *Sefer Ha-Emunot*, Part I, Chapters 1 and 7; Joseph Yaabetz, *Or Ha-Ḥayyim*, pp. 18 and 23.
8. Moses Alashkar, *Hassagot*, 6b.
9. Isaac Abravanel, in his *Yeshuot Meshiḥo*.
10. 103a.
11. In the introduction Albalag himself insists that he is not presenting a mere translation but, in fact, an independent work. He gave the work the Hebrew title *Tikkun Ha-Deot*. The manuscript which we employed, however, bears the title *Deot Ha-Pilosofim*. For some unknown reason Albalag did not finish the work. He completely translated and interpreted only the first parts, on logic and metaphysics. The third part, on physics, remained unfinished.

philosophy and religion recognize four central principles which must be considered universally acknowledged truths: (1) reward and punishment; (2) immortality of the soul; (3) belief in a single Creator who rewards and punishes; and (4) faith in divine providence which recompenses man according to his just deserts. The difference between philosophy and religion lies, in Albalag's view,[12] in the fact that philosophy grounds these principles scientifically through logical argument with the aid of speculative thought. The Torah, however, follows a completely different way. It addresses itself not merely to the select few but to the broad strata of the people. Its task is to influence the masses and lead them on the right way. It therefore employs the language of images and similes, and seeks to adapt itself to the conceptions and ideas of the ordinary man.

In the Torah, declares Albalag, every verse has a double meaning—one open to all, and the other a profound and hidden one; the first is for the common people and the second for thinking and understanding persons.[13] The Torah, Albalag further maintains, aims at the happiness and welfare of the multitude—so that it may avoid the evil and accustom itself to the good and the just, as far as it can according to its understanding. But his weak comprehension does not give the ordinary man the possibility of attaining philosophical truths in their pure form; he can only understand them in a corporeal garment, such that he can touch them with his hands and feel them with his senses. A simple, uneducated man is unable to imagine anything outside of space and time, without beginning or end. Just as a blind man cannot have any notion of color or a deaf person appreciate the sound of tones, so an uncultured man cannot comprehend abstract concepts with his dull mind. Hence, the Torah, in its great wisdom, endeavored to speak a language that would be understandable to such persons also. It compared the punishment for sin to burning fire. It portrayed the pleasures the soul would receive, as a reward for its righteous deeds, in corporeal forms, which alone are comprehensible to the multitude. God's attributes are also depicted in bodily images; His providence and will obtain a human garb; the divine thought is compared to man's. The mystery of "the work of creation," the origin of the infinite universe, is also concen-

12. The view is actually one which the Arabic Aristotelians, Avicenna and Averroes, had expressed before him.
13. *Deot Ha-Pilosofim*, Ms. p. 52. This opinion was shared by the majority of the rationalists of Maimonides' school. Levi ben Abraham, the author of *Battei Ha-Nefesh Veha-Leḥashim*, expresses an essentially similar view.

trated in a simple image of the birth and rise of petty and transitory creatures. But philosophy, whose function is not to instruct and educate the multitude but to guide perfect and thoughtful persons, to disclose to them the true bliss of pure knowledge and speculative thought, frees the profound truths hidden in the Torah from their physical garment and displays them in their pure, scientific, true form, which the masses cannot understand.[14]

This arrogant notion that the "ignorant multitude" can grasp the truth only in corporeal forms is repeated very frequently by Albalag. Typical is a passage in which he dwells on the dogma of the Trinity. One cannot deny, says Albalag, that a profound philosophic idea inheres in the concept of the divine tri-unity, in which are combined in one integral whole all three elements of knowledge: the knower, the act of knowing, and that which is known. But how crude this concept became among the masses, for whom the doctrine of the Trinity came to be the foundation of a false and noxious faith. This, however, Albalag insists, did not occur only among the Christians; it happens among every people. Everywhere we see the same phenomenon: the profound and noble ideas of the philosophers and thinkers eventually obtain, among the masses, crude and harmful forms. Among our people also this has unfortunately occurred quite frequently.

Albalag goes even further. He has the temerity to oppose the tradition hallowed by generations, and openly rejects one of the most fundamental elements of the Jewish religious world view, the creation of the universe in time. To believe in creation is an error in interpreting the plain meaning of the Torah, argues Albalag, and what the multitude think, i.e., that God created the world in six days, is nothing but "heresy" and "blasphemy." The foolish masses, he asserts, think that the philosophers believe in the eternity of the universe and thereby deny the entire Torah. In fact, however, the philosophers teach that the universe is daily created anew by God, as proclaimed in the Jewish prayer book: "In His goodness He renews every day continually the work of creation."

To be sure, Albalag must admit that not only the "foolish multitude" but even the great Maimonides believed that the philosophers consider the world eternal. He therefore attempts to show that Maimonides was also mistaken. Not of the eternity of the world do the philosophers speak, but of eternal creation and constant world-renewal. For, Albalag points out, the philosophers under-

14. *Deot Ha-Pilosofim*, preface. The same view is presented by an older contemporary of Albalag, the rationalist Moses of Marseilles, in his *Maaseh Nissim*.

stood very well that since God is eternal and infinite, He must also be eternal and infinite as Creator. His power of creation must be limitless, as must be His revelation as Creator. In this connection Albalag quotes the teaching of the ancient sages of India according to whom, in the course of infinite time, old worlds are destroyed and new ones born. Every seventy thousand years a link of the endless chain of time is closed, and on the ruins of the old world new life springs forth. An allusion to this, he adds, is also to be found in the words of one of the Talmudic sages who noted that before God created this world of ours He created many others and destroyed them.[15]

Thus did the philosophical speculation of the medieval Jewish thinker seek to break through the circle of the closed Aristotelian view of the world, with the immovable earth as its midpoint, and dream of the infinite vastnesses of the universe, pregnant with the mighty process of eternal creation and becoming, of the birth and destruction of worlds.

No less interesting is Albalag's view of the relationship between the Creator and the terrestrial world. In a special philosophical essay entitled *Maamar Le-Daat Elyon* Albalag discusses with great acumen the difficult problem of the divine knowledge and the divine will. He dwells first of all on the ancient question about which numerous thinkers carried on intense debates: whether God's creation is a "must," determined by the iron laws of necessity, like light "which is radiated from the sun," or whether it is a willed act, a manifestation of God's free choice. Albalag points out that the entire question has no foundation. It is pointless to speak here of free will and necessity in the human sense, for we must not forget that we denote both the human and the divine mind with the same word. In reality, however, we have to do here with two fundamentally different and in no way comparable entities. We, who owe all our knowledge to the phenomena we receive through our senses and the abstract representations of our human minds, are absolutely incapable of grasping either the essence of the divine will or the substance and nature of the divine knowledge. Our language does not and can not have the proper words with which to express these superhuman concepts and, therefore, when we speak of the divine nature, we employ the same words and terms by which we denote human acts and at-

15. Albalag here refers to the well-known dictum of Rabbi Abbahu. This dictum was undoubtedly influenced by Lucretius' famous poem *De rerum natura*, at the end of the second part of which the poet presents in powerful images a description of how, in the infinite distances of space and time, countless worlds are born and disappear.

tributes. This very frequently produces a tangle of tremendous errors and ridiculous misunderstandings. Many actually believe that because the same term and verbal concept are employed, the phenomena must also be the same, and are thus caught in a net of logical contradictions and misunderstandings.

In fact, we are incapable of comprehending the nature of the divine mind and will. But, Albalag insists, we see and understand how powerful and great is the connection between the Creator and His creation, the terrestrial world. Albalag is firmly convinced that not merely is the world in need of its Creator but that God Himself has great need of His own creation, which is His revelation. "Not only does the human species," he declares, "require, for its existence, the laws established by God, but God's will also requires the continued existence of the men created by it." But this view is in complete contradiction to Aristotle's on the relationship between the First Cause and the world. On the other hand, Albalag's view has strong affinities with that of the Kabbalah, which believes that man's deeds, especially the deeds of "the righteous of the generation," have a great influence on the upper worlds. But it is not in this point alone that Albalag shows himself a dubious adherent of Aristotle's system. To be sure, it may seem at first blush that we have before us a typical rationalist and follower of the allegorical method. Albalag, too, interprets the *tohu va-vohu* (waste and void) of the account in Genesis of "the work of creation" in the allegorical manner; *tohu* is hylic or primal matter, and *bohu* primal form. The "upper waters" are the spiritual world, the "lower waters," the material world. The "light" in the story of creation is absolute being. The six "days of work" are the six kinds of created entities: the four elements, gases, minerals, plants, animals, and men. The Sabbath is the symbol of the upper world of pure spirituality, etc. But after this comes a very characteristic remark: "I merely note that it is *possible* so to interpret the first chapter of Genesis that there will not be the slightest contradiction between it and the views of the philosophers; but I myself do not believe this."[16]

This rationalist and freethinker, who declares in his introduction to Al-Ghazali's work that philosophy teaches the same truths as the Torah, comes at last to the realization that no matter how strenuously one may endeavor to effect a compromise between science and faith, he must finally admit that they are strongly opposed to each other and that it is impossible to bridge the gap between the divinely revealed Torah and Aristotle's philosophy.

16. *Deot Ha-Pilosofim*, Ms. p. 47.

The "Natural Order" and the "Torah Order"

Not without reason did Albalag associate his life's work with the writings of the original Arabic thinker and mystic Al-Ghazali, who after many years of inquiry and meditation arrived at the conclusion that one cannot attain truth by way of philosophy and logical investigation and proceeded to enter the labyrinthine paths of mysticism and sophism. "I have long studied Aristotle's work," declares Albalag, "with the greatest care. I have found in it many solid proofs to the effect that there is an original dynamic power which is pure spirituality without any material element whatever, but it is nowhere shown that this First Cause is God."[17]

The rationalist Albalag thus arrives at the same conclusion as did Jehudah Halevi in his day, namely that there is a vast distinction between "the God of Abraham" and "the God of Aristotle." Albalag admits that God is not to be found either in Aristotle's *Physics* or in the "natural order," but in the "Torah order" (*Seder Ha-Torani*), i.e., not in the mechanical laws of nature but in morality and in its supreme and perfect disclosure—divine revelation. In nature everything proceeds according to established and regular processes that have no relationship either to good or to evil. But God's revelation and the "Torah order" grounded in it are based on the foundation of goodness, for "God's way is to desire only the good."

This antithesis between "physics" and "morality," between the mechanical laws of nature and the miracle of revelation, is incorporated by Albalag in two concepts: "philosophers" and "prophets." Our author does not tire of emphasizing the vastness of the distinction between these two categories of men. Not only their attitudes toward the world and the ways in which they seek to fathom it, but even their ways of thinking are fundamentally different. Philosophical truth is based on reason, on speculative thought, and is established through logical premises; the truth of the Torah, however, is founded on laws that transcend the mechanical order of nature, and its proof is the inexplicable miracle. Albalag attacks Maimonides because the latter refused to recognize the profound difference between philosophical thought and the religion of revelation. Maimonides, in Albalag's view, thereby arrived at grave errors. "He wished to explain the miracles rationally, in fact to deny them, and inserted his rationalist ideas into the words of the prophets."

Maimonides, Albalag argues, did not recognize the distinction between philosophical inquiry and prophetic ecstasy. He did not understand that with logical theories one cannot explain all the

---

17. *Ibid.*, Ms. p. 27.

mysteries hidden in the Torah. For, just as only a philosophically thinking person can best understand a philosopher, so only the prophet can feel most profoundly the experiences of prophetic revelation. One must bear in mind that their ways of thinking are not merely different but antithetical. The philosopher considers the world of feelings rationally, through common sense. The prophet, however, sees feeling, the spark of passion and inspiration, even in arid, rationalist thought. Completely divergent are their ways, and therefore fundamentally different are their worlds, their conceptions, and their views.

Albalag confesses that his *knowledge* is inconsistent with his *faith*, because their ways are different. While the former is ruled by the laws of nature, the latter is under the sovereignty of laws that transcend nature. On the basis of scientific inquiry, Albalag declares, I am *persuaded* of the truth of a given natural phenomenon; but on the basis of the prophet's words, I *believe* with complete faith in phenomena that are supernatural and antinatural. I believe in the sacred Torah with simple faith, without investigations and without logical proofs. But in the realm of philosophical inquiry and the natural sciences, I recognize the great importance of the laws of nature and logical demonstrations deriving from man's sober understanding.

Albalag thus realizes quite well that nature is ruled by iron law and that everything in it occurs with mechanical necessity; but the believer in him overcomes the rationalist thinker, and he has a strong faith that the divinely revealed Torah is more powerful than the mechanical laws of nature and human speculative thought, that the prophet's word is above the laws of nature, and that, with its aid, miracles may occur.

Albalag is convinced that the genuine bearer of divine truth is the prophetic word, and that only the man endowed with the holy spirit, the prophet singled out by God, can grasp the mysteries hidden in it. But how can an ordinary mortal find the road leading to divine truth, to that truth which is the twin of righteousness and justice? Albalag wanders about seeking this road. He becomes entangled in the labyrinth of doubts and inconsistencies between free speculative thought and theological tradition, and arrives finally at the speculative Kabbalah. The masters of the "esoteric wisdom" base themselves on the tradition of the fathers and assert that they have received as a legacy from previous generations the great truths which the prophets revealed in their divine inspiration. But even here Albalag cannot liberate himself from grave doubts. Among the Kabbalists of his day he knows not a few dreamers and visionaries who give forth the fruits of their own fantasies as divine truths received through the tradition of the fathers. Albalag is also too sober a thinker to be able to accept the practical Kabbalah. He speaks with great scorn of the "calculators of the end" and those who occupy themselves with "combinations of letters," *gematriot* and *notarikon*. "These Kabbalists," he asserts, "are equally distant from philosophy and science, on the one hand, and from prophetic revelation and genuine faith, on the other."

Graetz, who could not pardon anyone who manifested the slightest interest in mysticism and Kabbalah, dismisses Albalag with a few indignant words and declares him a "confused mind." More objective scholars, such as Moritz Steinschneider and others,[18] have attempted to compare Albalag's views with the doctrine of the "double truth" which had numerous adherents among scholars at the University of Paris in the thirteenth century. The essence of this doctrine was that there are two completely different kinds of truth, the philosophical and the theological. These are quite inconsistent with each other, but each has independent existence and is sovereign in its own realm.[19]

A certain affinity may, indeed, be noted between this view and Albalag's. But there can be no talk of any influence here. In the late Middle Ages, under the influence of Arabic philosophy, a tendency toward free thought gradually became discernible in the world of Christian scholasticism. Ever more prominently harbingers of the new era of revival which drove away the leaden shadows of the Middle Ages appeared. It would, however, be erroneous to think that the intellectual awakening in the Christian world also influenced the Jewish quarter and contributed to a renewal in it as well. We have noted previously that free thought arose among the Jews in the Middle Ages earlier than among the Christians and, indeed, the Jewish freethinkers, the rationalists of Aristotle's school, contributed a great deal to familiarizing learned Christian circles with the rich world of Arabic philosophy which contained the seeds of free thought and inquiry. But the battle for freedom of thought proceeded in the Christian milieu under conditions significantly different from those in the Jewish circles. The official bearers of "theological truth," the cardinals

18. *Jewish Encyclopedia*, I, 320.
19. See Albert Lange, *Geschichte des Materialismus*, II, Part Two, Chapter 3; Maywald, *Die Lehre von der zweifachen Wahrheit*; Renan, *Averroes*. In point of fact the principle of the "double truth" is much older than the thirteenth century. It had already been presented by some of the Arabic Aristotelians, chiefly Avicenna and Averroes. See Stöckl, *Geschichte der Philosophie des Mittelalters*.

and bishops, fought against free thought with fearful weapons, the chains and pyres of the Inquisition. To express one's own independent opinion on religious questions, to have a critical attitude toward the authority of the Church and its representatives, often involved martyrdom. Not everyone had the courage to give up his life and walk the thorny road of the martyr. Compromise was thus necessary, and here the best solution was the doctrine of the "double truth" which had been created by the Arabic thinkers. This doctrine served as a protective wall behind which one could hide in time of danger, save oneself from Inquisitorial hands, and refute the grievous charge of heresy. But the condition of the Jewish freethinkers was far more favorable. The Jewish bearers of "theological truth" did not have at their command the terrible weapons of their Christian counterparts. The power of the rabbis and heads of the Talmudic academies in Spain was limited. They were dependent on the Jewish plutocrats and courtiers, and in fact the Jewish freethinkers, as we have already noted, had numerous supporters in these circles. The court Jews were respected and honored among the Christian rulers, and the majority of the latter promoted freethinking tendencies among the Jews, believing that these would weaken attachment to Judaism and contribute to the conversion of Jews to Christianity.

Albalag expressed his ideas, which so enraged the pious and orthodox, openly and fearlessly. It was not external power nor the fear of persecution that brought him to the doctrine of the "double truth," but the inner conflict of his disquieted spirit, the "rent in the heart" produced by the struggle within him between free, rationalistic thought and the longing for the tradition of the fathers and the mystically hidden. A restless and constantly searching man, he was full of contradictions, and the proud rationalist who regarded the "benighted multitude" with contempt and scorn was frequently transformed into the deeply believing penitent who humbly declared, "I believe with perfect faith."

CHAPTER SEVEN

Isaac Ibn Pulgar and Joseph Ibn Kaspi

HE struggle waged by the adherents of the rabbinic tradition and Kabbalah against the freethinkers was stilled only for a while after the tragedy that suddenly befell French Jewry. Genuine peace between the two factions could not be concluded. The ban of the rabbis of Barcelona, with its strict prohibition against the study of philosophy, remained in full effect, and the orthodox strata of the population honored it. Mystical tendencies attracted constantly wider circles, intensifying the hatred the rationalists felt for these tendencies.

One of the most typical representatives of the contemporary freethinkers was the talented polemicist Isaac ben Joseph Ibn Pulgar (or Polkar), who completed Isaac Albalag's work and translated the last part of Al-Ghazali's *Makazid al-Falasifa*. All of Pulgar's works have a polemical character. He argues against Christian scholars and astrologers, and carries on disputes with Kabbalists and especially with apostates from Judaism who persecuted the people and blasphemed the faith of their fathers. Particularly well known is his polemic against the famous convert Abner (Alphonoso) of Burgos, who in his old age became a bitter enemy of the Jews and oppressed his erstwhile brethren.¹ Under the influence of the Aristotelian-Maimonidean world of ideas Abner became a freethinker. Like the author of *Livyat Ḥen*, Levi ben Abraham of Villefranche, he was also an ardent devotee of astrology and believed that man's fate is governed entirely by the stars and planets. This brought him to the conviction that "everything is foreseen" and that man has no free choice, because his will as well as all his activity and behavior are dependent on, and predetermined by, an eternal cosmic power that rules over him with ineluctable necessity.

"The Aristotelian-Maimonidean philosophy," Graetz justly notes, "to which Abner devoted himself, and perhaps also astrology, which was so precious to him, completely destroyed his religious feeling, and he became utterly indifferent not only to Judaism but to all faith." A man with a weak moral sentiment but with a strong desire for the enjoyment of life and worldly pleasures, Abner adopted the Catholic faith, to which he was no less indifferent than to the religion of his fathers. After his conversion he published a Hebrew work, *Iggeret Ha-Gezerah*, in which he endeavored to show that he was not morally responsible for his conversion. Not through his own free will had he done this; it was a matter of decree (*gezerah*) by an external power. From his birth it had been preordained by the spheres and planets that he would abandon the religion of his fathers and adopt Christianity. It was this theory of fatalism and the moral non-responsibility of man for his deeds that Abner's personal acquaintance,² Isaac Ibn Pulgar, sharply attacked. Abner considered it necessary to reply to Pulgar's critique with a counter-critique entitled *Minḥat Kenaot*, which he personally dispatched to Pulgar. The latter promptly sent his former associate a caustic satire entitled *Iggeret Ha-Ḥarifot*, accompanied by a pointed epigram in which Abner is compared to the Biblical adulteress whose shame and sin are displayed before all through the "cursed waters."³

---

1. Typical is the legend presented in Gedaliah Ibn Yaḥya's *Shalshelet Ha-Kabbalah*, describing Abner's encounter with his former teacher, the famous Naḥmanides.
2. In the first part of his *Ezer Ha-Dat* Pulgar mentions his acquaintance-ship with Abner: "Once I associated with a certain man who, as I live, was clever and well versed in religion and philosophy. Toward the end of his life he fulfilled his desire, and his heart inclined him to turn away from the religion of our Torah. His name formerly was Rabbi Abner."
3. The epigram is printed in *Taam Zekenim*, V. Pulgar's satire has not

Five Types of Opponents

Pulgar realized quite well, however, that men such as Abner were not the only threat to Judaism. The Jewish faith, he was convinced, had numerous enemies in various camps, and against all these he polemicized in his large work *Ezer Ha-Dat*. Pulgar divided this work, he explained, into five parts, because the opponents of Judaism belong to five classes. The first consists of ignorant men who have no conception whatever of faith and cannot appreciate its value. The second class are the heretics and deniers who think that the faith of Israel is completely inconsistent with the sciences. To the third class belong those who have been led astray by the astrologers and are so foolish that they actually believe that, even before a man is born into the world, his fate is determined in all details by the spheres and planets and that he cannot alter by a hair's breadth what these have decreed for him. The fourth class consists of deluded men who believe only in the deceitful products of their imagination and are incapable of distinguishing between falsehood and truth; these men regard with scorn those who refuse to be led astray by their foolish tales and ridiculous exaggerations.[4] To the last class belong the freethinking materialists who believe neither in immortality nor in reward and punishment; they cast off the yoke of religion and proclaim that "there is no judgment and no judge."

The most interesting parts of Pulgar's work are the first two, for in these the personality of this gifted rationalist of the first half of the fourteenth century is revealed most clearly. Many of our antagonists, says Pulgar in the fifth "gate" or section of the first part, when desiring to show how false and vain Judaism is, always stress the terrible plight of the Jews. These are so small numerically, forever live in exile, and are persecuted and despised by all. Yes, Pulgar proudly answers, the nobler and higher the religious outlook, the fewer the number of its adherents, for the masses believe only in the superstitious and supernatural, in bizarre exaggerations and miracles, which excite their unbridled imagination. Precisely for this reason, the cruder the faith and the more supernatural and incomprehensible to common sense the miracles, the more beloved are they by the multitude and the larger the number of their followers. Judaism has naturally not found favor among the broad, unenlightened masses, for it is

---

been published. Several other epigrams of his were published in *Literaturblatt des Orients*, 1840, pp. 249–50.
4. Pulgar here means the Kabbalists. He constantly endeavors to show his contempt for the mystics. Typical are these words of his: "These men have been impudent enough to compare their vain and worthless tales to the sacred books."

extremely strict and demands of man that he hold his desires and passions firmly in check; this obviously cannot please the mob. We Jews are weak and persecuted by all—that is true, for our faith has taught us how to overcome lust and educated us in the ways of truth and righteousness. In the course of many generations it has weaned us away from bloodshed, suppressed the desire for robbery and rapine, and aroused the sentiments of compassion and lovingkindness. We have gradually removed ourselves from the bow and the sword and devoted ourselves ever more to spiritual activity. We became a people of the spirit, but around us lived men who refused to know anything of the "qualities of righteousness" and remained the plaything of their unbridled lusts. *Their* faith has not weakened but rather aggravated their cruelty and increased their fanatical hatred. Is it any wonder, then, that we, a small, weak group, a community that lives by the slogan "peace and justice," are the victim of the barbarous and bloodthirsty people who recognize only one power, the power of the sword? It is not this that should surprise us. What should make us wonder rather is the fact that, despite the horrible cruelty of the peoples surrounding us, our name has not been blotted out and our courage and spirit have not been broken. Ask anyone of the nations among whom we live whether he desires that this people (the Jews) should be annihilated from the earth. Some will answer, We are prepared to give up all our possessions for this. Others again will tell you, We are ready to tear them to pieces. Yet our people lives; its spirit is not snuffed out.[5]

The second part of *Ezer Ha-Dat*,[6] which is written in the form of a debate between a *Torani*, a pious old man, and a "philosopher," a young freethinker, who expresses the views of the author, is also interesting. The debate, conducted before the gates of Jerusalem, is written in *makama* style, i.e., rhymed prose into which verses of poetry are interwoven. Pulgar, to be sure, was no poet, but he undoubtedly had a certain degree of literary talent and his debate is written in fresh and vivid language.

Pulgar's old man is not merely a man of Torah but also an ardent Kabbalist. In his youth he had allowed himself to be led astray by the "wisdom of the Greeks" and believed that one can fathom everything through reason. He soon realized, however, that he was following a false path. He heard a voice calling to him: If you wish to attain true knowledge, you must go to God's prophet. So he followed the path of divine prophecy and

---

5. *Kuntras Ha-Rambam* (1893), pp. 27-31.
6. Published in *Taam Zekenim*.

there great wonders, mysteriously deep and hidden, were revealed to him.⁷ The rationalist Pulgar endeavors to represent the *Torani* and Kabbalist as a fanatical opponent of all secular knowledge: "Better madness," he cries out, "than logic. Better affliction and sorrow than mathematics. . . . Better pain and terror than natural science. Better plagues and abscesses than metaphysics."⁸

The charges which Pulgar's *Torani* makes against the rationalists are particularly interesting: "They mock that in which we believe. They deride our wisdom and our sages. They refuse to take part in our commandments. They do not fulfill God's laws. They do not observe the precept of *tzitzit* and *tefillin*, and the doors of their homes have no *mezuzot*."⁹ To these charges the young rationalist, through whom the author himself speaks, replies with arrogant contempt: You ought not to speak of science, just as a blind man cannot speak of colors or a eunuch of love. It is true that religion is a major guide for man, but it cannot be compared with the value of science, and far more important than the discussions of Abbaye and Rava in the Talmud is *maaseh merkavah* (i.e., philosophy). The rationalist does not deny the *Torani*'s accusation that the freethinkers despise many commandments of the Torah. But the value of the commandments, he maintains, is measured by their utility; the religious laws were given only in order to make man better. God, however, has no need of them. It is ridiculous to believe that for observance of the commandments a reward is prepared in the "other world." Fulfilling the commandment, the *useful* commandment, is itself man's reward, declares Pulgar's "philosopher." The question so often posed why the righteous suffer while the wicked prosper has, therefore, no meaning, for in the very act of behaving justly lies man's happiness and in transgression his greatest evil.¹⁰

When the *Torani* insists that "not study but deed is the chief thing," his young adversary argues that the most important thing for man is to know God. And to perceive His light, to comprehend His wonders, is possible only with a keen mind and with critical speculative thought. To be sure, the rationalist mockingly informs the *Torani*, it is not you, whose eyes are blinded by fantastic foolishness, who can penetrate into the temple of science and knowledge, not you who can understand that in the realm of inquiry and thought deeds are not the essential thing but rather abstract philosophical concepts, and that, indeed, only in

7. *Taam Zekenim*, 15–16.
8. *Ibid.*, 14.
9. *Ibid.*
10. *Ibid.*, 14b.

the realm of philosophy does man's soul attain the ultimate degree of perfection and is it illuminated by the light of immortality.[11]

The debate between the aged *Torani* and the young philosopher is long drawn out. The old man argues fervently that only through *devekut* (cleaving to God), through prophetic ecstasy and "combination of letters," can one fathom the profoundest mysteries, and the young man declares that these are pure follies. That "the sage is better than the prophet" is an ancient truth. The only sure guide for man, the philosopher affirms, is sound common sense, lucid understanding; and he who refuses to rely on it crawls about in the swamp of darkness. All talk about "wonders and exaggerations," about the miracles that can be performed with "divine names," *gematriot* and amulets—all this is pure deception and child's play stemming from Germany and France, and false, treacherous men lead you astray with this swindlery.

The debate concludes with the stubborn disputants being brought to the king for a decision as to who is right. The learned judge naturally holds the same rationalist view as the author. Two ways, he declares, were given man to conduct him from darkness to light: philosophy and religion. These are not enemies but sisters who aid one another. The elder, however, is philosophy. The Torah educates man and prepares him so that his philosophical understanding may develop and, freed from its material vestment, unite with its Creator; in this consists man's immortality.[12] Without wisdom or science religion has no meaning. The philosopher, however, can also not dispense with the Torah, for only with its aid can he come into contact with his environment and not be like "one solitary in the wilderness."[13] "Live in peace and tranquillity"—so the judge concludes his judgment. But it is in fact just this *makama* of the thoroughgoing rationalist Pulgar that demonstrates most clearly that there could be no peace, for the antithesis between the two factions was too strong.[14]

11. Pulgar here adopts the view of Averroes and expresses the idea that the soul of the individual is not immortal in itself but only as a part of the world spirit.
12. *Taam Zekenim*, 17b.
13. *Ibid.*, 18b.
14. This, apparently, was felt by Pulgar himself, and in the closing words of his *makama* (*Kuntras Ha-Rambam* [1893], p. 36) he relates how a fanatical *Torani* ran after him and reviled and cursed him for his attempt to effect a compromise between the philosopher and the man of Torah, and for having the presumption to "compare the true faith with heresy and atheism."

Joseph Ibn Kaspi

On the sharp conflict between these sides, a contemporary of Pulgar's also expresses himself very clearly: "There are now two classes among us Jews. The first are the 'philosophizers' [*mitpalsefim*] who mock our sages, observe none of the commandments, and regard the narratives of the Torah as mere parables and allusions. The other class consists of men who despise the sciences and wish to know nothing of Aristotle and his views." These lines are from an interesting "human document," the *Sefer Ha-Musar*, which Isaac Ibn Pulgar's contemporary, Joseph ben Abba Mari Ibn Kaspi (c. 1279–1340) sent as a "testament" to his young son. Ibn Kaspi (his Provençal name was Don Bonafos) was one of the typical "seekers" of whom we spoke in the first chapter of this volume. He was born in Argentiers (whence his Hebrew name Kaspi, which means "of silver") in Provence, which at that time was the major center of free thought in the Jewish world. His insatiable thirst for knowledge, however, drove him from land to land. Well-to-do,[15] Ibn Kaspi spent his entire life journeying to various places. He lived in Arles, Tarascon, Aragon, Catalonia, and on the island of Majorca. In 1314 he travelled to Egypt for the sole purpose of studying philosophy in the city where Maimonides' *Guide for the Perplexed* was written and the philosopher's grandsons lived. There, however, a great disappointment awaited him. He relates sadly how he soon became convinced that the great thinker's grandsons were indeed "completely righteous men" but concerned themselves very little with the sciences.

Returning from Egypt to Provence, he almost perished there at the time of the *Gezerat Ha-Roim* (the Persecution of the Shepherds) when bands of the so-called Pastoureaux destroyed many communities.[16] As a middle-aged man, in 1332, Ibn Kaspi again set out for Africa upon learning that Maimonides' *Guide for the Perplexed* was studied in Moslem philosophical schools in Fez.

Despite the fact that Ibn Kaspi was a constant wanderer, he was an extremely prolific writer. Up to the year 1332 he composed more than thirty works[17]—commentaries to Ibn Ezra, to

---

15. Kalonymos ben Kalonymos calls him in his well-known open letter "our nobleman, our chief, our prince."
16. See the introduction to *Kevutzat Kesef*.
17. Twenty of these are listed by the author himself in his *Kevutzat Kesef*, which has come down to us in two versions. The first was published by Benjacob in his *Devarim Atikkim* (pp. 41–44) and reprinted by Isaac Last in the introduction to his edition of Ibn Kaspi's works.

Maimonides' *Guide*, to the Pentateuch and many other Biblical books.[18] He also wrote explanations to Ibn Jannaḥ's grammatical works, composed a textbook on logic and on Hebrew philology,[19] and reworked Aristotle's *Ethics* and Plato's *Republic* into popular form.

The possibility of obtaining a more or less clear picture of this interesting and gifted personality came only in modern times, after Isaac Last published part of Ibn Kaspi's literary legacy, which had lain for centuries buried in the dusty pages of old and extremely rare manuscripts. All of Ibn Kaspi's works are permeated with the greatest admiration for the renowned author of the *Guide for the Perplexed*, who "spreads light over the whole world." He laments the fact that he did not have the privilege of living at the time of Maimonides,[20] and expresses the wish[21] that he may at least in the "next world" be able to sit at the feet of the great scholar and enjoy his wondrous light.

Men, however, create gods for themselves after their own image, wishing to see in them that for which their own souls yearn. Ardent disciples very frequently read into their beloved master and guide words and ideas that are precious to *them* but were foreign and unknown to the teacher himself. Joseph Ibn Kaspi eagerly employs Maimonides' terminology and, completely in his spirit, declares that through scientific knowledge and tireless investigation man unites with the "active intellect," and that it is in this that human immortality consists. In his commentary to Maimonides' *Guide* he even expresses such a "heretical" idea as that "God is reason and reason is God" (*Elohim hu ha-sechel veha-sechel hu Elohim*). But the same Ibn Kaspi wrote mystical

---

The second, more complete version was published from a manuscript in Parma in Renan-Neubauer, *Les Écrivains juifs français*, pp. 535–44. Also listed are thirty works of Ibn Kaspi and the content of each is reported (pp. 482–535; see also Steinschneider, in Ersch and Gruber, *Encyclopedia*, Series II, XXXI, 61–73). Until the beginning of the twentieth century only his double commentary on Maimonides' *Guide for the Perplexed* (*Ammudei Kesef* [1848]) and his *Sefer Ha-Musar* (in *Taam Zekenim* [1854]) were published. It was only in this century that Isaac Last made a significant part of Ibn Kaspi's work available. In 1903 he published in two volumes *Asarah Kelei Kesef* (a collection of nine of Ibn Kaspi's commentaries); in 1905, *Mishneh Kesef*; in 1911–12, *Adnei Kesef*; and in 1914, *Taam Ha-Kesef*.

18. On Ibn Kaspi as a Bible commentator see W. Bacher's study in *MGWJ*, 1912 and 1913.
19. The introduction and several fragments of this work were published in *Literaturblatt des Orients*, 1847, pp. 481–86.
20. *Menorat Kesef*, in *Asarah Kelei Kesef*, II, 91.
21. In his *Sefer Ha-Sod*.

commentaries to numerous Biblical books,[22] steeped himself in the mysteries of the *maaseh merkavah* (the lore of the divine chariot or throne),[23] and declared quite openly that we ought not to be at all disturbed by the fact that the Bible is inconsistent in certain respects with the views of the philosophers, for the highest authority is, after all, the divinely revealed Torah, and for us, "who base ourselves on divine revelation—what does it matter that Plato, Aristotle, and their followers do not agree with us?"[24]

Like Abraham Abulafia and many other mystics, Ibn Kaspi was firmly convinced that in the original Hebrew of the Biblical text, and particularly in the letters of the divine names, vast creative powers are hidden.[25] Hence there can be no comparison between the sacred original of the Bible and its Latin or Arabic translations.

The fact that Ibn Kaspi was so eclectic and inconsistent explains why, on the one hand, he was considered by such orthodox writers as Rabbi Simeon bar Tzemah Duran, Joseph Yaabetz, and Isaac Abravanel a dangerous heretic, and why, on the other hand, the well-known Kabbalist Yohanan Alemanno believed that Ibn Kaspi's commentaries should be read by everyone who holds the esoteric wisdom precious, and so traditionally pious a poet as Moses Rieti, who in his *Mikdash Meat*[26] bars the gates of heaven before such "heretics" as Isaac Albalag and Gersonides, assigned Ibn Kaspi an honored place near the celebrated Talmudist and opponent of Maimonides, Rabbi Abraham ben David (the author of *Hassagot*), and the saintly Jehudah Hasid.

At first blush it might seem that Albalag's doctrine of the "double truth" was also adopted by Ibn Kaspi. This, however, is not quite correct. Ibn Kaspi was not an original thinker but a man of substantial talent. With his great thirst for knowledge, he could not and would not permit himself to be enclosed in the world of strictly rationalist ideas, which were alien to his impressionistic, volatile spirit. Hence we encounter in his writings a very unique phenomenon. He idolizes Maimonides and is an

22. His *Tirat Kesef* (or *Sefer Ha-Sod*), *Adnei Kesef*, *Mizrekei Kesef*, and *Matzref Le-Kesef*.
23. *Menorat Kesef*, 75–142.
24. *Ibid.*, 75.
25. *Shulhan Kesef*, 2. The same idea is reiterated in *Menorat Kesef*. Along with these purely mystical conceptions Ibn Kaspi develops the idea that no translation of any masterpiece is capable of rendering the spirit and unique beauty of the original. It is also noteworthy that Ibn Kaspi was the first Bible commentator who pointed out that there are two versions in the opening chapters of Genesis—the "Yahwist" and the "Elohist."
26. 103b.

ardent devotee of the "wisdom of the Greeks." He is dazzled by their persuasive power and their harmonious integrity. But without himself realizing this, their ideas receive in him an altogether different vestment and thereby their content and essence are also not infrequently greatly altered. Moreover, one must take into consideration a very characteristic feature: Ibn Kaspi did not write his works for the reading public, neither for the masses nor for the elite. He wrote because for him writing was a necessity, because he was a born writer with a considerable power of creation which inevitably drew him to pen and paper. The reader did not interest him at all. It is quite possible that his attitude toward the public was substantially influenced by the indignant reception which greeted his first work, *Sefer Ha-Sod*, written in 1317. *Sefer Ha-Sod* was intensely repugnant to the orthodox circles, and two Talmudic sages of Salon, Moses of Beaucaire and Abba Mari Sen Astruc, assailed Ibn Kaspi and declared that in *Sefer Ha-Sod* are expressed ideas that are noxious to the ordinary masses, "who must be allowed to live in the traditional conceptions in which they have been brought up." But these scholars were not content with this attack and, at their instigation, their disciple Kalonymos ben Kalonymos came out against Ibn Kaspi with a special polemical work.[27]

These attacks enraged Ibn Kaspi. Not without reason does the Kabbalist Yoḥanan Alemanno testify that he had never seen the like of Ibn Kaspi, who so openly and fearlessly expressed his convictions. "Where it is a matter of attaining the truth," declares Ibn Kaspi, "I will take account of no one."[28] "In questions of faith," he further says, "I will not defer to any opinion which this or that great scholar has expressed."[29] Like Jacob Anatoli in his day, Ibn Kaspi also declares that "the truth may not be timorous and bashful." "These poor little people," he bitterly replies to his critics, "always maintain that they admonish me out of love and compassion, so that I might walk on the right path. However, I know very well that if I were to kill a man, rob him of his money, and give it to them, they would declare that there is no one on earth as honest and righteous as I."[30] Hence, he declares that he has no further desire to write, either for wise men or fools, "for fools will remain ignorant and it is superfluous to teach the wise."[31]

27. Kalonymos' composition was published by Perles in 1879 (*Kalonymos ben Kalonymos: Sendschreiben an Josef Kaspi*).
28. *Shulḥan Kesef*, 170.
29. Ibid., 136.
30. *Menorat Kesef*, 77.
31. *Hatzotzerot Kesef*, I, 131.

All the works that he later wrote were specially intended for his own children. Almost every one is dedicated either to his elder son who lived with his sister in Barcelona or the younger who was being educated in Tarascon.[32]

As a result, Ibn Kaspi's writings have an intimate, tender character. The author frequently breaks off in the middle of a discussion and turns to his sons with words of instruction, teaching them how to respond to various problems of life and utilizing the rich experience of his own wandering existence. A man of many-faceted culture, as well as possessed of a keen eye and a capacity for literary portrayal, Ibn Kaspi has much to relate. Indeed, he is not at all chary of words. His works are filled with interesting descriptions that reflect the cultural life of the lands of the East and southern France in that era.

In Ibn Kaspi's time the pope was expelled from Rome and had to go into exile to southern France and settle in the city of Avignon. Ibn Kaspi relates with fine humor what an upheaval was called forth in the agriculture of the region by the residence of the "holy father" and his associates. All the fields in the area were turned into vineyards. "Wine became dirt cheap," he relates, "and bread became very expensive." There is no doubt, however, Ibn Kaspi adds sarcastically, that as soon as the pope returns to Rome, the vineyards will again be transformed into wheat fields.[33]

"For the sake of God," he admonishes his son, "do not dare to enrage fools, and may He protect you from the notion of attempting to show a fool that he has no sense." To add authority to his admonition, Ibn Kaspi relates a story which forcibly reminds one of Immanuel of Rome—how he once happened to stop in a benighted and foolish community on precisely the day when one of its members, a very rich man but a terrible ignoramus and miser, was being buried. Ibn Kaspi sits among the seven elders

---

32. Instead of customary introductions in which the author addresses the reader, these works contains letters sent as a gift from father to son. Some of these letters are written in an intimate, tender style. For example, in the introduction to his popular reworking of Aristotle's *Ethics*, written for his elder son, we find the following lines: "Providence has granted you a wondrous gift; you are privileged to have as your life's companion the most perfect and loveliest of all women. I trust that all your thoughts and desires will be directed to one goal—spiritual perfection and purity of heart. I am confident that you will strive to be worthy of your wife and endeavor to be the most perfect of men, as your wife is the most perfect of women" (see Steinschneider, *Hebräischen Übersetzungen*, pp. 226–27; cf. *Les Écrivains juifs français*, p. 487.
33. *Hatzotzerot Kesef*, 196.

of the city while these recite eulogies over the corpse. The more
they praise the deceased, the clearer it becomes to him what a
crude fellow, what a drunkard and glutton, this man was, and he,
the only person of sense among fools, listens with an earnest mien
and holds his peace. "I did not laugh at them. This would not
have helped in any way; they would have only become my enemies forever."[34] No less typical is the comical scene in which
godfearing pietists warn the author of the grievous punishment he
will have to suffer in the "next world" for his heretical talk:

They surround me and taunt me, saying, "You will not be privileged
to enjoy the pleasures of the world to come." I bow before them
and beg them to allow me at least a small portion. I say: "Surely, all
the fish of the seas are prepared for you and you will enjoy the
banquet of Leviathan, you will eat the geese of Rabbah bar bar Hana,
the stuffed hens and capons. You will drink the best wines; the wine
preserved from the six days of creation awaits you. At least permit
me to look on from a distance and let me eat some dried-out
carobs and drink some plain water." But they will not yield. They
begrudge me even this and sternly declare: "No, you will have to go
hungry."[35]

Sarcastically he addresses his Jewish brethren: "Yes, we have
become truly an odd people—indeed, unique in the world, a
people of complete fools and good-for-nothings. We are distinguished from one another only in nuances, in degrees, of foolishness." When Ibn Kaspi mentions in one of his commentaries the
ancestor of the patriarch Abraham, Eber, whose eldest son was
called Peleg (from a Hebrew word meaning "to divide"), "for
in his days the earth was divided,"[36] he sadly adds, "We all are
the best witnesses that our ancestral mother was, indeed, Peleg's
wife, for we are in fact *benei Peleg*, children of separation and
conflict, and as far as disunity and constant bickering are concerned, we have not our like among all the peoples of the earth."

Ibn Kaspi's words concerning "Jewish faces" in the lands of
exile breathe a quiet sorrow. "The Christians," he says, "immediately recognize the Jew with his melancholy aspect, for the Jew
has an altogether different appearance than the Christian. His face
is pale, cast down, and his eyes are not bright like those of a man
illuminated by fortune."

Endowed with a fine critical sense, Ibn Kaspi, as a Bible exegete,
was a sharp opponent of the allegorical method so popular at that

34. *Ibid.*, 37–38.
35. *Ibid.*, 18–19.
36. I Chronicles 1:19.

time in rationalist circles. He frequently insisted that the interpreter must, above all, take account of the literal meaning of the text and the principles of logical thought.[37] Ibn Kaspi definitely rejects Maimonides' view that the Book of Proverbs is to be interpreted in an allegorical sense. I have no doubt, he declares, that Proverbs was written in the same style as other didactic books, without mysteries or secrets but with a pure, simple meaning. In it everything is plain and clear, without philosophical allusions, metaphysical profundities, and mysterious references. When a profligate woman is discussed, she is meant to be taken literally, not as an allusion to sinful matter. When King Solomon speaks of wisdom, he means common, practical understanding—not divine or metaphysical wisdom. For the Book of Proverbs, like other moral-didactic books, concerns itself exclusively with practical morality, not with philosophical-theological problems.[38]

Ibn Kaspi, moreover, points to the extremely undesirable results that the allegorical method may produce.[39] It is manifestly impossible to set any limit to it, so as not to lose scientific ground and wander in a labyrinth of fantastic webs. If the Book of Job or Proverbs is interpreted as pure allegory, why should not any narrative or description in the Bible be considered the same? Indeed, Ibn Kaspi notes, we observe that even Jacob and his sons have been transformed into an allegory.[40] But this will bring it about that we remain with nothing at all. We shall have neither Torah, nor prophets, nor holy writings.[41] "To us Jews," he cries out, "nothing, after all, has been left except Moses and his Torah."

Ibn Kaspi therefore sharply attacks the rationalistic allegorists of his time. "I know them well," he calls out,

the little foxes of our generation, who have obtained a pinch of superficial knowledge of philosophy and the sciences and at once consider themselves authorities in philosophical-theological matters. They mock Jewish scholars, deny the miracles of the Torah in public speeches, and interpret all the narratives of the Bible as mere parables. Abraham and Sarah, they say, are nothing more than figurative expressions for the concepts of matter and form. Not enough that they themselves sin; they also lead others astray. And it is this that brings it about that the general public has adopted an attitude of hostility toward the sciences, for ignorant persons believe that science and inquiry lead one to denial of religious truth. They do not realize that

---

37. *Hatzotzerot Kesef*, 83, 122.
38. *Ibid.*, 83, 131.
39. *Ibid.*, 83, 94, 131, 137–38.
40. *Ibid.*, 131.
41. *Shulḥan Kesef*, 138; cf. *Hatzotzerot Kesef*, 94.

men of thorough and genuine knowledge will never allow themselves to come forward with such speeches. This is done only by half-informed people who desire to display their learning before women and ignoramuses.[42]

Ibn Kaspi has no doubt that the supreme level of perfection that man can attain is prophetic ecstasy.[43] Not the philosopher, with his cold speculative thought, but the inspired prophet is, in his view, the highest ideal. Aristotle, he declares, certainly attained the summit of investigative thought, but there is no doubt that, with regard to spiritual perfection, he cannot be compared to Moses, the greatest of the prophets.

Our author gives very little thought to effecting a compromise or reconciliation between philosophy and religion. This question, which was extremely urgent for the majority of the rationalists of that era, did not trouble him at all, for he was certain that the ultimate truth is the truth of religious revelation and that philosophy, as a scientific discipline, can only ground, but not contradict, the highest revealed truth. Ibn Kaspi cannot understand why most of the rationalists of his generation, while deeply interested in Greek-Arabic philosophy, remain completely indifferent to the Talmud and its commentators. "How is it possible," he asks,

to keep constantly on one's tongue Aristotle and Averroes and Themistius and Theophrastus and Euclid and Galen and Hippocrates, and entirely forget Bar Kappara and Nittai the Arbelite and Samuel Ha-Katan, Abbaye and Rava and Simeon ben Lakish, and Rabbi Yoḥanan and Rabbi Akiba and Rabbi Eliezer? We Jews forget our own great and holy men, and content ourselves merely with eminent figures belonging to other peoples.[44]

With his intense thirst for knowledge, however, Ibn Kaspi was a definite opponent of those who perceived in Greek-Arabic philosophy a source of dangerous heresy. "Do not, my son," he writes to his elder son in Barcelona,[45]

believe the pietists of our generation who assert that one who devotes himself to the "seven wisdoms" mocks our sages and despises the commandments and precepts of the Torah. The ignorant of our people are so firmly persuaded that all educated men are alike in this respect that they are amazed when they see a philosophically learned

42. Ḥatzotzerot Kesef, 19.
43. Shulḥan Kesef, 169.
44. Ibid., 174-75.
45. Ḥatzotzerot Kesef, 16. Cf. Shulḥan Kesef, 171, 176.

man praying before God. Astonishedly they ask, Do philosophers also pray? These ignoramuses do not realize that the meaning of the word philosopher is "lover of wisdom," and that it is precisely the man of thorough knowledge who knows how properly to appreciate the value of the commandments and religious precepts.

While Maimonides and his disciples clothed Judaism in Greek-Arabic dress, in Ibn Kaspi Greek-Arabic philosophy obtains a Judaic appearance. The former attempted to make the Torah a commentary to Aristotle's philosophic system; Ibn Kaspi, however, was convinced that Aristotle was faithful to the Torah. "Why," he asks, "should we push Aristotle away when he desires to hold fast to the religion of Moses?"[46]

In this respect his previously mentioned *Sefer Ha-Musar* is of particular interest. When Ibn Kaspi in 1332 set out on a long journey which, in that age, was associated with many dangers, he sent his young son who was then living in Valencia a unique "testament," a large *kuntras* or notebook entitled *Sefer Ha-Musar*, in which he sets forth his philosophy and indicates the way to live a righteous and ethical life. In this work also Ibn Kaspi insists that seeking and knowing God is the chief commandment of Judaism and that its fulfillment is the supreme goal of human life. "But," he admonishes, "may God preserve you from the heretical thought that, if this commandment is the basic purpose of the entire Torah, of what further benefit can all the hundreds of other commandments be?" He endeavors to show his son that this fundamental precept can be fulfilled only with the aid of all the other commandments, both practical and theoretical,[47] for man consists, after all, of body and soul and "the soul has no existence without the body."[48] Knowledge and understanding, he further declares, cannot be attained by man without the aid of his senses, and concepts are created only out of feelings and impressions. Therefore, the commandment "And thou shalt know the Lord" can also be fulfilled only when knowledge and understanding go hand in hand with observance of the precepts of the Torah. Ibn Kaspi does not tire of insisting that thought alone is insufficient; no less important is deed. Only through the act of will, through doing, does thought obtain true fulfillment. Only through embodiment in deeds does knowledge reveal itself. Action alone crowns the highest moral and spiritual attainments. In Ibn Kaspi's view, abstract knowledge, critical inquiry, and intellectual

46. *Shulḥan Kesef*, 174.
47. Cf. *ibid.*, 150, 171.
48. *Taam Zekenim*, 50a.

perfection by themselves cannot satisfy man; the knowledge one has obtained must be incorporated in real life, in ethical deeds.

Ibn Kaspi is firmly persuaded that even Aristotle and his disciples strongly admonished men to fulfill everything contained in the Torah and the prophets.[49] He deems it superfluous to demonstrate that the teaching of Judaism is consonant with the foundations of Aristotle's philosophy, because he has no doubt that Greek philosophy itself derives from Hebraic sources. He relates, as a well-known fact, that Aristotle himself wrote commentaries on the laws and precepts of the Torah and drew his entire wisdom from King Solomon's work and from the sages of Israel who lived in the days of the Second Temple.[50] Even if at first Aristotle did not agree with them on the question of the eternity of the universe, he later changed his mind,[51] and in regard to this matter also came at last to the conviction that the view expressed in the sacred books through prophetic inspiration, which is far higher than philosophical inquiry, is indeed correct, for "the prophets received their knowledge directly from the Lord of the universe, not like we philosophers, the representatives of speculative wisdom."[52]

Thus, in this unique rationalist and ardent disciple of Maimonides, naive, simple tradition is interwoven with philosophical inquiry, the practical commandments of the Torah with critical speculative thought. Ibn Kaspi attacks with equal indignation the "half-informed" who, with their frivolous attitude to religious commandments and customs, "awaken hatred for science among the people," and those who regard the sciences contemptuously and wish to know nothing of Aristotle and his philosophical views.

49. *Ibid.*, 52a.
50. *Ibid.*, 50a, 51a, 52b. The legend that Aristotle, and Plato as well, derived their wisdom from Jewish sources was very widespread not only among Jews but among other peoples also.
51. The legend that Aristotle, at the end of his life, renounced his doctrine of the eternity of the universe derives from the fact that in the Middle Ages he was considered the author of the then very popular work *Teologia*, which inclines toward the view that the universe was created in time.
52. *Taam Zekenim*, 52a.

CHAPTER EIGHT

Moses Narboni and Gersonides

T the time Joseph Ibn Kaspi wrote his *Sefer Ha-Musar* a new attempt was made in his native land, Provence, to raise the standard of that free investigative thought which wishes to know of no compromises and refuses to recognize any traditions and accepted authorities in seeking the way of the truth, the *rationalist* truth. In Ibn Kaspi's home city, Perpignan, where a special society of freethinkers was then established,[1] his younger contemporary, Moses ben Joshua[2] Narboni (his Provençal name was Maestro Vidal Bell-

---

1. Ibn Kaspi frequently refers to the members of this society. Moses Narboni indicates in the introduction to his translation of Averroes' work on physics, *Ha-Derushim Ha-Tiviyyim*, that he translated it at the request of the philosophical society (which he calls the "order of the brethren"). In the introduction to another translation he mentions "the honored men of the society of seekers of wisdom in the city of Perpignan." See Steinschneider, *Hebräischen Übersetzungen*, pp. 226, 312; *ZHB*, XIII, 124; Munk, *Mélanges de philosophie juive et arabe*, p. 504.
2. The printed edition of Moses' commentary to Maimonides' *Guide for the Perplexed*, as well as the manuscript in the Asiatic Museum in Leningrad, begins with the words: "Thus said Moses the son of Rabbi

shom), was born at the end of the thirteenth century and spent his childhood. While still a youth Moses studied Maimonides' *Guide for the Perplexed* with his father's aid.[3] He received his further philosophical education from Moses and Abraham Caslari,[4] both prominent members of the local "philosophical society." Moses spent most of his life in various Spanish cities—Toledo, Valencia, Soria, and others—engaged in the practice of medicine.[5]

Moses' literary work consists almost entirely of commentaries to the works of the major Arabic thinkers, Al-Ghazali,[6] Avicenna, and Averroes.[7] Of his few original works, the most interesting is his essay on free will, *Maamar Ha-Behirah*,[8] which is directed against the convert Abner of Burgos and the latter's book *Iggeret Ha-Gezerah*. In a fine philosophical-dialectical manner he shows that man's freedom of will and divine omniscience are not at all inconsistent. In this connection Moses ingeniously utilizes Maimonides' arguments[9] to the effect that all the confusion and difficulties in this question derive from the fact that most men fall into anthromorphic ways of thinking and speaking; i.e., when they think and speak of God's knowledge they measure it with a human yardstick. In this, however, lies a great error, for the divine knowledge is utterly different from man's, even though both are designated by the same term in our language. Man's mind receives its knowledge from the external world. It obtains its concepts of things and phenomena from the things themselves, through arduous analytic and synthetic effort. God's knowledge, however, is of an altogether different kind. Through self-con-

---

    Meir the son of Moses the son of Abba Mari the son of Mar David of Narbonne." It has been established, however, that after the phrase "Thus said Moses" the words "the son of Rabbi Joshua" are missing (see Steinschneider, *Cat. Bodl.* [1867]).

3. In the introduction to his commentary on the *Guide* he notes: "From my youth my father brought me up on it."
4. For a discussion of the scholarly Caslari family, see Renan-Neubauer, *Les Écrivains juifs français*, pp. 644–50.
5. In Moses' medical work *Orah Hayyim*, which he wrote in 1350, one frequently encounters such phrases as "and I discovered" or "and I tested" and the like. Here Moses also indicates that he studied medicine with Abraham Caslari, who was a prominent physician (see Renan-Neubauer, *op. cit.*, p. 677).
6. In his commentary to Al-Ghazali's *Makazid al-Falasifa* Moses laments the destruction of many Jewish communities in Provence that occurred in his time and speaks of the martyrdom of their members (see *ZHB*, XIII, 124).
7. On Moses' commentaries, see Steinschneider, *Hebräischen Übersetzungen*, pp. 156–57, 311–19, and Renan-Neubauer, *op. cit.*, pp. 668–81.
8. Written in Soria in 1362; published in *Divrei Hachamim*.
9. *Guide for the Perplexed*, Part III, Chapters 19–22.

sciousness, through grasping His own essence, His nature as the First Cause or the creative and dynamic power of the universe, God grasps the whole universe, the infinite chain of phenomena, which are finally nothing but His own revelations. The divine knowledge also at one and the same moment embraces the entire universe as a single, unitary whole, while man's knowledge is limited to single elements extending like links in the iron-bound, regular chain of causes and effects.

At the conclusion of his essay Moses proudly declares: the morally clean and strong man will not depart from the path of right, will make no compromises, and, despite the most serious obstacles, will not surrender what his moral sentiment and self-consciousness demand of him. If Abner, who has abandoned the faith of his fathers and rejected his people, wishes to hide under the cloak of fatalism and the idea that "everything is foreseen" in order to cast off moral responsibility, this merely demonstrates the pettiness and falseness of his sinful soul. A true scholar and sage will never reject his own people, even if he finds no support among his brethren but only estrangement, hatred, and ignorance.

In these last words a tone of restrained anger is discernible. In Spain, where at that time a hostile attitude toward "Greek wisdom" was already quite prominent in certain circles, Moses Narboni, the freethinker and ardent disciple of Averroes' rationalist system, did not everywhere receive a friendly welcome and was not infrequently compelled to carry on sharp debates with orthodox scholars. This accounts for the indignation with which he speaks of the "backward fools who consider themselves sages in Israel but in truth are the most ignorant of men." These words are from his famous commentary to Maimonides' *Guide for the Perplexed*,[10] on which he worked the last seven years of his life. He began this commentary in Toledo in 1355 and completed it in Soria in 1362 on the way to his native land.[11]

The *Guide for the Perplexed* was, for Narboni, the divine book, "the glory of our exile." He was thoroughly persuaded that the text of the Torah has a double meaning, one for the multitude, the other, an esoteric one, for the elect few. For this reason, he

10. Commentary on Part I, Chapter 32.
11. These details are provided by Moses in the interesting epilogue which, unfortunately, is missing from the printed edition of his commentary. Part of this epilogue was published by Jellinek in his *Kuntras Ha-Mafteah*, pp. 32–34. It is contained in full in both of the manuscripts we have employed. One of these is in the Asiatic Museum in Leningrad; the other, written on parchment, is in the library of the Society for the Dissemination of Enlightenment Among Jews, in the Kaufmann Collection.

insists, it might appear at first glance that there is a contradiction between the Torah and philosophy. The contrast between the notions which the multitude received from the literal meaning of the Biblical text and the philosophical ideas of the Greek thinkers was too great. Numerous expressions in the Torah, in their literal meaning, produced great agony for the philosophically enlightened among our people until "the light of the exile," Maimonides, appeared. He opened the eyes of our sages and illuminated the surrounding darkness with his brilliant work which disclosed the true form and content of the Torah.

Maimonides, however, provided only brief hints and allusions. Narboni therefore undertook to reveal and explain these hints for "understanding" and "chosen" persons. His explanations, which were deliberately written in obscure, difficult-to-understand language,[12] were too free, too "heretical," for that age.[13] Hence, it is not surprising that such a pious and orthodox figure as Isaac Abravanel speaks with great wrath of the heretic Moses,[14] and the author of *Akedat Yitzḥak*, Isaac Arama, concludes that he deserves to be burned, together with his writings, because of his godless thoughts.[15] The incisive and perceptive Joseph Solomon Delmedigo, when speaking of Moses as the most profound of all the commentators who expounded Maimonides' *Guide for the Perplexed*, insists that he is a *megalleh sod* (revealer of mysteries) who refuses to recognize any authorities.[16]

No less liberal in his views but of greater stature and significance than Moses Narboni was his countryman and contemporary, the celebrated philosopher Rabbi Levi ben Gershon or Gersonides (also called Ralbag), known in the world of medieval Christian scholarship by the name Magister Levi de Bagnols or Magister Leo Hebraeus. He was a man of universal knowledge, a living encyclopedia of his age. A famous Talmudist and Bible exegete, Gersonides was also a natural scientist, a physician,[17] an astronomer, a mathematician, and—above all—a profound thinker.

12. Moses at times adopts Abraham Ibn Ezra's manner of writing in enigmatic terms and employing parables of ambiguous meaning. A medieval writer, Samuel Cohen, the disciple of Elijah Delmedigo, already noted this affinity between the style of the two scholars.
13. Moses endeavors to explain the miracles of the Bible rationally and expresses his regret that it speaks of miracles at all.
14. See Abraham Geiger, *Melo Chofnajim*, pp. 66–67.
15. See Steinschneider, *Hebräischen Übersetzungen*, p. 313.
16. See Geiger, *op. cit.*, p. 18.
17. It is very likely that Gersonides earned his living from the practice of medicine. Isaac de Lattes speaks of him as a practicing physician in his *Shaarei Tziyyon* (Buber's edition, p. 48).

Gersonides the Encyclopedic Scholar

As in the case of most of the great Jewish figures of the Middle Ages, we know very few details of Gersonides' life. It has been established that he was born in 1288 in the Provençal city of Bagnols into a very prominent family. On his mother's side he was a great-grandson of Nahmanides and, in the opinion of many scholars, his father was the learned Rabbi Gershon ben Solomon of Arles, the author of *Shaarei Shamayim*, an encyclopedic work on natural science very popular in the Middle Ages.[18] Gersonides spent his life in the Provençal cities of Orange, Perpignan, and Avignon (at that time the capital city of the pope) and died in 1344. A man with a tremendous capacity for work, Gersonides composed numerous works in the most varied fields of knowledge.[19] His work on astronomy, *Sefer Ha-Techunah*,[20] in which an important instrument for precise astronomical measurement that he invented is described,[21] attracted the attention of Christian scholars even in the author's lifetime and, at the command of the pope, that part of the *Sefer Ha-Techunah* which deals with Gersonides' instrument was translated into Latin in 1342.[22] The celebrated Italian humanist Conte Pico della Mirandola, on becoming acquainted with this work, spoke with great enthusiasm of the "famous and extraordinary mathematician" (*insignis et celeber mathematicus*), and the great Kepler sought to familiarize himself with the "astronomical treatise of Rabbi Levi."[23] At the

---

18. The work consists of three parts: the first, on animals and plants; the second, on astronomy; the third, on metaphysics. The learned author assiduously collected in his work the scientific knowledge of his day. *Shaarei Shamayim* was first printed in Venice in 1547. On Rabbi Gershon and his work, see Gross, *MGWJ*, 1879; Steinschneider, *Hebräischen Übersetzungen*, pp. 9–16; Renan-Neubauer, *Les Rabbins français*, p. 985.
19. The author of *Ha-Yuhasin*, Zacuto, speaks of Gersonides' "innumerable books." In Renan-Neubauer, *Les Écrivains juifs français*, pp. 596–642, there is a list of Gersonides' works, as well as of their subject matter. Some of them were translated into Latin in the Middle Ages.
20. *Sefer Ha-Techunah* later formed the first section of the fifth part of Gersonides' *Milhamot Adonai*. The first publisher of *Milhamot Adonai*, however, printed it without *Sefer Ha-Techunah*, which is in fact an independent work. *Sefer Ha-Techunah* has remained in manuscript. The outline of all its 136 chapters, which Gersonides himself made, is printed in Renan-Neubauer, *Les Écrivains juifs français*, pp. 624–32.
21. Gersonides called his instrument *megalleh amukkot* (revealer of depths). Its invention so affected the taciturn and calm Gersonides that he even wrote a special poem (the only one he ever wrote) in praise of it. The poem, "Al Ha-Makel," is published in *Divrei Hefetz*.
22. *Hebräische Bibliographie*, XI, 55.
23. In his letter to Johann Ramus, Kepler wrote: "Utinam apud Rabbinos invenio passes tractatum R. Levi quint defensionum Dei."

wish of the distinguished musicologist and theoretician Philip de Vitry, Gersonides in 1343 composed a special work on the intervals in the musical scale.[24]

Despite Gersonides' significant achievements in astronomy and mathematics, his greatest importance lies in another realm, that of philosophic thought. As the author of *Milḥamot Adonai*, he is the last distinguished Aristotelian not only in the Jewish world but in all of medieval Europe. He was a man with a remarkably incisive, analytical mind, for whom the highest authority was that critical thinking which dissects and examines everything, and whose chief pleasure is courageously and fearlessly to investigate the truth for its own sake without any external motives. "To think is to live" (*ha-hassagah hi ha-ḥayyim*)—this was Gersonides' motto. The fullness and richness of life is measured according to the perfection of knowledge, for, in his view, knowledge is the only source of true joy and delight.[25]

Gersonides was convinced that there is no power in the world that can prevent man from striving to explore scientific truth, for in this consists his supreme bliss. Let no one think that the Torah can keep us from recognizing as true what common sense obliges us to believe. It is clear that where logical thought brings us to conclusions that are inconsistent with the plain meaning of the Torah, the latter cannot prevent us from speaking the truth, for how can a religious law code compel us to believe what is false?[26]

"I have no doubt," Gersonides adds ironically,

that my views will not find favor among many people. These views are overly strange to them, and it is too difficult to harmonize them with their habit of not thinking independently but living on ideas received from others by way of tradition. My words, however, are not for this class of people. For them, to believe is sufficient; inquiry and thinking are not for them.[27]

It also appears incomprehensible to Gersonides that one can keep to himself the truth he has attained and not disclose it to others. "This is the greatest shame," he cries out; and he adds that his entire striving is to remove the obstacles that hinder men on the path of inquiry and keep them away from their highest bliss.[28]

24. See *ZHB*, VIII, 23–24.
25. *Milḥamot Adonai*, p. 279.
26. Ibid., pp. 6–7.
27. Ibid., pp. 3–4.
28. Ibid., p. 6.

Also let it not be said, Gersonides urges, that man, with his weak intellect, is incapable of attaining the truth. On the contrary, his essential purpose, his supreme happiness and delight, is to come as close as possible to the truth, to ascend ever higher on the difficult but luminous ladder of knowledge.[29] Gersonides can also in no way assent to the humble view that "if the ancients were like men, we are like asses," and that we ought not to presume to grasp what they, the sages of long ago, could not attain. Such a view, he declares, is not only a sign of intellectual weakness, but also a complete denial of progress in the realm of knowledge. If we accept the idea that we cannot expand the realm of knowledge inherited from our predecessors and are incapable of investigating what remained hidden for our fathers, this means to condemn all the sciences to death, to disbelieve in their further advancement.[30]

In regard to this point, Gersonides diverges from his teacher Aristotle and Aristotle's Arabic interpreter Averroes. We have noted that Gersonides was the last important Aristotelian in medieval Europe. He was also the only one among the Jewish disciples of Aristotle who accepted the entire Aristotelian system[31] (in the form which it received from Averroes),[32] including those particulars that contradict certain fundamental principles of the Jewish world view. Nevertheless, as a free and original investigator, Gersonides even in his youthful years manifested considerable independence in his critical explanations of Aristotle's and Averroes' works.[33] His philosophical inquiries begin at the point where Averroes, in the general medieval philosophical world, and Maimonides, in the rabbinic-religious world, halted. Gersonides was not satisfied with the solutions the Arabic and Jewish Aristotelians had presented to the problems that so disturbed the keenest minds of the Middle Ages: the immortality of the soul, the nature of prophecy, divine omniscience and providence, the nature of the heavenly spheres, and the question of the eternity of matter. He attempts to provide his own answers to these problems in his

29. *Ibid.*, p. 5.
30. *Ibid.*, p. 4.
31. In this respect Gersonides went even further than Maimonides.
32. It is almost certain that Gersonides knew Averroes' works only in their Hebrew translation. Most scholars (Neubauer, Steinschneider, and others) believe that Gersonides had a good knowledge of Latin but was unfamiliar with Arabic.
33. For a discussion of these explanations, see Steinschneider, *Hebräischen Übersetzungen*, pp. 65–73, 118–19, 155, 508.

famous philosophical work *Milḥamot Adonai*, on which he labored for twelve years (1317–29).[34]

The most characteristic trait of Gersonides as a man and thinker is his understanding of the progressive nature of science. Here he diverges completely from the Aristotelian system, which was a powerful and harmoniously organized structure, but one strictly closed and hemmed in, without spaciousness or life or movement. Aristotle, the brilliant architect and systematizer, was convinced that his scientific structure would endure for all ages and that a satisfactory solution to all significant problems had been provided in it. The concept of dynamic development and advancement in the realm of science was absolutely alien to his system. Everything always revolves around the same point in this closed circle. This spirit of congealment was particularly well adapted to the stagnant world of ideas of the Middle Ages. The sum of human knowledge, according to the prevalent view, was completely determined for all time. The source of wisdom lay in Holy Scripture and in the writings of the Fathers of the Church, the founders of the Christian faith. Philosophy is merely a handmaiden to the "mistress"—theology (*ancilla theologiae*). And the foremost teacher and high priest of this science, Aristotle, with his monumental system, obtained among the scholastics an altogether Christian appearance. In his medieval vestment the great Greek philosopher became the central pillar of the Church, her pious and obedient servant. The final goal of investigative thought in the Middle Ages was not to extend the boundaries of knowledge but to systematize and bring into order the sum of religious and philosophic knowledge inherited from the fathers.

But Gersonides, who in this respect was the harbinger of a new era, could not be content with this. He understood—to be sure, not clearly or completely consciously—that human knowledge must be considered not in its static, congealed state but in its dynamism, in its process of becoming, in its drive toward further development. His restless thought could not be satisfied with the melancholy belief dominant in the Middle Ages that the human mind is destined to remain forever within the enchanted circle which the great and inspired men of former ages had already defined. Gersonides refused to assent to Aristotle's doctrine of the eternity of the universe and to the idea that the history of man on earth has extended throughout infinite time. How is it possible, he asked, for the world and man to be so old when the

---

34. These dates are indicated by Gersonides himself (*Milḥamot Adonai* [1868], pp. 219, 291, 417).

sciences are still so young? Given the restless probing of human thought, with its constant drive for knowledge, it was incredible that man could have wandered for an infinitely long time lost in the total darkness of barbarism and that the sciences should have appeared only at such a late stage of human history.[35]

Gersonides, however, was also dissatisfied with the classical Jewish religious idea of *creatio ex nihilo;* the notion that the First Cause, which is pure spirituality, should have created not only the forms but matter as well appeared incomprehensible to him. He therefore adopted Plato's view that formless matter is eternal. On the other hand, in agreement with Aristotle's doctrine of form and matter, he believed that formless matter existed only potentially and that this existence disclosed itself in actuality only at a definite moment, namely, when the formless matter obtained real being by coming into motion, i.e., by being united with form. And form is the reflection of the divine thought; it is the idea embodied in matter which is actualized through motion.[36]

Gersonides' intense faith in the constant progress of human knowledge and in the fruitful, creative power of free speculative thought brought it about that, despite all his enthusiasm and admiration for the profound Arabic philosopher Averroes, he could not accept the latter's teaching on the immortality of the soul. Averroes, in effect, denied personal immortality. In his philosophy the soul does not, after a person's death, survive as an independent substance but only as a tiny spark of the eternal world spirit, the "active intellect." In the living individual merely the potentiality for immortality exists, and only after his death and its own separation from matter does the soul unite with the active intellect. To this view Gersonides cannot give his assent. This, in his opinion, is an enchanted circle of tedious and monotonous confusion. If, immediately after the death of any man, no matter who he may be, whether a fool and good-for-nothing or a sage and scholar, his soul unites with the active intellect, what sense or meaning has our unquenchable thirst for knowledge, our drive to seek and attain the truth? It is foolish to believe that this precious gift with which man is endowed is completely vain and useless. Nature, Gersonides insists, is not a wastrel and does nothing in vain; everything in it is counted and measured.[37]

---

35. *Ibid.*, pp. 356–58.
36. In Aristotle's terminology the actualization of matter through form is called entelechy.
37. *Milḥamot Adonai*, p. 26. It may be noted that Isaac Albalag came forward with similar arguments against Averroes.

The problem of immortality occupies a highly important place in Gersonides' philosophical system. In discussing it he first gives a thorough critical overview of the opinions which the most eminent philosophers had expressed on the subject. He himself inclines toward the system of the famous commentator on Aristotle, Alexander of Aphrodisias, who lived at the end of the second century C.E. This Greek thinker distinguished two kinds of intellect: (1) the material (or hylic) intellect, which does not exist in actuality but only in potentiality and can, like matter, take on various forms through development, and (2) the acquired intellect, which arises out of the material intellect through inquiry and reflection and, as a result of the fertilization of thought, passes from mere potentiality into actual being. Basing himself on this fundamental idea, Gersonides develops with great dialectical acumen his own doctrine on the nature of the human intellect and soul.

It must be borne in mind in this connection that Gersonides was a convinced Aristotelian and that, in Aristotle's system, the intellect is a "king in his chamber," completely isolated from all the other functions of the human organism. Feelings have no part whatever in the cognitive process. They can only sense and receive impressions from without and have to do merely with phenomena. The intellect alone is capable of receiving what transcends feelings and sensations. Just as, with regard to the external universe, our world, the planet Earth, occupies the focal point in Aristotle's system, so in the realm of the sciences, the human, thinking "I" is sovereign. It is the center of all. Its concepts and ideas are regarded as the final and true reflection of the external world. Every object stands open and exposed before the searching "I," which discloses through the keenness of its thinking the object's real essence and nature. Gersonides is also firmly convinced that the true essence, the *divine* essence, of everything that is consists of *thought*. Only general concepts, the so-called universals, are the real essence of being. The "material intellect" is, in Gersonides' view, merely a "possibility" (*hachanah*) with which man is born, and the bearer of this possibility is the "power of representation or imagination" (*ha-tzurah ha-dimyonit*), which is itself merely a part of the "sensitive soul" (*ha-nefesh ha-margeshet*), the capacity for feeling or sensation with which not only human beings but animals as well are endowed.

This *hachanah* or possibility is lost simultaneously with a man's death if he has not, in his life, properly employed it and transformed it into the "acquired intellect" through inquiry and thought. And it is the acquired intellect of the thinking person that is, according to Gersonides, individually immortal, despite the fact that it has obtained abstract concepts with the aid of the material part of the human spirit (*ha-tzurah ha-dimyonit*). For concepts and ideas concerning the universal and general have not the slightest trace of matter, and whatever is not associated with matter but is pure spirituality (*tzurah*) is eternal. Following the scholastic mode of thought prevalent in the Middle Ages, Gersonides was certain that thinking cannot be separated from the object of the thinking process, and what man's acquired intellect thinks is the intellect itself, i.e., *thinking* and the *thought* or idea are one and the same.[38]

But Gersonides recalls and considers it necessary to insist that our acquired intellect, which is a result of the universal "active intellect," is strictly dependent on our *nefesh ha-margeshet*, i.e., our feelings and sensations.[39] This Aristotelian and thoroughgoing rationalist, with his critical mentality, came to the realization that the concepts of the thinking and inquiring individual do not yield a completely true and valid picture of the nature of the objects which the human understanding investigates. For man, flesh-and-blood mortal that he is, does not possess such a completely "pure" understanding that he can receive and grasp the absolute and abstract, the general or universal, without the aid of feelings and sensations. To grasp in full measure the universal spirit, to unite completely with the active intellect,[40] is, for the human acquired intellect, impossible, since its knowledge is finally dependent on man's limited sensations and feelings.[41] Man, says Gersonides, can only strive as far as possible to approach true and complete knowledge. And the greater his success in this respect, the closer his abstract concepts (*muskalot*) come to the ideal unity of knowledge in which the essence of the active intellect consists, the stronger grows his joy and the greater his happiness. But as long as man lives, matter obscures the spiritual vision with its earthly demands, and joy and happiness are therefore incomplete. Only after death does full and unhindered bliss begin for man's immortal spirit, his acquired intellect. And this bliss is all the greater

38. *Milḥamot Adonai*, p. 82 ff.
39. Gersonides was undoubtedly familiar with Thomas Aquinas' thesis: "Omnis nostra cognitio intellectualis incipit a sensu."
40. It must here be noted that in Gersonides' system the active intellect (*sechel ha-poel*) has a more important place than in Maimonides. According to Maimonides, the active intellect occupies the lowest level among the heavenly spheres (*galgalim*) which emanate out of one another. In Gersonides' view, however, all the spheres are at the same level, for all emanate directly from the First Cause.
41. *Milḥamot Adonai*, p. 86 ff.

and stronger the more the individual has in life obtained abstract concepts and ideas and sought to draw near the active intellect. After the death of the person, however, his spirit, or acquired intellect, can no longer enrich his knowledge. He is no longer capable of obtaining new concepts, for, as Gersonides explains, he now lacks the senses, the organs of feeling and sensation, which are the essential instruments for human attainment of knowledge.[42]

The level of immortality is therefore strictly correlated with the level of acquired knowledge.[43] Man's immortal spirit, his acquired intellect, is the greater, the more extensive the knowledge he has obtained in life. Like Maimonides, Gersonides was convinced that only the elect few—who through seeking and acquiring logical or rational truths, have transformed their "possibility" (*hachanah*) into an active spiritual power and in whom the material intellect has been changed into the eternal acquired intellect, which is completely spiritual and without the slightest trace of matter—merit personal immortality. And only these chosen few enjoy the privilege of having divine providence rule over them. For Gersonides, in full agreement with Averroes' teaching about the divine knowledge, maintains that God's exalted thought includes only general phenomena, the laws of the entire universe which embrace the most important, the universal, the genus, but not particulars, or the accidental, the incomplete, and the material.[44] The degree of God's special providence over every creature is therefore correlated with the intellectual development of the individual in question; the more his spirit or acquired intellect is developed, the more his thought is directed not to the accidental and the personal but to the general and the all-embracing unity, the greater the measure in which divine providence rests upon him. The elect few who have developed their understanding to the point where it is adapted to attaining the highest abstract concepts are under the rule of individual providence, but all the rest, who grope in darkness and have not utilized their spiritual possibilities (the material intellect), are governed merely by the general laws that are valid for the human species as a whole.[45]

42. *Ibid.*, p. 90.
43. In his commentary to Ecclesiastes 7:1 Gersonides also considers it necessary to emphasize: "and wisdom or knowledge is the final goal of man and his immortality, as we first explained in the book *Milḥamot Adonai*."
44. This idea is also expressed incidentally by Abraham Ibn Ezra in his commentary to the Pentateuch (Genesis 18:21): "God, blessed be He, knows everything in a general way but not in a particular way."
45. *Milḥamot Adonai*, pp. 164–65.

It is also from a purely rationalist standpoint that Gersonides considers the gift of prophecy (*shefa ha-nevuah*). He is firmly persuaded that the source of the prophetic spirit is the same as that of every other knowledge or science—perfection of intellect, complete and universal understanding.

Gersonides several times repeats his point: to be a prophet one must be a wise man and proficient in all the sciences; the "matter of prophecy requires perfection of the intellect"; to the level of prophecy he only can attain whose powerfully developed mind allows him to rule over his senses and imagination to such an extent that he is able, at any moment, to free himself completely from their influence and, unhindered, immerse himself in the revelations of the active intellect.[46] The prophet is in greater proximity and relationship to the active intellect than all other men. He is the person with open eyes who, thanks to his great wisdom, can predict what is yet to occur. As a result of the influence of the active intellect, the prophet is also able to perform miracles. Miracles, however, Gersonides insists, are not accidental phenomena that contradict firmly established laws of nature. They are merely phenomena of another, *higher* type which are also subject to a definite regularity, but of a more exalted kind very different from the mechanical regularity governing nature.[47]

Characteristic of Gersonides also is his controversy with Maimonides over the question of God's attributes. Maimonides endeavored with great acumen to demonstrate that, in relation to God, it is possible to speak only of negative but not positive attributes. Gersonides can in no way agree. We have already quoted his statement, "To think is to live." Elsewhere he asserts that in searching, in fathoming the true nature of everything around oneself, consists man's supreme bliss.[48] And since the source of all knowledge is God, He is also the source and the highest degree of life, happiness, and joy, as our sages declare, "For joy is in His habitation." To God such attributes as unity, being, and bliss, which express His perfection, are therefore appropriate.

In his commentaries on the Bible, however, Gersonides appears as Maimonides' faithful disciple. Here also he rejects all compromise, and even where Maimonides speaks only by way of allusion and "reveals one hand-breadth while concealing two hand-breadths," Gersonides expresses himself clearly, and openly and fearlessly draws all the logical conclusions that follow from his free, investigative thought. There is, after all, only one truth, the

46. *Ibid.*, Part II, Chapter 6.
47. *Ibid.*, Part VI, Chapters 11-12.
48. *Ibid.*, p. 115.

rationalist truth. Hence, it is obvious to Gersonides that, since the Torah bears the impress of divine wisdom, its teaching can in no way be inconsistent with philosophy. "It is clear," he asserts, "that one must believe only in that whose truth is demonstrated through logical argument, and when it happens that the literal meaning of the Torah contradicts this truth, the text must be so interpreted that it will fit the logical-philosophical conclusions."[49] "And not just once," he adds with great delight, "have we become convinced that the very conclusion at which we previously arrived by way of inquiry agrees completely with the views of our Torah."[50] A typical rationalist, Gersonides was persuaded that the Torah itself contains, in fact, the very ideas that he developed with such profundity in his *Milḥamot Adonai*.

Men see what they wish to see, and Gersonides found in the Torah his own doctrine concerning creation, God-seeking, providence, and the heavenly spheres, as well as his rationalist view of miracles. When Joshua the son of Nun says, "Sun, stand thou still upon Gibeon," the verse intends only to relate that Joshua expressed the wish that the enemy's defeat might occur before the sun set. The patriarch Jacob's wrestling with the angel, Gersonides is convinced, occurred in a dream, not in reality. The story of the Garden of Eden in which the first man lived is an allegorical, symbolic portrait of the material intellect and the acquired intellect. In the Song of Songs the author of *Milḥamot Adonai* sees the essence of his own philosophical system. Jerusalem is the symbol of thinking man who is like the holy city—elected to serve God; the "daughters of Jerusalem" are the qualities of man's soul; King Solomon is the rational part of man, etc.[51] Like Maimonides, Gersonides sought in every commandment its practical purpose, its utilitarian result, and in every Biblical story its moral and didactic meaning. His commentary to the Torah is therefore written according to the following order: first comes an explanation of the words, afterwards a systematic exposition of the text (*biur ha-parashah*), and finally an indication of the philosophical ideas and useful ethical lessons (*toaliyyot*) which may be derived from each individual section.

The ethical-didactic part of Gersonides' commentary is written in such a moving tone and popular style that the freethinker and Aristotelian philosopher became, among later orthodox and pious generations, one of the most beloved of Bible exegetes. His

49. *Ibid.*, p. 6.
50. *Ibid.*, p. 7.
51. It must, however, be emphasized that Gersonides made relatively little use of the allegorical method.

Milḥamot Adonai and the philosophical ideas expressed in it evoked bitter opposition, but his *toaliyyot* were read with great enthusiasm and delight. They were compared to the "most precious stones" and the "best perfumes."[52] In order that the common people might also be able to enjoy them, they were translated into Yiddish and printed together with the well-known translation of the Bible into Yiddish by Yekutiel Blitz.[53]

52. See the introduction by Jacob Markariah to the first edition of Gersonides' *Toaliyyot* (Riva di Trento).
53. Published in Amsterdam, 1679.

BOOK TWO: 1348–1492

CHAPTER ONE

The Cultural Decline of Spanish and Provençal Jewry

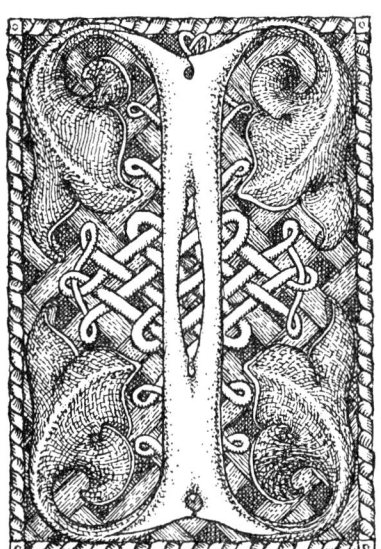

IT suffices merely to compare the fate of Maimonides' *Guide for the Perplexed* and Gersonides' *Milḥamot Adonai* to obtain a clear conception of the great cultural-historical changes which occurred in the Jewish world in the course of the one hundred fifty years separating these two important religious-philosophical works. We have noted that in Maimonides' time, under the influence of the Arabic civilization which then reached its zenith, there emerged in the Spanish as well as in the Provençal Jewish community a highly educated intelligentsia with a far broader world outlook than that prevalent among the common people. In the intellectual circles and in the upper strata of society, liberal ideas and conceptions that needed to be brought into harmony with the tradition of the fathers, the religious notions of ancient times, made themselves at home. If this harmonizing were not to take place, there was a danger that the intellectuals would become altogether alienated spiritually from the national culture, and the barrier between them and the mass of the people would grow constantly greater. The fulfillment of this task—the reconciliation of the old religious conceptions with the new philosophic ideas—was undertaken by Maimonides in his classic work. His *Guide for the Perplexed* enjoyed immense success and soon became the best-loved book in the circles of the enlightened. The Jewish intelligentsia in Provence, who did not read Arabic, took energetic steps, as we have observed, to obtain Maimonides' work in Hebrew translation as quickly as possible.

Gersonides' *Milḥamot Adonai* was produced under entirely different circumstances. This work was written in Hebrew, and only when one compares its style with the heavy and rather wooden translations of the Ibn Tibbons (Jehudah and Samuel) can one properly appreciate the great progress made in the development of scientific terminology in Hebrew in the course of the intervening century and a half. *Milḥamot Adonai*, however, lacked the most important things—a suitable audience and positive social response. It remained solitary and neglected, and the intellectual positions for which it fought so courageously were already surrounded by the enemy and hopelessly lost. Gersonides battled for free investigative thought. He wished to demonstrate that there is only one truth, rationalist truth, and that there are no contradictions between philosophy and Jewish religious teaching. But he obtained the completely opposite result; his relentless rationalism, which refused to admit any compromises, intensified the conflict between philosophical inquiry and religious belief. His *Milḥamot Adonai* (Wars of the Lord) was soon branded by furious adversaries as *Milḥamot Im Adonai* (Wars Against the Lord), and it was decreed that it is "deserving of being burned."[1] Even those who spoke with great enthusiasm of Gersonides' profound Talmudic knowledge, e.g., the well-known Rabbi Isaac bar Sheshet,[2] were extremely resentful of his philosophical views and indignantly declared that whoever studies them is guilty of a great sin.

Gersonides' "heretical" inquiries and his liberal, proudly rationalist world outlook were little suited to the restless times in which he was destined to live. He himself laments the severe persecutions of his day, under which it is impossible to occupy oneself peacefully with scientific investigations.[3] He had to witness the expulsion of the Jews from France and the massacres at the time of the disturbances accompanying the revolt of the "shepherds" (Pastoureux) and "lepers." All this, however, was merely a prelude to a far greater tragedy. In 1348, four years after Gersonides' death, the terrors of the Black Plague began. It

1. The title *Milḥamot Im Adonai* is first encountered in Shemtov Ibn Shemtov's Kabbalist book *Sefer Ha-Emunot*. Typical is the following characterization by David Messer Leon: "the *Milḥamot Adonai* of Rabbi Levi ben Gershon, in which he certainly fought against God, and which is deserving of being burned because of its numerous denials of all the foundations of the Torah, and especially because he said what he said openly and insolently, and explained the Torah illegitimately: for he denied the creation of the universe in time, miracles, and God's knowledge of particulars, as everyone who is familiar with the book knows" (see *Hebräische Bibliographie*, VIII, 64).
2. See his *Responsa*, No. 45.
3. *Milḥamot Adonai*, p. 3.

The Terrors of the Black Plague

was not only the "black death" that spread its wings over all of western Europe; on its heels strode its terrible twin brother, madness, with its "red laughter." The ignorant populace, crazed by fear, could not understand whence this terrible visitation with its poisonous breath of death and destruction came and who was responsible for the catastrophe. Someone, it seemed obvious, *must* be responsible. Thus, men were ready to believe the wildest rumors, and the most preposterous of old wives' tales passed for pure truth. The barbaric superstition prevalent in the Middle Ages knew nothing of compassion and decency, and it drove the mob, filled with mad terror, to the cruelest massacres. A rumor was spread abroad to the effect that the Jews were responsible for the horrible epidemic; they were poisoning the wells and rivers in order to destroy their enemies, the Christians. And the benighted multitude believed the rumor and poured out all its fury on the defenseless Jews.

From eastern Spain to Poland, with its ancient cities of Cracow and Kalisch,[4] the deluge of madness and bestiality spread everywhere. The Jewish communities of Germany suffered more than all others from the mob. The afflictions which the German Jews experienced in the thirteenth century cannot be compared with the persecutions in the years of the Black Death (1348-50). The ancient Jewish communities of Worms, Mainz, Frankfurt-am-Main, Cologne, and others were destroyed. From Switzerland and Bavaria to Austria and Moravia, the Jews everywhere were mercilessly slaughtered, burned, drowned, and robbed of their fortunes. Once more the bloody scenes of the era of the Crusades were reenacted. The miserable victims preferred not to die at the hands of the enemy, and so themselves killed one another, burned their own homes, and found death together with their families and households in the flames. The Jewish ghetto became one great cemetery. Over three hundred communities perished in these years of madness and death.

The terrible tragedies completely shattered the creative cultural powers of the Jews of Germany. Even rabbinic learning could no longer thrive on the wasted soil of the German lands; it found a place of refuge in Austria, which suffered relatively less during the years of the Black Plague. In the place of the *yeshivot* or Talmudic academies which were destroyed in Germany, Rabbi Meir ben

---

4. In an old *kinah* or elegy of that era, in which the communities that were then destroyed are mourned, these Polish communities, as well as Glogau, are mentioned (see Landshuth, *Ammudei Ha-Avodah*, Supplement VI).

Baruch Ha-Levi,[5] a refugee from the city of Fulda, established new centers of Torah in Vienna, Krems, and Neustadt, and from these academies came the most eminent rabbis of later generations —Rabbi Jacob ben Moses Mölln (Maharil),[6] Rabbi Moses Minz, Rabbi Jacob Weil, and the great figure of the generation, the celebrated Rabbi Israel ben Petahyah Isserlein.

These leaders of the age had occasion to carry on a stubborn battle against numerous unsuitable and disreputable representatives of the rabbinate. In the years of destruction the wells of rabbinic knowledge had dried up. The number of Talmudic scholars was greatly diminished, and under such circumstances the rabbinic office was frequently occupied by persons completely unfit for it. Many who sit on the rabbinic chair, laments Rabbi Jacob Weil, have altogether slight knowledge of the Talmud and its commentaries, and they rule with great self-assurance over the communities and exploit their power for personal, egotistical ends. These men do not possess even those qualities which, according to the Talmud, every Jew ought to have, and especially so the rabbis and guides of the people who teach God's word and should be an example for all. Indeed, God's name is often desecrated through them, for people point to them and say: Look at these men who teach and interpret the sacred Torah and themselves do not fulfill its commandments and precepts.[7]

Another eminent rabbi of that period, the above-mentioned Israel Isserlein, attacks these men no less sharply. He also com-

---

5. This prominent rabbi led a restless life of constant wandering. His father, Rabbi Baruch, died as a martyr. Meir studied Torah with Alexander Ha-Kohen (known also as Zusslein of Frankfurt-am-Main), the author of *Sefer Ha-Agudah*, on *novellae* of Talmudic law. In his youth Meir served as rabbi in Erfurt and later in Frankfurt-am-Main. In 1383 he settled in Nuremberg, but two years later returned to Frankfurt, where he was imprisoned as the result of a slander. In 1392 he was freed at the command of King Wenceslaus, and the "document" that he and the leaders of the Jewish community of Frankfurt signed in this connection is one of the oldest official documents in Judaeo-German that has come down to us (it was published in *ZHB*, X, 107-12). At the end of 1393 Rabbi Meir settled in Vienna and there spent the last years of his life. For more details on his life and work, see J. Freimann's preface to *Leket Yosher*, p. 51; M. Wiener, *MGWJ*, 1868, p. 383; I. H. Weiss, *Dor Dor Ve-Doreshav*, II, 5; Graetz, *Geschichte der Juden*, Vol. VIII; and M. Güdemann, *Geschichte des Erziehungswesen und der Kultur der abendländischen Juden während des Mittelalters und der neuern Zeit*, Vol. I.

6. Born c. 1360, died in Worms in 1427. For biographical details on this important rabbinic figure, see *Literaturblatt des Orients*, 1848, pp. 395–400.

7. Weil, *Responsa*, No. 163.

plains of the "corrupt judges" (*dayyanim mekulkalim*) of his time and stresses the sad fact that "many have received rabbinic ordination, but few are genuine scholars."[8] Isserlein deems it necessary frequently to remind these "corrupt judges" that one can persuade others of the correctness of his view otherwise than through oppression and bans,[9] and that one is not permitted to protect the honor of the Torah and respect for the rabbinate through the power of the external government authority.[10]

To prevent the rabbinic office from being held by unfit persons, the founder of the Talmudic academies in Austria, Rabbi Meir ben Baruch Ha-Levi, sought to introduce the custom of *semichut*, i.e., that only a scholar whom recognized rabbinic authorities had "ordained" and certified as suited to be a rabbi could occupy a rabbinic post in any community.[11] But apparently this ordinance was of little avail, and Rabbi Meir's disciples were still compelled to fight against "corrupt judges."

The literary productivity of the era consisted entirely of works intended to increase the severity of laws and precepts, to make the fences and restrictions of Jewish life ever stronger, and to isolate the Jewish community as much as possible from the hostile world surrounding it. No breath of fresh life was felt. "And the mean man boweth down, and the great man humbleth himself" (Isaiah 2:9). Men became numb with sufferings and sorrows. The affrighted power of thought sought no solution, no answer to the questions gnawing at grieved hearts. The leaders of the age saw before themselves one task only: to be faithful guardians of the heritage of the fathers, to preserve with punctiliousness the most insignificant customs of previous generations. They were unalterably opposed to any change whatever in the religious cult. "I have never seen nor heard of altering a custom" and "a custom is not to be changed," one of the rabbinic authorities of that era, Israel Bruna, constantly repeats.[12] "A custom is stronger than a

---

8. Isserlein, *Pesakim U-Ketavim*, No. 255.
9. *Ibid.*, No. 253.
10. *Ibid.*, No. 64.
11. David ben Solomon Gans, the author of *Tzemah David* (1592), when discussing the institution of *semichut* or ordination, writes: "This ordination was introduced among the Ashkenazim because at that time there were many who were engaged in matters of marriage and divorce even though they were not familiar with the particularities of the relevant laws; hence, this ordination was instituted as a sign to all Jews throughout the Ashkenazic lands that no one who has not been ordained to the title *morenu* [our teacher] is permitted to decide legal questions of marriage and divorce."
12. Bruna, *Responsa*, No. 73. "I was asked," Israel Bruna here further

law," the same author categorically declares.[13] While the celebrated Talmudist Joseph Colon, who lived in Renaissance Italy, found no prohibition against Jews wearing the same dress as Christians,[14] his contemporary, Israel Bruna, decreed that whoever goes bareheaded violates the teaching of the Jewish religion, for a Jew ought to be distinguished from other men not only in his clothing but even in his footwear, and he who does not comply is a heretic and ought to be excommunicated for the sake of Heaven.[15] The most popular works which derive from that benighted era, Jacob Mölln's *Minhagim* (or *Minhagei Maharil*), Israel Isserlein's *responsa Terumat Ha-Deshen*, and *Leket Yosher*[16] by Isserlein's pupil Joseph ben Moses, are permeated with the same strictly orthodox spirit.

There is, however, one exception. This is the polemic work *Sefer Ha-Nitzaḥon*, whose author was the rabbi and head of the Talmudic academy of Prague, Rabbi Yomtov Lipmann Mühlhausen.[17] For the scanty biographical information about him that we possess we are indebted mainly to *Sefer Ha-Nitzaḥon* itself. In its last nine sections it is related that in the year 1399 the rabbi and many other prominent leaders of the community were imprisoned because of a slanderous denunciation on the part of an apostate named Peter to the effect that the Jews had blasphemed the Christian faith. At the trial Rabbi Yomtov Lipmann brilliantly proved the falsehood and groundlessness of the denunciation. Nevertheless, the incident ended in the most tragic way. On the twentieth of Elul, 1400, seventy-seven members of the community were condemned to death, and the next day three other prominent men of the city were burned at the stake.

Numerous passages in *Sefer Ha-Nitzaḥon* testify that its author was well acquainted with the Gospels in the Latin translation of the Bible, and that he frequently carried on disputations with Christian priests and scholars on religious matters (sections 225, 260, etc.). It must be borne in mind that precisely at that time, at

---

relates, "by a rich Jew from Russia whether it is permissible to make a silk prayer shawl colored red or yellow in honor of the Sabbath and festivals, and I replied that this should not be done."
13. Bruna, *Responsa*, No. 23.
14. Colon, *Responsa*, No. 88 (Venice edition, 1519).
15. Bruna, *Responsa*, No. 34.
16. This collection of laws, which is extremely interesting from a cultural-historical point of view, was completed in 1470. It was first published in 1903–4 under the auspices of the Mekitzei Nirdamim Society by J. Freimann.
17. Lipmann also served for a time as rabbi in Erfurt, Cracow, and other cities (see J. Kaufmann, *Ha-Rav Yomtov Lipmann* [1927], pp. 15–16).

the beginning of the fifteenth century, in the learned Christian circles of Prague, the ideas of the great English reform preacher Wycliffe aroused intense interest. His followers and opponents carried on heated debates with each other in the halls of the University of Prague, where the famous John Huss then began his epoch-making activity. The religious ferment in Christian society evoked by the widespread feeling of dissatisfaction with the Church and its official leaders made a great impression among Jews as well. Many wished to see in this "the beginning of the redemption," and hoped that it would bring about the downfall of Christianity and the triumph of Judaism. A Christian chronicle of that era complains that "all the Christians and Jews, whether of the higher estate or of the common people, are going over to the side of the Hussites and no authority can therefore overcome them." In the year 1419 the question of the "bond between the Jews and the Hussites and Waldensians" was discussed in the theological faculty of the University of Vienna.[18]

That this was not simply a libel on the part of the Catholic clergy against the Jews, whom they so despised, is attested by the historical fact that in the religious disputations with the theologians of Prague the Kabbalist and liturgical poet, Rabbi Avigdor ben Isaac Kara, who obtained renown with his penitential poem "Et Kol Ha-Telaah," in which he laments the great massacre in Prague of 1389, frequently participated. The Hussite movement aroused such enthusiasm in him that he translated his poem on God's unity, "Eḥad Yaḥid U-Meyuḥad El," into German, and the Hussites used to sing this hymn in both languages. They were especially charmed by the lines

> Jew, Moslem, and Christian as well
> Know that God is incorporeal.[19]

The friendship of Rabbi Avigdor Kara with the Hussites gave birth to a legend, which was accepted even among Jews, to the effect that the entire Hussite movement emerged under the influence of the Jewish poet.[20]

---

18. According to Ignacy Schipper, *Die Yiddishe Velt* (1928), I, 124–25; see also Schipper's *Kulturgeshichte*, pp. 67–69.
19. In *Sefer Shirim Zemirot Ve-Tishbaḥot*, in which Avigdor's poem is included, these lines are missing.
20. This legend is reported by an unknown author of the fourteenth century. It was published by S. D. Luzzatto in Polak's *Halichot Kedem*, pp. 79–80. See also *Iggerot Shadal*, p. 866, and *Emek Ha-Bacha*, p. 75 (1852 edition).

It was just at that time[21] that Avigdor's disciple and colleague, Yomtov Lipmann, composed his *Sefer Ha-Nitzaḥon*,[22] in order to provide his brethren with the weapons they needed to defend the foundations of Judaism in religious disputations and successfully refute the criticisms of their antagonists. Lipmann himself was a skillful polemicist. He collected all the verses and passages in the Hebrew Bible which the Christian theologians endeavored to clothe in Christian garb and in which they sought to find solid proof that theirs is the only true faith. Lipmann relentlessly destroys their entire structure. With great acuteness he shows, at every point, how groundless their interpretations and subtleties are. The Christian theologians regarded the author of *Sefer Ha-Nitzaḥon* as their mortal enemy. They translated his work into Latin and for generations employed their foremost polemicists to overthrow the arguments of the rabbi of Prague and to dull the points of his finely honed arrows.[23]

It is characteristic of that difficult era that this clever polemicist, in whose battle against Christianity a certain rationalist spirit is discernible, was also an ardent mystic. Yomtov Lipmann wrote a special work on the mysteries concealed in the letters of the alphabet,[24] in which he calculates the "end" and asserts that the Messiah will come no later than the year 1430, when vengeance will be taken for the innocent blood of all the martyrs who sacrificed themselves for the sanctification of God's name. He also wrote a commentary on the "work of creation" (*maaseh bereshit*) and the "work of the chariot or throne" (*maaseh merkavah*),[25] in which he shows that only through the wisdom of the Kabbalah can one attain the highest level and fathom the deepest mysteries. He was even persuaded that Maimonides was a convinced Kabbalist.[26]

21. That *Sefer Ha-Nitzaḥon* was composed before 1410 may be seen from section 335, where the author notes that many contemporary "calculators of the end" assert that the redemption will come in the year 1410.
22. The work consists of 354 sections—corresponding to the number of days in the lunar year, according to the author's own explanation.
23. Against Lipmann appeared such works as *Triumphator vapulans sive exfulatio; Anti Lipmanniana; Disputatio contra Lipmanni Nizzachon;* and many others. For details, see J. Kaufmann, *Ha-Rav Yomtov Lipmann*, pp. 109–10.
24. The work is entitled *Sefer Alfa Beta*, and was printed at the end of the book *Baruch She-Amar* (Shklov edition, 1804, pp. 17–52).
25. *Sefer Ha-Eshkol*, first published by J. Kaufmann in 1927.
26. *Ibid.*, p. 165. Apparently Lipmann was also familiar with Solomon Ibn Gabirol's *Mekor Ḥayyim* (undoubtedly through Falaquera's *Likkutim*). See *Sefer Ha-Eshkol*, p. 128: "Know that our sages proved that matter and form cannot exist without one another."

Israeli, Bonfils, Parḥi, and Ibn Ardutial

The Jewish community in Spain suffered relatively little in the terrible years of the Black Plague, but the destruction which befell the German and French Jews had a powerful influence on the spiritual mood of the Jews of northern Spain. The major center of Jewish free thought, Provence, experienced all the horrors of the persecutions. With the economic destruction, the level of cultural creativity also declined.[27] Even in Castile the narrow spirit of isolationism which the celebrated Talmudist Rabbi Asher ben Yeḥiel imported with him from Germany was felt even more sharply. The ban of Rabbi Solomon ben Adret remained in full force, and even many Spanish Jews already considered it dangerous to study philosophy and natural sciences because they might lead one to heresy and atheism. An exception was made for mathematics and astronomy, since these were associated with determining the new moon and calendric calculations.[28] In fact it was in this field that a disciple of Rabbi Asher ben Yeḥiel wrote the only genuine scientific book that Spanish Jewry produced in the first half of the fourteenth century. This is Isaac ben Joseph Israeli's *Yesod Olam*,[29] which was extremely popular among Jews until modern times. Israeli was the first among European scientists in the Middle Ages who showed that one must calculate the position of the moon in regard to different points of the earth,[30] and it was only the renowned astronomer Kepler who first properly appreciated the full significance of his principle.

A contemporary of Israeli's was the Jewish astronomer and mathematician Immanuel ben Jacob Bonfils of Tarascon, whose major astronomical work, *Shesh Kenafayim*, played a very important cultural role in Muscovite Russia. In the year 1406 a Latin translation of *Shesh Kenafayim* appeared. From Latin Bonfils' work was translated into Russian, and the Russian version, entitled *Shestokriil*, became the chief source from which Muscovite Russia for ages drew its astronomical and mathematical knowledge.[31]

---

27. A melancholy portrait of the cultural decline in Provence at the end of the fourteenth century is given by the physician Leon Joseph of Carcassone in the introduction to his translation of Gerard de Solo's medical works.
28. Even Abba Mari and his followers at the height of their struggle against the rationalists considered it necessary to underscore the great utility of such sciences as mathematics and astronomy (see Simeon ben Joseph's letter in the *Zunz Jubelschrift*, p. 165).
29. The best scientific edition appeared in Berlin in 1846–48.
30. Employing what, in astronomy, is called parallax.
31. In his old age Immanuel translated into Hebrew the celebrated "Alexander of Macedon romance," which in the Middle Ages was con-

The Cultural Decline of Spanish and Provençal Jewry

Yesod Olam and *Shesh Kenafayim* are both connected with problems relating to Jewish ritual (the laws of sanctifying the new moon and determining the dates of the festivals). Religious interests were also served by another important scientific work of that era, *Kaftor Va-Feraḥ* by Estori ben Moses Parḥi. Estori's father was a Spaniard born in the city of Florence,[32] but he himself was apparently born in Provence, since he calls it "the land of my birth."[33] He received a well-rounded education, studying Judaism with his grandfather, Nathan of Tronquetelle, and afterwards with the "martyr" Eliezer of Chinon, and also with Rabbi Asher ben Yeḥiel, when the latter lived in Montpellier. The general sciences, as well as Arabic and Latin, he studied in Montpellier with his relative, the well-known astronomer Jacob ben Machir. After the expulsion of 1306 Parḥi spent a brief period in Perpignan and thereafter lived for seven years in Barcelona, where he translated numerous medical works from Latin into Hebrew, among them the handbook *De remediis* of Armengaud Blaise, which was extremely popular at that time.[34] In 1312 Parḥi again took up the traveller's staff. He spent a short time in Cairo and from there set out for Palestine. In a moving manner he relates[35] how he became a wanderer over strange lands among unfamiliar peoples until he finally managed to arrive in the holy land of the patriarchs, for which his heart had yearned greatly. For seven years Parḥi roamed over the ancient, ruined land.[36] He explored every corner and

---

sidered an ancient work and attributed to Kallisthenes, the pupil of Aristotle. Immanuel translated his *Toledot Aleksander* from the Latin version, the *Historia de Prelis* of the presbyter Leo. In the introduction to his translation Immanuel declares: "I have undertaken to translate this work which is so beloved among the Christians that they have adorned it with beautiful and colorful illustrations in gold and silver. Most readers believe in everything that is written here, but I take a different view. In any case, this is a useful work and certainly deserves to be translated. But let the reader not think that I do this out of ambition or in order to acquire fame; I do it simply out of pleasure. I think to myself: When I have occasion to sit in the midst of a noble company or even among ignorant men, I will relate to them the events of this book, and great will be their pleasure, sweeter to them than honey will be its words" (see *REJ*, VI, 729, and Renan-Neubauer, *Les Écrivains juifs français*, pp. 692–99).

32. It is from the word *flora* that the Hebrew name *Parḥi* comes.
33. The year of Parḥi's birth is unknown. It is conjectured that he was born in the middle of the 1280's.
34. For a discussion of Parḥi's translations, see Steinschneider, *Hebräischen Übersetzungen*, pp. 778, 835, and Renan-Neubauer, *Les Écrivains juifs français*, pp. 405–9.
35. In the introduction to *Kaftor Va-Feraḥ*.
36. *Kaftor Va-Feraḥ*, 46b: "I spent about two years in Galilee searching

noted down everything of interest for the past history of the country. The fruit of this diligent labor was his famous work *Kaftor Va-Feraḥ*, completed in 1322 in Beisan (ancient Beth-Shean).[37]

Parḥi's work is a genuine treasure trove for the study of Palestine. He presents highly important information on the flora of the land, on measures and weights, on coins from various periods, and on numerous matters connected with archaeology. His book also provides many interesting items of knowledge about chronology, various sects in Palestine, and the like.

In all other fields of literature and science the symptoms of decline appeared ever more clearly. The well of Hebrew poetry dried up entirely in Castile. Where once the song of Jehudah Halevi had resounded, the most honored place was now occupied by such slightly gifted versifiers as Shemtov Ibn Isaac Ardutial, who in 1345 appeared with his colorless *makama* entitled *Milḥemet Ha-Et Veha-Misparaim*.[38] Even in the realm of Talmudic knowledge no new creative figures appeared, but mere collectors, whose only task was to order and systematize the vast material accumulated in the course of earlier generations. We have observed how, from the time that Asher ben Yeḥiel, who had fled from Germany, obtained the post of chief rabbi in Toledo, the largest Jewish community of Castile, the influence of the *Nusaḥ Ashkenaz*, the German-French style, began to be felt ever more strongly in Spanish Jewish life. This soon became noticeable even in the literature of the Poskim, the collections of religious laws and precepts by rabbinic authorities. We have seen that Maimonides' *Mishneh Torah* even in its own day did not entirely satisfy the German-French Jews. In France Moses of Coucy soon appeared with his *Sefer Mitzvot Gadol*, which, in his view, was more suited to the customs and way of life of French Jewry. In Germany the *Or Zarua* of Isaac ben Moses of Vienna and the *Sefer Mordechai* of Mordechai ben Hillel were widely accepted. In the fourteenth century, however, the *Mishneh Torah* could no longer completely satisfy even the Spanish communities. Maimonides, who had only the slightest sense of historical evolution, was certain that with his

---

and investigating, and another five years in the rest of the lands of the tribes. I did not refrain for a single hour from exploring the land. Blessed be the divine Helper" (quoted from Edelmann's edition).

37. *Kaftor Va-Feraḥ* was first published in Venice in 1549, according to the only manuscript which has survived and which is filled with errors. It was reprinted by Edelmann in Berlin in 1852, and by Luncz in Jerusalem in 1897 with a corrected text. In 1912 L. Grünhut issued the corrected text with a German translation.

38. Published in *Divrei Ḥachamim*, pp. 47–55.

Mishneh Torah he had created a collection that would endure for all ages and proudly expressed his strong confidence that his work would "doubtless be accepted by the entire Jewish people, which would utilize it alone and no other book whatever." History, however, proved Maimonides mistaken. Major changes took place in the way of life and the ideas of Spanish Jewry in later generations. Talmudic knowledge in Spain was greatly developed by such outstanding scholars as Naḥmanides, Rabbi Solomon ben Adret, and Rabbi Asher ben Yeḥiel. With their keen *novellae*, distinctions, and *responsa*, in which the strong influence of the Franco-German Tosafists is discernible, they enriched rabbinic literature to such a degree that a new code, a "catchall" collection of Jewish laws and statutes that would properly employ this tremendous mass of new material, became necessary. This need was splendidly fulfilled by Rabbi Asher's son, Rabbi Jacob. In the 1330's his *Arbaah Turim*, which had a vast influence on all of later rabbinic literature, appeared.

Rabbi Jacob ben Asher was neither a great scholar nor an outstanding dialectician and "uprooter of mountains," as was his famous father. However, he possessed the skill of the excellent systematizer and, as a result of this, became a notable figure in Jewish history; his work came to occupy one of the most honored places among the legal codes of the Middle Ages. Jacob excluded from his collection all the laws and commandments which no longer had any practical application in his day. On the other hand, he gave the most careful attention to numerous customs and practices that were particularly popular in the German communities. All the vast material of his code was divided by Jacob into four parts: (1) *Tur Oraḥ Ḥayyim*, dealing with the conduct of a person from his rising in the morning until retiring to sleep at night, and all the laws and customs of Sabbath, new moon, and festivals; (2) *Tur Yoreh Deah*, containing the laws of ritual slaughter, clean and unclean animals, and what is forbidden and permitted (*issur ve-hetter*); (3) *Tur Even Ha-Ezer*, concerning family matters, laws of women, marriage, divorce, and levirate marriage; and (4) *Tur Ḥoshen Misphat*, concerning civil law, the laws governing relations between a man and his neighbor and between the individual and the community. Thanks to its clear, easily comprehensible language and the excellent order according to which the tremendous mass of material is organized, *Arbaah Turim* was soon accepted throughout the Jewish world.[39]

39. It was one of the first Jewish works to be printed (in Pieve di Sacco, 1473).

Bahya ben Asher and the Strengthening of Mysticism

In time it displaced all the other legal collections which had appeared earlier. It also became the foundation on which Rabbi Joseph Karo's *Shulḥan Aruch*, with all its commentaries and appendices, was constructed.[40]

This sober, arid collection of laws and rules, however, could not satisfy everyone. To be sure, Jacob ben Asher was himself mystically minded and frequently introduced arguments from the Kabbalah.[41] But generally his style is pallid and monotonous, without a spark of enthusiasm or poetic sentiment. He did not have the eloquence of the fiery preacher, as did Moses of Coucy, who knew how to clothe the laws and commandments in a garment of moving ethical instruction and inspiration. But what the diligent scholar and collector Jacob ben Asher lacked, his contemporary, the mystic and preacher of Saragossa, Rabbi Bahya ben Asher, who was a disciple of Rabbi Solomon ben Adret, possessed in full measure.

Bahya ben Asher set himself the task of writing "a work which would revive hearts wearied by the grievous exile and great afflictions." Men's minds, he declared, have been depressed by great sorrows and cannot calmly delve into the sea of the Talmud and search out its words, which are more precious than gold and pearls, in order to become versed in all the commandments and laws; their souls long for the refreshing springs of homilies and stories.[42] To this end Bahya wrote his work *Kad Ha-Kemaḥ*. In its sixty chapters he considers, following the order of the alphabet, sixty major commandments and principles which man requires for guidance on the road of life. The way of morality and justice, faith and love of God, trust in divine providence and its marvelous ways, the beauty of prayer and the synagogue, the importance of humility and purity of heart, the vanity of pride and flattery, loving one's neighbor as oneself, honoring father and mother, peace and repentance, charity and good deeds, the bliss of the hope for redemption and the holiness of the Sabbath—all these Bahya ben Asher discusses in the colorful language of the ardent preacher and adorns them with moving parables and moral instruction gathered from the Aggadah and Midrashim.

The unique qualities of Bahya's style appear even more clearly in his well-known commentary to the Torah, thanks to which he became one of the most popular personalities among the Jewish

40. For a discussion of *Arbaah Turim*, see I. H. Weiss, *Dor Dor Ve-Doreshav*, V, 115–20.
41. See, e.g., *Tur Oraḥ Ḥayyim*, Sections 6, 35, 51, 113, 115, 120, 121, et al.
42. Introduction to *Kad Ha-Kemaḥ*.

masses. "Rabbenu Baḥya says"—this phrase is encountered on virtually every page of the "women's Pentateuch" in Yiddish, the *Tze'enah U're'enah*. The ordinary reader in his naiveté believed that the commentator so frequently quoted in the *Tze'enah U're'enah* was the Baḥya Ibn Pakuda who composed the greatly admired ethical work *Ḥovot Ha-Levavot*. In this way the two authors, who lived in different eras, were united by popular tradition into one person, the beloved "Rabbenu Baḥya." Numerous legends were created about the "holiness" of Baḥya's commentary; it was believed to have come into the world accompanied by miracles and wonders.[43]

Not unjustifiably does Baḥya ben Asher indicate in the introduction to his commentary that, of all previous commentators, the most important for him is Naḥmanides, whom he takes as his model. Even more frequently than Naḥmanides Baḥya introduces arguments from the Kabbalah and relies, in his explanations, on the "esoteric wisdom." Naḥmanides was unwilling to have the mystical secrets revealed to ill-prepared readers and therefore veiled them in allusions that are difficult to understand. Baḥya, however, took the position that the time had come for the mysteries of the Kabbalah to be disclosed to all Israel, and he explains them in clear, easily comprehensible language and interweaves them with legends and parables from various Midrashim. In this effort to familiarize the masses with the truth of the "hidden wisdom" the spirit of that age is clearly discernible. In the course of the few decades separating Naḥmanides from Baḥya ben Asher the influence of the Kabbalah had grown so powerful that even many rationalists and representatives of radical philosophic thought began to take note of the mystical world of ideas. Even so thoroughgoing a rationalist as Moses Narboni speaks with respect of the Kabbalists of his time, and in his commentary to Maimonides' *Guide for the Perplexed* defends the men of the Kabbalah against the philosopher's sharp criticism. Just as the earlier Aristotelian rationalists sought to clothe the legends of the Talmud in philosophical garb, so Moses Narboni attempted to do the same with such Kabbalist works as *Shiur Komah* and others.[44] Even Gersonides, after witnessing with his own eyes the expulsion of the Jews from France, cried out passionately, "Happy is he who waits for the advent of the Messiah and will live to see him arrive!" Indeed, in his commentary to the Book of Daniel he cal-

---

43. The legend of the wondrous "revelation" of Baḥya's commentary is given by Ghirondi in his *Toledot Gedolei Yisrael*, p. 62.
44. See Narboni's essay published by S. Pinsker in *Kochevei Yitzḥak*, XXX, 23–33.

culates the "end" and indicates that the redeemer will come in the year 1358.

Many of Gersonides' younger contemporaries who devoted all their energies to philosophic and scientific investigations could be satisfied neither with the *only* rationalist truth nor with Isaac Albalag's "double" truth. Some of these still sought to unite what cannot be united, to join antithetical elements—philosophic rationalism with astrology, mysticism, and the like. Others again inclined increasingly toward the idea that there is, indeed, only one truth—the truth of revelation, which burns with the fire of inspiration and is illuminated with the mystical light of the *razin de-razin* (secrets of secrets), the sacred wisdom of the Kabbalah.

A typical representative of the first group was the philosophically educated David ben Yom Tov Ibn Bilia. Ibn Bilia was productive in the most varied fields of knowledge. He wrote a work on logic (*Kelalei Ha-Higgayon*), on ethics (*Tziyyurim*), and on the relationship between medicine and astrology (*Kelal Katan*). He composed a handbook on poetic meter, and in 1338 translated a work on the medicinal qualities of the skin of snakes, *Maamar Be-Segulat Or Ha-Naḥash*. Ibn Bilia was also involved in Jewish studies, writing a philosophical-astrological commentary to the Pentateuch entitled *Meor Enayim*, in which the influence of the Kabbalah is evident.[45] In a special essay, *Yesodot Ha-Maskil*,[46] he discusses Maimonides' "thirteen principles" of Judaism and presents, in addition, his own "thirteen foundations of the enlightened man." These twenty-six foundations together, Ibn Bilia underscores, equal the same number as the letters of the Ineffable Name of God (the Tetragrammaton) and the twice-repeated word *eḥad* (one) in the Biblical phrase "the Lord shall be one and His name one."

Ibn Bilia takes pains to stress that he deems it necessary to base his views not on arguments from the sages of the peoples of the world but on statements from "our sacred Torah," for the philosophers must first prove the correctness of their ideas and assumptions through logical theories and arguments from physics and natural phenomena, whereas the Torah transcends these laws and reveals itself through miracles and wonders. Ibn Bilia constructs his "foundations" on the high ethical principle that a man should not expect any special reward for his righteous deeds; the supreme recompense is the consciousness that his activity is in

45. Ibn Bilia's commentary is frequently quoted by Samuel Ibn Zarza in his *Mekor Ḥayyim*. S. Sachs provides interesting details in his *Ha-Palit*, pp. 31–33.
46. Published in *Divrei Ḥachamim*, pp. 56–60.

complete harmony with what the moral sentiment demands of him. In general, however, Ibn Bilia's work already reflects the spirit of decline and eclecticism.

More typical in this respect is Ibn Bilia's younger contemporary, the physician Meir ben Isaac Aldabi, the author of the popular religious-philosophical work *Shevilei Emunah*. Of Aldabi's life we know only the few details given in this work. His mother was the daughter of Rabbi Asher ben Yeḥiel, and he quotes him very frequently in his work under the title "grandfather."[47] Aldabi was born in Toledo, but for some unknown reason had to flee his birthplace and was a wanderer in foreign countries, where he lived in dire poverty. In the year 1360 he completed his *Shevilei Emunah* abroad and spent his last years in Palestine.

In modern scholarly literature Aldabi has been accused of plagiarism.[48] However, he is not at all guilty of the charge. The fact is that in the Middle Ages there was still no clear-cut boundary between a personal, original work and a simple reworking or compilation. In medieval scholarly circles men had an altogether different notion of plagiarism and literary theft than in modern times. Even first-rate writers considered it proper to appropriate and rewrite entire chapters of other men's work, without even mentioning the name of the original author (e.g., Albertus Magnus in regard to Maimonides' *Guide for the Perplexed*). More than one work which acquired great renown in the Middle Ages was in essence merely a compilation of other works and of ideas expressed by scholars other than its author. But Aldabi leaves no reason for error. In his introduction he openly declares that his task is merely to present, in popular form, the essence of works which his predecessors wrote. He declares,

I have not thought this out myself, and not with my own mind have I arrived at it, but I gathered it from precious books, translated it from foreign tongues, and copied it from great scholars. I have no desire to glory in strange clothing, and do not intend to acquire a reputation and become known through this book.

And immediately after the introduction is an acrostic poem, into which the author's name is woven, containing the statement that it should testify "that I composed this commentary [*biur*]."

A "collector" from "foreign books" and "copier" of "great scholars," Aldabi is, in fact, the typical eclectic. It does not even

---

47. See *Shevilei Emunah*, Netivim 3, 7, and 11.
48. See Brüll's *Jahrbücher für jüdische Geschichte und Literatur*, II, 166–68; Steinschneider, *Hebräischen Übersetzungen*, p. 16.

occur to him to blend the various elements into one mold. He simply mingles them mechanically and has no notion whatever that his material is not unitary and that there are gross inconsistencies in it. His work is divided into ten chapters which he calls "paths" (*netivim*) and every "path" or *nativ* is further divided into "tirals" (*shevilim*). In the first chapter, in which God and His attributes are discussed, Aldabi emphasizes, in the spirit of Maimonides, the divine unity, unchangeability, and absolute freedom from all material elements. But he grounds this idea in an altogether unique way, through "combinations of letters," *notarikon* and *gematriot*. When he deals with the questions of miracles, providence, and free will, he introduces a mixture of the most varied opinions, and relies on authorities holding completely contradictory views, e.g., Nahmanides on the one side, and Aristotle and Maimonides on the other. This is repeated in connection with other problems, for instance, with regard to reward and punishment (Chapter Nine). Here Aldabi makes no distinction between the crude, material conceptions the common people have about heaven and hell and the more abstract notions of Maimonides, Hillel of Verona, and others.

In the first six chapters of *Shevilei Emunah* we see before us, first of all, the natural scientist. Aldabi provides information in popular form about various natural phenomena, describes the course of the spheres and planets, explains the laws of eclipses of the sun and moon, discusses physiology, pathology, and hygiene, and thereby manifests his competence as a practicing physician. In the seventh chapter the natural scientist suddenly disappears and we find before us the pietist and godfearing ethical preacher. In the heartfelt style of Asher ben Yehiel's "Testament" and the ethical instruction of Rabbi Eleazar of Worms, the author of *Rokeah*, Aldabi teaches how a man must fulfill his highest goal: service of the Creator. With three things, Aldabi teaches, man can properly serve God: with prayer,[49] the fulfillment of the commandments, and humility. "Put off the garment of pride," he admonishes, "and wrap youself in the cloak of humility. Then will it be well with your soul. . . . For God's sake, be lowly in your own estimation, for hated by God are those with proud hearts. . . . Be of those who are shamed and mocked but not of those who shame and despise another. . . ."

This tender and humble tone, however, is abandoned by Aldabi in the eighth chapter, in which "the Oral Torah given on Mount

---

49. For prayer, Aldabi insists, is the foundation of the world (*ha-tefillah ammudo shel olam*).

Sinai" is discussed. The great miracle of "the giving of the Torah at Sinai," Aldabi insists, is confirmed through the sacred tradition which passes from generation to generation and is the foundation of Judaism. He knows, however, that in his day there are many "who occupy themselves with the wisdom of the philosophers of the nations," and these wish to explain the miracle through rational inquiry. Albadi is convinced that this can only lead to the "destruction of the Torah" and therefore issues forth with great indignation against the "erring spirits," the lost and deluded "philosophizers" (*mitpalsefim*), who assert that observance of the commandments and statutes of the Torah, in which the covenant God made with the congregation of Israel is manifested, is of merely secondary importance, since they are intended only to purify man's mind so that he may more easily understand and know. These "philosophizers" and "erring ones" consider the "subtleties of Abbaye and Rava" and the principles which the sages of the Talmud have set down in regard to performance of the commandments an "unimportant detail" (*davar katan*). Regarding all the commandments and ordinances merely as symbols, they have actually nullified the observance of such precepts as prayer, the wearing of phylacteries, and things permitted and forbidden (*hetter ve-issur*). They devote themselves only to "the wisdoms of the books of the sages of the nations," to philosophy and the natural sciences, seeking in them the secret of *maaseh merkavah* (the lore of the divine chariot or throne). But this, Aldabi cries out, is the way of death and corruption, and those who follow it thereby exclude themselves from the congregation of Israel. He considers it his sacred duty to warn against this dangerous way and to save men from heresy and the denial of religious truth.

Aldabi is thoroughly persuaded that not only the Torah of Moses was given at Mount Sinai but the whole Oral Torah as well. "You must believe with perfect faith," he declares, "that everything written in the Mishnah and the Talmud is the clearest truth, the words of the living God [*divrei Elohim hayyim*]."

"In the Gemara is everything"—this is Aldabi's deepest conviction. "Observe carefully," he writes, "and you will be persuaded that all wisdoms and sciences without exception are to be found in the Talmud, but the philosopher who is of the sages of the nations of the world cannot grasp these things." Aldabi assails with intense bitterness the philosophically educated men of his time who pursue foreign wells and explore the sciences of the non-Jewish peoples, in the hope that the foundations of the hidden truth will thereby be revealed to them. They run after false and erring lights, and the living source of light, the only foundation of true knowledge, the sacred Torah, they have forsaken. These lost and wandering men do not understand that all the wisdoms and sciences of the gentile sages are merely refuse and crumbs fallen from the table of Jewish scholars.

With naive simplicity Aldabi relates how the "philosophizers," i.e., the freethinkers with whom he carried on debates, laughed at him and his associates and pointed out mockingly that only gross ignoramuses who cannot comprehend the "external wisdoms" fight against them. They compared them to the cat of the fable who declared a good piece of meat rotten and spoiled because it was suspended too high above her and she could not reach it. Aldabi further recounts how, in order to know "what to answer the heretic," he diligently studied the "external books" and with great astonishment noted that among many false theories contradicting the "words of the sages" he found also some correct opinions, with which our sages are in agreement. Aldabi relates candidly,

This was a great surprise to me until I found an explanation in an old book. It tells that when Jeconiah [Jehoiachin], the king of Judea, was banished, the men of the Sanhedrin and other sages of Israel went with him into exile . . . and it was with their wisdom that the sages of Greece became familiar, and they employed it in their books of investigation. . . . It is further related there that the great philosopher Aristotle, whose system all the scholars follow and whose books they read, was the teacher of Alexander of Macedon who ruled the entire world. When Alexander conquered Jerusalem, he appointed Aristotle superintendent of King Solomon's archives, which had survived. Aristotle studied Solomon's manuscripts, transcribed them, made various additions, and gave them out as his own works; and in order that the truth not be known he hid the originals.

An opponent of the "philosophizers," Aldabi was a fervent adherent of the Kabbalah. He believes in transmigration of souls, speaks eloquently of "the secret of the letters" (*sod ha-otiot*), and complains of "some of our philosophizers" who deny the existence of demons. In the closing chapter of his *Shevilei Emunah* Aldabi relates the story of Armilus and of Messiah ben Joseph and Messiah ben David, as written down in the book *Raziel*. He also speaks of the great "Sabbath day," the seven thousandth after the creation of the world, and the "deep mystery" inherent in it. The sages of the "hidden wisdom" received this mystery by tradition from the prophets, but it may not be revealed; it may not be told or investigated, because not all are worthy of it.

But the "mysteries" of the "hidden wisdom" began increasingly to dominate Jewish minds in that era. Just as Aldabi was convinced that all the sciences derive from Jewish scholars, so others sought to prove that the "hidden wisdom" is the only valid and true philosophy. Abraham Abulafia had long before declared Maimonides one of the greatest Kabbalists.[50] He considered his *Guide for the Perplexed* a book filled with mystical "terrible secrets," and his *Hayyei Ha-Nefesh* is devoted to expounding these.[51] Following Abulafia, other Kabbalists also claimed that Maimonides in his old age became an ardent devotee of the "esoteric wisdom." Rabbi Solomon ben Adret's disciple, the Kabbalist Shemtov ben Abraham Ha-Levi, relates in his *Migdal Oz* (a commentary to Maimonides' *Yad Ha-Hazakah*) that he saw in an old manuscript Maimonides' own words which proved definitely that the philosopher, toward the end of his life, became a Kabbalist and immersed himself in the "secrets of the chariot."[52] Others tell of another manuscript in which Maimonides confesses that, in his old age, an elderly man came and revealed to him the profound mysteries of the Kabbalah. "If my books had not already long been spread all over the world," Maimonides then declared, "I would have erased much that is written in them."[53] This, however, was still not enough. Men "discovered" entire mystical works written by the "penitent," the author of the *Guide* himself, e.g., the apocryphal *Megillat Setarim*[54] which Maimonides is alleged to have sent to his favorite pupil, Joseph Ibn Aknin. In this mystical "scroll" the thoroughgoing Aristotelian and fierce adversary of mysticism is made to assert that philosophy may—God forbid—lead men away from

50. In his *Hayyei Ha-Nefesh*, Part I, Chapter 1. Like most of Abulafia's works, *Hayyei Ha-Nefesh* has remained in manuscript. We have utilized the manuscript in the Firkovich Collection, No. 185. The last pages of the first part and the first pages of the second part of this manuscript are missing.

51. See the introduction to *Hayyei Ha-Nefesh:* "And I will declare to you thirty-six mysteries and future marvels . . . as I gathered them from the *Guide for the Perplexed.*"

52. See Weiss, *Dor Dor Ve-Doreshav*, V, 57; Zunz, *Gottesdienstlichen Vorträge*, second edition, p. 417.

53. See Isaac Abravanel, *Nahalat Avot*, end of the third chapter; Meir Ibn Gabbai, *Avodat Ha-Kodesh*, p. 33 (the Cracow edition, 1577); Gedaliah Ibn Yahya, *Shalshelet Ha-Kabbalah*; and Joseph Delmedigo, *Matzref Le-Hochmah* (1629), p. 16.

54. *Megillat Setarim* was first published by Moses Ha-Goleh of Kiev in his *Shoshan Sodot*, pp. 32–36 (the Koretz edition, 1774). It was reprinted in *Iggerot Ha-Rambam*, III, 35–36.

the right path, and that only the way of Kabbalah is free of stumbling blocks and that the danger of temptation is excluded from it.

The complete victory of the Kabbalah and tradition over philosophical rationalism was especially furthered by political events in Spain in the second half of the fourteenth century. Of these we treat in the next chapter.

CHAPTER TWO

The Clerical Reaction in Spain and the Literature of Polemics Against Christians

THE tempestuous political events which occurred in Castile in the second half of the fourteenth century were the harbinger of a new era, an era of religious reaction and severe persecution for the Jews of Spain. For generations the Castilians carried on an obdurate struggle with an enemy adhering to another faith. Devotedly they fought for every foot of Spanish soil, and the war was not yet over. In the 1330's Christian Castile was still in grave danger. In the Moslem south the Arabs of Granada made a treaty with the sultan of Morocco and, with combined forces, sought to recover the provinces which Castile had previously wrested from them. But the Moslems suffered a great defeat; their army was vanquished by the courageous Castilian general Gonzalo Martinez, who was known to be a bitter enemy of the Jews.

Hatred of Jews was intensified in various strata of the Christian populace at that time. It would be erroneous, however, to believe that religious motives alone brought this about. The Spanish nobility, which for generations carried on a stubborn battle with the Moors, was extremely militant. The Castilian knight spent most of his days on horseback, encased in armor, his hand never without a spear or sword. Though a skillful and valiant warrior, he had very slight knowledge of financial or political matters. Trade was considered dishonorable; money on interest could be borrowed only from Jews and Moors.

It is therefore not surprising that in the Christian kingdoms of Spain—Castile and Aragon—Jews played a very important role in all realms of political and civic life. Jewish tax gatherers, whom the government empowered to collect the taxes and excises throughout the land, Jewish bankers, fiscal agents, advisors, and emissaries were prominent at court. But these courtiers or *hatzranim*,[1] as they are called in the contemporary rabbinic literature, were of an altogether different type from the Jews who had held office in Moslem Spain, e.g., Ḥasdai Ibn Shaprut and Samuel Ha-Nagid. Raised in the rich Arabic civilization, the latter knew how to appreciate cultural treasures. They were connoisseurs and patrons of art and science, and their influence on the development of Jewish civilization was very extensive. But Christian Spain in the Middle Ages was at a significantly lower level of culture. Spanish literature was still in its infancy. In the field of science, as well as in official documents, Latin was still dominant. Among the Jews Spanish was merely a vernacular, not the language of culture.[2]

1. The terms *ḥatzran* and *ḥatzranim* are encountered quite frequently in the *responsa* of that era. Rabbi Isaac bar Sheshet, for instance, relates how some members of a rabbinic court who refused to validate a certain election that seemed improper to them were coerced by a certain *ḥatzran* who had them seized and imprisoned.
2. To be sure, King Alfonso X in the middle of the thirteenth century invited some Jewish scholars to translate Arabic scientific works into Castilian. But it is highly probable that only the scientific knowledge of the Jewish scholars and their proficiency in Arabic were employed in this enterprise; the translations themselves appear to have been made by Christian scholars. Historians such as Renan, Dozy, and others long ago showed that most medieval translations from Arabic into Latin were made not by persons who were competent in both languages but usually by two collaborators, an Arab or a Jew who knew very little Latin, or had no knowledge whatever of the language, and a Christian scholar who was a good Latinist but understood no Arabic. In the later period Jewish converts and also a few Jews did, indeed, contribute to Spanish literature, e.g., the gifted poet Rav Santo (Shem Tov), who dedicated to King Don Pedro the Cruel (1350–69) his famous poem "Danra general de la muerte" (for a discussion of this poet see M. Kayserling, *Sefaradim*, Chapter Two). Nevertheless, in the fifteenth century the scholar Joseph ben Shemtov still found it necessary to translate Hasdai Crescas' polemic work *Tratado* from Spanish into Hebrew "because Jews are accustomed to read scholarly works not in Spanish but in Hebrew only."

Moral Decline of the Jewish Aristocracy

The Jewish ḥatzranim at the Castilian and Aragonian courts were interested only in adopting the external glitter of the Christian nobility. The parvenu Jewish magnates, the tax collectors who had become wealthy from state excises and leases of customhouses, the financiers, moneychangers, and bankers lived in great luxury, imitating the Christian grandees. They clothed their wives and children in gold and pearls. They loved to ride in richly ornamented carriages, surrounded by hosts of outriders and servants, and their balls and banquets were renowned for their dazzling splendor. But beneath this outward brilliance was moral corruption and emptiness. Many reliable sources of the period testify how greatly petty jealousy, vainglory, and barbaric passions dominated the milieu of the Jewish ḥatzranim and "men of might." Every man begrudged his fellow, and their constant intrigues, gossip, and slander multiplied controversies in the communities and created an atmosphere of hatred and oppression. To obtain complete power over the communities, the Jewish officials tried to limit the authority of the rabbinate through all the means at their disposal. Recognized at court, they found it easy to have the government designate them the chief representatives of the Jewish community. Such representatives bore the titles *rav* (rabbi) and *mara de-atra* (master or teacher of the place),[3] even though they were common ignoramuses and led a debauched life. These community leaders adopted an attitude of contempt toward the spiritual guides of the people[4] and denied them material means, so that they had to live in great poverty.[5]

"For the barbarism of our orphaned generation," laments the famous rabbi of that time Isaac bar Sheshet, "our rich men, great lords, and courtiers are more responsible than all. Their entire thought is only of their wealth and glory, and they refuse to remember God and His commandments."[6]

"Righteousness and justice," Rabbi Isaac calls out in another place, "are trodden underfoot, liars shame the most honorable persons, profligate and base men go about with proudly raised heads; and for this our grandees and princes are responsible."[7] "Controversies," we further read, "grow ever greater. Everyone wishes to

---

3. David Messer Leon relates in one of his *responsa:* "In Spain they used to give the title rabbi to anyone who was appointed by the king even though he was not proficient in the laws or pious and of good conduct" (see *REJ*, 1892, p. 135).
4. See Rabbi Isaac bar Sheshet, *Responsa*, No. 373.
5. See Solomon Alami, *Iggeret Ha-Musar*.
6. See his *Responsa*, No. 373 (beginning).
7. *Ibid.*, No. 267.

seize power, to be the 'pestle of the mortar,' and the one sacred Torah they have split into a thousand Torot."⁸

An even more melancholy picture of the moral corruption of the Jewish aristocracy is given by Solomon Alami in his *Iggeret Ha-Musar*.⁹ The majority of the "great men of the community" who became intimate with the courts and were entrusted with the keys of the royal counting houses and treasuries, laments Alami, promptly forgot their earlier estate. They gloried in their greatness and wealth, and dismissed from their minds their poor brethren and the people from whom they stemmed. They built splendid palaces and rode in rich carriages and on mules adorned with precious stones, clothed in gorgeous robes. They decked their women and children like princesses and hung the most precious pearls and loveliest diamonds on them. Out of pride and desire for dominance, they sowed hatred and jealousy, denounced one another to the king, and did not refrain from the shedding of innocent blood in order to fulfill the desire for vengeance and the lust for the possessions and treasures of others. Arrogantly they violated the commandments of the Torah and publicly desecrated the Sabbath, and whoever had the courage to issue forth against their shameful deeds had a bitter end and perished through their denunciations. They hated the Torah, despised knowledge, and looked with contempt on those who live by their own labor. They employed all means to free themselves from taxes and cast the entire burden on the poor.¹⁰

Controversies, persecutions, and denunciations became very common occurrences in the Jewish communities. It is sufficient to note that, through a false denunciation, seven of the most eminent rabbis of that time were imprisoned in 1374, among them such scholars as Rabbenu Nissim ben Reuben (Ran),¹¹ his disciple Rabbi Isaac bar Sheshet, and the famous philosopher Ḥasdai Crescas, the author of *Or Adonai*.¹² In this connection it must be taken into consideration that the Jewish communities in Spain had

---

8. *Ibid.*, No. 222. See also Nos. 234, 251, 387, 447, and 477, and Profiat Duran, *Maaseh Efod*, Part V, p. 193. On the bitter struggle between the Jews of Aragon and their government-appointed "rabbi," the *ḥatzran* Solomon Alconstantini, see Jean Regné, *Catalogue des actes de Jaime I, Pedro III, et Alfonso III, rois d'Aragon, concernant les juifs*, No. 2551.
9. *Iggeret Ha-Musar* was written in 1415, but mainly the conditions prevailing before the catastrophe of 1391 are portrayed in it.
10. *Iggeret Ha-Musar*, pp. 44-47 (according to the Vilna edition of 1878).
11. For a discussion of Rabbenu Nissim, see Weiss, *Dor Dor Ve-Doreshav*, V, 132-37.
12. On this incident, see Rabbi Isaac bar Sheshet, *Responsa*, No. 376.

their own courts of rabbis and judges, authorized by the government. These Jewish courts were empowered to act even in capital cases. To be sure, in such cases the verdict could not be executed without the consent of the king, but for the Jewish courtiers or *hatzranim*, who were experts in palace intrigues, it was not at all difficult to obtain the royal seal of approval.[13]

The Jewish courts, with their rabbis and judges, were actually a plaything in the hands of the Jewish "princes, officers, and men of wealth." These grandees exploited them in their intrigues and for the promotion of their petty personal interests. In this demoralized environment the spiritual leaders of the people did not have the courage to fulfill their obligation, publicly to oppose the Jewish officials and "strong men" and fight against their unjust deeds. Many of the rabbis were not at a particularly high moral level and followed the same paths as the *hatzranim*. "Some of our rabbis," Alami complains in his *Iggeret Ha-Musar*,

have entered on crooked ways. Out of hatred for, and jealousy of, one another, they sell the Torah and put it to shame.... What one permits, the other forbids, and they make of the single Torah two different ones.... They multiply mountains of decisions, *novellae*, and subtleties that no one needs and that can be of no value to anyone. They spin useless webs day and night to reveal their pettiness and baseness. Their eyes are blind and their hearts stopped up, so that they do not open the eyes of the people and disclose to them the shame and sinfulness surrounding them.[14]

In addition, the rabbis endeavored to be strict constructionists in interpreting the law, terrorizing people with excommunications and bans for every petty violation. This intensified the controversies and increased denunciations and slanders. "I looked on," laments Meir Aldabi in the preface to his *Shevilei Emunah*, "and saw the people lost in darkness, the educated becoming ever fewer, the wise disappearing, and men of the fist and violence dominant and performing their shameful deeds."

The leaders were so little concerned for their communities that ignorance continued to spread. According to Rabbi Isaac bar Sheshet, the Jewish masses in Castile became so backward and

13. In this way, for example, the tax collector-general Joseph Pichon was put to death. His enemies succeeded in fraudulently obtaining from King Juan I an order to inflict the death penalty on a certain "dangerous person." They lied to the king about the name of the condemned man, and on the authority of this order the unfortunate Pichon was beheaded in 1379.
14. *Iggeret Ha-Musar*, p. 41.

ignorant in his day that they could not even read the ordinary prayers.¹⁵ One must here bear in mind the fact that in the fourteenth century a rather significant percentage of the Spanish Jews were ordinary laborers, field workers and artisans. Virtually entire communities were engaged in weaving and dyeing.¹⁶

The *ḥatzranim*, however, had a demoralizing effect not only on the internal life of the Jewish communities; they also produced a great intensification of hatred for Jews within the Christian populace. The Spanish nobility looked with jealousy and enmity on the arrogant Jewish officials and court counselors who were in fact the masters of the kingdom's finances. Hostility toward them was also widespread among the common people. The constant wars consumed colossal sums of money; these had to be provided by the masses, the peasants and artisans. The taxes and excises grew constantly heavier, and at the head of the royal treasuries were Jewish courtiers exclusively. The Jewish tax farmers appointed agents to collect the excises and payments, and these agents (mainly members of their own families and relatives) were merciless creditors and also permitted themselves all kinds of deception and fraud. Hence the common people carried over their hatred for the Jewish agents and fiscal officers to the Jews as a whole. "There is no doubt," insists Alami,

> that for all the oppressions and afflictions which we have suffered in recent times, impudent wretches from among our own people are at fault. They have covered us with shame through their disgraceful behavior toward the Christian populace. We who live in exile among foreign people have desecrated God's holy name among them, for we have committed all kinds of falsehoods, deceptions, and frauds against them. For this reason we have become despicable in their sight. They regard us as a band of thieves, liars, and deceivers, and every shameless act or vile deed is among them called Jewish trickery.¹⁷

The Catholic Church, whose influence grew constantly greater in Spain, exploited the hatred of the masses of the people for the Jewish aristocracy with great success; it understood how to sharpen it not only against the Jewish men of wealth but against all Jews. Anti-Jewish agitation on the part of the Catholic clergy

15. See his *Responsa*, No. 37: "Because the majority are ignorant and can pray even out of a book only with great difficulty . . . therefore all of them pray together with the precentor of the congregation."
16. See Graetz, *Geschichte der Juden*, VIII, 199. For the decree of King Juan II, see also Regné, *Catalogue des actes* . . . , Nos. 1289, 1946, 1953, 2054.
17. *Iggeret Ha-Musar*, p. 48.

was intensified after the dynastic struggle between Alfonso XI's two sons, Pedro and Henry de Trastamara. In the battle for the Castilian throne the Jewish courtiers took a leading role, and their involvement in the palace intrigues and the struggle of the two pretenders had the most melancholy consequences for all of Spanish Jewry. The Jews sided with Pedro because Henry, who was supported by the clerical party, was extremely hostile to them. In the course of the conflict many Jewish communities, among them the largest in Castile, that of Toledo, suffered intensely. When the struggle ended in 1369 with the death of the legitimate heir Pedro, and his brother Henry ascended the throne, the Jews had to pay dearly for having been partisans of the dead king.

A clear picture of the afflictions and terrors that the Jewish populace endured during the "wars of the brothers" is given by a writer of that time, Samuel Ibn Zarza, the author of the well-known commentary to the Torah, *Mekor Hayyim*. In the introduction to his commentary on the legends of the Talmud, *Michlol Yofi*,[18] Ibn Zarza relates:

The year 1368 was a time of trouble for all the communities of Castile and Leon. All the curses of the Biblical list of anathemas were fulfilled among us because of our great sin. In the holy community of Toledo, the ornament and crown of our people, more than ten thousand persons perished during the two months that King Henry besieged the city. Tender-hearted women killed their own children and appeased their hunger with their bodies. The famine was so great that the scrolls of the Torah and all other books and objects of leather were consumed. Even woolen objects were singed on the fire and eaten. Many left the city and surrendered to the enemy. "Better," they said, "to die by the sword than of hunger!". . . Numerous holy communities perished of famine, and many in this time of terror abandoned their people. We were robbed and plundered. We were left naked and bare. We are barely alive, and the son of David [the Messiah] still does not come!"[19]

On the Jewish communities which had suffered so grievously, large assessments were imposed after the war. Furthermore, the

18. The introduction was first published in *Otzar Ha-Safrut*, II, Part 3, pp. 121–23.
19. The terrors of the famine in Toledo in 1368 are also recounted by another contemporary, Menahem Ibn Zerah, in the preface to his *Tzedah La-Derech*. He, too, describes how mothers slaughtered their own children and assuaged their hunger with them: "The holy community of Toledo was so sorely afflicted that they ate the flesh of their sons and daughters, and about eight thousand persons, old and young, died in the period of distress from famine and want."

clerical party, with whose aid the young Henry obtained the crown, exercised its influence with the king to have anti-Jewish decrees promulgated in 1371. These included a prohibition against Jews bearing Christian names, a reconfirmation of the old ordinance requiring them to wear a special badge on their outer garments, and many other restrictions. To incite the mob against them even more, the Catholic clergy, with the consent of the king, forced the Jews to carry on public disputations on religion. The situation of the rabbis was an extremely critical one. They were compelled to fight with bound hands, more accurately, with closed mouths. In these debates they had to take great care not to offend the honor of the Christian religion by so much as a word, lest they enrage the priests and arouse vengeful feelings in the mob. One had to be the cleverest dialectician, expert in the most subtle refinements and sophisticated devices, to be able to dispose of all the foolish questions and crude attacks on Judaism made by the clergy and at the same time not offend or criticize Christianity and its dogmas. In consequence of this situation, a special polemic literature was created. Handbooks teaching battle strategy, the method of conducting religious disputations, appeared.

In 1374 Moses Ha-Kohen of Tordesillas[20] issued his *Ezer Ha-Emunah*, in which he presents, in the form of a debate between a Jew and a Christian,[21] an account of a disputation which he was forced to hold in the city of Avila in a Catholic church where many Christians, Moslems, and the entire Jewish community were assembled. Most interesting is the last (the twenty-eighth) chapter, where various passages of the Gospels are analyzed polemically, and the Catholic custom of confessing to a priest all the sins one has committed is also sharply criticized.[22] The author dispatched his work to the community of Toledo so that its members might utilize it in religious disputations, and along with this strongly admonished the Jewish participants in debate to guard themselves against using overly sharp expressions, for, as he emphasizes, the Christians, after all, have power and can compel the truth to silence.

20. At the time of the dynastic war Moses Ha-Kohen was taken captive and withstood all the trials and ordeals through which his captors sought to force him to convert to Christianity.
21. The debate between the Jew and the Christian is carried on from the third to the twenty-fourth chapter.
22. Manuscript, 104. *Ezer Ha-Emunah* has not been printed. We have utilized a manuscript found in the Asiatic Museum in Leningrad in the Friedland Collection. The manuscript consists of 104 pages. On the title page is written: "*Ezer Ha-Emunah* of Rabbi Moses Ha-Kohen of Tordesillas, dialectics concerning the Christian faith, written in 1374."

Six years later, in 1380, Shemtov Ibn Shaprut of Tudela completed his *Even Bohan*,[23] in which he describes his public disputation with Cardinal Pedro de Luna (later Pope Benedict XIII) on the subject of "original sin" and the question of reward and punishment. As an aid to Jewish disputants, he also translated the first four books of the New Testament into Hebrew and added critical comments. Ibn Shaprut wrote, in addition, a special commentary, *Pardes Rimmonim*,[24] on some legends of the Talmud. In the Talmudic literature, as is known, there are numerous stories written in an altogether fantastic style (e.g., Rabbah bar bar Hana's exaggerations). These legends and miracle stories were eagerly employed by Christian disputants as polemic material, to demonstrate that Judaism is full of absurdities and old wives' tales. Saadiah Gaon in his battle with the Karaites had already taken the position that a faithful Jew is not obliged to give credence to all the legends of the Talmud. Nahmanides also, in his disputation with Fra Paolo (Pablo Christiani), publicly declared that he did not believe in the literal meaning of all the legends.[25] Yehiel of Paris, too, in his disputation with the apostate Nicholas Donin, declared: "The Talmudic legend on which you rely in your attack on the Jewish faith is for us by no means 'a law from Sinai.' Whoever so wishes, believes in it; as for one who does not, no one will interfere with him, and he will not be considered a heretic." Moses of Tordesillas had noted in the introduction to his work that numerous Talmudic legends bear the same character as the parables and words of instruction in *Kalilah Ve-Dimnah;* in others, again, a deeper, concealed meaning doubtless inheres, but the faithful Jew is not obliged to believe in them. Ibn Shaprut takes the same view. He merely attempts to demonstrate in his *Pardes Rimmonim* that in many of the legends of the Talmud, which astonish one with their exaggerations and crude notions, profound philosophical ideas are hidden.

These frequent public disputations, with their bitter attacks on Judaism, intensified hatred of the Jewish populace in the Christian milieu. More restrictions were constantly imposed on the rights of Jews, and new persecutions of them undertaken. After the tragic death of Joseph Pichon, the right to deal with criminal matters was taken away in the name of the king from the Jewish courts.

23. On the different versions of *Even Bohan*, see *Yad Va-Shem Le-Zecher Avraham Zalman Freiduss* (1929), pp. 265–70.
24. This work first appeared in Sabbionetta in 1554 and was reprinted by Eleazar Zweifel in Zhitomir in 1866.
25. See *Milhemet Hovah*, p. 3: "And I answered and said: I do not believe in this legend at all."

In 1385 a decree was issued to the effect that no Jew or Moslem could occupy the position of treasurer at the royal court. The old prohibition of the Church forbidding Jews to live together with Christians was renewed. Clericalism in Spain became ever more influential and its power increased daily. The Catholic priests who formerly had fought only against the overly strong influence of the alien civilization became constantly more demanding and aggressive. They were no longer content with defending Christian culture but sought to annihilate every vestige of the alien cultures. Their slogan became "one kingdom," and they maintained that Christianity alone must rule the entire Spanish land and that all foreign elements, belonging to another race and faithful to another religion, must be ruthlessly destroyed with the sword. But this dream of a unified Catholic Spain conflicted sharply with the important role which the Arabs, and even more the Jews, then played in Christian Spain. The Catholic Church was afraid to proceed with strong measures against the Moslems; these, after all, could avenge themselves on the Christians who lived in Arabic Granada and North Africa. On the other hand, the Church felt free to vent all its fury on the defenseless and powerless Jews. The clergy were no longer content with accusing the Jews of stealing from the royal treasuries and destroying the land; in the name of the faith they demanded that the Jews be either annihilated or compelled to undergo baptism. The priests realized quite well how easy it was to arouse fanaticism and the flame of religious hatred in the Spanish people which, for many years, had carried on such a relentless struggle against an enemy belonging to another faith and suffered under the heavy exactions which their creditors and tax collectors, mainly Jews, wrested from them.

"Death or baptism!"—this slogan of the militant Catholic clergy found an enthusiastic and indefatigable champion in the fanatical, half-crazed priest of Seville, Fernando Martinez. From the pulpit of the church Martinez hurled fire and brimstone at the "enemies of Christ" and preached with great ardor that every pious Christian is under obligation to compel Jews to adopt the Christian faith. Little Jewish children must be taken away from their parents and their souls saved through baptism. Jewish synagogues and houses of study must also be seized and turned into churches. The poisonous seeds which Martinez and his numerous accomplices sowed fell on fertile soil, and greatly magnified within the Christian populace the intense hatred of Jews which had accumulated through generations as a result of religious, political, and economic factors.

The Marranos and the Informer-Apostates

In 1391 the fearful storm which ultimately brought total destruction to the Jewish community in Spain broke. The tragedy began in Seville, where Martinez preached his fanatical sermons. The enraged mob there massacred several thousand Jews. The slaughter in Seville was the first harbinger, the initial spark of the fire that soon broke out and later enveloped the entire land. Most of the other communities in Castile and Aragon had the same horrible end as that of Seville. In Toledo, Cordova, Valencia, and other cities the mob attacked Jewish homes and killed, pillaged, and burned without restraint. More than seventy communities were destroyed at that time. The terrors of the Crusades were repeated. But the Jews of Spain were not able to endure them with the fanatical stubbornness of their brethren in Germany.

The German Jews went the way of martyrdom and sacrificed their lives for the faith of their fathers. Only a few adopted Christianity, and this only ostensibly; as soon as the danger was past, they returned penitently to Judaism. The situation in Spain, however, was different. There also many in the orthodox circles sacrificed themselves. In Toledo, for instance, Rabbi Asher ben Yehiel's great-grandson, Jehudah ben Asher, slaughtered his entire family with his own hands, and afterwards he and his pupils took their own lives.[26] But tens of thousands of Spanish Jews who lived in wealth and prosperity did not stand the test when the sword hung over their necks and saved themselves through baptism.[27]

Among these new Christians, there were many who accepted Christianity only externally, "until the storm would pass," hoping that as soon as the danger was over, they would be able to return to the faith of their fathers. Some of these ostensible Christians in fact eventually succeeded, despite the Church's spies and inquisitors, in escaping from Spain and publicly declaring themselves Jews in other lands. But those who remained in Spain had officially to play the role of pious Christians. Secretly, in hidden rooms, however, they held fast to Judaism and its practices and despised

---

26. See *Yuḥasin* (Filipowski's edition), p. 225; Ḥasdai Crescas' letter in *Shevet Yehudah* (Wiener's edition), p. 129. In a long elegy, in which practically all the communities of Castile and Aragon which suffered in that terrible year are enumerated, the martyred Jehudah ben Asher is also mentioned. This elegy was published in *Letterbode*, VI, 33–37. The massacre at Seville is also lamented in another elegy which was published in *Ginzei Nistarot*, I–II, 56–57. In addition, the destruction of 1391 is also mourned in many other laments and elegies which have been preserved in manuscript.
27. According to certain sources, the number of those Jews who converted in 1391 was close to two hundred thousand.

the cross which had been violently forced upon them. Thus, the unique phenomenon of the people known as *Anusim* or Marranos appeared in Spain. In the struggle against these Jewish Christians the flame of the executioners' pyres soon flared up, and the Inquisition, together with the pious representatives of the Church, covered the land with shame for generations with their bloody deeds and inhuman cruelty.

Not all the *Anusim*, however, dreamed of the opportunity to return to their former faith. Among the Jewish intelligentsia in Spain, there were many who, under the influence of rationalist philosophic ideas, assumed an attitude of indifference to the tradition of their fathers and to religious matters in general. When in 1391 the question was sharply put before them—either martyrdom and death or adopting the Christian faith and peacefully enjoying the pleasures of life—they did not hesitate long before choosing the latter alternative.

"The perfect Torah," laments Solomon Alami,

they [the Jewish rationalists] adorned with philosophic ideas and clothed in Greek garments. . . . They wished to combine the Law of Moses, the man of God, with Greek philosophy and thought they do our Torah great honor when they rob it of its grace and corrupt its beauty, when they make of it merely a ladder on which philosophy can rise. . . . They believe that we owe much more to Aristotle and Plato with their investigations and inquiries than to Moses our teacher and his Torah. . . . Is it, then, surprising that these men asked themselves whether it is worthwhile to sacrifice oneself for the Torah, to suffer the yoke and shame of exile which robs one of the possibility of quietly engaging in philosophical inquiry? On the contrary, only he who liberates himself from the heavy burden, throws off the yoke of exile, and withdraws from the grievously persecuted community, can breathe freely and immerse himself without hindrance in investigation and science.[28]

The moral stature of these converts was not especially high but, as far as knowledge and culture were concerned, they were the cream of the contemporary Jewish intelligentsia. These were writers, artists, scholars, physicians, and statesmen. Thanks to them, Christian Spain all at once obtained a large accession of intellectual energies which it urgently needed. Among these new Christians there were not a few careerists who wished to make of their baptism the magic key that would open to them all the treasures of life. To find favor among their new co-religionists, they took great pains to demonstrate their devotion to the Church

28. *Iggeret Ha-Musar*, pp. 41–42.

The Marranos and the Informer-Apostates

and Christianity. In this endeavor they did not recoil even from denunciations and often informed against the *Anusim*, charging that they were not genuine Christians but secret Jews. Many apostates became informers, slanderers, and fierce enemies of Israel. Various motives contributed to this phenomenon. Some wished to dissimulate their indifference to religious matters through persecution of their erstwhile brethren and the faith of their fathers. Others, with their denunciations of the *Anusim*, desired to rid themselves of some threatening competitor. Still others did so simply because they felt isolated and alienated in the new Christian environment and wanted the whole Jewish community to emulate them and go over to Christianity.

"Among the apostates," relates Rabbi Isaac bar Sheshet,

there are many who at first converted out of necessity but, in time, they have of their own free will denied the Torah, rejected its commandments, and followed alien precepts. But they have not only cast off the yoke of the Torah; they also inform against the unfortunate Jews who live among them, devise slanders against them in order to exterminate them and blot out the name of Israel. The *Anusim* who in their hearts remained loyal to their faith and hoped to free themselves from apostasy as soon as possible are also denounced by these wicked men, who hand them over to the government.[29]

In such converts the Catholic Church found the most desirable collaborators in its battle against Judaism. These were, after all, learned men, well versed in Jewish religious literature. Thus they would appear in disputations, carry on debates with the rabbis, and write calumnious tracts against the "false rabbinic doctrine." The Jewish scholars, naturally, could not remain idle bystanders. They responded to their adversaries with the same weapons—sharp polemic arrows, lampoons, and satirical tracts. The lampoons and polemic writings that were created in the heat of the struggle constitute the most interesting chapter in the Hebrew literature produced by Spanish Jewry at the end of the fourteenth and the beginning of the fifteenth centuries.

29. Rabbi Isaac bar Sheshet, *Responsa*, No. 11.

CHAPTER THREE

Lampoons in Religious Disputations; Joshua Lorki and Profiat Duran

AN apostate of that era who became one of the most rabid enemies of his erstwhile people, the physician Astruc Raimuch (Francisco Dios Carne), addressed a sarcastic letter to his former friend Shealtiel Bonafos in which he mocked the Jewish faith and praised Christianity and its dogmas to the skies. Bonafos replied in a rather gentle and restrained tone, taking care not to offend the Christian religion by so much as a word. But Bonafos' friend, Solomon ben Reuben Bonafed, the only talented Jewish poet in Spain of that time, responded with greater courage to Raimuch's letter.

Solomon Bonafed was a man of high culture. Well versed in philosophy, he was also virtually the first medieval Jewish scholar who drew his knowledge of Aristotle not from Averroes' work but from the Latin translation of Boethius. He was also familiar with the Roman classics and the great Arabic poets, and justly notes that his Muse was raised not merely on the fields of Judah, since "his heart also conquered Latin poetry and not infrequently roamed among the tents of Arabia." Bonafed wrote numerous love songs¹ and also composed, on the model of Horace's *Ars Poetica*, a didactic poem in which he presents the principles of the poetic art. Here he teaches that one must write poetry in clear language, comprehensible even to children, and that the verses must be refined and polished for a long time before being sent out into the world.² Among the Hebrew poets, Solomon Ibn Gabirol had the greatest influence on Bonafed, who frequently attempted to write in the former's style. Living in Saragossa, from which the young Gabirol had once been banished, Bonafed also came into conflict with the local community. The poet poured out his wrath on the "base fools" of Saragossa in a poem³ modeled after Gabirol's well-known "Niḥar Bekori Geroni." But he was not content with this poem alone and composed another lampoon⁴ against the men of Saragossa in which he portrays the community's way of life with caustic sarcasm.

Bonafed was a formidable adversary; his witty sallies struck their mark like well-aimed arrows and his epigrams were ingeniously honed, sharp and venomous:

> It happens not seldom that fools understand
> What great sages cannot grasp.
> Balaam did not notice God's angel,
> While his ass recognized him at once.⁵

To a certain informer who engaged in slanders and denunciations Bonafed dispatched the following epigram:

> From the bee you have obtained only its poison,
> And inflict painful wounds on all;
> But of its sweet honey
> Your poisonous mouth has not taken a single drop.⁶

The catastrophe of 1391 made a great impression on the poet. "In our western land," he laments,

---

1. Some of these were published by Joseph Patai in the Blau *Festschrift*, *Ve-Zot Le-Yehudah* (1926), pp. 220–23.
2. The only manuscript of Bonafed's *diwan* is in the library of Oxford University. Extracts of it were published by A. Kaminka in *Mi-Mizraḥ Umi-Maarav*, II, 109–27, and in the previously mentioned collection, *Ve-Zot Le-Yehudah*, pp. 288–95.
3. Published by Edelmann in *Divrei Ḥefetz* (1853), pp. 20–23; reprinted with a corrected text by Egers in *MGWJ*, 1884, p. 523.
4. Printed in *Otzrot Ḥayyim*, pp. 363–64.
5. See *Literaturblatt des Orients*, 1843, p. 689.
6. See Steinschneider, "Poeten und Polemiker in Nordspanien im 1400," *Hebräische Bibliographie*, XIV, 97.

the sun has set and will appear no more. How can one hope for joyous days when each day brings us new destruction? . . . Silenced is my happy song. The accursed time has embittered it and veiled my harp in sorrow. . . . How can I sing in the pitch-black night when the hope of the coming dawn is lost? . . . Hateful to me is life under the yoke of this cruel time. I am bent under the burden of hatred, oppression and destruction.

Deeply moving is his poem "Re'eh Susim Be-Lev Yam," which he sent to a comrade who had lost his entire fortune in the period of turmoil. He proposes to his friend that together they forsake the noisy regions of life, withdraw as far as possible from the tumult of men, and, on the bosom of the blooming fields, befriended by the birds of the forest, forget the sorrow of life, seek out the hidden mysteries, and quietly enjoy the wondrous elixir of wisdom.[7]

Like Solomon Alami, Bonafed saw in the destruction of 1391 a punishment for the fact that "the faith was snuffed out in numerous hearts and many of the Jewish intelligentsia undermined its foundations with alien ideas."[8] "These ideas," the poet declares, "have fruits like wormwood and their flowers are bitter as gall. They have poisoned hearts and, as in a snare, captured the feet of my friends."[9]

The conversionist letter of the apostate Astruc Raimuch greatly enraged Solomon Bonafed, and he expressed his indignation in a masterly lampoon filled with biting sarcasm and proud sentiment.[10] Bonafed's polemical talent is displayed here in all its brilliance. Cleverly he hurls pointed arrows at his adversary, and with keen irony criticizes the Christian dogmas which Raimuch had portrayed so enthusiastically in his letter. Bonafed cannot understand how it happened that God revealed Himself in human form, offered Himself up for man's sin and shed His innocent blood, and after this sacrifice the world became no better and is now, as before, steeped in shame and sinfulness. You confess your sins so frequently, Bonafed sarcastically writes, and your priests wash you clean like newborn children; thereupon you promptly begin to sin again and do all your shameful deeds. In your case, he sarcastically tells Maestro Astruc Raimuch and his friends, your eyes were suddenly opened and in the pitch blackness you all at once

---

7. *Ve-Zot Le-Yehudah*, p. 200.
8. *Mi-Mizrah Umi-Maarav*, II, 110.
9. *Ibid.*, p. 125.
10. The lampoon was published together with Raimuch's letter in *Kibbutz Vikkuhim* (1844).

saw great light. You ask no questions about your new faith, you accept the wildest notions without inquiry, and even if you are told that left is right and right left, you put on a pious mien and affirm that you believe with perfect faith; but then, of course, you are clever, practical people.

No less interesting is another tract by a contemporary of Bonafed, the open letter which the physician Joshua ben Joseph Ibn Vives Lorki sent to one of the most terrible apostate-missionaries, Solomon Ha-Levi of Burgos (1351–1435), who, after his conversion, adopted the name Pablo de Santa Maria and eventually became bishop in his native city. Well versed in Talmudic literature, Solomon Ha-Levi in his youth maintained a friendly correspondence with the Castilian king's court physician, Meir Alguadez,[11] and with the celebrated Rabbi Isaac bar Sheshet, who, in his *responsa*, is generous in praise of him and extols his wisdom and piety.[12] Solomon was in fact an extremely practical and shrewd man who understood how to display his piety when it could bring him some material benefit. To him glory and worldly pleasures were more precious than all else. When, in the bloodbath of 1391, he did not stand the test and adopted the Catholic faith, it was no secret to anyone that he did so only for the sake of "this world," and that he would know how to exploit his baptism so as to obtain an honored position in the life of the community.[13] Solomon himself, however, asserted that the profound works of Thomas Aquinas had opened his eyes and convinced him that the Christian faith is the only true one. That no one might doubt that he had gone over to Christianity wholeheartedly, he became the grimmest adversary of Judaism and ruthlessly persecuted his former brethren. He was the real instigator of the edict of 1412 which declared Jews pariahs without any rights.[14] Soon after his conversion Solomon Ha-Levi

11. Solomon sent Alguadez his humorous Purim gift "Esa Einai El He-Harim" (published in *Letterbode*, X, 78–84, and also in *Ha-Yekev*, pp. 40–42; reprinted with a corrected text by Abrahams in *JQR*, 1900, pp. 258–63). Graetz' theory that Solomon wrote this jesting piece after his conversion and that he intended to mock Judaism in it is absolutely without foundation.
12. *Responsa*, Nos. 187–92. Isaac bar Sheshet hails Solomon with these terms of praise: "A well of deep living waters, a distinguished scholar, a sage superior to a prophet."
13. Joseph ben Shemtov, when mentioning Solomon's name in his commentary on Profiat Duran's lampoon (of which we shall speak later), deems it necessary to insist: "Pablo did not believe at all in this faith and changed his religion for the sake of glory, wealth, and office."
14. According to this edict, Jews had the right to dwell only in special quarters (*juderías*), surrounded by a wall with a single gate. They

began to circulate lampoons and abusive writings against Judaism to his former acquaintances and friends, among them the court physician of the king of Navarre, Orabuena. This enraged his former disciple, Joshua Lorki, who addressed a remarkable polemic document to him.[15]

Lorki pretends to be a simpleton and begs Solomon to explain to him out of what motives he, his erstwhile teacher, "has changed the orders of creation" and assumed an alien faith. Was it because of a desire for wealth and honor, a yearning for earthly pleasures? Or was it perhaps your philosophical inquiries—he asks—that brought this about? Did you come to see in religious matters pure swindlery and foolishness and therefore choose for yourself the most comfortable way both for the body and the soul, so as to live without fear? Or was it perhaps the great misfortune that broke your spirit? You realized: terrible is our destruction, God has turned His countenance away from us, we have become food for the beasts of the earth and the birds of the heavens. And did you believe that our remembrance was already blotted out from the world?

Lorki pretends to have no doubt that Solomon Ha-Levi adopted Christianity out of genuine conviction. "I saw how you wrote to Orabuena of Navarre that already at the end of the period of the Second Temple the Messiah, the redeemer whom our ancestors awaited, appeared and with his life and death fulfilled everything that the prophets predicted about his revelation." Lorki puts to his former teacher eight questions, whose substance implicitly contradicts the foundations of Christianity. How, he asks in one of these, is the belief that the redeemer has already come to be reconciled with the assurance of the prophets that "in the end of days," when the Messiah will redeem the world, nations will no longer carry on warfare with each other, blood will no longer be shed, and no man will raise his sword against another, but peace and brotherhood will rule the world? Is the world not now steeped in blood perhaps even more than ever before? Does not every new day bring new wars, with massacres crying to the heavens?

---

were forbidden to occupy the post of tax collector, or to engage in credit enterprises, medical practice, optics, and various other professions and trades. Jews were also forbidden to have business partnerships with Christians and to employ Christian servants. They were further prohibited from having their own courts dealing either with civil or criminal matters. In addition Jews were not allowed to bear the honorary title "Don," to carry weapons, to trim their beards, etc.

15. Published in *Divrei Hachamim* (1849), pp. 41–46.

Lorki goes even further and puts before Solomon the following question: Is a truly religious man obliged critically to examine the principles of his faith? Can he rely entirely on the tradition of his fathers, or must he seek independently, on his own account, and decide for himself whether his faith is really the true one or whether perhaps an altogether different religion is the vehicle of divine truth? Apparently, Lorki writes, you have followed the second path, considering it the right one, and have therefore abandoned your old faith. But then a difficult and unanswered question arises: If so, no religious man can abide peacefully in the faith he has inherited from his ancestors; he must always be in doubt whether he may not be living in error, whether perhaps the true faith, the really divine truth, is still not hidden from him. You, Lorki adds with veiled sarcasm, after extensive probing and investigation, have discovered that Christianity is truer than Judaism. But why did you not go further and explore Islam and, indeed, many other religions as well? For it seems possible that not one of the three well-known faiths is the one actually revealed by God but an entirely different one. Perhaps, however, the first way is the right one and, after much balancing of opinions, we must come to the conclusion that every religious man ought to hold fast to that faith which has been hallowed for him through the tradition of his fathers, that each is sanctified and blessed with eternal life by serving God in his own way and faithfully fulfilling the commandments which his religion, the religion of his ancestors, requires of him.[16]

Lorki considers this humanist ethical idea, at which the mentality of medieval Europe did not for a long time arrive, the only logical one. Otherwise, says he, one would have to come to the awkward conclusion that God's judgment is unjust. For how can a man be punished and have the gates of eternal life barred to him for loyally fulfilling his duty, serving God with his whole heart according to the precepts of the faith in which he was raised and which he received by way of tradition from his ancestors? But, again, how is this to be reconciled with the Christian doctrine that only the Church and its servants have the keys to the gates of heaven? How also, he asks Solomon, is what you have done to be explained?

Imagine, Lorki further writes, a Christian believer living in an isolated corner somewhere on a distant island without any notion whatever that there are Moslems or Jews in the world. On other castaway islands live a Moslem and a Jew, each completely iso-

16. *Ibid.*, p. 46.

lated and neither aware that other faiths exist. Each is convinced that there is only one, single, divinely revealed religion, and that is his own, to which he is devoted heart and soul. But it is clear that one of them is mistaken and follows a false path, and that the tradition obtained from his fathers is not the true one. Yet how can one believe that such a genuinely religious, godfearing man will be severely punished for not having recognized the true faith, about which he did not and could not know? How could he repent when the ways of penitence were closed to him? And by what right does the Christian Church declare that whoever does not accept baptism is damned for eternity? Is it to be believed that God, whose essence is justice and righteousness, will condemn millions upon millions of souls to eternal suffering only because they were in error and did not know it?

Solomon Ha-Levi felt compelled to reply to this sharp attack. His response,[17] however, is so pallid and insignificant that it is not worth dwelling on. Characteristic is merely the subscription: "In earlier years, when as a Jew I still did not know the true God, I was called Solomon Ha-Levi, but now that my eyes see Him, I am Pablo of Burgos."

Further details about Joshua Lorki are not known to us. Some scholars believe that Solomon Ha-Levi's opponent is the Joshua Lorki who, after converting to Christianity, adopted the name Maestro Geronimo de Santa Fé[18] and became no less an enemy and persecutor of the Jews than Pablo of Burgos. But it is difficult to believe[19] that such a remarkable and brilliant polemicist, who fought so ardently against apostate-missionaries, should be so quickly transformed into the rabid enemy of Israel, because of whom the famous disputation at Tortosa, which lasted not quite two years (1413–14) and which served as the occasion for com-

17. Published in *Otzar Neḥmad*, II, 5–6.
18. For this reason Jews gave him the insulting title *megaddef* (blasphemer), constructed from the initial letters of his new Christian name.
19. That the scholars who so believe are in fact mistaken and that Joshua Lorki, the author of the tract discussed above, and the apostate Geronimo de Sante Fé were two entirely different persons may be demonstrated by the following point: Joseph ben Shemtov, when speaking in the introduction to his commentary on Duran's lampoon of the various principles employed by the Jewish polemicists, adds: "And this was the path trodden by the scholar Lorki in his disputation, according to what has come down to us from the letter that he wrote on it." These lines were written by Joseph ben Shemtov in 1451. It is extremely difficult to believe that he could have written in such a calm tone about the "scholar Lorki" if the latter had, in fact, later denied his people and come forth as a slanderer and oppressor of the Jews.

pelling thousands of Jews to undergo baptism by force, took place.[20]

Paul of Burgos was attacked by another very talented Jewish polemicist, Profiat Duran (his Jewish name was Isaac ben Moses Ha-Levi), also known as Efodi. Very little is known of his life. It is conjectured that he was a native of Catalonia and educated in Germany.[21] Apparently the style of learning there, which involved devoting oneself exclusively to the Talmud and in which even the Bible was not properly studied, was very uncongenial to him.[22] He soon returned to Spain and there received his further education. He studied philosophy and natural science thoroughly and obtained a good knowledge of Arabic, Latin, and Spanish. After the catastrophe of 1391, Profiat Duran appears among the *Anusim*, the Jews forced to convert to Christianity. He, too, became ostensibly a Christian. The fact that he did not stand firm in the hour of trial and outwardly denied the faith of his fathers caused him great anguish. He felt "the mark of Cain" on his forehead and was mortified by shame and regret. In 1394 he received the news that his good friend, the prominent communal leader Abraham ben Isaac Ha-Levi of Gerona, who suffered much in the turmoils of 1391, had died. Duran promptly sent a condolence letter to the son of the deceased. This letter is an extremely interesting human document in which is reflected very clearly the deep drama which the *Anusim* of Spain carried in their hearts. Duran writes in his eulogy:

Your father is dead. Gone from the world is the chosen and righteous man, who was so beloved and precious to me. But I must conceal my sadness from all; I must hide my tears. For great is God's punishment. He has filled me with the cup of gall and wormwood. The accursed waters of baptism have gone over my head, and my lips are rendered dumb. I am a living corpse who cannot raise his voice.[23]

20. The major role in the forced baptisms at the time of the disputation at Tortosa was played by the fanatical Dominican Vincent Ferrer. With cross in hand he would march at the head of a band of monks from city to city, rush into the synagogues and houses of study, and in a thundering voice demand of the terrified Jews that they convert to Christianity.
21. At the beginning of the second chapter of his *Kelimmat Ha-Goyyim* Duran writes: "I heard this in my youth when I was in many *yeshivot* in Germany." This phrase appears in both of the manuscripts which we have employed. Steinschneider, however, indicates that in the manuscript which he saw the phrase appears as follows: "I heard this from a certain German and from the men of the wisdom of the Kabbalah" (see *Hebräische Bibliographie*, X, 109).
22. See *Maaseh Efod*, p. 25.
23. *Ibid.*, p. 197.

Duran's Al Tehi Ka-Avotecha *and* Kelimmat Ha-Goyyim

Even the contemporary reader does not find it possible to read without emotion the heartfelt lines, suffused with despair and longing, in which this miserable Marrano touches his deep wound. With trembling words he speaks of the *Anusei Ha-Am*, the forced Christians, and from his heart bursts forth the painful question which gives his conscience no rest: Will God forgive the great sin? Will He pardon the miserable men who did not stand the test and under the threat of the sword denied His Torah? Or is the decree that they are lost forever already sealed? But surely God is an *El male rahamim*, a God full of compassion. To Him all hearts are open. He knows that the extremity was great and the persecutions fearful. He will surely forgive and grant mercy to the sorrowful with despairing hearts. But he is also the *El kana ve-nokem*, the jealous and vengeful God! He will pay the bloodthirsty enemy back for the innocent blood they shed, for the great and terrible sufferings they caused.[24]

Profiat Duran, too, insists that for the great national misfortune the leaders of the Jewish people, with their base deeds, their constant intrigues and controversies, bear a large portion of the blame. "These wicked shepherds of the people," he declares, "are responsible for everything!"[25]

Under the impress of the catastrophe he had experienced, Duran wrote a work, *Iggeret Ha-Shemadot*, in which he describes, in chronological order, all the persecutions and oppressions which the Jewish people had lived through from the destruction of the Second Temple to his own time.[26]

In 1396 Duran finally decided to throw off the Christian mask which he so despised and publicly declare himself a Jew. To this end he made arrangements with a friend, also a Marrano, David Bonet Bongoron, to leave Spain and go to Palestine. Duran arranged to meet his friend in one of the harbor cities of Provence, but Bongoron did not come. Instead, he sent a letter stating that Pablo of Burgos had persuaded him to abide in his new faith and advising Duran to do likewise. Enraged, Duran responded to his

---

24. *Ibid.*, p. 195.
25. *Ibid.*, pp. 193–94. In another passage (p. 5) Duran also speaks with great indignation of the Talmudists of his day who endeavored to exploit their learning for selfish purposes and desired the rabbinic office only in order to obtain power and thereby cast fear on the community, rule with a strict hand, and persecute their opponents with bans and excommunications.
26. Graetz was the first to demonstrate that Profiat Duran is the author of *Iggeret Ha-Shemadot* and that this work was utilized by the author of *Shevet Yehudah* and also by the poet Samuel Usque (see his *Geschichte der Juden*, VIII, *Beilage* 1).

former friend in a letter which is rightly regarded as the most brilliant satire in the entire Jewish lampoon literature of the Middle Ages, a masterpiece of irony and sarcasm. Every line reflects the contempt and scorn with which the author regards Bongoron. Duran considers him too petty, spiritually and morally, to enter into argumentation with him. Instead, he assails him with mockery and laughter, and each of his arrows aims not only at the apostate but at his seducer, Pablo of Burgos, as well. *Al Tehi Ka-Avotecha*, "Be not like your fathers"—with these words every section of the masterly letter begins. They also became the title under which Duran's satire passed from generation to generation and entered the history of Jewish literature. "Be not like your fathers," writes Duran, who believed in the one and only God who, with thunder and lightning, commanded, "Thou shalt not make any image." Be not like your fathers, who foolishly believed in God's unity and imagined that this is the real meaning of "Hear, O Israel, the Lord our God, the Lord is one." You realize that they were mistaken; you know the great mystery that one is three and three one. Be not like your fathers, who believed that God is pure spirituality and has no form or bodily image. They were confused and did not know the truth which has been revealed to you and your new teacher—that an innocent virgin was the mother of God and offered herself as a sacrifice. "Be not like your fathers . . ." Under the restrained and polished style, a deep, seething anger is discernible, and every phrase and sentence cuts like a powerful lash.

The court physician and translator of Aristotle's *Ethics* (from Latin into Hebrew), Meir Alguadez, immediately appreciated the biting force of Duran's satire and distributed numerous copies of it.[27] The Catholic clergy at first did not understand the true character of Duran's work and believed the author was serious when he said "Be not like your fathers" and praised the dogmas of Christianity.[28] Later, however, when the true significance of the work was explained to them, they publicly burned it. The illustrious philosopher of that era, Ḥasdai Crescas, in whose home Duran spent some time, was so enchanted with his talent that he requested him to write a special polemic work critically presenting the major principles of the Christian Church in a popular, easily

27. It was first printed in Constantinople in 1554 with a commentary by Joseph ben Shemtov and an introduction by Isaac Akrish; reprinted in Abraham Geiger's *Melo Chofnajim* (because of the censorship, not in all copies) and also in the collection *Kibbutz Vikkuḥim* (1844).
28. Among the Catholic clergy the satire was known under the corrupted title *Alteca Boteca*.

comprehensible form. Duran at once assented, for he had discovered that, under the influence of the missionary sermons, "the plague of heresy had blossomed in many Jewish minds." In 1397[29] he completed his work *Kelimmat Ha-Goyyim*, dedicating it to Crescas.

Testimony to the great impression that the tract made at that time is given by the well-known thinker and polemicist, Joseph ben Shemtov, who declares that he knows of no apologetic work comparable to *Kelimmat Ha-Goyyim*. Duran, who had himself lived through the terrors of 1391 and witnessed the cruel and bloody deeds of such fanatical Christians as Ferdinand Martinez and Vincent Ferrer, speaks with profound hatred and contempt of the "foolish people with the long sword" which believes that men can be brought to paradise through violence and massacres. Hence, Christianity is for him "the shame of the gentiles" (*kelimmat ha-goyyim ve-ḥerpat arelim*).[30]

As a former convert, Duran was quite familiar with Christian religious literature. With the keen eye of the fierce adversary he discloses all its inconsistencies and naive exaggerations, and destroys like a house of cards the clever, hairsplitting subtleties and scholastic theories of the Catholic theologians.[31] At times Duran demonstrates a genuine historical-critical sense; in several of his remarks about the first stages of the development of nascent Christianity there is undoubtedly a kernel of true scientific-historical criticism.

Kelimmat Ha-Goyyim, as we have observed, was dedicated to the profound thinker Ḥasdai Crescas. Duran also dedicated to Crescas' family his other books, his mathematical work on astronomy and reckoning the intercalation of the month, *Ḥeshev Ha-Efod*, and his major work, which was very popular among both

29. This date is given in the supplement of an anonymous copyist from Catalonia. The supplement in question is to be found in many manuscripts of Duran's work. It is also found in the older copy which we utilized. According to a report in *Kiryat Sefer*, VI (1929), 60, J. D. Eisenstein, in his *Otzar Ha-Vikkuḥim* (New York, 1928), published *Kelimmat Ha-Goyyim* along with other polemic works. Unfortunately, we have not had the opportunity to obtain Eisenstein's collection.
30. *Kelimmat Ha-Goyyim*, which was written in an extremely sharp and critical tone, could not be published in Christian Europe. The copyist's supplement and the table of contents were printed by Steinschneider in *Otzrot Ḥayyim*, pp. 364–65. The substance of the tract was presented by M. Zanger in *MGWJ*, III, 320–27. Zanger also noted that Profiat Duran's work was intensively utilized by Simeon Duran in his *Keshet U-Magen*. See also Steinschneider, *Safrut Yisrael*, p. 182.
31. Especially interesting in this respect are Chapters 7 and 10.

Jews and Christians, a philosophical-critical investigation of the Hebrew language entitled *Maaseh Efod* (1403).[32] A special cultural-historical value pertains to the author's lengthy introduction to the latter work, which was greatly admired in earlier times because of its presentation of fifteen principles explaining how to simplify for the memory the *darchei ha-iyyun* (ways of investigation or speculation) and *yediot ha-Torah* (knowledge of the Torah).[33] Of greatest interest to the historian of culture, however, is the clever portrayal that Duran provides in this introduction of various tendencies among the contemporary Jewish intelligentsia.

After the disaster of 1391 Duran, who was schooled in philosophy and was an ardent disciple of Maimonides,[34] became a penitent filled with remorse. He confesses in his introduction that he pursued a false path, and regrets that he did not follow his teachers and guides, and devoted too much time to philosophical inquiry.[35] He realizes, however, that the thirst for Greek philosophy and the natural sciences is strong among many of his contemporaries and that they are therefore in danger of departing from the straight path; they may become ensnared and completely lost. He therefore provides "the remedy for the sickness." He recommends to those who are eager for knowledge that, before embarking on philosophical speculation, they read through the splendid work of the great Jehudah Halevi and become familiar with Halevi's perceptive criticism of Greek philosophy in his *Kuzari*.[36]

Duran speaks of three tendencies which dominated the Jewish intellectuals of his time. The first group are the *baalei hochmat ha-Talmud*, the men of Talmudic knowledge, who are thoroughly persuaded that the only way leading to genuine beatitude and eternal life is to immerse oneself in the sea of the Talmud, to explore its treasures and uncover its hidden riches. Many of these go so far as to look contemptuously on all other sciences. They not only

---

32. Published with some supplements by J. T. Friedlander and Jacob Cohen in 1865.
33. Especially interesting are Principles 7–9, in which the author presents some very acute remarks on the role of rhythm in man's spiritual activity and creation.
34. His commentary to Maimonides' *Guide for the Perplexed* is well known. Duran is convinced that a work such as the *Guide* "has no peer among any people whatsoever."
35. *Maaseh Efod*, 25.
36. As several scholars have noted, Duran wrote comments and explanations to the *Kuzari*. See Renan-Neubauer, *Les Écrivains juifs français*, p. 751.

believe that it is regrettable to waste time on these sciences which, for them, have no value whatever; they are also convinced that whoever occupies himself with Greek philosophy and the natural sciences has hell prepared for him and is doomed to eternal damnation.

The second group are the *mitpalsefim* (philosophizers), who walk the way of the philosophers such as Aristotle and his adherents. They wish to resolve the contradictions between the Torah of Moses and the philosophy of Aristotle, and assert that in order to attain true perfection and virtue, one must above all be proficient in logic and philosophical inquiry and penetrate deeply into the world of ideas which the Greek thinkers created; in these ideas, they believe, the secrets of the Torah are concealed. In this they rely on the great authority of Maimonides and maintain that he agreed with their view, that he also believed that to engage in philosophical investigation is more important than to be concerned with the discussions of Abbaye and Rava in the Talmud. But Duran considers this a great error. Maimonides, he declares, has become for these philosophizers a "stumbling block," simply because they have not correctly understood the eminent scholar's ideas. He endeavors to show that Maimonides was very far from thinking that Aristotle's opinions are more important than God's word and the commandments set down in the sacred Torah.[37]

Duran is convinced that closer to the truth than the "philosophizers" are the "third group," the "men of the wisdom of the Kabbalah" who believe that the profound knowledge hidden in the Torah is transmitted from generation to generation, from Moses and the prophets to later times. This wisdom, which embraces all the divine and wondrous mysteries of God and His angels, of the "work of creation" and everything that fills the space of the world, cannot be attained by way of inquiry. It is a *revelation*, transmitted through tradition. And to grasp it, to understand in full all its marvelous secrets, is, in the view of the men of the Kabbalah, the summit of human bliss. Here man unites with his Creator. But the philosophers are not, with all their investigations and speculations, capable of fathoming these mysteries, for Aristotle and his disciples are far removed from the "God of Israel" and His revelations.

Duran believes that "the Torah, the prophets, and the sayings of the Talmudic sages agree much more with the views of this third group than with those of the *ḥachmei ha-meḥkar* [philosophers]." But he dwells on the weak points of the men of the

37. *Maaseh Efod*, 9.

Kabbalah which Isaac Albalag had already noted: the chain of the sacred tradition was broken under the burden of exile; universal agreement is lacking; the teachers of the Kabbalah have differing opinions on major questions and each declares the other mistaken. Duran therefore concludes that the only sure way that can lead man to eternal beatitude is the divine word, the living and eternal word of the book of books—the Bible. It is not the mysteries of the Torah that are to be explored but the Torah itself: "And thou shalt meditate on it day and night." One must constantly study the sacred books and lovingly carry their words in his heart. The mere reading of the text of the Bible, Duran asserts, itself calls forth "the divine influence" (*shefa elohi*), for the Bible is the holy of holies of the Jewish people. It is their protection and fortress, which has saved them in the long, hard exile. Only the Bible gave them the power to endure all the terrible persecutions visited upon them. Because of it, "God forgives the sins of the Jewish people." But the Bible is intertwined with its language, and Duran is convinced that in the marvelous connection of the divine *thought* with the Biblical, Hebraic *word* a mysterious, incomprehensible power is hidden. No translation is comparable to the Torah in its original language.

Another characteristic feature is interesting: Duran is clearly displeased with, and coldly disposed toward, the Talmud. A number of times he quotes the old sarcastic expression: "It is written in the Bible, 'He hath made me to dwell in dark places' (Psalms 143:3)—this means the Babylonian Talmud." Duran maintains that the Talmud and its commentaries take up too much time, and that men therefore neglect the Bible.[38] He speaks with great bitterness of the German and French Jews who concern themselves exclusively with discussions of the Talmud and are so absorbed in *pilpul* (dialectical hairsplitting) and *novellae* that they remember the Bible only once a week when, on the Sabbath, they read the weekly portion of the Pentateuch "twice in Hebrew and once in the Targum." Duran further suggests that it may be that it is precisely because they forsook the sacred books and thereby weakened the holy bond that God has turned away from them and that the wrath of "banishments, oppressions, and apostasies" has been poured out upon them. Perhaps for the same reason, the great misfortune has struck the Jews of Spain also. We have forgotten His divine books, he suggests, and so God has hidden His face from us. It may be that the communities of Aragon remained at peace and were not struck by the terrible

---

38. *Ibid.*, 14.

Three Tendencies Among the Jewish Intelligentsia

storm because the sacred prayers and the hymns of the Book of Psalms were constantly on their lips. The living word of the Bible was their palladium and protected them in the time of great peril.

Of all this Duran speaks in his introduction, in order to make clear the task he set for himself in his work. Properly to understand the text of the Bible, one must first become thoroughly familiar with the spirit of the language and with the laws governing it. To this end he decided critically to examine the material which his predecessors had collected in this field and adapt it to the general laws of human speech and logical thought, and then present it in a clear form, comprehensible to all.

CHAPTER FOUR

Ḥasdai Crescas and His Era

WE have observed that the tragic events in Spain toward the end of the fourteenth century brought even such lucid and philosophically educated minds as Profiat Duran's to moods of penitence which, in turn, led to the ways of mysticism. Grieved hearts sought consolation and hope in the miraculous and supernatural, and men thirstily fell on the magical spring of the "hidden wisdom." The *Zohar* was widely regarded as a sacred book, created through the holy spirit by the saintly Tanna Rabbi Simeon ben Yoḥai. On the social scene appeared such mystics and miracle-workers as Moses Botarel, who mystified the public, fabricated "ancients" and "saints" who never existed, and gave them out as authors of Kabbalist books which were never written. In his commentary to the *Sefer Yetzirah*, composed in 1409 especially for his friend the Christian scholar Maestro Juan,[1] he cites as convinced adherents of the "hidden wisdom" numerous

---

1. At the end of his introduction to the commentary Botarel writes: "And because I see this man Maestro Juan crowned with the crown of virtue . . . I wished to disclose the secrets of the Torah, for the sages of the Talmud said that a gentile who occupies himself with the Torah is like the High Priest who enters the innermost sanctuary" (quoted according to the manuscript in the first Firkovich Collection, No. 325).

Amoraim, Geonim, the *paytan* Eleazar Kallir, and other great figures, to show that the wisdom of the Kabbalah was esteemed and loved by the Jewish people already in ancient days.

At this time the following statement was even set forth as a motto: "Whoever does not seek God by way of the Kabbalah is of those of little faith. . . . Such a man has no clear conception of whom he serves, and God's specific providence, therefore, does not rest upon him."[2] This idea was expressed by an ardent mystic of that era, Abraham ben Isaac of Granada, in his work *Berit Menuḥah*.[3] The author divided this book of his into twenty-six "ways" (*derachim*), twenty-six being the numerical value of the letters of the Tetragrammaton or Ineffable Name of God. In the introduction Abraham affirms that with the secret of the "holy name," with its letters, crownlets, and vowel points, everything in the world from beginning to end was created, and this secret was transmitted by way of tradition through the generations from the time of Adam to Rabbi Akiba and Rabbi Jehudah Ha-Nasi, who handed it over to Rabbi Simeon ben Yoḥai. Since Rabbi Simeon, however, the secret has been hidden, and only allusions to it were disclosed to a chosen few.

Especially characteristic of that era is a feature that appears very clearly in *Berit Menuḥah*—the hope for speedy redemption, and the conviction that the recently experienced afflictions and persecutions are nothing but the "pangs of the Messiah," the great woes under which a new and glorious era is being born, the era of the long-awaited "end," when God's emissary, Messiah the son of David, will save the world. A contemporary of Abraham ben Isaac, the poet Solomon Dapiera, who himself suffered much from the troubles of the time, concludes most of his lamentations and elegies on a joyous note in which the hope for the approaching redemption is clearly expressed. "Great is the ruin," he writes in one of his elegies,

terror and misfortune on all sides, lamentation and affliction surround us, Edom and Sodom rule over us. We are taken captive, grieved, exiled, bent and bowed. But do not despair, my dearly beloved; soon the faithful watcher will appear and announce, "Arise from your sorrow!" Rise, my loved one, leave the vale of sorrow to enjoy the sweetness of joy. Throw off the slavish robe of exile, appear in the splendid garments of beauty and bliss.[4]

2. *Berit Menuḥah*, p. 16 (we have employed the first edition, printed in Amsterdam in 1648).
3. Only the first ten *derachim* (chapters) of *Berit Menuḥah* were published. The work has also been translated into Italian (see Steinschneider, *MGWJ*, 1898, p. 515).
4. See Dapiera's elegy published by H. Brody in his monograph *Rabbi Shelomoh Dapiera* (1893), pp. 30-35.

Abraham of Granada also offers consolation to his afflicted brethren. "Our great troubles," we read in his book,

should not fill our hearts with despair. Let us not forget that just before the dawn the darkness grows deeper. We see this happening now: the more grievous our exile becomes and the greater injustice waxes in the world, the clearer and stronger is the indication of approaching redemption. Many of the enlightened, when they saw the terrible afflictions, quickly lost hope and forsook the faith of their fathers. We, however, the pious and godfearing, rely on God's grace. We know that He is the God of mercy. He will not abandon the remnant of Joseph. He will stand by us in the great trouble and help us through the pangs of the Messiah.[5]

The fact that the educated and enlightened, the "philosophizers," did not stand the test in the hour of catastrophe and many of them abandoned their people and converted to Christianity completely discredited, in the eyes of the people, not only the "wisdom of Greece," i.e., Greek-Arabic philosophy, but the natural sciences as well. Mystical tendencies became ever stronger, and from three different directions war was declared on rationalist Aristotelianism.

Philosophy and its "heretical" ideas were attacked, first of all, by the most prominent rabbinic authorities of that era. Menaḥem ben Abraham ben Zeraḥ, who himself lived through the terrors of the time of turmoil and with his own eyes saw murderers slaughter all of his family,[6] cries out with great indignation in the introduction to his *Tzedah La-Derech*:

God's holy name has become a mockery and a scorn. Many of the "philosophizers" mock the pious and godfearing who engage in study

---

5. *Berit Menuḥah*, p. 15.
6. Menaḥem's father, who was a native of France, settled in Navarre after the expulsion of 1306. In 1328 a massacre of the Jews there took place. In the slaughter Menaḥem's parents and four of his younger brothers perished. Menaḥem himself, who was then thirteen years old, lay severely wounded among the slain till late at night, when a knight who was an acquaintance of his father saved his life. The young orphan managed to reach Toledo, where he studied with Jehudah, the son of Rabbi Asher ben Yeḥiel. At the time of the struggle between the two brothers, Pedro and Henry de Trastamara, over the Spanish crown, Menaḥem lost his entire fortune. Thanks to the support of the wealthy patron and courtier Samuel Abravanel, he was given the opportunity to complete his collection of Jewish laws *Tzedah La-Derech*, which, according to his own report, was written especially for the Jewish officials and courtiers who, with their constant intercourse with the Christian nobility, were not infrequently compelled to violate certain commandments and customs (for details see the introduction to *Tzedah La-Derech*, first edition, 1567).

of Torah all their days. Why, they ask, do you spend all your time on laws and precepts, discussing what is clean and what unclean, what may be eaten and what may not? You are so concerned about the purity of the body; why do you not think of exalting the soul, liberating it from foolish superstition and barbaric ignorance? Drunk with the accursed, bitter waters which they have drawn from Greek wells, they arrogantly preach their heretical ideas to the people. They, who follow crooked paths and grope in the darkness, think that with their wisdom they have fathomed the secrets of the distant heavens and that all God's deeds are revealed to them. In order to cast off the yoke of the Torah and to fulfill the desires and sinful lusts of their debauched hearts without hindrance, they declare hypocritically that "God desires the heart," that not the deed, observance of the commandments, is important but understanding and knowing. Woe to those who sin and also cause others to sin!

The renowned Rabbi Isaac bar Sheshet (Ribash),[7] whose *responsa* we have quoted a number of times, attacked the "philosophizers" no less sharply. He was a rigorously orthodox scholar who battled against the slightest trace of free thought in the realm of religion. With loud protests he issued forth against the rabbi of Huesca, Ḥayyim Galipappa, charging him with "destroying the fortress of the faith" merely because he permitted combing one's hair on the Sabbath and was also inclined to be somewhat lenient in such matters as the wine of heathens.[8] Himself not unfamiliar with philosophy,[9] Rabbi Isaac was nevertheless antagonistic to the natural sciences, because they "destroy the foundations of the sacred Torah." Their capacity for leading men astray is so great, he insists, that even such eminent scholars as Maimonides and Gersonides left the right path because of them and at times expressed ideas that literally reek of heresy and that "it is forbidden to listen to." Especially in our time, Rabbi Isaac adds, we have seen that many of those who devoted themselves to these sciences cast off the yoke of the Torah and turned away from all the commandments and precepts.[10] We do not need to search and inquire,

---

7. Rabbi Isaac bar Sheshet was born in 1326 and served as a rabbi in Saragossa and Valencia. After the catastrophe of 1391, which he mourns in his elegy "Le-Shod Iri," he fled from Spain and settled in Algiers, where he died in 1408. From the farthest countries Jews applied to him with questions on various religious and social matters, and his *responsa* (numbering 518) are among the most important sources portraying the cultural situation of the Jews in Spain of that era.
8. Rabbi Isaac bar Sheshet, *Responsa*, No. 394.
9. See for example *Responsa*, Nos. 118 and 438–39, on the nature of God's knowledge.
10. *Ibid.*, No. 45.

says the embittered and homeless rabbi; we need, instead, to rely entirely on our sages, even when they say right is left and left right, for they have received by way of tradition "every man from the mouth of another, from Moses our teacher, peace be upon him," the correct interpretation and significance of all the commandments. We cannot and must not rely on the Greek and Arabic sages who merely express their personal views.[11]

With even greater wrath does the enthusiastic mystic Shemtov ben Shemtov, the author of the well-known Kabbalist book *Sefer Ha-Emunot*, issue forth against the rationalists and freethinkers.[12] In the introduction to his work Shemtov complains vehemently of the "philosophizers," charging that among them Judaism receives a philosophical garb and that, according to them, immortality is attained only by the person who occupies himself with "speculative sciences" and sharpens his thought with philosophical inquiries. It is clear, he argues, that the teaching of the Greek philosophers to the effect that only through philosophical inquiry does the soul unite with the "active intellect" really denies belief in reward and punishment. A man may be completely righteous with the noblest of virtues, and his whole life may be a golden chain of good deeds and self-sacrifice, but if he has not immersed himself in *muskalot* or abstract philosophical concepts, "nothing remains of him," and "he is as if he had never been"; his name is forgotten, and no memory of him survives. The wicked man, however, may do all the evil deeds in the world, but as long as this has not prevented him from obtaining scientific knowledge, his intellect is joined with the "active intellect," and he is under the influence of divine providence. "When I penetrated as far as possible into their thoughts," Shemtov declares,

the flame of indignation flared up in me. I realized that this doctrine is a terrible misfortune for the people of Israel and leads to apostasy and atheism. We have seen that when the great catastrophe took place and the wrath of persecutions and apostasies was poured out upon us, our learned men and "experts in investigation" at once denied their faith and became converts. There is no doubt that because of their guilt our communities were destroyed. They, the men of knowledge and the philosophizers, were the first breakers of the fence and repudiated the Torah, and many of the common people followed them. And we have remained desolate and forsaken. As soon as they came to the conclusion that "there is no justice and no judge," that

---

11. *Ibid.*, No. 447.
12. We here follow the first edition of *Sefer Ha-Emunot* published in Ferrara in 1556.

neither good nor evil is recompensed, that only philosophical inquiry is important, that it alone brings about the exercise of providence, they recognized that this can be attained far more easily when one is liberated and can lead a free and calm life, not remaining a slave in exile.[13]

More guilty than all others in this matter, in Shemtov's view, is Maimonides. "His books and position," he declares angrily, "were the cause of the children of Israel denying the God of their fathers."[14] Maimonides' views are far more dangerous than Aristotle's doctrine, for he was a brilliant Torah scholar, a great teacher in Israel, and with his vast authority led many astray.

It is noteworthy that Shemtov ben Shemtov puts forth as Maimonides' complete antithesis the author of the *Kuzari*, Jehudah Halevi. Whoever wishes to serve God, he asserts, must lovingly take up Halevi's book. The profound ideas expressed in it are diametrically opposed to those which the author of the *Guide for the Perplexed* teaches. Shemtov also harshly attacks another Jewish freethinker, Gersonides. "This man," he exclaims angrily, "had the lawlessness to reveal in his book *The Wars Against the Lord* [*Sefer Milḥamot Im Adonai*] such things as the earlier rebels considered it necessary to conceal."[15] Hence Gersonides, for him, is a "vile, wicked man."[16]

If philosophy is for Shemtov ben Shemtov a stumbling block for the Jewish people, he considers the Kabbalah the sacred and only true Torah, the foundation and support of all of Judaism. Like Abraham of Granada, Shemtov is persuaded that the mysteries of the "hidden wisdom" passed by way of tradition from generation to generation, on from Adam, to whom the secrets were first revealed and who wrote them down in the holy Kabbalist book *Raziel*.[17] With great devotion and reverence, this ardent mystic endeavors to report "letter by letter and word by word" the golden chain of the Kabbalist tradition, as "the sages and Geonim of the Talmudic academies in Babylonia" transmitted them. In so doing he bases himself not only on the *Zohar* and on the *Sefer Ha-Bahir*, which he regards as extremely ancient books; he also quotes very frequently, as authorities in the wisdom of the

13. *Sefer Ha-Emunot*, 4a.
14. *Ibid.*, Part II, Chapter 4. Many refused to pardon the ardent mystic for these harsh words against Maimonides. Two generations later the rabbinic writer Moses Alashkar deemed it necessary to attack Shemtov ben Shemtov in his *Hassagot*, in which the author of *Sefer Ha-Emunot* is declared a "liar, forger, and deceiver."
15. *Sefer Ha-Emunot*, IV, Chapter 19.
16. See *He-Ḥalutz*, VII, 93.
17. *Sefer Ha-Emunot*, III, Chapter 2.

Kabbalah, a certain "great scholar named Rav Keshisha,"[18] as well as the Kabbalists Rabbi Moses of Burgos[19] and Rabbi Isaac Ha-Kohen,[20] of whom Isaac Albalag also speaks with admiration.

A typical feature is worth noting here. This Spanish mystic takes special pains to emphasize the important role in the development of the wisdom of the Kabbalah played by the "sages of Germany," the Kabbalists of the Rhine provinces. In this connection he mentions not only Rabbi Jehudah Hasid and Eleazar of Worms, the author of *Rokeah*, but numerous other German mystics whose works have not come down to us. He is convinced that it was precisely these "sages of Germany" who were the faithful bearers of the true "chain of tradition." They obtained the secrets of this wisdom from Babylonia, from "the Geonim of the holy academy in Mata Mehasya [Sura]." From there they also obtained the holy *Sefer Ha-Bahir;* and it is thanks to these "sages of Germany" that this book became known in Provence and Spain as well.[21]

Like Rabbi Isaac bar Sheshet, Shemtov ben Shemtov insists that the chief thing is faith, blind and intense faith that knows of no doubts whatever and that accepts everything handed down from the fathers as pure truth. All the stories of demons and destroyers, of magic, of unclean powers and angels of destruction, of heaven and hell; everything that has passed by way of tradition from generation to generation, from the sacred books, *Sefer Ha-Bahir* and the *Zohar*, on back to Adam, and that is confirmed through the "assent of the multitude" (*be-haskamat ha-hamon*)—all this is sacred and must be believed in with perfect faith.[22] Only through such unquestioning belief can Israel be saved.

18. *Ibid.*, III, Chapter 14.
19. *Ibid.*, V, Chapters 1–2. On the mystic Moses bar Solomon bar Simeon, who was a rabbinic judge in Burgos, we have had until recently only the very scanty information which Shemtov ben Shemtov provided in his *Sefer Ha-Emunot* (Gate V, Chapters 1–2), and Steinschneider in his description of the manuscripts in the Royal Library of Berlin (p. 26). In 1932 the indefatigable Gershom Scholem published an article (*Tarbitz*, Vol. III) entitled "Rabbi Moshe Mi-Burgos Talmido Shel Rabbi Yitzhak," in which he provides for the first time a complete portrait of the world of ideas of this Kabbalist of the thirteenth century (Moses was born c. 1222–55 and died at the beginning of the fourteenth century). In his major work, *Sefer Ammud Ha-Semoli* (a commentary on the ten "left" or "unclean" *sefirot*), which was published by Gershom Scholem, Moses, a faithful disciple of Isaac Ha-Kohen, further develops the purely Gnostic elements in his teacher's system.
20. *Sefer Ha-Emunot*, V, Chapters 9–10.
21. *Ibid.*, III, Chapter 2; VIII, Chapter 9.
22. *Ibid.*, VIII, Chapters 1 and 20; VI, Chapter 8.

It is not necessary, argues Shemtov, to search and inquire, to listen to the learned and knowledgeable; the supreme authority is the "assent of the multitude." Such an adversary was, of course, not especially threatening to the philosophical-rationalist tendency. Shemtov was too old-fashioned, and interest in philosophic questions was still too powerful among the Jews of Spain for them to be satisfied with his teaching. But at the same time, in the philosophical camp itself, there arose a scholar, armed with encyclopedic knowledge, who first had the courage to storm the mighty fortress, revered for so many centuries, which the great Aristotle had constructed. This man, who ruthlessly shook the foundations of the Aristotelian system, which until him was universally considered forever invincible, was Ḥasdai ben Abraham Crescas.

Ḥasdai Crescas[23] was a scion of a very respected and prominent family in Barcelona. His grandfather Ḥasdai ben Jehudah, a distinguished Talmudist, was the teacher of Rabbi Isaac bar Sheshet. Ḥasdai himself, who studied Torah with the celebrated Rabbenu Nissim (Ran), was renowned as one of the greatest Talmudists of his time. The foremost rabbis, among them Isaac bar Sheshet, applied to him in Saragossa, where he lived for a long time, with religious questions. A man of comprehensive knowledge and philosophical education, Crescas occupied an important position at the court of the king of Aragon, James I.[24] The catastrophe of 1391 struck him with special force: his extremely gifted twenty-year-old son perished in Barcelona as a martyr. In a letter sent to the communities of Avignon,[25] Crescas reports the tragic death of his beloved son in tender words: "Many sacrificed themselves for the sake of God's name, among them my only son, a young bridegroom. As an innocent lamb did I offer him up; I accept the judgment and console myself that it is well that the lot fell upon him, and that his portion is sweet and bright." His son's death and the persecutions suffered by the Spanish Jews doubtless had a great influence on Crescas' religious mood. Popular legend portrays the famous rabbi and philosopher as a godly and holy man who could perform miracles and through these "hallow God's

---

23. The year of Ḥasdai's birth is unknown. It has been conjectured that he was born around 1340. He died shortly after 1410.
24. Joseph Yaabetz in his *Or Ha-Ḥayyim* (Chapter 12) writes of his prominent position at the court of Aragon.
25. This "letter" sent by Crescas in Ḥeshvan 1392, in which the horrible details of the massacre that occurred in 1391 are reported, is an extremely important historical document. It was published in *Shevet Yehudah* (Wiener's edition, 1855).

name."[26] His townsman Solomon Dapiera declared in his eulogy at Crescas' death: "Gone from us is the anointed cherub! . . . Departed on account of our sins is the holy ark with the tablets."[27]

Crescas was completely devoted to his people and his faith, and to their defense he dedicated his immense spiritual and intellectual powers. In 1396, the same year that Profiat Duran completed his *Kelimmat Ha-Goyyim*, Crescas published in Spanish his brilliant polemic work *Tratado*,[28] in which the central principles of the Christian faith[29] are sharply criticized. Like his contemporary, the author of *Sefer Ha-Nitzahon*, Crescas exposes the numerous inconsistencies in the accounts of the four Gospel writers. Especially characteristic of the philosopher are the indignant lines in which he polemicizes against the admonition that "whosoever shall smite thee on thy right cheek, turn the other to him also" (Matthew 5:39). Crescas exclaims:

How now, should one voluntarily surrender himself to shame and degradation? This is a sin, a grievous violation of the commandment, "Thou shalt love thy neighbor as thyself." Every man is obliged to treat his own personality with love and reverence. Furthermore, one ought not to bring another man into temptation nor give him the possibility of besmirching himself with injustice and sinning against the image of God that inheres in every man. To cause another to sin is a double sin.

No less sharply does Crescas assail the doctrine of the apostle Paul that God's anger could be assuaged only through the innocently shed blood of His own son. The idea that the death of God's righteous son alone could appease Him and turn His hatred and wrath against sinful men into love seemed to Crescas dreadful

26. See the work of Joseph Yaabetz mentioned above; also Joseph Michael, *Or Ha-Hayyim*, pp. 421-22; I. H. Weiss, *Dor Dor Ve-Doreshav*, V, 139.
27. H. Brody, *Rabbi Shelomoh Dapiera*, p. 28.
28. The original was lost. Only the Hebrew translation entitled *Sefer Bittul Ikkerei Ha-Notzerim*, completed by Joseph ben Shemtov in 1451, has come down to us. Crescas indicates that he composed this work at the wish of some prominent courtiers (apparently Jewish): "Princes and honored men entreated me to compose an essay noting the doubts and disparagements that the observers of the Torah of Moses make against the Christian faith." It is difficult to accept Graetz' theory that Crescas is here speaking of Christian "princes and honored men."
29. The original sin of Adam, the Savior as a sacrifice, the Trinity, God in human form (the Incarnation), the virgin birth, the symbolic benefit of the divine sacrifice (the Holy Eucharist), baptism, Jesus as redeemer or savior, the New Testament, the belief in spirits and demons.

and bizarre. He considered immoral the notion that an innocent victim could be desired and accepted by God as a complete atonement for all the sins to be committed by future, corrupted generations.

Crescas himself witnessed how many in his day converted, repudiated their ancestral faith, and became rabid enemies of their former brethren. In the defection of these "apostates out of spite" and informers, an especially prominent role was played by the leaders of the rationalist-philosophic circles. But Crescas could not be satisfied with the conclusions to which other pious men of his time came: that it was necessary to prohibit all investigation and inquiry, to declare every science heresy and a denial of God deriving from foreign, "poisoned" sources. Not to *forbid* but critically to *illuminate*, not to isolate himself from all foreign ways but courageously to explore them, to disclose their false goals, their stumbling blocks and pitfalls in the light of science—this was the task that the rabbi of Barcelona set himself.

Crescas clearly understood the futility of all the attempts of the compromisers to demonstrate that the Torah of Moses rests on the same foundations as Aristotle's philosophy. The latter, he was convinced, is alien to, and utterly different in nature from, the Jewish faith. He concluded, therefore, that an end must be made, first of all, to the "confusion of borders"; the boundaries separating the religious from the speculative-philosophic realm must be clearly drawn. But successfully to fulfill the task he had set for himself, Crescas ventured an undertaking that in the Middle Ages appeared to be unheard-of arrogance: to present a sharp criticism of Aristotle's absolute authority, to demonstrate that the grand Aristotelian structure, seemingly so solid and so greatly admired by all, is built on extremely weak foundations.

In the introduction to his major work, *Or Adonai*, Crescas writes:

Many of our people have adorned with alien ideas the words of our prophets and the mysteries concealed in them. Even our foremost men, led by the great Maimonides, have enthusiastically done this. With all his profundity and extraordinary knowledge of the Talmud, Maimonides was so enchanted by the world of philosophical ideas that he put forward, in his *Guide for the Perplexed*, many of its altogether weak and ungrounded assumptions as the cornerstones on which the foundations of the Torah rest. While his intention was certainly good, among his followers numerous rebellious slaves appeared who falsified and corrupted the teaching of their master and made heresy and atheism out of God's living word. In the great turmoil and confusion everyone sought to read into the text of the Bible a different meaning. All among us became so dazzled by Greek philosophy that no one had the courage to endeavor critically to illuminate it. Therefore I, whose eyes have been enlightened, have decided to examine the cornerstones on which our Torah is based, to explore the focal point which brings everything into motion, and to do this objectively, without any ulterior motives, seeking nothing but the plain truth.

Crescas considers it necessary to insist that he has no intention of quarreling with Maimonides, whose name is loved and revered by him.[30] "But," he adds,

the truth is more precious to me than everything, and where desecration of the name of God is involved "one does not give honor to the master." And since the major cause of all Maimonides' errors derives from Aristotle's doctrines and assumptions, I have set myself the task of demonstrating to the entire world that these assumptions of the Greek philosopher are false and ungrounded, and that in religious matters only the Torah can give a satisfactory answer and bring light into all obscure questions.

To this end Crescas composed his famous *Or Adonai*. He labored more than five years on this book,[31] which, according to his plan, was to have been merely the theoretical part of a comprehensive work, *Ner Elohim*, a kind of summation of Jewish knowledge like Maimonides' *Mishneh Torah*. Crescas, however, was not destined to write this larger work, for he died shortly after completing *Or Adonai*.[32]

30. Nevertheless, his work provoked great displeasure among the followers of Maimonides, and Crescas deemed it necessary to request his disciple Zerahyah to give a special address on his behalf in order to calm the enraged adherents of Maimonides (see *He-Halutz*, VII, 96–101).
31. According to an addendum at the end of the manuscript utilized by the publisher of the Vienna edition of *Or Adonai*, the work was completed in 1410. Crescas himself, however, indicates that several chapters of his work were already written in 1405 (e.g., Chapter 8 of Maamar Shelishi [Book III]).
32. *Or Adonai* was first printed in Ferrara in 1555 and reprinted in Johannesburg in 1861. In 1860 *Or Adonai* also appeared in Vienna in an edition for which the publisher employed an old manuscript. Unfortunately, the text of *Or Adonai* is seriously corrupted in all editions. As an example, it is sufficient to note the following. In the first edition of Ferrara, at the end of Maamar Sheni (Book II), two columns are erroneously interchanged. The ignorant publishers of the later editions did not notice the error, and in this way a considerable part of the last chapter of Maamar Sheni was inserted into the middle of the introduction to Maamar Shelishi (Book III) without any rational connection. H. Flensberg's very long commentary to Maamar Rishon (Book I) of

Ḥasdai Crescas and His Era

In *Or Adonai* Crescas actually gives considerably more than he promises. At first blush it may appear that the author takes his stand on the orthodox view that one cannot touch a jot or tittle of the sacred tradition and of what the ancients ordained. This, however, is only the external vestment. The orthodox rabbi was also a profound thinker who not only undermined the powerful Aristotelian system but also laid the foundations of a new kind of philosophy and enriched the world of speculative thought with fertile and original ideas which the great genius Baruch Spinoza[33] utilized so successfully later on.

Crescas begins with a critique of Maimonides' dogmas. Already in his introduction (*Hatzaah*), he notes that Maimonides errs in considering the belief in God as the ruler of the world among the *taryag mitzvot* (613 commandments). The very word *mitzvah* (commandment) implies that there is a *metzavveh* (commander) who ordains it. The belief in God the Creator is the foundation stone, the basis and origin of all the commandments and precepts of the Torah. Crescas is also dissatisfied with the thirteen principles of Judaism which Maimonides had propounded.[34] He maintains that his predecessor confused two different kinds of dogmas; together with principles lacking which the faith cannot endure, he also set forth some which are, indeed, extremely important and which the believer is obliged to accept on pain of being called a

---

Or Adonai (Vilna, 1905–7) is also of little use in enabling the reader to penetrate into the profound substance of the often baffling text, which is written in obscure and difficult language. A better fate befell only that part of Maamar Shemi in which the problem of free will is discussed. This section was issued with critical comments and with a German translation by Ph. Bloch (*Die Willensfreiheit von Chasdai Kreskas*, Munich, 1879). Bloch points out, incidentally, that in the manuscript of *Or Adonai* in the Halberstamm Collection there is an interesting addendum by one of Crescas' disciples, in which it is noted that the master used to give lectures on philosophy before a small group. The disciple complains that Crescas would read his lectures in the same terse and difficult-to-understand language as that in which his book is written. In the work of H. A. Wolfson, *Crescas' Critique of Aristotle* (Cambridge, 1929), the text of that part of *Or Adonai* in which Crescas criticizes Aristotle's physics is scientifically illuminated and corrected on the basis of eleven manuscripts.

33. On Crescas' influence on Spinoza, see the interesting work of M. Joel, *Don Chasdai Creskas religionsphilosophische Lehren* (Breslau, 1866). On page 71 he writes: "All the germs forming the most characteristic aspects of Spinoza's system are already to be found in Ḥasdai." See also the same author's *Spinozas Theologisch-Politischer Tractat*, and D. Neumark's article in *He-Atid*, II.
34. *Or Adonai*, Maamar Shelishi, 45a (we quote according to the Johannesburg edition).

heretic, but the rejection of which does not make him a denier of a root principle of Judaism, since the Torah can still exist without them. Proceeding from this standpoint, Crescas divided his work into four books (*maamarim*). The first deals with the fundamental principle which is the cornerstone of every religion, the belief that there is a God. The second considers the basic dogmas of the revealed religion of Judaism. Crescas sets forth only six such dogmas (*ikkarim*), aside from the belief in God and the divinely revealed character of the Torah: (1) God's omniscience; (2) His providence; (3) His omnipotence; (4) prophecy; (5) free will; and (6) the purposefulness of creation. In the third *maamar* the principles which every Jewish believer is in fact obliged to accept, although they cannot be considered fundamental dogmas of the faith, are discussed. In the last are examined the opinions and views which have come down by way of tradition and reason obliges us to accept but which, despite the fact that they have great significance and value, are not essential, and everyone may adopt whatever attitude he pleases toward them.

Maimonides, as we know, was convinced that everything Aristotle had taught in regard to the terrestrial, sublunar world is pure truth, which no one can possibly dispute. Taking this view, he relied, in order to demonstrate through logical argument the existence of the one God who is completely spiritual and free from the slightest trace of matter, on twenty-five propositions of Aristotle's *Physics*. These propositions, Maimonides insisted, "are all firmly proven and no one can have any doubt concerning them."[35] But it was precisely against these "firmly proven" propositions that Crescas issued forth with a shattering critique. With immense brilliance he exposed all the weak aspects of Aristotle's *Physics* and demonstrated how obsolete and scientifically ungrounded its basic assumptions and conceptions were.

The ancient Greek world, it must here be noted, saw in number not a concept created by man's thought but something that is itself a creative substance, an independent being. It must also be borne in mind that numbers, among the ancient Greeks, were not concepts of extension, of spatial relationships, but rather, sharply defined unities that could be touched by the hand and seen by the eye. Every number was a boundary, a division, a closed integer. To conceive the nature of extension non-corporeally, but as distance, as spatiality, was alien to the Greek mentality. Hence, the idea of infinite space, of a universe with boundless distances, was also alien to it.

---

35. *Guide for the Perplexed*, beginning of Part II.

On the Greek notions outlined above Aristotle's *Physics* is based. The Stagirite views the external world as a sharply defined and closed sphere, at whose center is the planet Earth. Aristotle demonstrates through logical argumentation that outside this self-enclosed sphere nothing else can exist. He defines space (which, incidentally, is not clearly distinguished by him from the concept of "volume" and "place") as the boundary between the body which contains or surrounds and that which is contained or surrounded. As for time, this, for him, is the number of motions in regard to "earlier" and "later." Proceeding from these principles, Aristotle arrives at the theory that beyond our sharply delimited universe nothing else can exist, neither space nor time, that empty space without corporeal being is inconceivable, for "nature abhors a vacuum." And this bounded universe must have a single guide or ruler, for Aristotle (and Maimonides after him) was persuaded that an infinite chain of causes and effects is utterly unimaginable.

Step by step Crescas demolishes this Aristotelian structure. Hundreds of years before the famous experiments of the Italian physicist Torricelli, the medieval Jewish thinker demonstrated how groundless are Aristotle's assumptions that a vacuum is an impossibility and that no movement can take place in it.[36] Crescas also shows with great acuteness how full of contradictions Aristotle's doctrine is concerning the "natural place" of each of the elements, such as water, air, and the like, which surround the earth, according to the philosopher's *Physics*, in the form of concentric layers.[37] All this, he points out, derives from the fact that Aristotle had a completely false understanding of space. He erred when he believed that space is the boundary between the body which contains or surrounds and that which is contained or surrounded. True volume or space, says Crescas "is vacuity, emptiness." Every being, every entity in the universe, he maintains, is surrounded by infinite, indivisible, empty space.[38] What with Isaac Albalag was merely an obscure presentiment or feeling is with Ḥasdai Crescas a certainty, a basic principle on which he constructed his conception of the universe. He was the first medieval thinker who broke through the narrow, bounded Aristotelian universe and whose eye envisioned the infinite vastnesses of space.

Crescas also came to the original conclusion that extension is one of the attributes of God. Many of the ancients, he notes,

36. *Or Adonai*, Maamar Rishon, Kelal Sheni, 9a.
37. *Ibid.*, 10.
38. The concept of empty space in the older Hebrew literature is designated by the term *ḥalalo shel olam*, "the hollow of the world."

taking the position that volume and extension give every entity its definite form, designated by the word *makom* (place) the form, i.e., the nature and essence, of the thing.[39] Because God is "the form of everything that exists," because He creates, defines, and limits everything, the sages of the Talmud called God Himself *Ha-Makom* (the Place) and frequently employed the phrase *Baruch Ha-Makom* (Blessed be the Place). God, in their view, was the "place of the universe." This analogy of the Talmudic sages, Crescas observes, is indeed remarkable, for just as emptiness or vacuity permeates the smallest parts of every material substance, so all parts of the universe are permeated with God's radiance, as is said in the Bible: "The whole earth is filled with His glory." God is the foundation of everything that exists.[40]

Crescas also challenges the principle proclaimed by Aristotle that an infinite chain of causes and effects is impossible. He clearly enunciates the idea which became so significant and fruitful in modern science, that what, according to man's understanding, is called an infinite chain undoubtedly can exist.[41] Crescas also rejects Aristotle's view that our world is the only existing world; one can easily imagine, he maintains, that other worlds may also exist. We shall see later how Crescas, proceeding from this idea, a most original one for a thinker of the Middle Ages, arrives at some extremely interesting conclusions. In the meantime, however, we merely note his conclusion that if the *singleness* of the world is not demonstrable, we have no proof that the dynamic power setting it in motion is also a single one.

Thus, step by step, through ingenious dialectic and profound logical analysis, Crescas concludes that the unity or oneness of God is simply not demonstrable in a philosophic-speculative way.[42] In this matter, he declares, "the doors of speculation are closed." Firm, unshakable conviction can be given us only by faith. "The Torah has enlightened the eyes of us, the congregation of believers, and driven out every doubt from our hearts with its declaration: 'Hear, O Israel, the Lord our God, the Lord is one.' "[43]

---

39. Like all other medieval scholars, Crescas believed that the essence and real nature of everything is its form.
40. *Or Adonai*, 10b. This idea is later found in Spinoza: "Extension is an attribute of God, or God is an extended thing" (*Ethics*, Part II, Proposition 2).
41. *Or Adonai*, Maamar Rishon, Kelal Sheni, Chapter 3, 12a.
42. The Arabic thinker Al-Ghazali had come to the same conclusion in his *Tahafut Al Falasifa*. See S. Munk, *Mélanges de philosophie juive et arabe*, p. 376.
43. *Or Adonai*, Maamar Rishon, Kelal Shelishi, Chapter 4.

Crescas proceeds to subject to a sharp critique Maimonides' doctrine that God, who in His essence is unity itself—and this without any trace of corporeality—may in no way be vested with various and diverse attributes. In order not to belong to those who commit the sin of anthropomorphism, Maimonides maintained, one may not represent divinity with any positive attributes whatever, but only with negative ones. Crescas, however, shows that not everything that appears to be various and diverse is actually so, and that the fact that, in our human perception, God's attributes are reflected as various and diverse is no proof that they are also such, rather than a harmonious unity, in their bearer.[44] He cannot understand, furthermore, why one may not employ, in relation to God, such attributes as have in fact no substantive content but are purely conceptual or logical, e.g., eternity, oneness, existence, etc.[45] Moreover, Crescas acutely adds, the negative attributes of which Maimonides speaks are nothing more than dialectical hairsplitting, without any real content. Modern thought recognizes that a total negation is an impossibility, for every negation is simply the result of the comparison that is made between real things that admit of comparison. Only through comparing them does one come to the negative conclusion that *this* is not similar to *that*. Everything surrounding man provides his thought with positive values only; negation can therefore be merely the result of the struggle occurring between these values in human consciousness.[46] Man, for instance, arrives at the conclusion that this or that thing is dark and not light only through comparing it with others which are bright and radiant—this truth was already grasped by our Jewish thinker of the fourteenth century. When we assert that God's knowledge is not limited, that He is not powerless, etc., we actually affirm, Crescas insists, something quite positive; we thereby declare that God is wise, powerful, etc.[47]

In regard to the question of positive divine attributes, Crescas, we thus observe, is entirely in agreement with Gersonides. But when he proceeds to explain what he understands by these attributes, it becomes evident how diametrically opposed are the philosophies of these two most significant Jewish thinkers of the Middle Ages after Maimonides. Gersonides maintains the purely rationalist view of Aristotle, who was convinced that the creative

---

44. *Ibid.*, 17b.
45. *Ibid.*
46. For a discussion of this see A. Potebnya, *Misl I Yazik* (Russian), fourth edition, pp. 178-79.
47. *Or Adonai*, 17b.

power of the universal divine spirit can reveal itself only in the realm of thinking, for every other kind of creation has a goal beyond itself, while the universal spirit, which is the acme of perfection, must have its highest goal in and not outside itself. The thinking of the supreme intelligence cannot be merely potential; it must be a constant and uninterrupted active process. And the object of the divine thought can be nothing but the universal spirit itself, for the value of every thought is measured by its content and essence. The highest value conceivable is possessed only by what is completely perfect, namely, the universal divine spirit itself. The divine thought is therefore, in Aristotle's view, "thinking about the highest level of thinking"; in constant reflection on itself, in investigating its own "I," consists the incomparable bliss of divinity.

Accepting the fundamental Aristotelian idea that intellectual inquiry is the supreme level of creativity and that the greatest and finest pleasure imaginable consists in speculative thought, Gersonides, as we have seen, considered joy or bliss one of the major attributes of God. The divine bliss, in his view, however, transcends the feeling of joy which a common mortal experiences when he delves into the world of thought by as much as the divine thinking incalculably transcends man's thinking and reflection.

Crescas attacks this notion with the weaponry of his keen dialectic. He demonstrates, first of all, that Gersonides, who constantly insists that the deity may not be clothed with any corporeal conceptions, here himself lapses into anthropomorphism and perceives in God attributes that are clearly connected with bodily senses. It is remarkable how acutely the medieval scholar analyzes the difficult problem of sense perception. Quite in the spirit of modern science, Crescas shows that the extent of the pleasure which a person experiences in obtaining a certain item of knowledge or a certain concept is correlated with the exertion of the nerves and the sum of energy expended to attain the knowledge or concept in question. The more difficult it is for us to grasp a scientific problem and the more energy we expend in comprehending it, the greater and more intense is our pleasure. Hence we are indifferent to knowledge we have already obtained long ago and it does not provide us any pleasure. It is clear, Crescas concludes, that one cannot conceive of any analogy between human and divine knowing. For in the case of God there can be no thought of Him, as it were, *obtaining* knowledge, of a transition in Him from ignorance to knowing.[48]

48. *Ibid.*, Maamar Rishon, Kelal Sheni, 19.

Knowing and thinking, Crescas teaches, are not the source of divine bliss. Only love, great and boundless love, is, as it were, the essence of God. Love is the source of all being, of everything that is. Out of His great love God is the *Creator* who unceasingly produces the perfect good, and in this ceaseless process of creating and bestowing the good, which is the symbol of His supreme perfection, lies the source of His infinite bliss; as is written in the Bible, "The Lord will rejoice in His works." The divine bliss, therefore, discloses itself in the consciousness of His great love, which is embodied in the uninterrupted process of creating what is truly good and desirable.[49] This idea that not knowledge but love is the link which unites man with God the Creator, whose essence consists in producing the good and the perfect, is the central theme of Crescas' philosophy. All his assumptions and arguments are connected with it. Hence, it is quite understandable that he is sharply opposed to the view of Maimonides and Gersonides that the special providence resting on the individual is strictly correlated with the degree of his understanding and proficiency in philosophical matters. Providence, Crescas affirms, is a result of God's love for His creatures, and this divine love is not caused by speculative knowledge.[50]

Crescas, moreover, does not agree with Maimonides that from God comes only good but not evil. The latter, in Maimonides' view, has no substantive reality, for just as darkness signifies merely the absence of light, so evil is merely the privation or negation of good. On this matter Crescas adopts the dialectical view of the Kabbalah, which knows of no absolute antitheses and recognizes no sharp distinction between good and evil. Evil is a stage toward good. What man considers evil serves the purpose of the good, for it is sent by providence to promote justice and righteousness, whether it be a punishment for the wicked or a test and warning for the righteous. Divine justice is the symbol of good.[51] Just as the commandments and precepts were given us so that we may demonstrate through them our love for God and thereby attain genuine perfection, so evil, which comes to us as a test, is actually nothing but good, for testing and trials alone provide us with the possibility of manifesting our great love. Furthermore, Crescas adds, only through trials does true love reveal itself, and we then clearly see that our previous love was not genuine love at all.[52]

49. *Ibid.*, 19b.
50. *Ibid.*, Maamar Sheni, Kelal Sheni, 28a.
51. *Ibid.*, 27–28.
52. *Ibid.*, 27b.

Here we suddenly and unexpectedly see in our calm, profound thinker the face, darkened by grievous suffering, of the miserable father who has just lived through a bloody ordeal and offered his only son as an "innocent sacrifice." Through fearful trials alone, Crescas declares, do we disclose our love; it was only after our father Abraham demonstrated that he was prepared to sacrifice his only son out of love for God that the divine voice called to him, "Now I know that you fear God."

In his apologetic work *Tratado* Crescas already speaks of the heavy burden of the legacy of "original sin" pressing down on the human species, which requires redemption. To this thought, in which the influence of the Christian world of ideas is discernible, Crescas returns in his *Or Adonai*. The binding of Isaac, the manifestation of Abraham's great love for God, Crescas declares, atoned for the entire Jewish community and saved it from "original sin." And the commandment of circumcision, the holy covenant of the Jewish people, serves as a symbol of this redemption and atonement.[53]

Proceeding from the assumption that the individual is answerable for the community, that his personal feeling of responsibility is intimately associated with the responsibility of the entire group, Crescas sharply attacks Gersonides' utilitarian rationalism which distinguishes philosophically thinking persons from the common multitude. According to Gersonides, providence is strictly correlated with the intellectual development of the individual. The more closely a man approaches the "active intellect" through his power of philosophic reflection, the more clearly does his mind understand how to remove itself from evil and approach good, and precisely thereby does this person find himself under the protection of *hashgahah peratit* (individual providence). We shall note presently the arguments that Crescas employed against Gersonides' rationalist system in general. Here we pause only at the idea, which he underscored, that the individual cannot free himself from responsibility for the community. It is not possible for the individual to be completely innocent when the community is completely guilty. The world, says Crescas, is judged according to the deeds of the majority, and the individual must be responsible for his generation and for the community in which he lives. In this he perceives the *yosher elohi* (divine justice).[54]

We now come to the most characteristic feature of Crescas' philosophy: his manner of resolving the contradiction between

---

53. *Ibid.*, 28–29.
54. *Ibid.*, 27b.

ascribing free will to man and the fundamental dictum of Talmudic tradition that *"ha-kol tzafui"* (everything is foreseen), that the Master of the universe is omniscient. Gersonides, as we have observed, found no solution to this problem other than to proclaim that God's knowledge does not apply to individual details. The divine knowledge embraces only general phenomena, the laws of the universe as a whole, which include only the most important, the universal, the entire genus or species but not particularities—the accidental, incomplete, and material.[55] A definite limitation of divine omniscience is in fact affirmed here. Crescas sharply rejects Gersonides' view. "Many words but little logic," he declares indignantly; "one need pay no attention to this view."[56] But before stating his own position, he dwells at length on the arguments of the representatives of the two opposing tendencies: (1) those who believe *"she-teva ha-efshar nimtza,"* that there is no predetermined necessity in the world, that every event is nothing more than a "possibility" and is merely *in potentia*, and that man's will is free to choose and can fulfill its decisions without hindrance; and (2) those who are persuaded that *"teva ha-efshar bilti nimtza,"* that everything occurs according to the ineluctable laws of necessity, that all events are merely links in the iron chain of causes and effects.[57]

Crescas in fact inclines toward the second position. He actually denies free will but considers it necessary to insist that this question must be approached with the greatest caution, for such a view openly expressed may be extremely pernicious, inasmuch as many of the common multitude may exploit it to defend the most shameful deeds.

Man, says Crescas, possesses freedom of will to the extent that he can really choose, on his own, one of two completely different, even antithetical, possibilities. But this choice, he insists, is basically not a product of the free, unlimited human will, but a result of definite conditions and circumstances which compel him to take just this decision and not another. The decisions of the human will are free merely insofar as we do not feel any compulsion and necessity, have no consciousness of being coerced. In fact, however, our decisions are not completely free; they are necessitated, the definite consequences of definite causes.[58]

Every event or phenomenon taken in itself, Crescas maintains, is merely an accident, a possibility; but considered as a link in the

55. Gersonides, *Milḥamot Adonai*, Maamar Shelishi, Chapter 4.
56. *Or Adonai*, 23a.
57. *Ibid.*, Maamar Sheni, Kelal Ḥamishi, Chapters 1–2.
58. *Ibid.*, 35a.

chain of causes and effects, it is a necessity.[59] However, there can be no talk of fatalism here. One cannot say: if it is a matter of foreordained decree, for example, that this or that person will become rich, why should he exert himself and expend his powers and energy to acquire a fortune? Or: what sense does it make to observe all the commandments and precepts, if everything occurs according to the iron laws of necessity? One must bear in mind that the expenditure of energy in the first case, and the fulfillment of the commandments and precepts in the second, are themselves necessary links in the chain of phenomena; they are the causes through which this or that result becomes a matter of necessity.[60] With this also falls the argument that if there is no freedom of will, one must deny reward and punishment, since it would be the grossest injustice to punish men for sins they have committed without free choice. Reward and punishment, in Crescas' view, are themselves nothing more than necessary consequences called forth by definite causes. In the case of the first, the cause is the observance of the commandments and the performance of good deeds; in the case of the second, sinful acts and transgressions. To come forward here with arguments about injustice has as much sense as to blame the fire for the "injustice" that it commits in burning the person who has unintentionally come too close to it.[61]

To be sure, Crescas realizes quite well that a very serious objection still remains unanswered. We do, after all, make a sharp distinction between acts done through one's own volition and those committed not out of free will but out of compulsion and necessity. We say that a man is responsible only for the former and not for the latter. But if the first kind of act is distinguished from the second merely by the fact that the person *thinks* that he acts freely but in fact here also acts not out of free will but out of necessity, then there is no distinction to be made between the two kinds of acts, and one can again pose the question: why should there not also be punishment for such deeds as are done not freely but through compulsion? Here also the cause must necessarily call forth the definite result.[62] How, furthermore, is this difficult problem to be resolved: we know by tradition the severe punishment that awaits heretics and sectarians for their false opinions, for their not believing in the Torah or in the resurrection of the dead; but how can there be any talk of punishment for "things

59. *Ibid.*, 35b; cf. 24b.
60. *Ibid.*, Maamar Sheni, Kelal Ḥamishi, Chapter 3.
61. *Ibid.*, 35a.
62. *Ibid.*, Chapter 5 (beginning).

that are in the heart," for questions of belief? It is certainly clear to all that in matters of faith free will is paralyzed; a man cannot compel himself to believe in this or that religious dogma.[63]

Crescas' reply is typical of his religious outlook. We know how highly mysticism in general and the Kabbalah in particular value the moment of emotion, the feeling of religious enthusiasm, the flame of "separation from corporeality." Crescas shares this valuation. God, for him, is pure love, the absolute good. In His infinite love God gives man commandments and precepts to arouse in him the desire to do the good and the right, so that he may become similar, as it were, to Himself. God in His boundless love creates the good, and acts in conformity with it are the source of infinite joy and bliss. To perform good and just deeds, to follow His ways, is what is meant by imitating God—doing good to fulfill His will, to increase His joy and pleasure. The feeling of bliss at such a moment brings a man close to God; the lack of it removes him from God. With iron necessity, as ineluctable consequences of definite causes, we have in the first case what we call reward, and in the second case, punishment. Not the deed itself, whether good or bad, is the chief thing, but the intention (*kavvanah*) associated with it, the emotion, the feeling of pleasure which fills the soul when it is done. Mere performance of a commandment does not mean fulfilling God's will. It is accepted by God only when it is accompanied by enthusiastic intention and is permeated with the sentiment of joy. To be sure, intention and the fire of enthusiasm also do not arise out of man's free, unlimited will; they, too, are a result of a definite sum of closely interwoven causes. But the same is true of reward and punishment; these do not come as recompense for a man's act done out of his free, unlimited will, but as necessary consequences of the world order which is born out of the divine love and in which intentions and strivings that lead one close to God bring reward and opposite strivings that remove one from God bring punishment. But when, in our deeds, the *consciousness* of freedom is absent, when our act is called forth not by our own volition but through compulsion, without any desire and inward flame, there can be no talk either of approaching or removing oneself from God or of the reward and punishment associated therewith.[64]

We may now understand why religious convictions are also associated with reward and punishment. To be sure, in such convictions, there is no free choice. But they are "things that are

63. *Ibid.*, Chapter 5.
64. *Ibid.*, 37a.

in the heart"; they bring into play the deepest soundings of the soul, arouse great enthusiasm, and endow man with the sweet sentiment of bliss and joy. If a man's religious convictions are able to bring his soul closer to God, the source of love and good, then comes reward; but if his religious views are pernicious and only besmirch and lead astray his soul, which is thereby removed from God, then punishment inevitably awaits, just as fire must burn the man who comes into too close contact with it.[65]

Crescas proceeds to deal with the last of the six principles on which, in his view, all of Judaism rests. This is the question of "purpose." In what does the goal and final purpose of the entire "work of creation," of the giving of the Torah, and of man's existence consist? We know, to be sure, that the Torah aims at improving man, bringing him to moral and intellectual perfection. It is concerned with man's physical and spiritual happiness; through fulfilling its commandments and precepts he attains eternal life. But what is the single and unique, the final and supreme, goal? Is it one of those just mentioned or another one altogether?[66] And if another, what is the relationship between it and the other goals which serve merely as preparatory stages to this highest and ultimate goal? It is clear that the most important of the goals listed above is immortality. All agree that physical happiness is merely a forestage. Also, no one will dispute that moral perfection, which purifies the soul of all dross, is more important than material bliss. However, Crescas insists, with regard to the goal of intellectual perfection we must speak at more length, "for at this point some of the sages of our people stumbled."

Crescas here presents a very incisive critique of the rationalists of Maimonides' school, especially Gersonides. The rationalists, he says, proclaim as a firmly established principle the notion that thought alone is the agent of immortality, that only through philosophical inquiry and honing of the mind with abstract concepts (*muskalot*) does one obtain the "acquired intellect" which alone, being without any particle of corporeal admixture, is immortal. And the richer the "acquired intellect" is in philosophical concepts, the greater is its bliss.[67] The precepts and commandments are considered by the rationalists merely means to aid man in obtaining philosophical ideas and conceptions. Those commandments, however, which cannot promote the sharpening of the mind have, in their view, no sense, and it is not worthwhile to

65. *Ibid.*, Chapter 5 (end).
66. *Ibid.*, Maamar Sheni, Kelal Shishi, Chapter 1, 38a.
67. *Ibid.*, 39a.

fulfill them. According to these opinions, Crescas concludes, the righteous and saintly persons who sacrificed themselves for the sake of God's name must not hope for immortality if they did not sharpen their minds and occupy themselves with philosophical inquiry; but base men, informers and slanderers, if they had obtained philosophical enlightenment and thereby attained the "acquired intellect," must necessarily be eternal.[68] For on this view it would be the greatest logical inconsistency that the "acquired intellect," which is immortal because it is free of the slightest trace of matter, should be held responsible and punished for the sins which the bodily part of a man committed while he lived on earth.

Crescas, however, is not content with demonstrating how strongly all this contradicts Jewish tradition and is opposed to the Jewish world outlook. With all the acuteness of his dialectic he also attempts to show how ungrounded these conceptions are from the scientific-philosophical point of view.[69]

According to Gersonides, the "acquired intellect" is completely separated from the "material intellect" as well as from its bearers, the *nefesh ha-margeshet* (sensitive soul) and the *tzurah dimyonit* (power of imagination or representation); these, along with man himself, are mortal. It appears, Crescas remarks, that on this view, in the transitory and mortal is created, in some incomprehensible fashion, something entirely new and extraordinary, something immortal and not ephemeral. This immortal spirit lives its separate life. It gathers, and enriches itself with, ever new general concepts, the so-called universals (*muskalot*); and these are the essence of the immortal soul. In short, that which has just been thought by man, the abstract concept, becomes the thinking spirit itself; it becomes the father and creator of these concepts, and derives the greatest pleasure from acquiring them. We have here a kind of magical circle, a tangle of scholastic spiderwebs.[70]

The rationalists wish to assure us, Crescas further notes, that these abstract concepts are the basis of the principles of our Torah. But if immortality is obtained only through philosophical *muskalot*, and if these alone are the immortal spirit which survives man, what need is there of the whole Torah, with its numerous commandments and precepts? Universal concepts may be found in far greater measure in the works of astronomers, mathematicians, and other learned representatives of abstract thought.[71]

68. *Ibid.*, Maamar Sheni, Kelal Sheni, Chapter 2; cf. *ibid.*, 25a, 39b.
69. *Ibid.*, 39b.
70. *Ibid.*
71. *Ibid.*, 37a.

"Thou Shalt Love the Lord" as Basic Principle

These scholastic notions which the abstract thinking of the philosophers produced, Crescas insists, have misled some of our sages, who did not realize that they thereby undermined the fortress of the Torah and destroyed its fences—and all for the sake of ideas which themselves have no firm foundation.[72] These sages, he further notes, were so powerfully influenced by rationalist ideas that, in their view, even the source of prophecy is the same as that of every science—intellectual perfection.[73] Every prophet must necessarily be a profound thinker, a philosopher: "it is a prerequisite of the prophet that he be a wise man," and "the attainment of prophecy is dependent on perfection of the mind." But, if this be so, the question arises: why did the prophets appear precisely among the Jewish people and not among the Greeks and other nations in whose midst philosophy and the other sciences reached such a high level?[74]

It is obvious, Crescas concludes, that knowledge, intellectual perfection, is, like the fulfillment of the commandments, not the highest, final goal of the divine teaching. Both are merely means to the supreme goal. "Small in extent is this goal but enormous in significance; it belongs both to the realm of knowledge and the realm of practical activity, and it is—*love of God*."[75]

Of the two commandments in the Torah, "Thou shalt know the Lord" and "Thou shalt love the Lord," Crescas considers the second the more important. It is written, "And thou shalt love the Lord thy God with all thy heart"; this is the foundation of the whole Torah, the ultimate goal of man's life. And the essence and purpose of all the commandments and precepts consists in awakening this love in our souls, strengthening the feeling of enthusiasm and attraction toward the Creator. In this love, this fervent feeling, Crecas maintains, lies the source of our immortality.

Employing the traditional terminology, Crescas regards the soul as man's "form," i.e., the content and essence of his being. He declares, "As spiritual substance, it [the soul] is potentially capable of intellectual development but is not yet developed in actuality." As a spiritual entity, the soul cannot be destroyed. But it is not through abstract thinking that it obtains immortality; not thereby does it reveal its true nature and pass from a state of mere potentiality to embodiment in real being. Thought and universal concepts do not constitute the highest level of the soul's perfection or its supreme goal and purpose. Because the source of the

---

72. *Ibid.*, 40a.
73. Crescas here polemicizes mainly against Maimonides and Gersonides.
74. *Or Adonai*, 34a.
75. *Ibid.*, 40a.

highest perfection in the world, God, is the essence of love and goodness, and His boundless love is the cause and dynamic power of His ceaseless activity and creation, the supreme measure of the soul's perfection is its love and its striving for the good. And the higher the degree of the soul's perfection, the stronger is its love, the more passionate its drive toward the primordial source of love.[76]

Crescas turns once again to Gersonides' doctrine of the "acquired intellect," which, for him, is merely sophistical hairsplitting without actual substance. He also regards as "pure sophistry" Gersonides' views to the effect that, as long as a man is alive, and matter prevents him from freely devoting himself to abstract thought and science, his pleasure and joy in intellectual inquiry is imperfect; that only after death does the eternal "acquired intellect" enjoy complete and unhindered bliss; and that the degree of this bliss is the greater and stronger the more universal concepts the "acquired intellect" has obtained in the man's life. Crescas demonstrates in the most incisive fashion that the feeling of joy and bliss in our life is intimately associated with our consciousness that what has been striven for and longed for has been attained. Our sense of joy in obtaining knowledge is a result of our exertion of the will (*hamratzat ha-ratzon*), of the intense desire with which the emotional part of our soul is permeated. In the discharge of the strained energy with which our passage from ignorance to knowledge is associated, in the sudden transition from restless exertion to peaceful satisfaction, lies the source of our sensation of pleasure, just as a melody in music is all the more pleasant to our ears the more varied its tones and the greater the intervals between them. But with the "acquired intellect," as Gersonides and his followers represent it, there can be no possibility of feeling pleasure or joy after death, for they conceive it as being without strivings or desires. For them it is simply abstract thought, without a trace of will or emotion.[77]

Crescas repeatedly insists that he has no intention whatever of denying the important role of inquiry and knowledge. He wishes merely to remind men that these do not constitute the whole of human life, that they are merely the means of awakening and strengthening the love of God. Not understanding, not man's intellect with its abstract thought, give him joy and happiness, the bliss of attained love, but rather desiring and wishing, the fervor of "cleaving to God," the drive of the will.[78] And the greater a

---

76. *Ibid.*, 40–41.
77. *Ibid.*, 41b.
78. *Ibid.*

man's desire, the more ardent the longing of his soul for God, the stronger becomes the bond of love between God and himself; for God is not merely thought and wisdom but also love, creative love, which discloses itself in the ceaseless process of creation, in the love of producing the good.[79] This love is, as it were, God's pleasure and bliss. The good, which is created by God, is thus the source of a twofold bliss: on the part of Him who produces it and on the part of him who receives it.[80] In point of fact, Crescas here adopts the position of the Kabbalah, which declares that, without the cooperation of man, God's grace cannot reveal itself, for "no influence descends from above unless it is preceded by a stimulus from below" and "never is there any awakening of the attribute of mercy from above without an awakening of the heart below." Crescas therefore also underscores, along with the Kabbalists and mystics, the great significance of prayer. In the outpouring of the human heart before its Creator, in the emotion of "cleaving" (*devekut*) with which man unites with God, he attains the supreme degree of joy. In this connection, Crescas adds, the sages of the Talmud are justified in saying that "the Holy One, blessed be He, desires the prayer of the righteous."[81] It is therefore quite understandable that Crescas constantly proclaims that a man's love for God arouses in him not only *shelemut ha-deot* (perfection of opinions), intellectual knowledge, but the moral deed, the fulfilling of ethical commandments. The Torah, he declares, shows the right way of love not only for *mushlamim*, men of great knowledge, but for each individual believer.[82]

In sum, the love of God, of the ultimate degree of absolute good, is the highest goal of the Torah. It is also the only goal, for if there were still another, that would be the more important and higher. Only now does Crescas consider it possible to express his view completely. It is the love of God alone, not reward and the hope of the world to come and heaven, that is the supreme goal. This love "that is not dependent on anything" must be boundless. It must not be associated with any recompense, with any external motives, nor with any other purpose; otherwise, this purpose would be the most precious and beloved.[83] Not without reason, Crescas insists, did the sages of the Talmud affirm that "one hour of repentance and good deeds in this world is more precious than all the life of the world to come."

79. *Ibid.*, 41a. From this idea Spinoza later developed his doctrine of the "intellectual love with which God loves Himself."
80. *Ibid.*, 19b.
81. *Ibid.*
82. *Ibid.*, 42b.
83. *Ibid.*, 42a.

Crescas, however, in no way denies that the world to come and eternal beatitude are the highest and loveliest reward. In this, from his point of view, there is no contradiction whatever. We know that he considers the good created by God a mutual bliss: happy is not only he who receives the good but also He who bestows it. Man's highest and most beautiful goal is indeed boundless love for God, without expectation of any recompense. But as for God, who creates and bestows the good, His bliss consists in the infinite and boundless bestowal of happiness and the ceaseless pouring out of the abundance of His love on men. In this divine purpose man's immortality lies hidden.[84]

Closely associated with the question of the ultimate purpose of the giving of the Torah is Crescas' extremely interesting solution to a further problem: what is the purpose of man and the whole "work of creation"? The customary answer, accepted by all pious men in the Middle Ages, that the world was created for the sake of man so that he might serve God, was already regarded as unsatisfactory by Maimonides. He pointed out that such an answer is really no answer at all, for one can ask further: what purpose does man's service of God really promote? Is God's greatness increased thereby?[85] Maimonides regards the problem as insoluble. We must, he says, declare: So God willed, or so His wisdom decreed. Crecas himself emphasizes that, in regard to this matter, he diverges completely from Maimonides.[86] He was the first and only thinker of the Middle Ages who clearly and sharply maintained that this question concerning purpose and goal has no meaning whatever, for there can be no talk of any goal external to, or transcending, life. The pious rabbi of Saragossa was the first person courageous enough to express the view that the supreme goal of man on earth is nothing other than life itself, the ongoing process of living and striving. Precisely because God is love and the absolute good, He must, by His nature, constantly and uninterruptedly create. Hence the question, for what purpose was the world or man created, makes no sense. The act of creation is itself the ultimate goal, for God's nature is love, and His essence is revealed in what we designate by the concept "the good," i.e., in the endless and unbroken act of creation. As for the creature, he can have no other goal than to love the creative power and to be united with the Creator through the bond of love.[87]

84. *Ibid.*
85. Maimonides, *Guide for the Perplexed*, III:13.
86. *Or Adonai*, Maamar Sheni, Kelal Shishi, Chapter 5. Through an oversight of the editors this passage at the end of Chapter 5 was printed in the middle of the introduction to Maamar Shelishi (see note 32 above).
87. *Ibid.*

Creation of the World as Necessity

Here Crescas' original idea that the "work of creation" is an *act of necessity* appears very clearly. Creation is, for God, a *must*; He cannot do otherwise than create. He must pour out His infinite power, disclose all the vastness of His love, for in so doing His nature or essence consists. Crescas frequently repeats this fundamental idea.[88] He considers it necessary, however, to insist that when he speaks of necessity, he does not intend to deny God's will.[89] His explanation of what he means by the divine "will" is reminiscent of Solomon Ibn Gabirol, for whom the concept of "will" is merged with wisdom or divine understanding. God, in Crescas' view, creates without any compulsion or demand from any cause outside Himself. He embraces with His thought, and comprehends and knows, everything He creates. He is fully aware that everything is produced through and only through Him; and this *thinking* principle, the conscious *agreement* to create, is what is called will.[90]

It should now be obvious why Crescas does not consider *emunat ha-ḥiddush* (belief in temporal creation) one of the essential principles of Judaism. To be sure, he approaches this problem, about which the orthodox theologians and believers raised a stir in their struggle against the rationalists, with exceeding caution. Thoroughly, gradually, and with great incisiveness, as is his way, Crescas expounds the views of Aristotle, of Maimonides, and especially of Gersonides with regard to the question of the creation of the universe. Gersonides, as we have observed, actually denied the traditional Jewish dogma of *creatio ex nihilo*, i.e., the idea that the first cause, which is pure spirituality, created not only form but matter as well. Hence he adopted Plato's view that formless and motionless matter has existed throughout eternity and that only at a specific moment is this matter summoned out of chaos and does it obtain actual existence—and this through motion, i.e., through the form that is born out of the divine thought. Crescas puts into sharp relief the weak side of this view, and shows that it must lead to the grossest inconsistencies. There is and can be only one single, free and independent first cause; but if we make the assumption that a formless matter which is not created by the first cause exists eternally, then we actually concede that there are two "first causes," one with full perfection, and the other its complete antithesis.[91] Crescas notes that whether

---

88. See, e.g., *Or Adonai*, 19b. This idea was later expressed by Spinoza in his statement, "Will cannot be called a free cause, but only a necessary cause" (*Ethics*, Part I, Proposition 32).
89. *Ibid.*, 52a.
90. *Ibid.*, 53a.
91. *Ibid.*, 51b.

matter is eternal or was created in time is not the main issue; the essential point is that matter is not, and cannot be, an independent or self-subsistent first cause. In short, we must arrive, whether we will it or not, at the conclusion that both the spiritual and the material, both form and matter, arise out of a single first cause, and that the spiritual, the form, summons the material into being.[92] And this is what the Biblical statement about "creation out of nothing" means—not that at the time of the "work of creation" the creative act worked on some passive, formless, yet eternal "nothing," but that both form and matter were called forth out of the "nothing," out of non-being, to their real existence through the everlasting and primordial power, the first cause.[93]

Gersonides faithfully followed the Aristotelian system which sharply distinguishes form from matter and regards the former as the complete opposite of the latter. Therefore, as we have seen, he could not give his assent to the idea that the highest level of spirituality, God, could be the creator of His complete antithesis, matter, which is utterly alien to His essence. In regard to this question Crescas, however, adopted the more dialectical position of the Kabbalah, which did not see in matter the total antithesis of spirit. The Kabbalah did not consider matter an independent and separate entity, for in it, too, it perceived sparks of spirituality, though in a less pure form. We have already observed that Crescas considers the concept of space or extension one of the attributes of God. He develops this idea still further, and in this regard also adopts the view of the *Zohar*. According to the *Zohar*, even the *kelipot* (shells) bear the stamp or seal of God, because everything is forged into one unity, everything bears the reflection of light and spirit, and all levels strive and yearn toward each other, for each wishes to be raised and exalted, to attain the summit of perfection. Crescas is also firmly persuaded that the matter created by God cannot be entirely alien to His nature. In all the multiplicity and variety of the creatures there must be, in Crescas' view, an element that unites them and makes them brothers. In both spiritual and material entities there must be something that binds all of them to the absolute unity, the source of all being—God. And this is love, which gives birth to goodness and grace. The entire universe is a revelation of God's nature, the absolute good; and everything bears the stamp of this nature—both spirituality and materiality.[94]

92. *Ibid.*
93. *Ibid.*, 52a.
94. *Ibid.*, 53a.

Infinity of the Universe

Only now does Crescas return to the question regarding the "novelty" or "creation" of the world that he had previously touched upon—whether the world was created in time or whether it is eternal. For Crescas, the Jewish tradition is of course extremely precious, and he knows very well that, according to this tradition, God created the world in time. Yet he must concede that if the "work of creation" is a necessary act, one is forced to the conclusion that it is an eternal one.[95] The "work of creation" is, according to Crescas, a conscious act of the deity, and the Creator's will cannot be inconstant and changeable. If creation is a necessary consequence of the divine nature, if the first cause must create because it cannot do otherwise, then the creative process must be an eternal and uninterrupted one and the flux of time can have no dominion over it.[96] Crescas thus comes to the same conclusion as Isaac Albalag did in his day, namely, that creation is an eternally ongoing process. God as bearer of the absolute good cannot cease to create. "He acts out of His abundance and renews constantly; with conscious will He brings into being everything that exists."

This idea of the eternal and continuous work of creation leads Crescas to extremely original conclusions. Who knows, he asks, whether the world in which we live will endure forever? One can imagine that this world will be destroyed and a new one, a more fitting and so much more perfect a world as living things are more perfect than plants, will arise in its place.[97] Crescas nowhere mentions Isaac Albalag. It is possible that he was not familiar with his work. On the other hand, however, he refers to Jehudah Halevi[98] when he mentions the famous Talmudic legend given in the name of Rabbi Abbahu to the effect that our world was not the first, for "God created worlds and destroyed them, created other worlds and again destroyed these." Jehudah Halevi, Crescas emphasizes, noted that this legend is not at all incompatible with the Biblical account of creation, for the Torah begins only with the moment when the world in which *human* life began was brought into being.[99]

95. *Ibid.*, 65a.
96. *Ibid.*, 52a.
97. *Ibid.*, 53a.
98. *Kuzari*, I:67.
99. It is quite characteristic that Maimonides, as a faithful adherent of the Aristotelian system, regarded this Talmudic legend with utter contempt and declared the idea of the destruction and creation of new worlds "indecent" and "ugly" (*Guide for the Perplexed*, II:30). David Kaufmann conjectured (*MGWJ*, 1884, pp. 208–14) that the passage in the *Kuzari* quoted by Crescas was corrupted by the translator and that

But if our world is a result of God's infinite goodness, how can one assert that the divine power of creation is limited to it? It is more credible that, along with our world, there are in the infinite vastnesses of the universe countless very different ones.[100]

So this profound medieval thinker penetrated into the secrets of the new world, the world of novel conceptions and ideas which the geniuses of a later time, Copernicus and Kepler, revealed.

---

in the Arabic original the text in question had a completely different meaning. This conjecture, however, is not confirmed by the new scientific edition of the *Kuzari* which appeared under the editorship of Zifronovitz (Warsaw, 1911), who again compared the Hebrew translation with the Arabic text.

100. *Or Adonai*, 66a.

CHAPTER FIVE

Simeon Duran and Joseph Albo

BEYOND all doubt, Ḥasdai Crescas, who laid the foundations of a new philosophical world view, is one of the most original and significant thinkers of medieval Europe. But he was too far in advance of his time; hence, in his own day his ideas found little response. Only centuries later did a descendant of the Spanish exiles, the brilliant Baruch Spinoza, successfully employ the profound ideas of the half-forgotten medieval thinker in constructing his monumental philosophical system. For his own time Crescas' significance consisted mainly in the fact that, with the power of his philosophical dialectic, he shook the ancient Aristotelian structure. The boundless faith in Aristotle's philosophical and scientific assumptions, which had prevailed for centuries, was stripped of its force. Thereby the struggle of Jewish tradition against rationalist philosophy also gradually lost most of its impetus as well as its bitterness. The majority of the Jewish scholars who appeared after Crescas were no longer either Aristotelians or anti-Aristotelians but merely philosophically educated theologians who set themselves one definite goal: to defend Judaism in the face of the onslaughts of its adversaries, the Catholic clergy and the apostates from their own midst. These scholars were no longer concerned with making peace between faith and rationalist philosophy. Their task was to bring into systematic order the foundations of Jewish doctrine, to establish on logical grounds the principles of the structure called ḥochmat ha-yahadut, the "wisdom" or "science" of Judaism.

The most significant of these learned theologians was doubtless Crecas' younger contemporary, the celebrated rabbi of that era Simeon bar Tzemaḥ Duran (Rashbatz).¹ Simeon was the scion of a prominent family which had emigrated from Provence and settled in Spain. Born in 1361, he spent his youth on the island of Majorca, which belonged at that time to the kingdom of Aragon. Besides Talmud, the young Duran studied logic, philosophy, mathematics, and astronomy.² He also studied medicine, and for a period was engaged in medical practice³ in Majorca and later in Aragon, where he became personally acquainted with Crescas.⁴ In the catastrophe of 1391 Duran lost his entire fortune but managed to save his life.⁵ Together with many other refugees he settled in Algeria, and after Rabbi Isaac bar Sheshet died in 1408 the community there elected him its chief rabbi.

While still a young man Duran attained high renown in the rabbinic world, and after the death of Isaac bar Sheshet was universally recognized as the foremost Talmudic authority of his day. From everywhere Jews applied to him with religious as well as social questions, and his three volumes of *responsa* are a genuine treasure trove for all interested in the cultural history of the Spanish and North African Jewish communities of the first half of the fifteenth century.⁶

This distinguished Torah scholar was also well versed in Jewish and Arabic philosophy. But it was not philosophic questions that engaged his mind and spirit. He was, above all, a theologian, for whom the divinely revealed Torah needed no authorization whatever from philosophy. For him the foundations of the Jewish faith were strong enough not to require any external support. In Duran's view, philosophy can contribute only to clarifying re-

1. On Rabbi Simeon's life and work see H. Jaulus, "Rabbi Simeon bar Tzemaḥ Duran," *MGWJ*, 1874–75, and J. Guttmann, "Die Stellung des Simeon bar Tzemaḥ Duran in der Geschichte der jüdischen Religionsphilosophie," *MGWJ*, 1908–9.
2. See Duran's *Responsa*, Part II, No. 52.
3. Duran mentions his medical practice a number of times. See, e.g., his *Magen Avot*, Part IV, 62a (Jellinek's edition of 1863).
4. See his *Responsa*, Part III, No. 30.
5. See *Magen Avot*, Part IV, 62a. Echoes of the great catastrophe are also heard in Duran's *kinot* or elegies (see Zunz, *Literaturgeschichte*, p. 521). Duran was in general quite proficient in the technique of composing verses. Several of his letters of friendship written in verse have come down to us (published in *Tzofnat Pa'aneaḥ*, pp. 20–32, and *Kovetz Al Yad*, VII [1896]). See also Kaufmann's notice in *MGWJ*, 1897. On Duran's *teḥinnot*, see *Literaturblatt des Orients*, 1844, p. 451.
6. Duran died in 1444. On his Talmudic works, see I. H. Weiss, *Dor Dor Ve-Doreshav*, V, 184–98.

ligious problems and to sharpening the mind and polishing its thought. Himself a practicing physician and proficient in the natural sciences, Duran insists that "one must remain faithful to tradition but also not refrain from inquiry." "Man," he declares,

> was created by God as a creature of intellect, and he therefore has the obligation to investigate all things with his thought. He ought not to be like one who has his own eyes but keeps them closed and relies on the competence of his guide. Our Torah has not commanded us to proceed in this fashion; it does not forbid the way of inquiry.[7]

Elsewhere Duran says, "Let no one be suspicious of the fact that, along with verses from Holy Scripture, I also introduce opinions of the sages of the world. In this there is no guilt whatever, for the duty of every understanding person is to recognize the truth, taking no account of who its author may be."[8] However, he also deems it necessary to insist that among the *baalei ha-meḥkar* (philosophers, or investigators) the truth is mingled with many false ideas which lead to doubts, for man's mind is, after all, extremely limited, and "the philosophers are as far removed from the prophet as speechless creatures are from man who is endowed with the word." Duran quotes with approbation the Arabic thinker Al-Ghazali, who regarded faith as superior to philosophy and believed that the secret of the holy spirit can be attained only by the prophet, and that just as a child cannot understand the speech of an adult, so the philosopher cannot comprehend what God reveals to the prophet through the holy spirit.

Duran speaks indignantly of the philosophizers who believe only in what the mind obliges and reject what cannot be demonstrated through logical argumentation.[9] For him it is obvious that Jehudah Halevi is right in asking, "What has the God of Abraham to do with the God of Aristotle?,"[10] for "the Torah that is from heaven revealed numerous divine mysteries that the human intellect cannot attain by mere inquiry." These mysteries which man's mind cannot grasp lie hidden in the letters of the Ineffable Name of God as well as the other divine names, and the key to them was transmitted generation after generation from the prophets to the men of the Kabbalah.[11] Duran has no doubt that the author of the *Zohar* is the saintly Tanna, Rabbi Simeon ben Yoḥai,[12] and that

---

7. *Ohev Mishpat*, Chapter 6, 11a.
8. The introduction to *Magen Avot*.
9. *Magen Avot*, Part II, Chapter 3, 22a.
10. *Ibid.*, 4.
11. *Ibid.*, 30a.
12. See, e.g., his *Responsa*, II, No. 128; III, No. 20.

the Kabbalah is the profoundest science, to which no other is comparable. The wisdom of the Kabbalah, he declares enthusiastically, is the only true wisdom. Pure and peerless, it is the wisdom of our prophets. It alone brings man close to God. It is the pride and glory of mankind. It discloses the profound mysteries of the "work of creation," and through "combinations of letters"[13] it casts light on the marvelous ways of the "work of the divine chariot or throne." Compared to it, all other wisdoms are merely preliminary; it is the mistress, and they are its servants.[14]

As a renowned Talmudist and expert in philosophy, Duran speaks with deep respect of Maimonides. He considers him great, however, only as a legal codifier and thinker, and refuses to recognize his authority in questions of religious ethics. In this realm, in "matters of the heart" (*devarim she-balev*), in questions of the inner experiences of the soul, where flaming enthusiasm, burning hopes, and tender dreams are involved, Duran applies not to Maimonides but to men of great ecstasy and passionate sentiment—the mystics and Kabbalists.

Like Profiat Duran, Simeon bar Tzemah Duran turns very frequently to the author of the *Kuzari*, Jehudah Halevi,[15] and even more frequently to the masters of the Kabbalah, chiefly Nahmanides, whom he calls the angel of God.[16] It is on the authority of Nahmanides that he relies when he speaks of the advent of the Messiah,[17] transmigration of the soul,[18] and similar matters. He can in no way assent to the view of Maimonides and Gersonides that the measure of divine providence over a person is correlated with the level of his perfection in dealing with philosophical questions and that God, as it were, turns His countenance away not only from men who are wicked and stained with sin but also from those who have not endeavored to sharpen their minds and attain as many abstract ideas (*muskalot*)[19] as possible. Duran finds Maimonides' discussion of this matter "obscure and incomprehensible," and speaks with even greater dissatisfaction of Gersonides' philosophical system and his theories about the "acquired intellect."

13. On the mysteries of "combinations of letters" see his *Responsa*, III, Nos. 54, 55, 56, and many others.
14. *Responsa*, II, No. 52.
15. On the subject of Jehudah Halevi's influence on Simeon Duran, see Guttmann's previously cited work, *MGWJ*, 1908, pp. 671–72.
16. *Magen Avot*, Part III, 88b.
17. *Ibid.*, 88–92.
18. *Ibid.* See also Duran's *Responsa*, II, No. 1, and *Magen Avot*, Part III, 83–84.
19. *Ohev Mishpat*, Chapter 18, 26a.

In this connection Duran utilizes the acute arguments of Crescas,[20] but without mentioning him by name. Apparently he was not a disciple of Crescas. In the roster of his fourteen works which he put together as an eighty-year-old,[21] he indicates that in 1439 he wrote a polemical work, *Or Ha-Hayyim*, directed against Crescas' *Or Adonai*. A year later he wrote two other brief works on the same theme. These have not come down to us, but there is no doubt that in them Duran polemicized particularly against those ideas in *Or Adonai* through which Crescas appears not as a theologian but as a free and independent thinker, seeking new paths. Duran, however, is quite far from the fanatical Shemtov ben Shemtov, who branded Crescas' ideas as pernicious heresies. Here we encounter the most interesting aspect of Duran's outlook, his attitude toward dogmatics, the *ikkarim* (principles) of Judaism.

In the extensive introduction to his commentary on the Book of Job,[22] Duran criticizes, as does Crescas in his *Or Adonai*, Maimonides' formulation of the thirteen principles of Jewish faith. Among the dogmas of Judaism Duran distinguishes the fundamental principles that he calls *avot* (fathers) from the so-called *toledot* (results or conclusions), which are merely logical consequences of the *avot*. If one counts both groups together, then their number, in Duran's view, is far more than thirteen. But the basic principles, the *avot* or sources of all the rest, are only three: (1) the existence of God; (2) the divine revelation of the Torah; and (3) belief in reward and punishment. But it is not about the *number* of the fundamental dogmas that the controversy between Duran and Maimonides revolves. Duran chiefly attacks the notion that one who does not acknowledge any of Maimonides' thirteen principles is a heretic and an atheist.

We know, Duran notes, that among the sages of the Talmud there were those who denied the coming of the Messiah.[23] Were they therefore accused of heresy? They were not, nor were those who declared, in total contradiction to ancient Jewish tradition, that the world is eternal or that before our world many other worlds were created and destroyed by God.[24] One cannot argue,

20. *Magen Avot*, 82, 86.
21. This list is printed at the end of his *Responsa* (Amsterdam edition, 1734).
22. This commentary, entitled *Ohev Mishpat*, was composed by Duran in 1405. It was printed in Venice in 1590.
23. Duran here refers to the statement of Hillel II: "Israel has no [future] Messiah, for it already enjoyed him in the days of Hezekiah, king of Judah" (*Sanhedrin*, 98a).
24. *Ohev Mishpat*, Chapter 9, 14-15.

Duran holds, that whoever rejects the creation of the world also denies miracles. "The Torah does not oblige us to believe in false opinions."[25] If we concern ourselves with the problem of "the work of creation," we must seek truth alone and take no cognizance of extraneous motives.[26] And if, indeed, it be demonstrated through solid arguments that the world is eternal, then we shall interpret the relevant passages in the Torah accordingly, as we do in explaining those places in which God is spoken of in overly corporeal terms.[27] Duran finds this kind of interpretation of the Biblical text perfectly justifiable.

Duran's view appears in its full logical power only when he poses the question, Who is a heretic and an atheist, and who is merely mistaken or confused? His reply is highly remarkable for a pious medieval rabbi. A heretic, in Duran's view, is only one who *deliberately* "cuts down the plants" and declares war against the Jewish faith, as, for instance, Elisha ben Abuyah, who publicly preached belief in "two powers" and realized quite well, in doing so, that he thereby undermined the chief foundation of the Torah which proclaims that "the Lord our God, the Lord is one." But it is otherwise with thinkers who stand firmly on the ground of Judaism. They seek truth only and do not even consider, no matter at what conclusions they arrive, that the truth they attain may be incompatible with the divine words of the Torah. They are completely persuaded that the meaning of the Torah is entirely congruent with their truth, that the meaning must be so and cannot be otherwise. It may in fact be that these seekers are mistaken, that their conclusions are false, that their views are utterly inconsistent with the tradition. But they believe in the truth of the living word of the sacred Torah, and thus they are not heretics and atheists. May God protect us, Duran exclaims, against branding as apostates those who are in error and do not believe in the creation of the world or who think that the prophecy concerning the "days of the Messiah" was already fulfilled in the time of King Hezekiah. And we cannot, and may not, charge Maimonides with heresy for thinking that the story of Balaam and his ass is merely a parable, or Gersonides for believing in the eternity of matter. Furthermore, we certainly cannot agree with Maimonides when he brands as atheists those who represent God as having corporeal attributes. To be sure, these people are mistaken, but they are not atheists or heretics, for they are firmly convinced

---

25. *Ibid.*, 15.
26. *Magen Avot*, Part III, 93b.
27. *Ohev Mishpat*, 15.

Joseph Albo and His Ikkarim

that they remain loyal to the Jewish faith and abide under its roof.[28]

These views, which Duran expresses in the introduction to his *Ohev Mishpat*, were developed further in his major work, *Magen Avot*,[29] in which he set himself a double task: first, to serve as a champion of Judaism and defend it against the slanders of its enemies, and second, to provide his own people a clear and purified understanding, in popular form, of the basic principles of the Jewish religious outlook. In consonance with Duran's teaching concerning the three basic principles of Judaism, his work is divided into three parts.[30] The first, entitled *Ḥelek Eloha Mi-Maal*, deals with the prime foundation, God, and the four *toledot* or "conclusions" associated with it: (1) the reality of God; (2) His unity; (3) His eternity; and (4) His attributes. The second part, which bears the subtitle *Ḥelek Shosenu* and discusses the dogma of the Torah as divinely revealed, has a purely apologetic character. The author here argues against the Karaites as well as against Christian and Moslem theologians. He polemicizes especially against the view of the Christian theologians that once the Gospel came into being Judaism lost its validity.[31] The third and largest part, *Ḥelek Yaakov*, discusses, as "conclusions" associated with the doctrine of reward and punishment, the problems of (1) God's omniscience, (2) divine providence, (3) the coming of the Messiah, and (4) the resurrection of the dead.

Duran hoped that his *Magen Avot* would become a popular book, but this expectation was not fulfilled. His work was soon displaced by another apologetic book which appeared immediately after it and became one of the most beloved and widely read works among Jews. This is the *Sefer Ha-Ikkarim* of Ḥasdai Crescas' pupil Joseph Albo.[32]

28. *Ohev Mishpat*, Chapter 91, 14–15.
29. Composed in 1423–25 and printed in Leghorn in 1785.
30. The fourth part, a commentary on *Pirkei Avot*, is in fact a separate composition, written in a tender, heartfelt tone and filled with moral instruction.
31. Chapter 4 of Part II, where Duran sharply criticizes Christian doctrine, was banned by the censor and is missing in the Leghorn edition. Duran's son, Solomon, inserted the chapter under a special title *Keshet U-Magen* in his work *Milḥemet Mitzvah*. It was also later published in the polemic collection *Milḥemet Ḥovah*, pp. 38–60. The part of Duran's work in which he polemicizes against the Moslem theologians was published by Steinschneider under the title *Setirat Emunat Ha-Yishmaelim* in *Otzar Tov*, 1881, pp. 1–35. The German translation, *Islam und Judenthum*, was published in *Magazin* . . . , 1880.
32. On Albo's life we have very scanty information. It is known only that he was born in Monreal in Aragon and that as a young man he partici-

Not only men but books as well have a unique fate, and the ways of fate are extremely strange. Hasdai Crescas' profound and monumental work was printed only once, in 1556, and three hundred years elapsed before a new edition appeared. In the course of these centuries the author of *Or Adonai* was so thoroughly forgotten that even such an outstanding nineteenth-century scholar in Jewish philosophy as Solomon Munk does not mention Crescas' name in his historical work.[33] Simeon Duran was renowned in later generations as a great Talmudist, but his religious-philosophical works were almost entirely forgotten. Quite different was the fate of Joseph Albo's *Ikkarim*. One of the first Jewish books to be printed, it was afterwards reissued numerous times. Generation after generation was nourished on it. Numerous commentaries were written on it,[34] and many songs of praise sung over it.[35] It was translated into various languages, and there was even one scholar (S. Back) who enthusiastically declared Joseph Albo to be "the first Jewish thinker who had the courage to effect a compromise between religion and philosophy and to show how similar to each other they are."[36]

All this occurred despite the fact that, already at the end of the fifteenth century, Jacob Ibn Habib, the author of the universally known *En Yaakov*, publicly accused the author of *Sefer Ha-Ikkarim* of plagiarism, showing with cogent arguments that Albo employed his teacher's work *Or Adonai* very extensively and nowhere even mentions Crescas' name.[37] That Ibn Habib's charge is well founded was demonstrated in modern times by M. Joel[38] and afterwards by H. Flensberg in his commentary to *Or Adonai*.[39] The same conclusion emerges when one compares *Sefer Ha-Ikkarim* with Simeon Duran's work. Earlier H. Jaulus[40] and then J. Guttmann[41] showed in detail how in the most important

---

    pated in the historic disputation at Tortosa (1413-14). He completed his work in 1428 in Oria, where he served as a preacher. According to some sources, he died in 1444.

33. S. Munk, *Mélanges de philosophie juive et arabe*, pp. 461–511.
34. By Jacob ben Koppelman in 1584, Gedaliah Lipschitz in 1761, and others.
35. E.g., by Jehudah Aryeh (Leo) de Modena in Gedaliah Lipschitz' edition.
36. See the *Russian-Jewish Encyclopedia*, II, 117.
37. See M. Joel, *Don Chasdai Creskas' religionsphilosophische Lehren* (Breslau, 1866), p. 78.
38. *Ibid.*, pp. 76–78.
39. *Otzar Hayyim* (Vilna, 1905-7), p. 22.
40. *MGWJ*, 1874, pp. 457–63.
41. *MGWJ*, 1909, pp. 58–60, 67–69.

questions, those forming the cornerstones of his entire work (the three basic principles of the faith, reward and punishment, etc.), Albo utilizes the work of Duran, in places verbatim, and indeed always without quoting him and nowhere even mentioning his name.[42] Albo also frequently stumbles and falls. The arguments and views that he introduces on his own are utterly inconsistent with the basic ideas which he drew from others and gives out as his own. For example, he repeats practically verbatim[43] Simeon Duran's brilliant passage in which the latter explains who may be considered an atheist and heretic and who not. Further on, however, Albo forgets this passage and lists[44] six *emunot* (beliefs) which do not even belong to the *ikkarim* (principles) of Judaism but each of which he declares it obligatory for every Jew to believe, on pain of being considered a "heretic" for whom "there is no share in the world to come." Here Albo also declares as a *kofer be-ikkar* (denier of the root principle, or atheist) one who belongs to the *magshimim* and attributes corporeal forms to God.

Nevertheless, *Sefer Ha-Ikkarim* is an important phenomenon in the realm of Jewish theology. Its author was not, to be sure, an original thinker or writer. On the other hand, he possessed in significant measure what both Crescas and Duran lacked, namely, the talent of the systematizer and popularizer. A skilled preacher, Albo deals with religious-philosophical problems in such a clear, popular form that they become accessible and comprehensible to all. While he did not enrich Jewish religious-philosophical thought, he provided what none of his predecessors had done: the Jewish religious outlook as an integral structure, a unified system—and this not in the form of a profound book of speculation but in a popular work permeated with the heartfelt accents of the inspired preacher.

We have already noted that Albo proceeds from Duran's view that every religion is founded on three basic principles: (1) the existence of God, (2) revelation, and (3) reward and punishment.[45] Not every faith, however, which acknowledges these

42. Guttmann even deems it necessary to note that in regard to the question of reward and punishment Albo introduces an argument not to be found in Duran (on the purification or refinement that the human soul obtains through "chastisements of love"). But Guttmann is mistaken in thinking that Albo is here original. This argument was also taken by him from someone else—not, to be sure, from Duran but from Crescas (see Chapter 4, above).
43. *Ikkarim*, I, Chapter 2.
44. *Ibid.*, Chapter 23.
45. For this reason Albo's work, like Duran's *Magen Avot*, is divided into three parts, according to the number of the fundamental principles.

three principles, Albo maintains, can be regarded thereby as the true and correct faith. The truly divine faith (*dat elohit*) is only that which recognizes, along with the three principles, the "roots" (*shorashim*) and "branches" (*anafim*) that are their logical consequences. For example, four conclusions derive from the fundamental principle of *metziut ha-El*, the existence of God: His complete unity, His absolute spirituality, His independence of time, and His total perfection. But the doctrines of the Trinity, God's incarnation in human form, etc., are utterly inconsistent with these conclusions. The second dogma, revelation, is also, according to Albo, closely associated with the concept of the divine knowledge, the idea that God is omniscient, as well as with the doctrine of divine self-disclosure through prophecy and the principle that the Torah of Moses is valid for all time.[46] To this last point, that the Mosaic Torah is eternally valid and will never be abrogated, Albo deems it essential to give special emphasis for polemical reasons. For all of eleven chapters[47] he discusses this matter, coming to the conclusion that "the Torah of the Lord is perfect, lacking nothing, throughout all generations." But he is not content with this. He also wishes to show that the Jewish religion alone is based on authentic tradition, that it alone acknowledges the three basic principles (*ikkarim*) with all their logical consequences. Along with this, he sharply criticizes Christianity in the form of a debate with a Christian theologian. Later on, Christian censorship considered it necessary to ban these polemical chapters (Book Three, Chapters 25–26), and directed its agents to tear out the heretical pages from every printed copy of *Sefer Ha-Ikkarim*.[48]

> These are preceded by a separate introductory section which Albo originally wrote as an independent work. Only later, Albo himself relates (at the close of Part I), did he rework the questions touched upon in this introductory section into three separate parts, following the request of his friends.

46. *Ikkarim*, I, Chapter 13.
47. *Ibid.*, III, Chapters 13–23.
48. Mortara quotes from *Sefer Ha-Zikkuk* the following verdict of the Catholic censor: "*Sefer Ha-Ikkarim*, III, Chapter 25, deserves to be erased entirely; even better, it ought to be completely removed from the book" (see *Hebräische Bibliographie*, V, 99). This verdict was in fact executed. From all six editions of the *Sefer Ha-Ikkarim* which had been printed up to that time the heretical pages were excised, and in the later editions the chapter in question was printed in greatly abbreviated form. It was published in its entirety only in 1876 in Leghorn by Giuseppe Jaré, in *Vikkuaḥ Al Nitzḥiut Ha-Torah*.

The Significance of Albo's Work

Albo asks, In what does the supreme goal of religion and the highest purpose of man consist?[49] The same question, as we know, was raised by Ḥasdai Crescas. Albo's answer lacks the profundity and acuteness of his master's, but it is extremely interesting, for contemporary intellectual moods are very clearly reflected in it.

The goal of man lies in perfecting himself, and the way of human perfection consists not only in the principle "And thou shalt love thy neighbor as thyself" but also in the striving to become similar to the supreme symbol of perfection, God, who created man "in His own image and form."[50] This striving for perfection is the source of eternal bliss. But the highest level of perfection does not consist merely in knowledge and philosophical thinking. The philosophers, says Albo, claim that only through abstract thought and philosophical inquiry does one merit immortality. For this only one in a thousand, a few individuals in a whole generation, are suited. But those who do not attain this level of knowledge are comparable to the beasts and, like the beasts, these millions of persons perish and are lost. Hence, an entire generation exists only for the sake of a few philosophers, e.g., Plato and Socrates. But if a generation is so orphaned that it does not produce any significant thinkers, then the entire human species has no justification for existence, and the memory of it is erased.[51] The philosopher believes, Albo further asserts, that only the philosophically thinking man is in fact immortal, that his soul alone is united with the thinking spirit. But Moses taught, "All you who cleave to the Lord your God are alive this day" (which Albo interprets to mean "All you who are alive today are united with God").[52] "Faith," Albo affirms, "is the cause of our bliss; it is also the cause of our eternal life." Man, after all, is not pure spirit; he is flesh and blood, inextricably associated with matter. Hence, he cannot attain true perfection without concrete deeds. Through good acts, through doing the good and the right out of love for God the Creator, through loving fulfillment of God's will and commandments in practical life, Albo frequently insists,[53] man achieves perfection. "Love for God," he reiterates the dictum of his teacher, "is the purpose of the whole Torah." And this love is mutual; God is also imbued with great love for the children of men, and not without reason do the letters of the

49. *Ikkarim*, III, Chapter 2.
50. *Ibid.*, I, Chapter 34.
51. *Ibid.*, III, Chapter 3.
52. *Ibid.*, I, Chapter 21.
53. *Ibid.*, III, Chapter 4, 5, 27, 28.

word *eḥad* (one) have the same numerical value in *gematria* as the letters of the word *ahavah* (love).[54] And yet, Albo concludes, no matter how vast God's love for the human species in general, it is not to be compared to the ardent love He has for His chosen people Israel.[55] To be sure, the sorrows of this people are great and its sufferings endless, but these are merely "chastisements of love," sufferings imposed as a trial which only serves to strengthen the bond of love.

The situation of the Jews in Spain became increasingly precarious in Albo's time. Black clouds covered the sky over the Jewish quarter. The heavy, choking terror of the approaching storm was already palpable, and the day was close when the pyres of the Inquisition would flare up over the entire land with their diabolical flames and the air would be filled with the agonized death cries of thousands of victims whom the pious executioners tortured and cast into the fire in the name of love of man and eternal bliss. On the threshold of the bloody drama, before Spanish Jewry was compelled to drink to the dregs the bitter cup of suffering and shame, the preacher Joseph Albo offered the cup of consolation to his brethren with a loving hand. "You may not, you must not, lose hope," Albo constantly reminds them. To be sure, the sufferings of the people are immense, its sorrows measureless. "We are slaughtered like sheep, the burden of exile has become intolerable, and troubles press upon us like heavy clouds." We have become a mockery and a scorn, we are trodden underfoot, we are cast into the deepest abysses of degradation; it is impossible for us to fall lower.[56] Nevertheless, Albo declares, we must drive away despair from our hearts.[57] Trust and hope—these are our protection and support. Because we have reached the nadir of shame and degradation, because we have been cast into the lowest depth of the abyss, we must surely hope for speedy redemption. "We must receive the vastest grace," for our God is the God of graciousness and justice, the God of lovingkindness and truth, of love and compassion. He will accept us and pour out His great mercy upon us, His dejected and exhausted servants.

Solid and strong, Albo further affirms, is our bond with God, and so long as we carry the sign of our covenant with Him on our

---

54. *Ibid.*, IV, Chapter 45. Both words are equivalent in *gematria* to the number 13.
55. *Ibid.*, III, Chapter 37.
56. *Ibid.*, IV, Chapter 50.
57. *Ibid.*, IV, Chapters 46–47.

bodies,[58] no matter how great our troubles and afflictions, we may not lose hope that the day of redemption will come. We are now like one grievously ill who lies on his deathbed and for whom hope has been abandoned; but so long as a spark of life continues to glow, hope is not really altogether gone. All the people regard us as already lost, but so long as we bear the sign of our covenant with God, we know with certainty that there is still life in our people, that the old force is still not snuffed out, and that we will be revived and restored to our former estate.[59]

The resurrection of the people, however, is bound up with the belief in the coming of the Messiah. Here we encounter an extremely interesting point in Albo's outlook. He is not in complete agreement with Simeon Duran that faith in the advent of the Messiah cannot be considered one of the fundamental dogmas of Judaism. Though he polemicizes against those religions in which faith in the appearance of the redeemer is the chief cornerstone,[60] he considers that to believe in the coming of the Messiah is the duty of every Jew. Whoever denies it is a heretic (*min*) who forfeits his share in the world to come, for this belief is sanctified by the tradition, the entire historical past, of the Jewish people, and the survival of the people is bound up with it. Not entirely clearly and consciously, but quite strongly, Albo expresses the idea that faith in the coming of the redeemer is not a religious but a national symbol. The long-awaited redeemer will come, must come! "We suffer so much from the peoples around us," and we wait and hope for him faithfully and firmly "like the watchman who stands on guard; he waits for the dawn and is certain that the night will pass and morning with its sunlight arrive."[61] And it is not for the Jewish people alone that the Messiah will come; as the redeemer of the world, he will bring light and perfection to all mankind.

When we read such words, the fact that Joseph Albo's *Sefer Ha-Ikkarim* was so deeply loved and admired by later generations of Jews ceases to be a mystery.

58. The covenant of Abraham, i.e., the covenant of circumcision.
59. *Ibid.*, IV, end of Chapter 45.
60. *Ibid.*, I, Chapters 4, 15, 23 (end).
61. *Ibid.*, IV, Chapters 47, 48, 50.

CHAPTER SIX

Preachers and Defenders of the Faith

FROM the work of Simeon bar Tzemah Duran and Joseph Albo it is clear that these writers had two major purposes: first, to provide their brethren with a clear conception of the Jewish religion and its principles, and second, to defend Judaism against the strictures of Christian theologians and the slanders of Jewish apostates. These apostates, as newly baptized Christians, took to their missionary work with intense zeal and in fact achieved a certain measure of success here and there among the ignorant and backward strata of the population. The Catholic Church became ever more militant and aggressive, and Jewish scholars had to carry on an unremitting defensive struggle both orally and in writing. They were obliged to carry on disputations, give public addresses, and write apologies and polemical tracts. This accounts for the luxuriant growth in the middle of the fifteenth century of controversial and apologetic writing, which attracted the best literary talents in the Jewish community of that era.

An honored place in this literature is occupied by Joseph Albo's contemporary Hayyim Ibn Musa, who was born in 1380 in Bejar, near Salamanca. As a physician,[1] he had access to the royal court, where he had frequent occasion to engage in debates on religious themes. In his old age in 1456 he composed his polemic

---

1. A translation that he made of an Arabic medical work has been preserved (see Steinschneider, *Hebräischen Übersetzungen*, p. 706).

tract *Magen Va-Romaḥ*, which was extremely popular at the time.[2]

At the beginning of his work Ibn Musa writes:

> Since ignorant men, who have little proficiency in religious disputations, easily allow themselves to be led astray by Christian theologians, especially by the arguments of such clever polemicists as the apostates Abner, Solomon of Burgos, Geronimo Lorki, and others, I decided to write a work refuting all their arguments and nullifying the proofs which they introduce from Jewish sources, so that our brethren may be supported and clearly see how groundless the charges of our enemies are. . . . And since one of the chief authorities among the Christian controversialists is Nicholas de Lyra,[3] I commence with his work and attack his arguments.[4]

Our author's response to the Christian polemicists who rant and rave about the "moral corruption" of the Jews is typical:

> They complain that we lead a sinful life, and bring proofs thereof from the Bible. But for forty years now I have frequented the courts of the kings and princes as a doctor, and it is quite impossible to relate the horrible acts of immorality[5] which I witnessed in them, not to mention all the robberies, murders, and thieveries committed there.

Ibn Musa sets forth twelve principles for his comrades who carry on disputations with Christian theologians. If one wishes to succeed in these disputations, he insists, he must hold fast to them. The most important of the principles are the following: (1) the Jewish debater must keep to the literal meaning of the Biblical text and not enter into allegorical subtleties; (2) he must at once declare that Jews do not recognize the authority either of the Aramaic Targum or of the Greek translation of the Bible (Septuagint); (3) he must make clear that Jews in no way consider the homilies of the Aggadah as "laws given to Moses at Sinai" and

---

2. The work has come down to us only in manuscript, and this not in complete form. Several fragments were published by Graetz in his *Geschichte der Juden* and by D. Kaufmann in *Bet Talmud*, II, 113–16.
3. A Christian scholar descended from Jews (1270–1340). He was the author of a polemical work against Jews entitled *De Messua Ej usque Adventu Praeterito*.
4. *Bet Talmud*, II, 113–14.
5. As an example of the cynical debauchery which he observed among the Christian nobility Ibn Musa relates: "And I must write about a certain man who lay with a woman and commanded that her husband should have a horse's bit put in his mouth and eat straw like an ox while he had intercourse with his wife in the husband's presence by the light of two candles."

that there is no obligation to believe in them; and (4) he must stipulate that Jews do not recognize arguments from the Gospels and the apostolic histories, since they do not regard these as reliable.

The first major principle that Ibn Musa proposes explains why, in his own polemical works, he often assails the freethinking Jewish preachers who eagerly ornament their sermons with allegorical interpretations and quotations from gentile scholars. "These new-fangled preachers who ascend the pulpit before the reading of the Torah and give sermons on speculative, philosophical themes," he complains, "never stop talking of such philosophers as Aristotle, Alexander of Aphrodisias, Themistius, Plato, Averroes, and Ptolemy, but the names of Abbaye and Rava are never mentioned by them. And the Torah, alas, lies on the reading desk and waits, as a neglected wife waits for her husband who spends his time with his paramour and pays no attention to her."[6]

Ibn Musa also complains strongly of the preachers who, relying on the well-known dictum of Hillel II to the effect that the Messiah had already appeared in the days of King Hezekiah, adopt a critical attitude toward the belief in his coming and thereby distress the hearts of their simple listeners. In that time of troubles, when persecutions became so grievous and numerous, Ibn Musa considered it especially dangerous to undermine the faith in national redemption. In his long letter to his son Jehudah,[7] and in his *Maamar Ha-Yiudim* (which eventually was lost), he takes pains to point out how strong and sure is the belief in the advent of the redeemer who will save the exiled people.

The position on which the Jewish polemicists so strongly insisted—that in disputations one must be faithful to the literal meaning of the Biblical text—brought it about that precisely at that time the first Bible concordance in Hebrew appeared. Like Ḥayyim Ibn Musa, Isaac ben Kalonymos, of the Provençal family Nathan which produced a whole series of scholarly translators, engaged frequently in debates with Christian theologians and even wrote two polemical works.[8] The Christian disputants would constantly introduce arguments from the Bible in their debates. To be able to reply to them at once, Isaac Nathan believed it

---

6. *Bet Talmud*, II, 118.
7. Published in *Bet Talmud*, II, 117-25.
8. These two works, *Tochaḥat Mateh* and *Mivtzar Yitzḥak*, in which Isaac Nathan polemicizes against the apostate Geronimo Lorki, have not come down to us. His ethical work *Me'ammetz Koaḥ* has remained in manuscript. For a discussion of Isaac Nathan see Renan-Neubauer, *Les Écrivains juifs français*, pp. 582-85.

would be extremely helpful to compose a handbook in which all the verses of the Bible were grouped alphabetically, according to the first word of each verse. In this way the Jewish disputants would find it easy immediately to locate and compare the Biblical quotations introduced by their adversaries for apologetic purposes. Isaac labored more than ten years on his handbook, and in 1447 his *Meir Nativ*, which served as a model for all later concordances,[9] appeared. In this work the scriptural books are for the first time divided into chapters, following the pattern of the Latin translation of the Bible.[10]

Undoubtedly the most significant of the scholarly polemicists who lived in the middle of the fifteenth century is Joseph ben Shemtov, the son of the zealous Kabbalist, Shemtov ben Shemtov. Joseph was a man of wide-ranging knowledge, one of the most learned personalities of his age.[11] He was thoroughly familiar with the natural sciences and proficient in the philosophy of Aristotle and all his Arabic, Christian, and Jewish interpreters.

A native of Castile, where he was born around 1400, Joseph ben Shemtov lived for a long time in Toledo and other Spanish cities. He relates[12] that for a while he occupied a position at the royal court and was frequently sent on missions to various cities. Before Passover of 1452 he was dispatched to Segovia, there to avert the threat of popular riots against the Jews. For some unknown reason disfavor was cast upon him at court, and he had to endure great troubles and lead a wanderer's life. In his scholarly work he strained his vision to such an extent that for a time he was in danger of permanent blindness. It was apparently then that he became a professional preacher and travelled around giving sermons in various Jewish communities. Because of his eye trouble he did not write but dictated to a copyist his interesting work *En Ha-Kore*, the first systematic handbook on homiletics in Hebrew literature. Here the principles of oratorical art are presented

9. In the view of some specialists, Isaac Nathan employed as a model for his work the Latin concordance which the Franciscan Arlotus de Prato had made in 1290.
10. It is characteristic that Isaac Nathan's contemporary Peretz Trabot deems it necessary to stress in the introduction to his textbook *Makrei Dardekei*, first published in 1487, that he also intended to be of assistance to Jewish disputants. We have employed the rare copy of his work located in the Asiatic Museum in Leningrad.
11. For a complete list of Joseph ben Shemtov's work, see Steinschneider, *Ersch und Gruber Lexikon*, Series 2, XXVII, 92; S. Munk, *Mélanges de philosophie juive et arabe*, pp. 507–9.
12. In the conclusion of his Hebrew reworking of Crescas' polemical work written in Spanish which he entitled *Bittul Ikkerei Ha-Notzerim*.

in a methodical way. Joseph explains, through numerous quotations and examples, how the preacher must utilize the plain meaning of the Bible text.[13] When his sight was cured, he resumed his scholarly work and died, according to Heinrich Graetz' conjecture,[14] as a martyr in 1460.

Intimate with the royal court, Joseph ben Shemtov had occasion to come into close contact with Christian scholars and theologians, with whom, as he relates, he would frequently carry on religious disputations, according to the custom of that era, in the presence of the courtiers and royal family.[15] But he was not content with oral debates. To encourage his brethren and weaken the missionary activity of the Catholic clergy and the Jewish apostates, he popularized and made accessible to the general reading public two masterly apologetic works of the preceding generation. He wrote a commentary on and provided a lengthy introduction to Profiat Duran's celebrated tract *Al Tehi Ka-Avotecha*, and published a Hebrew reworking of Hasdai Crescas' *Tratado*.[16]

In fact, Joseph ben Shemtov's major scholarly work is closely connected with Crescas' philosophy. He was not only the most important thinker of Spanish Jewry in the fifteenth century; he was also Crescas' protagonist and disciple in the keen criticism that he directed against the rationalist system of the Jewish Aristotelians. In this particular his philosophical work *Kevod Elohim*, which appeared in 1442,[17] is of special interest.

Graetz, whose hostility to the Kabbalists is so intense that he completely abandons scientific objectivity in discussing them, asserts that Joseph ben Shemtov opposed his father, the orthodox Kabbalist, and the latter's followers.[18] But if we read *Kevod Elohim* carefully and without extraneous motives, it becomes clear that Graetz' assertion is quite unjustified and that just the opposite is the case. Joseph frequently invokes his father.[19] He agrees entirely with his battle against the rationalists, and explicitly

13. See the introduction to *En Ha-Kore* published by A. Jellinek in *Kuntras Ha-Mafteah*, p. 31. *En Ha-Kore* has remained in manuscript. Numerous quotations from it are given by the Kabbalist Meir Ibn Gabbai in his *Avodat Ha-Kodesh* (see Part II, Chapter 5; Part III, Chapter 67; and many other places).
14. Graetz, *Geschichte der Juden*, VIII, Note 4 (end).
15. Joseph writes of these at the end of his commentary to Aristotle's *Ethics* (see *MGWJ*, 1883, p. 81) and in his introduction to Profiat Duran's *Al Tehi Ka-Avotecha*.
16. Published in *Kibbutz Vikkuhim* (1844).
17. Printed in Ferrara in 1555.
18. See the Hebrew edition of Graetz' *Geschichte der Juden*, VI, 179.
19. On one page (28a) the author quotes his father three times.

insists that his father was perfectly right when he charged the "philosophizers" with the destruction of numerous Jewish communities.[20] He believes merely that the method which his father employed in his polemic was incorrect. If one wishes to overcome his adversaries, Joseph says, one must proceed from assumptions and major principles recognized by both sides; his father, however, adopted premises which the opposing side definitely rejected.[21] Joseph himself practiced what he preached, making use of Crescas' scientific method.[22]

We know how thoroughly Maimonides was persuaded that everything Aristotle taught regarding the terrestrial, sublunar world is indisputable truth.[23] For this reason he set forth his well-known twenty-five "propositions," taken from Aristotle's *Physics*, with the aid of which he attempted to show in a purely philosophical way the existence of a single creator of the universe. To undermine this firm support of the Jewish rationalists, Hasdai Crescas with great acumen disclosed the weak and contradictory aspects of Aristotle's *Physics*. But Joseph ben Shemtov goes even further. To destroy entirely the foundation of the Jewish rationalists, he also proceeds from Aristotle—not, however, from his *Physics* but from his *Ethics*. It is very characteristic that Joseph comes forward not as Aristotle's opponent but, on the contrary, as his ardent admirer. Enthusiastically he declares that we must thank God for "having bestowed of His wisdom upon a common mortal, a sage of the nations of the world."[24] Aristotle's *Ethics* was one of Joseph's favorite books and, in order to make this work accessible to all, he wrote a rather long commentary,[25] on which he

20. *Kevod Elohim*, 27: ". . . and this is what happened at the time of testing long ago. . . . For men endeavored to acquire these branches of knowledge and their attention to them was the cause of the destruction of the congregations of Jacob in most [of Castile and Aragon] and the greatest and most exalted among them left the community [and became apostates]." The words in brackets were stricken out by the Catholic censor. Time, however, proved stronger than the censor's ink; it ate through the color of the ink, and the stricken words reappeared. On this, see our article in *Kto Silntse*, No. 2 (1918), *Novii Put*.
21. *Kevod Elohim*, 3b.
22. Joseph ben Shemtov refers to Crescas at the beginning of his work (3b).
23. *Guide for the Perplexed*, II:22.
24. *Kevod Elohim*, 15a.
25. We have employed an old manuscript of this commentary. The manuscript was completed in the summer of 1470 by one David Maimon. It is included in the first Firkovich Collection, No. 379, and contains 319 pages in quarto. Joseph ben Shemtov's introduction is missing in the manuscript.

worked day and night for more than three months, to the Hebrew translation which the learned Jewish court physician Meir Alguadez had published.

In his *Kevod Elohim* Joseph begins with a thorough analysis of the moral assumptions which Aristotle expresses mainly in the first and last chapters of his *Ethics*. Only then does he raise the question whether these assumptions are in fact compatible with what is taught by the Torah of Moses.

With verbatim quotations from the *Ethics*[26] Joseph shows that, in the Greek thinker's view, man's supreme bliss and goal consist in attaining knowledge, in perfecting the mind. The joy yielded by the power of inquiry is not only the highest and most beautiful; it is also the only free and independent bliss that is not subject to anyone else's will or control. The patron or philanthropist, for example, to be able to do good, requires both means and persons on whom he may bestow his generosity. The mind, however, is a world in itself; free and unhindered, it soars to the exalted realms of thought. But the degree of perfection in science is dependent not only on the power of inquiry but on its *object;* the higher the entity with which a man's thought concerns itself, the greater and more perfect is his bliss. And since the highest and most perfect entity is the spirit of God, the investigation of God's nature, the fathoming of His greatness, is the summit of human perfection and the acme of human bliss.[27]

But does one thereby attain immortality? Have we here proof that the highest, intellectual part of man's spirit survives his death? Here Joseph touches with great acuteness on the most obscure and confused aspect of Aristotle's philosophy—his teaching about the nature of the human soul. Aristotle regards the soul as the realization or actualization of an organic body which possesses life merely potentially.[28] This disclosure in actuality of a living organism, which before was merely *in potentia*, contains in itself, as supreme level of creation, all the lower levels as well. The function of plants consists only in drawing nourishment and growing. In animals the capacities of feeling, motion, and will are added. In man there is also the highest principle, the principle of spirit or mind (*nous*) which rules over all else. But is this spirit of each

26. He utilizes the Latin translation.
27. *Kevod Elohim*, 8, 10, 13.
28. In Aristotle's terminology this is called entelechy. In *De Anima*, Book II, Chapter 1, the nature of man's soul is explained in the following statement: "The soul is the first grade of actuality of a natural body which has life only in potentiality." On this, see also *De Anima*, Book I, Chapter 3.

individual person eternal? Does Aristotle acknowledge the immortality of the soul? Joseph ben Shemtov insists that Aristotle provides no answer to this question or, more accurately, that the question is not even raised by him. Joseph was quite familiar with the literature on Aristotle. He knew the views that had been expressed in regard to this question by Aristotle's interpreters and commentators, such as Alexander of Aphrodisias in ancient times and Averroes in the Middle Ages. He even wrote a commentary to Averroes' work on the individual human intellect and its capacity for union with the "active intellect."[29] "I do not intend," he writes,

> to enter into speculations as to how far all the explanations of these commentators are correct. Here only this question is raised: does it follow from everything Aristotle says about man's highest goal and greatest happiness that the human soul is immortal? I affirm that in all his works, whether in his *Physics*, *Metaphysics*, or *Politics*, not a single proof of this is adduced.[30]

From Aristotle's teaching, Joseph further declares, one can only conclude that man's supreme bliss is connected with the thinking part of his soul, that only in inquiry, in sharpening the mind, is the true nature of man, which raises him above everything else on earth, revealed. Just as, in a great singer the best and loveliest that he has consists in his singing, so in a man endowed with a keen mind the chief thing is his inquiring spirit, his speculative thinking. This alone can be inferred from Aristotle's teaching. But he does not deal at all with the question whether this bliss will endure eternally, even after death. When we say that the beautiful melody is the supreme gift with which the singer is endowed, we do not thereby touch on the question whether this loveliness is eternal. So also when we speak of the supreme bliss which the thinking and inquiring part of the soul provides man, we do not associate this with the question whether this part is immortal.[31] Man's inquiring spirit raises him to the heights. The most exalted level of perfection is attained by the individual when his thinking fathoms the depths of the divine nature. This is the supreme bliss, the acme

29. On this commentary, entitled *Perush Al Ha-Milah Le-Efsharut Ha-Devekut*, see Steinschneider's article in *MGWJ*, 1883, pp. 459–79, 514–20, where extensive quotations are given. Joseph ben Shemtov concludes that Averroes is indeed a great thinker but full of inconsistencies.
30. *Kevod Elohim*, 15–16. The same idea is underscored by Joseph in his commentary to Averroes, *Efsharut Ha-Devekut* (see *MGWJ*, 1883, p. 467).
31. *Kevod Elohim*, 16a.

of joy. But how is it necessary that this perfection also be immortal? Do we not observe that trees live much longer than animals, though animals are on a higher level than plants? And how often do we see that a common, ignorant man lives far longer than a great sage, "for bliss is not measured by the yardstick of length and duration but by the value of its own nature." Gersonides, as we have observed, categorically rejected Averroes' view that, in regard to immortality, there is no difference between the soul of a wise man and the soul of an ignoramus. Joseph ben Shemtov, however, believes that Gersonides' arguments have no substance. Gersonides wished to show that the "acquisition of wisdom" must be associated with immortality, but he was mistaken. Wisdom and the perfection of knowledge are, in themselves, high goods. Even here, in our life on this earth, we enjoy far more happiness when we are rich in knowledge than when we grope in the darkness of ignorance, regardless whether this happiness is eternal or not.[32]

In short, Joseph insists that in Aristotle's doctrine of the supreme bliss attained by man through intellectual perfection there is no indication that this bliss endures beyond death. To be sure, Aristotle's disciples and interpreters endeavored to fill this void in their master's system, but the very fact that each offers a different interpretation demonstrates most clearly that Aristotle left the problem open and did not even attempt to solve it. We are fully entitled to affirm, Joseph concludes, that immortality is promised not by Greek philosophy but by the Torah of Israel. It alone brings eternal beatitude; its ways alone lead to that highest joy over which death has no dominion.[33]

This competent student of Greek-Arabic philosophy also sharply stresses the extent to which the ways of philosophy and the ways of the Torah diverge. "These two paths," he asserts, "are totally different in character and nature." Hence, he complains strongly of Maimonides[34] and his followers, who endeavored to show that speculative philosophy and religion are essentially identical and strive toward the same goal, though employing different means. In their view, the Torah, which addresses itself to the plain, uncultured masses, must conceal philosophical truths under the veil of allusions and parables, while philosophy, which is directed to the elite, enunciates clear statements and has no

---

32. *Ibid.*, 17a.
33. *Ibid.*, 17b.
34. Joseph also opposes Maimonides in his commentary *Efsharut Ha-Devekut:* "We saw the godly rabbi, the teacher of righteousness, very hard pressed in all this" (see *MGWJ*, 1883, p. 464).

need to employ metaphors and symbols. Even when they saw that the contradictions were immense, Joseph maintains, they attempted to cover them and sought to demonstrate that philosophy and the Torah live together in complete amity. The mysteries of the Torah were transformed into philosophical syllogisms; *maaseh bereshit* (the work of creation) and *maaseh merkavah* (the lore of the chariot or throne) were changed into physics and metaphysics; and all the positive and negative commandments in the Torah were regarded as aiming at the same moral principles as Aristotle's *Ethics*.[35] This conclusion of the rationalists that there are no inconsistencies whatever between religion and philosophy, Joseph insists, is completely untrue, and he notes that his father long ago showed in his book what thoroughly false and pernicious results it is capable of producing.[36]

The perfection and happiness of man, according to Joseph ben Shemtov, consist of various aspects or categories. The first arises from considering man as a link in the chain of the phenomena of nature and as a constituent of society. To live as a useful member of the organized community according to certain laws, through which one is raised above other living creatures, is the initial category of perfection and the happiness associated with it. A second and higher level is the perfection of knowledge, which arises when man seeks to investigate with his mind the phenomena of the universe according to the order and laws of nature, and to employ the results in life for the sake of his happiness and welfare.[37] These categories of perfection can be attained by man with the aid of his own natural intellect and require neither revelation nor the spirit of prophecy. But Joseph is profoundly convinced that man's highest ideal of bliss and perfection cannot be content with earthly, practical life and the mechanical order of the world, governed by the iron laws of nature. And it is precisely this ideal, which lives within man and strives towards the heights, that provides the most powerful evidence that there is another world with an altogether different chain of possibilities, beyond the mathematical order of the processes of nature.

This supreme ideal, the ideal of eternal justice and the realization of the imperishable and absolute good, can be attained only

---

35. *Kevod Elohim*, 18a. Cf. *MGWJ*, 1883, p. 464.
36. *Kevod Elohim*, 22a. There is no doubt that in Joseph's arguments is discernible the influence of the Arabic thinker Al-Ghazali, whose *Tahafut al Falasifa* he quotes, further declaring that he considers Averroes' reply to Al-Ghazali's work too weak and unconvincing (*ibid.*, 24a).
37. *Ibid.*, 21a.

through revelation, through the Torah given from heaven. The religion of divine revelation, Joseph asserts, has its own regularity and lawfulness. It is subject not to the laws of nature but to other, higher laws; and it is just these, the laws of divine justice, not the mechanical laws of mathematics and the natural sciences, which are the revelation of the supreme truth. This, he insists, does not however mean that the religion of revelation is inconsistent with the foundations of logical thought or rejects the premises which reason obliges us to accept.[38] The Torah, according to Joseph, is simply not under the dominion of the mechanical laws of nature. It is governed by special divine laws, and "Naḥmanides was quite right when he declared that the Torah consists wholly of miracles."[39] The great mysteries of the Torah,[40] which are revealed in their entire essence only to prophets and men of the holy spirit, Joseph is convinced, are symbolically incorporated in the commandments and precepts. And only through deed, through action and performance, he insists, does the wish or thought obtain its consummation, its real being.[41]

Those who think that one can rationally explain all the divine commandments and precepts are mistaken. Through utility and the promotion of practical goals alone, Joseph maintains, it is impossible to account for the commandments, which are not the product of natural laws but of divine revelation. Even in nature, he adds, we encounter such phenomena as we are at a loss to understand and whose nature we cannot explain. This is exemplified by the force of magnetism. We see how iron is attracted by this force; we do not doubt that it exists, but its essence is hidden from us.[42] Nevertheless, Joseph insists, it does not at all follow that the laws of the Torah were given through revelation as an arbitrary "decree of the king" without any order or reason, and that they are not subject to a definite regularity of causes and effects. This regularity, however, is of a different type and, given our simple and limited understanding, we are incapable of com-

---

38. *Ibid.*, 19a. This idea is repeated by Joseph in his introduction to Profiat Duran's *Al Tehi Ka-Avotecha*. He here notes that there is a great difference whether we say that prophecy *transcends* human reason or that prophecy *contradicts* human reason.
39. *Kevod Elohim*, 21a.
40. Joseph, like Naḥmanides, is firmly persuaded that in the words and letters of the Torah profound mysteries are hidden. This idea is expressed especially clearly in his commentary to Averroes. See *MGWJ*, 1883, p. 466.
41. *Kevod Elohim*, 20a.
42. *Ibid.*, 22b.

prehending it without the aid of the prophets or of their disciples and spiritual heirs.[43]

Joseph ben Shemtov sharply attacks Maimonides and his followers, who portray the prophets merely as thinkers and scientists, and consider the spirit of prophecy "the union of the active intellect with the power of imagination." The holy spirit or prophetic revelation, says Joseph, is not a product of abstract philosophical thought, and it is not through scientific knowledge and proficiency in speculation and inquiry that one attains the level of the prophet. Like Ḥasdai Crescas, Joseph emphasizes that philosophy achieved its flowering in Aristotle's time. The greatest of the Hebrew prophets, however, were much earlier, preceding Aristotle by centuries. "We know," he adds,

that among the Greeks and Arabs there were remarkable thinkers. These lived calmly and securely under the protection of their countries, yet not one of them was privileged to enjoy the spirit of prophecy. But as for our sages, who were unable to occupy themselves peacefully with the sciences—upon them the *Shechinah* rests, and it accompanies them in their wanderings.[44]

Recalling the agonies which his generation had to endure, Joseph cries out with emotion: "And even now, when God has poured out His wrath upon our people, and our exiled nation finds itself in the mouth of the lion, is it not the greatest miracle that, of so many powerful peoples, even their name has been forgotten, while Israel has still not perished?"[45]

The prophet, we have seen Joseph maintaining, is higher than the philosopher, and the spirit of prophecy is not associated with scientific inquiry. He considers it necessary, however, to insist that "only a man without understanding can think that the sciences are superfluous."[46] Here he sets forth the very principle which centuries later, in the period of the Haskalah, was so prominent in the program of the enlighteners or *maskilim* concerning the twofold obligation of the Jew, as *man* and as *Jew*. The laws of Aristotle educate the *man;* the laws of the Torah, the *Jew*. The Jew requires scientific knowledge not as an adherent of Judaism but as a rational being; if he wishes to become perfect, he must strive for general knowledge and become proficient in philosophy and natu-

43. *Ibid.*, 22–23.
44. *Ibid.*, 21a. The same idea is expressed by Joseph in his previously mentioned commentary (*MGWJ*, 1883, p. 575).
45. *Kevod Elohim*, 22a.
46. *Ibid.*, 26b.

ral science.⁴⁷ As a follower of the religion of Moses, the Jew is not obliged to seek out and demonstrate through argumentation "reasons for the commandments," but as a man endowed with speculative thought he inquires and thinks about the purpose and significance of each commandment. It was not, however, because of Israel's great learning in the sciences and general wisdoms that it became a "peculiar people and holy nation" and was characterized as "a wise and understanding people." In this realm, Joseph insists, other peoples accomplished far more. The Jews obtained these special titles on account of their "Jewish wisdom" (*ḥochmat Yisrael*), by reason of the fact that Israel is the bearer of the sacred Torah, which is the highest category of perfection.⁴⁸

The philosophically educated author realized quite well that no limits or restraints can be placed on man's free speculative thought. But he lived in a difficult time. The enemies who assailed the Jewish community and its religion from all sides became ever more arrogant and ruthless, and apprehension for the survival of his people compelled this encyclopedic scholar to join the company of the orthodox "defenders of the faith." "One must admit," writes Joseph,

that the attractive power of speculative philosophy is great, and it is quite easy to become lost and confused in the ingenious philosophical web of "Greek wisdom." We know very well the terrible destruction produced by the teaching of our rationalists to the effect that in devotion to the sciences and in philosophical inquiry consist man's supreme goal and the secret of his immortality.⁴⁹ We have seen how many of the most prominent people in the Jewish communities allowed themselves to be led astray by the philosophers and thinkers, looked with contempt on religion and tradition, did not stand the test, and refused to make any sacrifices. They took the position that not in religion but in philosophical thought lies the highest level of perfection—and that, indeed, here, in *this* world. Hence they abandoned the faith of their fathers and caused the ruination of many great communities in Castile and Aragon.⁵⁰

"We also know very well from history," he adds,

that in those countries into which the philosophical-rationalist ideas did not penetrate, thousands and tens of thousands of our brethren

47. *Ibid.*, 22b.
48. *Ibid.*, 25a.
49. Joseph here aims above all at Maimonides. In one place he even mentions him by name (7a).
50. *Kevod Elohim*, 27a.

sacrificed themselves for the sanctification of God's name and perished by fire and sword. So, for example, Gersonides relates[51] that in the Jewish communities of France hundreds of thousands gave up their lives for the sole Creator and His holy name, but among us in Spain this did not happen, and precisely for the reason indicated.

Taking this into consideration, Joseph ben Shemtov further declares, "the wondrous scholar Maestro Rabbi Asher" (ben Yeḥiel) was not unjustified when he thanked God for having kept him from contact with the secular sciences. It was precisely for this reason also that Rabbi Solomon ben Adret and his followers proscribed study of the natural sciences in one's youth. These great scholars were not enemies of secular knowledge; they appreciated its value and utility. However, they saw where the "philosophers" with their preachments and writings were leading: "that the whole land was turned to heresy."

Thus the circle was firmly closed. Under the burden of the persecutions and troubles which Spanish Jewry endured, those who were far apart came together and opponents forgot their differences of opinion. The most significant Jewish thinker of the fifteenth century in Spain joined the strictly orthodox party and publicly espoused the fanatical view taken by the typical representative of the pious and enlightenment-hating Jews of Germany.

The other authors of Joseph ben Shemtov's generation who wrote on religious-philosophical themes are rather uninteresting, from both a scholarly and literary point of view. Nothing original is to be found in their work; they merely reiterated the ideas of their predecessors and wrote extensive commentaries to them. The most typical of these figures is the broadly educated Abraham ben Shemtov Bibago, a native of Saragossa. Very few details of his life are ascertainable. We know merely that his first work (a commentary on a composition by Averroes) was completed in 1446 in the city of Huesca. In the 1470's he was the head of a Talmudic academy in Saragossa,[52] and died in 1489.[53] Like Joseph ben Shem-

---

51. Joseph here undoubtedly refers to the passage in Gersonides' commentary to the Pentateuch: "'And I will scatter you among the nations ... and your land shall be a desolation ... while you are in your enemies' land' (Leviticus 26:33–34): this points to the great afflictions endured by our people, many of whom died as a result of the destruction of some of the holy communities and the expulsion of the Jews from France; in consequence of these things twice as many perished from hunger and pestilence as went out from Egypt."
52. See S. Munk, *Mélanges de philosophie juive et arabe*, p. 507.
53. Steinschneider wrote a monograph on Bibago's scholarly activity (*MGWJ*, 1883, pp. 79–96, 125–42).

tov, Bibago also carried on disputations with Christian theologians, and while still a youth, as he relates,[54] he debated with a "great scholar" at the court of the king of Aragon, Juan II. In his old age he completed a large work in three parts, entitled *Derech Emunah*,[55] in which he endeavors systematically to expound the nature of Judaism, and incidentally defends it against slanders and attacks. Bibago here displays great learning, not only in Judaeo-Arabic literature but also in Christian theological writings.[56] Nevertheless, after the work of Simeon Duran and Joseph Albo, it is difficult to find anything new in Bibago's *Derech Emunah*. A typical eclectic, Bibago includes in his work material of all kinds. He quotes, one after the other, the Greek philosophers and Kabbalists. The "spheres" and the "active intellect" are intermingled in his work with such Kabbalist works, "incomparable in their divine wisdom," as *Sefer Heichalot*, *Shiur Komah*, and *Sefer Ha-Bahir*, which "are more precious than gold and pearls."[57] *Maaseh bereshit* (the work of creation) is associated with *notarikon*, *gematriot*, and "combinations of letters," whose profound mysteries "are known by the true Kabbalah."

A certain cultural-historical interest pertains only to the passages in *Derech Emunah* in which Bibago complains of "some of the contemporary scholars who keep the husk and throw away the kernel and, to demonstrate to the multitude their piety and reverence, speak contemptuously of Maimonides and his followers."[58] To the frequently preferred charge that the philosophically enlightened constituted the largest percentage of converts and apostates, Bibago replies:

But I also saw a great many learned man who drew all their scholarship from the sea of the Talmud and never concerned themselves with philosophy, and yet these also denied the religion of their fathers and forsook their people. I do not even speak of those who are common boors and ignoramuses, and who in their palaces and courts commit the most shameful deeds.[59]

54. *Derech Emunah*, p. 99.
55. Printed in Constantinople in 1521.
56. Bibago quotes the Latin works of Eusebius, Boethius, Duns Scotus, Occam, and many others. In general, it may be noted that the Jewish scholars of that era diligently studied the Christian scholastics for purely polemical purposes. A contemporary of Bibago's, Elijah Haviliah, translated many works of Thomas Aquinas and Occam into Hebrew so that Jewish scholars might be able to obtain familiarity with the famous Christian savants.
57. *Derech Emunah*, p. 64.
58. Ibid., p. 43.
59. Ibid., p. 45.

Like Joseph ben Shemtov, Abraham Bibago was also a preacher. During one Sabbath sermon which he was giving in the synagogue (apparently in Saragossa) a Christian mob attacked the local Jewish populace, and he was unable to conclude his sermon. The final act of the bloody drama, when Spanish Jewry was struggling in its death agony, had already begun. The two kingdoms of Aragon and Castile had just been united under the crown of Ferdinand and Isabella, and the pyres of the Inquisition flared up with their infernal fire over the entire land. The Jewish communities were already accustomed to attacks and riots from the incited mob, and the following Sabbath the congregation requested Bibago to finish his interrupted sermon. Then Bibago, "in order to comfort and strengthen hearts wearied by tumults and terrors," delivered a sermon on the sanctity of the Sabbath day, which is the crown of "the work of creation," of the revealed divine grace. *Zeh Yenahamenu* (this will comfort us)—so the sermon which he gave on the Sabbath after the riot was called.[60]

In the realm of preaching, too, a firmly closed circle was formed. From the time of Samuel Ibn Tibbon and Jacob Anatoli the Jewish Aristotelians had attempted to utilize the synagogue pulpit as a forum for disseminating their rationalist ideas. We have noted the sharp controversy that this provoked in orthodox Jewish circles. After the catastrophe of the Seville massacre, at the end of the fourteenth century, completely new tendencies became manifest in Jewish homiletics. The battle of the Catholic Church against Judaism became ever more relentless. The Church was no longer satisfied with compelling Jewish scholars to conduct public disputations with apostates on religious issues. At its urging, a law was passed obliging Jews to come and listen to conversionist sermons. Resentment at such oppressive acts was expressed among the Jews in a strongly developed polemic-apologetic literature, and also found a sharp echo in the homiletic explanation of the Bible and in the sermons given in the synagogues and houses of study. The Jewish preachers sought to counteract the influence of the missionary sermons, to strengthen trust in the foundations of Judaism in the hearts of their listeners. Precisely for this reason, as we have already noted, almost all the Jewish scholars of that era were also preachers, and Joseph ben Shemtov even wrote a handbook on homiletics.

60. Printed in 1522 with the following on the title page: "This composition entitled *Zeh Yenahamenu* was composed by the great sage Abraham Bibago, may his memory be for a blessing." The sermon, which is divided into fifteen parts or "gates" (*shearim*), is now extremely rare. We have employed the copy located in the Asiatic Museum in Leningrad.

But it was not apologetic goals only that the Jewish preachers set themselves. Their task was more than a struggle against missionary sermons. We have noted in regard to Abraham Bibago's preaching how clearly one motif resounds in it: *zeh yenaḥamenu*, this will comfort us, this will strengthen grieved hearts. Preaching acquired a distinctively didactic character. Its fundamental motive was moral instruction and religious conduct. In the history of culture, however, one frequently encounters the unique phenomenon which Aḥad Ha-Am once designated by the phrase "names emptied of their content." By this he meant the power of the tradition inherited from previous ages. For generations sermons among the Jews of Spain had borne a speculative-philosophical character; this was a result of the cultural situation of the era. But the form or dress often outlives the content; the "names" remain, even though their substance has been consumed by the teeth of time. The philosophical spirit in Spanish Jewry had long since died, but the garment, the philosophical form as traditional and established style of preaching, survived. The ethical-didactic homilies of Abraham Bibago's era, the pious, godfearing sermons so Jewishly orthodox in their content, still carried the philosophical form which had lost its erstwhile substance long ago.

The most typical representative of this unique ethical-philosophical type of preaching is Isaac ben Moses Arama, author of *Akedat Yitzḥak*, one of the most popular Jewish books of speculation. For the scanty information we have about Isaac Arama's life we are indebted chiefly to the author's introduction to *Akedat Yitzḥak*. Born around 1420, Arama was, while still a youth, the head of a Talmudic academy in the city of Zamora and afterwards rabbi and preacher in Tarragona and Traga. In his old age he was rabbi and head of the academy in Calatayud. Following the great expulsion of 1492, Arama settled in Naples, where he died in 1494. Of the great reverence in which his contemporaries held him, testimony is provided by the inscription placed on his tombstone:

> This is not a heap of stones but an altar;
> Isaac comes forever, and God sacrifices.

Arama was quite familiar with Arabic-Jewish philosophy but was much more impressed by the wisdom of the Kabbalah. For him the *Zohar* was great and holy, and he declared "truly divine" not only Rabbi Simeon ben Yoḥai but other Kabbalists as well.[61] *Akedat Yitzḥak*, which was admired by many generations of Jewish readers, provides evidence that Arama was doubtless a skilled and gifted preacher, but without originality or genuine inspira-

---

61. *Ḥazut Kashah*, 27b (we quote according to the Pressburg edition).

tion; the stamp of tedious mediocrity lies over the whole of his five-part composition.[62] Arama constructs his sermons on the basis of verses from the Torah and interweaves them with Talmudic legends, ethical principles, and philosophical-theological maxims. But these various elements remain merely a mechanical mixture, without being forged together into a unitary, organic whole. An epigone of the era of decline, Isaac Arama lacks the naive simplicity of the Franco-German school and the passionate ardor of the Kabbalists, as well as the systematic consistency of the freethinkers and rationalists. He is always neither hot nor cold, and it is only rarely that he rises above the superficial plane of banal preachment, seasoned with scholastic hairsplitting. He generously employs the allegorical method so favored by the rationalists, and at the same time carries on an intensive battle against the rationalists and issues forth against the "plague of philosophy" in a tract entitled *Hazut Kashah*.

This acerbic tract undoubtedly has a certain cultural-historical interest. Typical is Arama's description of how Jews were compelled to listen to conversionist sermons and how he himself engaged in a disputation with a Christian theologian on the question of God's grace.[63] Also characteristic is the pious author's complaint about the contemporary Talmudic academies. "I consider it the greatest misfortune," writes Arama,

that at the very time we are oppressed and persecuted in exile and fall ever deeper into the abysses of sorrow as recompense for ancient sins, our own protectors and champions deceive us. Like traitors, they lead us astray into alien ways filled with snares and nets; with false words they undermine the foundations of the faith and destroy the trust in the hearts of the people. Now, in a time of distress, when misfortune increases so fearfully in the house of Jacob, a new infectious disease is spreading ever more widely among the leaders and elders of our people. Ever larger grows the number of those who devote themselves to foreign sciences, which are the most dangerous adversaries of our Torah and faith. It is not enough that they study all these things in their original languages, but the majority of our youth are raised on strange tongues, and this is presently the major concern in our *yeshivot*. The Torah and Talmud are forgotten there, and no one is interested in them.[64]

The tract is written in the form of a dream, a "grievous vision" (*hazut kashah*), which is actually an allegorical commentary to the

62. *Akedat Yitzḥak* was written in the form of a commentary to the Pentateuch.
63. *Hazut Kashah*, Chapter 4.
64. *Ibid.*, 34a.

Biblical story of Sarah and Hagar. Sarah is revealed religion, the Torah from heaven, and Hagar is philosophic wisdom, whose task is merely to serve: to explain and to facilitate the attainment of religious truths. But the "maidservant" soon became arrogant, "and her mistress became despised in her eyes." Then the offended Sarah demanded of Abraham that he remove the impudent servant.[65]

Very characteristic is the point, underscored by Arama himself, that, in his hostility to free philosophical thought, he is not altogether uninfluenced by the zealous and militant Catholic Church. Medieval scholastic philosophy at that time was in a critical period of transition, with clear signs of temporary decline, while the Catholic Church in Spain became ever more aggressive. Arama suggests that Jews, in this matter, might learn a lesson from the Catholic theologians. These maintain the principle that philosophy is merely the servant of theology and therefore acknowledge only those philosophical assumptions that are consistent with the faith; they are persuaded that the divine religion transcends philosophical speculation, which is quite incapable of attaining the marvels of revealed faith.[66]

Arama believes that the Christian theologians hold a far more proper view and are less dangerous than the *bogdei Yehudah* (deceivers of Judah), the Jewish rationalists. The former "have chosen the way of faith" and have not surrendered, for the sake of philosophy, so much as a hair's breadth of it—unlike the Jewish "philosophizers" and freethinkers. Especially despised by Arama are the *pashranim* (peacemakers or compromisers) between religion and philosophical speculation. Outwardly these assert that they regard the Torah and its commandments as precious; in fact, however, philosophy leads them astray on altogether false paths leading to a total destruction of the faith. Everything in the Torah, all its miracles and prophetic words, Arama complains, they seek to interpret in a logical, naturalistic fashion, so that they will not be inconsistent with philosophy; everything must be adapted to what Aristotle taught. For the sake of philosophy, they ruthlessly destroy the foundations of the faith. The divine Torah revealed on Mount Sinai has been transformed among them into parables and allegories for the common multitude which, with its crude understanding, is incapable of grasping purely philosophical truths.

65. *Ibid.*, Chapter 11.
66. *Ibid.*, 15b and many other passages. It is interesting that Arama's contemporary, the orthodox and pious Joseph Yaabetz, also insists in his *Or Ha-Ḥayyim* (p. 40) that in this particular Jews might take a lesson from the Christian theologians.

And, according to them, only those commandments of the Torah that can be brought into complete congruence with philosophical theories need to be recognized.[67]

But if so, Arama asks, of what use is the divine Torah? Would it not be better both for it and for all Israel if it had not been revealed? For if one maintains the literal meaning of the text, he must come to the conclusion, according to the rationalists, that the whole Torah is filled with lies and old wives' tales, told in order to mislead the common people and to dazzle the eyes of fools with fantastic dreams, so that they grope in darkness like beasts and are unable to attain the truth and lead a conscious human life. On the other hand, if one interprets the text in an allegorical manner and discovers in it a hidden philosophical content, the question arises: if we already possess the philosophic truths, of what use to us is the Torah from heaven?[68]

We, however, declares Arama, will not follow these "men who pretend to be wise" and who wish to persuade us that "the plain meaning of the Torah is simply for fools."[69] We will not let ourselves be led by the "compromisers" and "deceivers of Judah" who make of the living, divine word an arid commentary to philosophic theories, and for whom the entire Torah becomes an extraneous accessory to speculative philosophy.[70]

Arama declares war against the "philosophical plague," against the "children who act corruptly," who "undertake to make a mockery of the Torah and its commandments and to deny its wonders."[71] These compromisers who have subordinated the Torah to philosophy, the author of *Akedat Yitzḥak* exclaims emotively, are responsible for the fact that the day of redemption is so remote. Since "the servant has inherited the place of her mistress," we fall ever lower and there is no end to our afflictions.[72]

---

67. *Ḥazut Kashah*, 16.
68. *Ibid.*, 16b.
69. *Ibid.*, 18b. It is characteristic that Arama also relies on Al-Ghazali's *Tahafut al Falasifa* and calls him the "divine philosopher" (*ibid.*, 12b).
70. *Ibid.*, 18a.
71. *Ibid.*, 30b.
72. *Ibid.*, 33b.

CHAPTER SEVEN

Kabbalists and Satirists

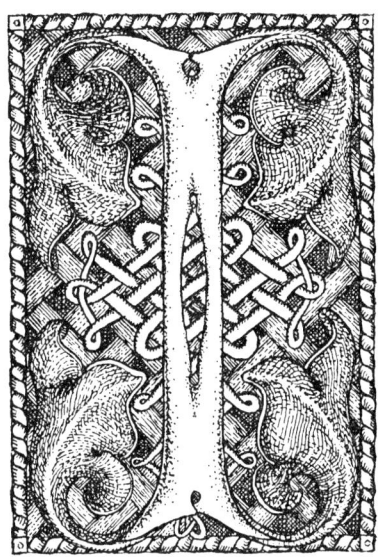

ISAAC Arama was deeply persuaded that the "compromisers" had delayed the messianic "end" and that it was their fault that the redemption had not yet arrived. But even before him, there appeared another zealous representative of the orthodox "defenders of the faith" who charged many, not only among the rationalist freethinkers but also in the camp of the rabbis, with responsibility for the fact that the exile had still not ended and the redeemer not yet come. This was an ardent Kabbalist whose name and life are veiled in mystery, the author of two popular and widely known Midrashim, *Sefer Ha-Kanah*,[1] a Kabbalist commentary on the commandments, and *Sefer Ha-Peliah*,[2] a mystical commentary on "the work of creation."

The name of the author is unknown. In *Sefer Ha-Kanah* he calls himself Kanah Aben Gador ben Naḥum, and in *Sefer Ha-Peliah* Elkanah ben Yeroḥam ben Avigdor of the family Ram. There is no doubt, however, that the name Gador here has a purely symbolic character, referring to the "restrainer," the protector who "builds a fence." Indeed, quite frequently, immediately following the name is the explanation, *baal ha-geder be-torat El*, "the maker of a fence around God's Torah."[3] In both works the

1. First printed in Poritzk in 1776.
2. Printed in Koretz in 1784.
3. The first author who quotes the works of this mystic, Moses Ha-Goleh of Kiev, refers to the author of *Sefer Ha-Kanah*: "This is what Avigdor wrote in his book on the commandments" (*Shoshan Sodot*, 28b). In another passage (*ibid.*, 46a) Moses writes: "Baal Ha-Gador in his work on the commandments by way of truth."

author declares that he is descended "from the family of Rabbi Nehunya ben Ha-Kanah," and in *Sefer Ha-Kanah* it is noted that the work was written "in the year 4000," i.e., in the third century C.E. Heinrich Graetz, however, has demonstrated with irrefutable arguments that both works come from one author, who lived in Spain, though he is somewhat mistaken when he writes that the anonymous writer flourished in the last quarter of the fifteenth century.[4]

Both works begin in a thoroughly fantastic, mystical fashion:

I was standing on the Mount of Olives and I heard a voice but did not see anyone. The voice said to me, "Elkanah, my son, go from here. Return to your home and your dwelling." It was a whole mile from there to my house. But the earth moved from its place and through a miraculous foreshortening of the way [*kefitzat ha-derech*] I immediately stood before my house. I saw before me an old man and was terrified, for he looked like a heavenly appearance. And he said to me, "Fear not; I am Elijah." Indescribably great was my joy. And he revealed to me what is hidden in the heavenly heights and permitted me to see great wonders. He led me to a large stone of infernal fire and showed me what is inscribed there in black fire on white fire. As soon as I saw the stone and the inscription, Elijah said to me, "Elkanah, my son, do you understand what is written here?" I said, "Yes."[5]

Even more fantastic in style is the introduction[6] to *Sefer Ha-Kanah*:

These are the words of Aben Gador, the man who made a fence around God's sacred Torah. I once boarded a ship and set out to sea. Under the ship I saw a great mountain swimming, and I said to the men on the ship, "What do you see?" They replied, "A large mountain is moving under us." I asked them further, "What is your occupation?" And they answered, "We are believers in God, and out of great love for Him we mourn our whole life long for the exile of the *Shechinah* and spend our days in fasting." When I heard these words I cried out, "There is none like unto Thee, O Lord, among the gods. Who can fathom Thy deeds? Thou hast begun to reveal to me, Thy

---

4. The bibliographers have shown that as early as the first half of the fourteenth century copies of *Sefer Ha-Kanah* and *Sefer Ha-Peliah* were known (see Steinschneider, *Hebräische Bibliographie*, XV, 59; XVIII, 4). Jellinek's arguments (in *Kuntras Taryag*, p. 41) that the author of the two Midrashim came from Italy are not at all convincing.
5. From the introduction to *Sefer Ha-Peliah*.
6. The introduction was published separately under the title *Keneh Binah* as early as 1610 (in Prague) with supplements and a commentary.

servant, Thy wonders. Explain to me, then, what this mountain which follows us in the midst of the sea means and who these men are." And God sent a great serpent, whose tail was in the sea and whose head reached to the heavens. It placed itself between the mountain and the sea, greeted me and said: "The mountain is the beauty of the people of Israel that descends to the crown of wisdom, which bears the name sea . . . and these men who spend the days of grievous exile in fasting and sorrow are the *sefirot*, which yearn for the heavenly waters, as the forlorn and languishing yearn for the refreshing spring."[7]

And my eyes hovered over the vastness of the sea and considered God's great and wondrous deeds. And when I found myself in the middle of the sea, there shone before my eyes a dazzling light, and I saw someone running toward me and proclaiming the tidings: "The Messiah will come in the year 5250 [1490 C.E.], when the crown will rule." When I disembarked from the ship and set out on my way, I met another man who greeted me and said, "My lord, in the year 5250, when the crown rules, Israel will be redeemed."[8]

Characteristic is the account, in the introduction, of how *Sefer Ha-Kanah* came into being. "In the year 4000 [from the creation of the world] my father heard in a dream: 'Your daughter-in-law, the wife of your son Kanah, is pregnant. She will bear a son, and you shall call him Nahum, as your father was named.' The daughter-in-law then gave birth to a boy, and he was given the name Nahum." When the child was only three years old, all mysteries were revealed to him. Then, the author further relates, three men appeared. One was black, the second white, and the third yellow. The grandfather and the father were terrified, but the wonderful child calmly approached them and asked: Why have you come here? The white one said, I have come to familiarize you with the Written Torah. The black one replied, I will acquaint you with the Mishnah and the Talmud. And the one with the yellow face said, I will expound to you the Bible during the day and the Mishnah at night. I will hand over to you the letters of the alphabet in the most marvelous combinations and associations. I will teach you the profound mysteries of *notarikon* and *gematriot*. Then you will understand that the *niglot*, the things that are open and revealed to all, must be destroyed, and the *nistarot*, the hidden and veiled, will again build out of the destruction a strong and perfect structure.

---

7. The comparison of wisdom and Torah with fresh spring water is very common among the Kabbalists.
8. *Sefer Ha-Kanah*, 15b. Ran is the year 5250 from creation according to the Jewish reckoning of time.

Kabbalists and Satirists

In this mystical account the major tendency of the unknown author is discernible. Graetz,[9] who so despised Kabbalists and mystics, attempts to show that the author of these two Midrashim, "out of arrogance and ignorance," dared to mock the Talmudists and numerous commandments of the Torah. But not without reason do the sages of the Talmud say that "hatred disregards the rules of conduct." Graetz' hostility toward the Kabbalists is so intense that, in this instance, he overlooks the most important obligation of the historian: to investigate the truth without prejudice or extraneous motives. In regard to the author of *Sefer Ha-Kanah*, Graetz allows himself things which no reputable scholar and investigator may do. He tears quotations out of context and chops them up, so that the thought comes out mutilated and distorted, and not infrequently obtains an appearance completely opposite from what the author in fact intended. Hostility blinded our historian to such an extent that he simply did not recognize the unique dialectical manner of the author's style of writing and debating. *Sefer Ha-Kanah* is written in the form of a polemic conversation between the grandfather, the son, and the wonderful child. One asks and the other replies, not infrequently with a new question, sharply pointed and sarcastic. The author is an excellent dialectician, and to demonstrate the truth of his favorite idea that the Kabbalah is the crown of all wisdoms he endeavors, in dialectical fashion, to make the view of his opponents appear ridiculous. Given this kind of writing, it is not at all difficult to show, with half-quotations torn out of context and accidental phrases, whatever one wishes—not only that the author mocks the men of the Talmud but even God himself, not to speak of the prophets, who are declared in *Sefer Ha-Peliah* to be plain "fools."

We read in *Sefer Ha-Peliah*:[10]

The son then said to the father, "The prophets are fools, for our sages have said that since the Temple was destroyed the spirit of prophecy is found only among fools." The father replied, "They are fools only in *inyanei de-alma*, worldly or profane matters, but they are great sages in divine things.... The Kabbalists are the heirs and disciples of the prophets. They are the bearers of the tradition which has been transmitted from generation to generation, on from the time of Moses our teacher, the first and greatest of all the prophets.... The true heirs of the prophets and genuine bearers of the tradition are *the men of the Talmud*, and only thanks to them has the true wisdom, the wisdom of the Kabbalah, come down to us, for in every

---

9. *Geschichte der Juden*, VIII, Note 8.
10. 1 (we quote according to the Koretz edition of 1784).

The "Secrets of the Talmud"

word of theirs the deepest and most marvelous mysteries are concealed."

Both works of the anonymous mystic are permeated with the idea that the men of the Talmud are the bearers and teachers of the "hidden wisdom." We read further:

Were it not for the sages of the Talmud who took over the mysteries of the Torah from the prophets, who had received them from Moses our teacher, who spoke with God face to face, we would be even more ignorant in knowledge of the Torah than all the peoples of the world. But our sages pointed out the right way for those who grope in darkness. They enlightened our eyes and we enjoy the radiance of the *Shechinah*, thanks to the revealed mysteries inhering in the wondrous, holy names.[11]

"The Tannaim and Amoraim," the author of *Sefer Ha-Peliah* further declares, "learned this wisdom in the heavenly academy. All of them stood at Mount Sinai at the time of the giving of the Torah, and afterward God sent them down into the world. They are true, and their Torah is true."[12]

"Only consider carefully the intentions of the men of the Talmud," we read in *Sefer Ha-Kanah*,[13]

and you will at once be convinced that all their words are only parables and figures of speech, and when they speak of common material things, these are allusions to exalted matters of pure spirituality. If, however, you insist on the literal meaning of their words you will destroy the entire structure, for it is the hidden mysteries that are the essence and foundation of their Torah, which seeks to exalt and enlarge God's greatness and power. For every word that issues from their mouths is burning fire.

"Woe, woe to him," the author of *Sefer Ha-Peliah* cries out, "who does not yearn and strive to penetrate into the *sitrei Torah* [secrets of the Torah]."

The author applies the full power of his dialectic to demonstrate the foolishness and ridiculous conclusions at which those who hold merely to the literal meaning and refuse to seek out the mysteries hidden in the depths must arrive. And not, indeed, "to mock" the sages of the Talmud, as Graetz supposes, but simply as a polemic against his adversaries does the author dwell on the debate con-

11. *Sefer Ha-Peliah*, 50b. Cf. 11b.
12. *Ibid.*, 74a.
13. *Sefer Ha-Kanah*, 3a.

ducted in the Talmud concerning the meaning of the word *or* (light)—whether the word signifies dawn or twilight. It is important for him to show that in translating this simple word "the Tanna concealed a profound mystery," for the "brightness of light" is the symbol of the "light of wisdom," with the aid of which man drives the unclean and noxious out of God's house.[14]

Graetz commits a similar error when he scores the author of *Sefer Ha-Kanah* for mocking the commandments of *tzitzit* (wearing fringed garments) and *tefillin* (phylacteries). In fact, the fervent mystic has no other intention than to show that these commandments were not given merely as a sign and memorial; in them also lies a profound symbolic allusion, for they are bound up with the secret of the "channels" (*tzinorot*) which convey the divine attribute of lovingkindness (*ḥesed*).[15]

Especially characteristic is the debate conducted in *Sefer Ha-Kanah* on why women are exempt from numerous commandments that are obligatory only for men:

The wondrous child said to this father and grandfather, "Either both of you destroy and I will build up, or I will destroy and you will build anew." They said to him, "What do your words mean? What do they intend?" The child replied, "One must lift his voice to heaven and ask God why He created miserable woman, whom neither reward nor punishment await. She has been exempted from observance of most of the commandments, even from that which is equal in importance to all the others combined, the commandment of studying the Torah. For it is said in the Bible, 'And you shall teach your sons,' from which the sages of the Talmud concluded that this does not mean children generally, but specifically sons and not daughters. And they were not content with this; they even ordained that putting on *tefillin* is equal in weight to study of the Torah, and from this commandment also they exempted women. It is written, 'you shall study the Torah, for it is your life and the length of your days.' How can this be? Should men live long and women not? And they were still not satisfied with degrading poor woman, with declaring her unworthy to fulfill important obligations and precepts. She was also compared to a slave, and it was publicly affirmed that every commandment obligatory on a woman is also obligatory on a slave. Explain to me, for God's sake, how they permitted themselves to compare a free daughter of Israel to a Canaanite slave?"[16]

The author returns frequently to this matter, asks questions of the men of the Talmud and of God Himself—and all with a defi-

14. *Ibid.*, 68.
15. *Ibid.*, 40–46.
16. *Ibid.*, 23 and 71. See also *Sefer Ha-Peliah*, 74.

nite purpose: to show that, in relation to this problem, one can make nothing of the literal interpretation of the Biblical text but that one contradiction after another must proceed from it. Only the wisdom of the Kabbalah is capable, in his view, of reconciling all these inconsistencies. The great difference in the obligations which apply to the two sexes in regard to observance of the commandments has a universal, cosmic reason, for it is bound up with the sexuality of the *sefirot* themselves. These, after all, are divided into male and female, active and passive.[17]

The anonymous author, who was so thoroughly persuaded that the profoundest mysteries are concealed not only in the Biblical text but also in the sayings of the Talmudic sages, speaks with contempt of those scholars who do not acknowledge the mystical content of the Talmud. "Know, my son," we read in *Sefer Ha-Kanah*, "even he who studies the *Sifra* and *Sifre* and the entire Talmudic literature remains an ignoramus so long as he does not try to fathom their true substance, to seek out the mysteries hidden in them."[18]

It is therefore not surprising that this mystic speaks with such wrath of the rationalists. "Those who attempt to explain the meaning of the Torah by way of natural science, i.e., according to the laws of nature, and assert that man's intellect unites with the highest intellect only lead astray and beguile the children of our sacred Torah."[19] Elsewhere the author indignantly declares, "Those who make allegories and dreams of everything—may their names be blotted out and their memory be forgotten in future generations!"[20]

This zealous mystic, however, is not content merely with carrying on a struggle against the rationalists. Like Abraham Abulafia, on whose work he very frequently relies,[21] the author of *Sefer Ha-Kanah* also sharply assails the rabbis and theologians. "In the heavens," he cries out, "the sins of the Talmudists who occupy themselves with vain and foolish things are marked down."[22] These have forgotten the tradition of the Tannaim and Amoraim,

17. *Sefer Ha-Peliah*, 74.
18. *Sefer Ha-Kanah*, 23.
19. *Sefer Ha-Peliah*, 45.
20. Ibid., 80a.
21. On the large extent to which this mystic utilizes the works of his predecessors, Abraham Abulafia and others, see Jellinek, *Kuntras Taryag*, pp. 40–41. This, however, does not justify the severe verdict which Steinschneider issues in regard to the author of *Sefer Ha-Kanah*: "The impudent plagiarist and fraud" (*Polemische und apologetische Literatur*, pp. 368–69).
22. *Sefer Ha-Kanah*, 2.

every one of whose words is holy. Some of the later Talmudists did not understand the mysteries hidden in the words of the sages or grasp how essential it is to attain these mysteries and reveal them to others.

The author attacks with particular severity a certain segment of the rabbis of his era, whom he calls in one passage "worthless and wanton men."[23] In his polemic against these rabbis, a unique feature that is very typical of the author of *Sefer Ha-Kanah* appears with special prominence: his ascetic mood, his hostility to those who devote themselves excessively to the pleasures of this world. "Woe," he cries,

to those who live in luxury and deck themselves in rich and colorful garments. They forget that we are in exile and are hated and persecuted by the nations of the world. They ought to be clothed in sorrow. They ought to weep and mourn rather than glory in the beautiful garments which tomorrow will be torn from them with mockery and shame. Even if they are buried in their finery, the enemy will exhume them from their graves and cast their bodies to the dogs and birds.[24]

Woe to those parents who allow their children to spend their time singing and dancing, arranging happy parties, enjoying the finest foods and best wines, and completely forget that death lurks for them and that the fate of perishing not naturally but through a horrible death may befall them.[25]

The mystic and reprover blames the rabbis of his time for all this:

Have you seen such a remarkable thing, my son? We always wonder why the exile lasts so long! But observe! Our rabbis, who are such strict disciplinarians, who fulminate with thunder and lightning for the least jot and tittle of every law, who multiply new interpretations of the law every day, eat and drink like wild animals and guzzle wine by the bucket. Their faces are bloodshot, covered with fat and flesh. . . . And they forget completely that the *Shechinah* is in exile. They do not guide the people or give them moral instruction. . . . They spend their whole life only in concern for the body and do not think of the soul at all. . . . They are learned and have knowledge, but they do not observe and fulfill. Even the Talmud they study with one purpose only: to make themselves great before the multitude, to say, "I am learned in Torah."[26]

23. *Ibid.*, 37b.
24. *Ibid.*, 122b.
25. *Ibid.*
26. *Ibid.* See also *Sefer Ha-Peliah*, 78b.

Especially interesting in this respect is the account by the author of *Sefer Ha-Kanah* of his encounter with a rabbi, a handsome elderly man. He requested the rabbi to permit him to come to his home that he might hear Torah from his lips.

Then the old man took me by the hand and brought me to his house, and his house was full of wives and concubines, of servants and maidservants. There were whole barrels of wine there, and the cupboards were filled with all kinds of delicacies. Then I said to him, "My lord, God has blessed you with everything good, but this is not the proper way for a scholar." Then he sat down opposite me and said, "My son, I see that you are confused and do that which God hates. By your appearance you are a son of worthy people, but your parents did great wrong in not guiding you in the ways of the world, in not accustoming you to the demands of real life. For God created man with all his senses, endowed him with eyes so that they might enjoy love and beauty, provided him with hands so that he would be able to fulfill his wishes, gave him desires and lusts; and man ought to satisfy these desires and enjoy all things, including feminine beauty. And now, my son, follow my advice. Not without reason did God create us. One should eat and drink and enjoy everything; otherwise, we will go to the grave hungry and unsatisfied." When I heard his ugly words, I prayed to God, and the house fell down and killed all its inhabitants. The city, however, I led to repentance.[27]

Graetz violently berates the "impudence and arrogance" of this "ignorant" author. Steinschneider regards him as a "shameless plagiarist and fraud." But neither of these eminent scholars recognized the valuable and remarkable things that this unshakable fanatic and zealous Kabbalist possessed—the flame of true dedication, of passionate devotion to his ideal, his *sanctum sanctorum*. His fiery feeling, his colorful, stormy, indignant style seized the reader with tremendous force, tore him out of his apathy, demanded and challenged him. And, indeed, in this turbulent temperament, in this aggressive polemical talent, lies the secret of the great popularity that these two Midrashim of the anonymous author enjoyed for many generations.[28]

27. *Sefer Ha-Kanah*, 26b.
28. After this chapter was already written in Russian (1918) an article by S. A. Horodetsky appeared (*Ha-Tekufah*, X, 283–329) in which he speaks very enthusiastically about the author of *Sefer Ha-Kanah* and *Sefer Ha-Peliah*. Unfortunately Horodetzky's essay demonstrates that not only enmity but love as well "disregards the rules of conduct." The article is not written in the form of a cultural-historical inquiry but in the fervent style of *Shivḥei Baal Shem Tov* and *Kahal Ḥasidim*. For Horodetzky the anonymous mystic is a "man of the spirit who is en-

In the person of the author of *Sefer Ha-Kanah* and *Sefer Ha-Peliah*, the Kabbalah of the Spanish Jews appears in a new vesture, the melancholy garment of asceticism that carries on warfare with "this world" and sees in the body and its desires sinfulness, the *sitra aḥara* (other side). The more grievous and gloomy the situation of Spanish Jewry became, the stronger did this tendency grow, and on its victorious march it trampled the shoots of free speculative thought and triumphantly laid its stamp on the rabbinic world outlook and made it its faithful follower and servant.

But the representatives of the opposing tendency, of rationalist philosophical thought, still refused to surrender. They fought devotedly for "a long-lost thing" and still dreamed of victory. At the same time that the manuscripts of *Sefer Ha-Kanah* and *Sefer Ha-Peliah* began to spread among the Jewish communities and Isaac Arama wrote his *Ḥazut Kashah*, the son of the author of the *Kevod Elohim*, Shemtov ben Joseph, carried on his scientific work.[29] In his lengthy commentary to Maimonides' *Guide for the Perplexed* he again endeavors to make peace between the "two lights," between the "intellect" (philosophy) and "law" (religion).[30] An ardent disciple of Maimonides, he declares with contempt that

> the bright memory of the great scholar cannot be obscured by the foolish rabbis who may have a reputation in their communities but know nothing and understand nothing and grope in darkness, while Maimonides' way is the way of radiant light which shines with its former brilliance to the present day.[31]

And Shemtov ben Joseph admonishes the reader "not to allow his thinking to be obscured, not to permit himself to be led astray with

---

    tirely holy, pure as crystal; he rests in God and speaks constantly with God" (*op. cit.*, p. 326). When the fanatical ascetic and moralist complains about the life style of his era, this suffices for Horodetzky to speak of the "corrupt milieu" in which this "man of God" was unfortunately fated to live.

29. Shemtov ben Joseph wrote commentaries to several works of Averroes and also a special work on the purpose of "the work of creation" and on the relationship between form and matter (1461). In 1489 he composed his *Derashot Ha-Torah* which went through three editions in the sixteenth century (see Steinschneider, *Polemische und apologetische Literatur*, p. 120, and also S. Munk, *Mélanges de philosophie juive et arabe*, p. 508-9).
30. See the introduction to his commentary on the *Guide*, and his comments on the *Guide*, III:51.
31. His commentary to III:26 (we quote according to the Jessnitz edition of 1742).

false opinions nor let himself be talked into believing that these are a whole Torah, as indeed happens with many ignorant rabbis of our time who think that they come close to God by believing in all kinds of falsehoods and empty dreams."[32]

The most interesting thing, however, is that Shemtov ben Joseph, the faithful Aristotelian, wishes nonchalantly to refute Hasdai Crescas' epoch-making work, his polemic against the foundations of Aristotle's *Physics*. The very raising of criticisms of the scientific authority of the great world genius is, for Shemtov, incredible impudence. Unable scientifically to refute Crescas' arguments, he contents himself with the assertion that "whoever is capable of distinguishing the true from the false with his mind will immediately perceive the errors of Rabbi Hasdai."[33]

Shemtov ben Joseph was a weak adversary, and his attack on the "foolish rabbis" made no significant impression. In his time, however, another fighter came forward who, in his battle against the orthodox rabbis and Kabbalists, employed the keenest weapons, the lash of satire and the arrows of mockery and sarcasm.

The name of this satirist has not been definitely established, for he appeared under a pseudonym, the first in Jewish literature, Palmon ben Pelet. Nevertheless, as we shall presently see, one can assert on the basis of well-grounded conjectures that his real name was Joseph ben Meshullam. The satirist indicates quite precisely the time of his literary debut, the spring of 1468. It was then that his satire *Alilot Devarim*, one of the most brilliant works of this genre in Hebrew literature, appeared.[34] According to the explanation of the author himself, the title of his work means "words of battle and anger." He declares war against all the foolish, obsolete customs of his day, everything that is contrary to common sense, that smacks of mold and mildew. His mockery and laughter, his satiric, venomous arrows are hurled at the camp of the "rebels against the light," the orthodox rabbis and Kabbalists. This richly endowed satirist, brilliant stylist, and master of Biblical prose was an Aristotelian rationalist of the extreme left wing. His credo was *shilton ha-sechel*, the unlimited, sole sovereignty of speculative thought. This is the only immortal thing in man, and what binds him to the world spirit, the "active intellect." To attain *muskalot*, abstract philosophical conceptions, is the supreme duty of man. For him, Maimonides and Gersonides are the greatest authorities. He is thoroughly persuaded that they alone have true conceptions of the nature of God, and that one can speak of God's omniscience

32. Commentary to II:47 (end).
33. Introduction to Part II, Hakdamah 1.
34. First published in *Otzar Nehmad*, IV (1863), 179–214.

only in the sense which Gersonides explicates, namely, that the divine knowledge embraces only the universal or general, not the particular or individual.[35]

In one significant respect, however, the author of *Alilot Devarim* is sharply distinguished from the majority of the rationalists of that era. He possessed the virtue which Maimonides and his followers lacked: a historical-critical sense, a feeling for historical development. He gives an altogether objective and, in general, accurate overview of the first stages in the development of the tradition. He presents an excellent characterization of Rashi's work and acutely emphasizes that Rashi's commentary to the Talmud has greater scientific value than his commentary to the Pentateuch, in which *peshat* (literal meaning) and *derush* (homiletic interpretation) are so naively mixed together.[36] The satirist has great respect for the sages of the Talmud and their work. On the other hand, however, he criticizes very severely their "weapon-bearers" and protagonists—the interpreters, decisors, codifiers, and Tosafists. He accuses the scholars and rabbis of later generations of having proceeded on crooked ways, of having distorted and perverted the meaning of the sayings of the Talmudic sages, and of having—on the authority of these—devised laws and precepts such as "your ancestors never dreamed of." These epigones created whole mountains of *novellae, responsa*, and all kinds of subtleties. They call this *pilpul* (dialectic), but it is more properly called *bilbul* (confusion), which confounds and entangles thought.[37] "The Bible and the Talmud," the author of *Alilot Devarim* laments, "lie in a corner. No one inquires about them and no one is interested in them; but whoever occupies himself with *pilpul* is held in great esteem, though he may know nothing besides *pilpul*." Inquire of the earlier generations, he continues, whether they occupied themselves with the *pilpul* in which you are so engrossed. Compare yourselves with them, contrast their cultural condition with yours; only then will you have some notion of how ignorant you are, how low you have fallen and keep falling ever lower.

35. *Ibid.*, pp. 191–92, 206–7.
36. *Ibid.*, pp. 182, 199.
37. *Ibid.*, p. 183. A contemporary of the satirist who belonged to the opposing camp, the orthodox pietist Joseph Yaabetz, also strongly deplores *pilpul* in his *Or Ha-Ḥayyim*: "They pay attention only to *pilpul* in order to display their mental agility and to purify the mind; in this they spend all their days, and they do not fathom the essence of the Torah. They gain no knowledge even of the laws applicable every day, not to speak of true piety and the essence of what is genuinely important."

The Author of Alilot Devarim

"O you poor leaders," he addresses those who are at the head of the people, "knowledge and enlightenment are hateful to you, for you are afraid that the people will have their eyes opened and realize how petty and ignorant you, its leaders, are." "O my people," he further exclaims emotively, "those who watch over you are those who enslave you. Your leaders are your misleaders. They have locked for you the gates of wisdom and knowledge, and not a single ray of light penetrates through to you."[38] The satirist and convinced rationalist attacks the Kabbalists with the same fierce indignation. He laughs at their preoccupation with "combinations of letters" and mocks the images and illustrations in which they gather the *sefirot*. "They are forever counting the letters of God's name, but God Himself is alien to them and they do not understand Him." These men, asserts the author of *Alilot Devarim*, are no better than the Baal worshippers of old; they are just as idolatrous as the latter were.

No matter how sharply the satirist attacks his ideological opponents, he is nevertheless compelled in places to speak merely in insinuations, to veil his allusions in Biblical quotations and similes. But he wishes clearly and sharply to dot every *i*, and devises ways of making his mockery all the more bitter and his arrows as pointed as possible. This he achieves in a very ingenious way. He composes a commentary to his satire and pretends that it was written by someone else, one Joseph ben Meshullam, who discovered an old, half-rotted manuscript and, since the content of the manuscript interested him, wrote a commentary to it. And the commentator, playing the fool, begs his readers not to complain of him if they should find in this work some heretical ideas; he, after all, is no more than an interpreter and cannot be responsible for the author's thoughts and conceptions. That all this, however, is nothing but a pretense to mystify the public is easy to see from the following dates. The satire, as we know, was written in 1468 and in Italy five years later, in the spring of 1473, the well-known Abraham Farissol copied the satire *together with the commentary*. Hence, the commentary was written not to an old, half-rotted manuscript but to something quite new. In fact, it is the commentary that most sharply points the arrows which the satirist hurls at his adversaries. It insists with ostensible naiveté that "in this book" the words *rabbi* and *ignoramus* are identical, that the word *morim* (teachers, guides) rhymes very well with *ḥamorim* (asses), and that by what are nowadays called "pious, godfearing men" are meant simply "boorish, ignorant masses," etc.

38. *Ibid.*, p. 183.

Kabbalists and Satirists

In the style of the Biblical prophets the satirist addresses the shepherds of Israel:

> You cannot even defend yourselves by pleading that you erred and sinned merely out of ignorance. For thus says the Almighty: "After the close of the Talmud I sent you a godly man, the second Moses [Maimonides]. He gave you his *Mishneh Torah*, in which he explained the entire Torah with all its commandments and precepts. He also created a book whose value is incalculable. This was to be a guide for all who are 'perplexed,' all who are in doubt and questing. . . . But you did not follow his ways. You turned away from him, arrogantly burned his wondrous book on the pyre, falsified his *Mishneh Torah* which embraces the whole written Torah and the entire Talmud, and corrupted its great beauty. You surrounded it with your commentaries and additions. You called this improvement and explanation, but you only mutilated and corrupted it. You did not explain, but rather obscured and distorted. For his way is not like your ways. His logic is not your hairsplitting, and you cannot attain his greatness."[39]

The satirist turns with his reproving words not only to the leaders of the people but to the people itself. With mockery and sarcasm he shows his contemporaries how deeply mired in ignorant and foolish superstitions they are, and the barbarism of their customs. These brilliant pages have not only an ethnographic interest; they are also of significant historical value. In modern European literature one not infrequently encounters works which bear the stamp of "stylization." An attempt is made, for instance, to imitate the unique form of the Italian novella writers of the Renaissance era or to write in the style of the German *Nibelungenlied* or of the old Russian *Vilines*. And, along with this, an effort is made not only to imitate the style and form of the old works of art but also to copy the archaic world outlook of the era in which they were composed. But in Hebrew literature, in the artistic creativity of the ancient, wandering people, we see a completely different phenomenon, something not to be found among any other people. Jewish culture in its millennial way experienced numerous ascents and declines. The tragic fate of the eternally roaming people very often cast them down from radiant heights into dark abysses; and from the depths they began once more, with great effort, to climb slowly upward. With such a zigzag course of rising and falling it happens not infrequently that in different eras, separated by many generations, the same cultural phenomena are repeated. Similar ideological tendencies, which obtain the same

39. *Ibid.*, p. 185.

literary dress and reveal themselves in analogous forms, appear under identical cultural conditions. Here there can be no question of "stylization" or "imitation." We have before us *one and the same style*. Now, anyone familiar with the modern Hebrew literature of the Haskalah period and recalling the ingenious satires of Isaac Erter's *Ha-Tzofeh Le-Bet Yisrael* will be literally overwhelmed by the brilliant pages of *Alilot Devarim*. He will be astonished not only at the extent to which these two writers, separated by almost four centuries, write in the same style and manner but at the fact that even the substance, the themes and phenomena of life against which they issue forth with the lash of their satire, are identical. Furthermore, in places it seems that the Spaniard of the fifteenth century breathes a freer atmosphere and that his eye has a wider range than that of the Galician *maskil* of the nineteenth century. And here there can be no question of any influence whatsoever, for *Alilot Devarim* was first published in 1863, twelve years after Isaac Erter's death. Erter's satires are frequently written in the form of dreams and revelations. In one of them he mocks Kallir's liturgical poems, with their barbaric, outrageous language whose meaning no simple mortal can understand. In *Alilot Devarim* also a fantastic dream is described[40] in humorous form—how before the Throne of Glory a miserable woman pleading for protection and help appears with great weeping. To the question, "Who are you, daughter?," the woman answers: In the land of Shinar, in Babylonia, was I born, a daughter of priests and prophets. My cradle stood in the tent of the Men of the Great Synagogue, and the last of the prophets raised me. Marvelous was my splendor and beauty, but see what the liturgical poets have made of me. They ripped off my magnificent garment, covered my body with wounds, boils, and abscesses. No complete limb has been left to me; I am mutilated and distorted. My appearance arouses dread, and my name is—Prayer.

In his *Tashlich* and *Telunat Sani Ve-Sansani Ve-Samangaluf* Isaac Erter mocks foolish customs—casting one's sins into the water, or hanging charms on the bed of a woman in childbirth to frighten away the witches and demons so that they will have no power over the newborn child. Against these same superstitions the author of *Alilot Devarim* issues forth with his mockery and laughter. Behold, he cries out, how Jacob's children come to the banks of ponds, there shake out their skirts into the water, and whisper prayers. Thus they throw their sins of a whole year into the depths, and with great joy run home, for they have purified

---

40. *Ibid.*, pp. 185-87.

themselves of all their misdeeds. And eight days later, on the eve of Yom Kippur, they seize a luckless fowl, every man a rooster and every woman a hen, and they twirl these around their foolish heads, and cry and shriek, "This in exchange for me!"

The satirist of *Alilot Devarim* passes on to other customs.[41] He mocks the gestures, the throwing oneself about in prayer and the shaking, done to fulfill the Biblical verse, "All my bones will speak." When the moon appears, we further read, the Jews run out, disperse over all the mountains and various regions, jump about like wild goats, and pray before the moon. When a woman gives birth to a child, they gird their loins with swords, make a circle around the mother and newborn child, and utter barbaric formulas and bizarre incantations. They mark the corners and the walls with illustrations, and draw pictures of Adam and Eve and the serpent. Thus they carry on warfare with the evil ones, demons and angels of destruction. If someone is sick, they do not turn to the doctor but to witches and exorcisers. They set fires around the sick person on all four sides and pull off his undergarments, spreading them toward the light of the moon. They measure him with ropes lengthwise and across. They make puppets out of these and keep on reciting formulas, uttering all kinds of incantations. They tear up graves and call to the dead. There is no limit to their wild follies.

Let this not be defended by saying, the author of *Alilot Devarim* continues,[42] that other peoples also have a great many foolish customs. Open the Law of Moses. Will you there find any mention of these? Is it not there admonished, "You shall not imitate the deeds of the land of Egypt and the land of Canaan"? Remove the foreign idols from your habitations. Wash yourselves clean from all this filth. Let yourselves no longer be led astray by the exorcisers who have so greatly multiplied among you. Innumerable are your superstitions, but you lack the one true belief.

Only with knowledge, cries out this thoroughgoing Maimunist, with the inquiring thought of the educated mind, can one truly serve God. But if you proceed further on the way of superstition, you will become like the Amalekites, Midianites, and other barbarous peoples. Only the name *Am Yisrael* (people of Israel) will you still bear, but perhaps even the name will also be forgotten.

41. It is difficult to say for certain whether all of the customs, so interesting from the ethnographic point of view, were practiced by the Jews of Spain. It is possible that the satirist also visited neighboring countries, such as Italy and others, and thereby became familiar with the customs of their Jews.
42. *Otzar Neḥmad*, IV, 188–89, 204.

Thwarted Hopes of Redemption

The closing pages of the satire are extremely interesting. The author portrays the intellectual and spiritual condition of his generation in pitch-black tones. He sees around himself only superstition and corruption. Yet he has not lost hope and believes in a brighter future:

Yes, we all grope like blind men in the dark. We are all drowsing and sunk in fantastic dreams. Yet I believe that somewhere, in a hidden corner, sits one who watches and that he, the wakeful one, will arouse all who sleep. We know, after all, how from one spark innumerable lights are kindled.

We have seen, the satirist further declares, the great wonders that one Maimonides performed with his works. The number of his adversaries was great, and his books were burned on pyres. Nevertheless, thanks to him, many became open-eyed. All his opponents could no longer snuff out the light which this man kindled; for great and indomitable is the power of knowledge and understanding.

The satirist dreams of the great day of redemption when the emissary filled with God's spirit, the shoot of "Jesse's stock" whose wisdom will be "broader than the sea," will appear. All will await his command. He will be the banner of all the peoples, the consolation of mankind as a whole. He will rouse all out of the sleep of darkness and ignorance. He will enlighten the eyes of the entire exiled people with his divine spirit. Under his protection wisdom will rule the world, strife and warfare will have no further dominion, and man, with open and understanding eyes, will march on the path of light and truth.

But what a bitter disappointment was in store for our gifted satirist! When he dreamed of the victory of light and knowledge, the terrible decree was already sealed, and the black wings of the Inquisition already covered Catholic Spain. It was not the "light of knowledge" but the infernal fire of the stakes at which men were burned that flared up on the Iberian peninsula, and not paeans and praises to the sovereign intellect and its accomplishments that ascended to the heavens but the groans and shrieks of thousands tortured to death.

The fate of the Jews was already determined. The armies of the pious Catholic King Ferdinand were besieging the last "city of refuge" of Arabic civilization and power in Spain, beautiful Granada. Its days were now numbered. And there, in proud Granada, the last Hebrew poet of Andalusia then lived and sang his song, the swan song of the Jewish muse in Spain. The catastrophe which soon befell Spanish Jewry choked his song. Its sounds were snuffed out, and only fragmentary chords have come down to us, not entire poems and lyrics but chance stanzas and mutilated verses. This is merely the weak echo of an extinguished song, a memorial of a poetic creativity which was destroyed in the time of the great tragedy.

The poet was Saadiah ben Maimon Ibn Danan. Like the author of *Alilot Devarim*, Ibn Danan was an enthusiastic disciple of Maimonides. A rabbinic judge in Granada, he devoted himself extensively to Hebrew philology[43] and wrote a work on Jewish history.[44] His true vocation, however, was poetry. In the literary creativity of this last of the Hebrew poets of Andalusia the long silent chords of the heyday of Hebrew poetry in Spain reawakened. Songs of ardent love and flaming passion were again heard. Ibn Danan writes poems of praise to the "daughter of the vine," with whom he has been in love "since his youthful years." But the poet is infatuated not with the daughter of the vine only, and it is not her alone that he celebrates in his poems. "Whosoever has a heart sick of love, let him seek recovery in the blooming fields, amidst the fragrance of flowers and the song of birds. Let him heartily embrace his beloved and cover her face with kisses; the trees with their thick shadows will conceal them and tell no one their secret." "Abide with me, my lovely one; you have captured my heart and soul. Stay in my chamber till your father returns; lie in my arms until your mother comes." "On my breast lies my beloved; close to her breasts she presses her lyre; her hand plays on the strings, and the strings of my heart she breaks and the wounds of love remain without healing." "My beloved dazzles like the sun; like the morning star she shines on my couch. Her rosy cheeks glisten like the rays of the moon, and her black locks hold my heart captive." "My beloved's brows are like strained bows. They hurl lightning arrows into the languishing heart. I longed to cover her lips with ardent kisses, and the flame of her breath has burned my heart."

A true poet, Ibn Danan cannot resist the impulse to creation. He must write his poetry when he feels inspired. "As soon as the muse's sacred fire touches my heart, I must sing, and I create my Hebrew and Arabic songs." Like Moses Ibn Ezra, Jehudah Alharizi,

43. His major work, *Sefer Ha-Shorashim*, has been preserved in manuscript. In the first chapter, entitled "Be-Mishkelei Ha-Shirim" (which Neubauer published in *Melechet Perek Ha-Shir*), Ibn Danan includes some fragments of his own poems.
44. His monograph entitled *Seder Ha-Dorot* was published in *Ḥemdah Genuzah* (1856).

and Immanuel of Rome in their day, so Saadiah Ibn Danan also speaks with emotion of the great significance of the gifted poet. The poetic art is for him genuine service of God. "Do you know, my brethren, who gave birth to the poets and whence their songs come? It may be that they are prophets, and God's word is on their lips." "The muse's beloved are the stars that illuminate the earth, and the holy Temple is their habitation. How lovely is their portion; they rule over the word, and the flame of inspiration is in their hearts."

Ibn Danan's gay, life-loving song harmonized very poorly with the dominant mood of the time, and many refused to pardon him for his erotic poems. His contemporary Abraham Gavison, who speaks with great respect of Ibn Danan as a Talmudist and calls him "the great rabbi, the light of Israel," reproaches him for his "sin" in writing "frivolous and erotic" songs.[45]

Hence the poet often felt forlorn and solitary. "I write," Ibn Danan complains, "and they will not read. I teach, and they will not learn. I disclose the treasures of my soul, but they will not believe. Though I may preach like Hillel, they turn away from me. My song may be sweeter than the Levites', but their ears are deaf to it." "I proclaim the truth," the poet laments in another song, "to a false generation. I call to them in vain; no one wishes to listen. I desire peace, and my contemporaries declare war on me. I am concerned for their welfare, and they devise evil against me. I uncover the depths of my soul, and they whisper slanders against me."

It would, however, be erroneous to think that the controversy between the poet and his contemporaries derived solely from the fact that he sang "frivolous" songs. Most of his adversaries were provoked by his satires and polemical tracts. Ibn Danan was not only a poet but a scholar. In philosophy and science the greatest authority for him was Maimonides. He regarded the anti-Maimunists and opponents of rational philosophy as "rebels against the light," as ignorant obscurantists, and he fought against them with the same weapon as the author of *Alilot Devarim*, the lash of satire and sarcastic laughter. One of his satires has come down to us in its entirety,[46] and it must be admitted that it harmonizes very little with the poet's assurance that he was a seeker of peace and wished to live in concord with all.

"Behold," Ibn Danan calls out,

---

45. *Omer Ha-Shikehah*, 131b.
46. Published in *Divrei Ḥachamim* (1849), pp. 81–82.

how these narrow-minded people despise all knowledge, hide themselves from the light of the sun, and like bats show themselves only in the shadow of night. These, the lost and confused, declare war against the *Guide for the Perplexed,* the pointer of the way. They blaspheme and shame the book which destroyed the fortresses of idolatry and superstition, which heals the deepest wounds, which is the tower of light to all who thirst for knowledge, which plants the tree of life and roots out thorns and thistles, which has revealed the great wonders and treasures of the Torah and made all heretics and deceivers a mockery and a shame.

The satirist further declares,

Those who whisper with their lips that "the Lord is one" and free from the slightest matter portray Him as sitting on a throne surrounded by hosts of angels. And when the *Guide* showed how ignorant and benighted they are and disclosed their shame before the entire world, these fools, who with their blind eyes could not appreciate its light and brilliance, poured out all their hatred on "Greek wisdom" and perceived in it the greatest danger. . . . If you blind and benighted ones could see and understand, you would know that our Torah is the source of wisdom and knowledge. It has shone with its light for all peoples, and the Greek thinkers, when they sought philosophical truth, discovered it in the religion of Moses.

CHAPTER EIGHT

Don Isaac Abravanel

SAADIAH Ibn Danan's native city fell. The cross triumphed over the flag of Islam, and our poet had to exchange the satirist's whip for the wanderer's staff. In 1492, when Christopher Columbus set out on the Atlantic to discover a new world, Granada, the last fortress of Arabic civilization in Europe, succumbed before the Christian armies. It was there, in the magnificent palace known as the Alhambra, that the last act of the tragic drama was concluded and the fate of Spanish Jewry sealed. The fanatical Inquisitor General of Spain, Thomas de Torquemada, blessed the pious royal couple, Ferdinand and Isabella, as they signed the edict of expulsion, decreeing that within four months all Jews refusing to adopt the Catholic faith must leave the three Spanish lands, Castile, Aragon, and Sicily.

All at once, the great cultural center which for over five hundred years had exercised spiritual and intellectual dominion over the entire Jewish diaspora was destroyed. Hundreds of thousands had to abandon their homes and set out for distant, unknown places where, in every corner, misfortune and dread lurked for them. Many of the affluent leaders of Jewish society did not stand the test and, in order not to have to leave the land, converted to Catholicism. Thousands of families delivered themselves from exile through apostasy,[1] among them the wealthy tax-farmer and

1. The liturgical poet of that era, Abraham Ḥayyun, laments this in one of his elegies: "From the day God created man there has been no such great apostasy among the Jews, to destroy them" (we quote according to the manuscript in the library in Leningrad of the Society for the Dissemination of Enlightenment Among Jews).

chief rabbi appointed by the Castilian government, Abraham Senior.

It is of this betrayal of their people by many of the Jewish grandees and intellectuals that a historian of that era, Abraham ben Solomon of Torrutiel, writes:

In the year 1492 God's wrath was poured out on his people Israel . . . for our sins had become fearfully great and our guilt reached to the heavens. . . . For the sake of the secular sciences the Torah was virtually forgotten, and only the poor and needy occupied themselves with the Oral Law. . . . And when the great catastrophe came, the majority of the Jewish nobles, leaders, and judges did not withstand the ordeal and, to save themselves from expulsion, forsook the true faith and exchanged it for idols. Leading the apostates was the chief rabbi of all of Spain, Don Abraham Senior—he, his son, and all his family. Thousands upon thousands imitated him. May their names be blotted out from the book of life, for they not only sinned themselves but caused others, who looked to them as their leaders and followed their ways, to sin. Of all of the prominent leaders and heads of the communities, only a few decided to sacrifice themselves for the sanctification of God's name. Chief among these was Rabbi Don Isaac Abravanel.[2]

With even greater wrath does another contemporary, the noted preacher of that era, Joseph ben Ḥayyim Yaabetz (died 1507), who after the expulsion migrated to Italy and travelled around among the various Jewish communities to give didactic sermons, speak of this.[3] "Listen, my brethren! I am one of the exiles of Spain, and I saw how ordinary women and unlettered men sacrificed their lives and their fortunes for the sanctification of God's name, but the majority of the cultured, who so glory in their knowledge, became apostates and desecrated their honor in the day of the great misfortune."[4]

Like Abraham of Torrutiel, so the deeply pious Joseph Yaabetz saw in the catastrophe God's just punishment[5] for the fact that Jews devoted themselves more to philosophy and secular sciences

2. See Neubauer, *Seder Ha-Ḥachamim Ve-Korot Ha-Yamim*, I, 111–12.
3. See his *Or Ha-Ḥayyim*, 2–3, 12a.
4. *Ibid.*, 5a.
5. The basic motif of "punishment" and "taking vengeance" on rebellious children is to be heard in most of the elegies and laments of that time mourning the great expulsion. In one elegy we read: "The father raised children—to take vengeance upon them." Another begins with the following words: "Who is the father who chastises his son with the chastisements of vengeance and pours out his wrath upon him mightily and with hot anger?"

than to the sacred Torah. And he pours out all his anger on the *mitpalsefim* (philosophizers) in his *Or Ha-Hayyim*. "These educated men, proud of their knowledge and learning in philosophic matters, cast off the yoke of the commandments and precepts of the Torah. They declared that these are merely for the multitude, not for persons who have enjoyed the tree of knowledge."[6] Yaabetz cries out with great anger:

How contemptuously these base men, with their very slight knowledge of secular sciences, looked at the sages of the Kabbalah and all the others who remained faithful to the tradition and refused to agree with them that the Torah is merely a commentary to Aristotle's *Ethics*! With what arrogance, mockery, and ridicule they regarded the pious, godfearing women in whose conceptions and understanding God took on human forms! But it was precisely these simple women who sacrificed themselves for the sanctification of God's name and also demanded the same of their husbands, while all the educated, who so exulted in their wisdom and philosophical speculation, did not stand the test and became apostates and converts.[7]

"I do not intend," Yaabetz further says, "to carry on controversies with the rationalists and philosophizers, to show how groundless their theories are. This has already been brilliantly demonstrated by the greatest thinker of his age, Hasdai Crescas. I wish merely to cry aloud: 'Hear and know, you are lost and erring!' "[8]

Joseph Yaabetz' *Or Ha-Hayyim* is interesting, because it reflects very clearly the moods which dominated the Spanish exiles. In its pages are heard their anger and indignation toward that segment of the Jewish intelligentsia in whom philosophical rationalism destroyed the religious sentiment and who, in the day of trial, preferred baptism to expulsion.

The fate of the Spanish exiles was an extremely painful and bitter one. The chroniclers and historians of that era provide horrible details of how the Jews who had been driven out of Spain perished by the thousands from cold, hunger, and all kinds of plagues and afflictions. Robbers and pirates lay in wait for them on the highways and the seas, plundered them, and ruthlessly slaughtered them or sold them into slavery. The cup of agony was filled to overflowing and those who survived were permeated with a single thought: This can no longer be endured!

6. *Or Ha-Hayyim*, 5a, 10b.
7. *Ibid.*, 12.
8. *Ibid.*, 23.

There must be a *finis* to the unbearable sufferings! The "end" must be near; redemption must come speedily. The terrible darkness is only the gloom before the approaching dawn; the fearful woes are the *ḥevlei ha-mashiaḥ* (pangs of the Messiah). The great, bright day of redemption is being born, and soon the redeemer, Messiah the son of David, the savior of the exiled people and the star of all mankind, will appear in all his marvelous splendor and beauty.

The inspired emissary and harbinger of these mystic-redemptive currents and hopes was the man who led the entire host and stood at the head of the Jews who were expelled from Spain, the celebrated Don Isaac Abravanel (born in 1437).

The life of this eminent figure was filled with exciting and dramatic moments.[9] Expert in financial and economic matters, Abravanel occupied a very important post at the court of the Portuguese king Alfonso V. After the king's death in 1483, however, he had to flee from Portugal. He settled in Castile and, thanks to his brilliant capacities, found favor with King Ferdinand, who appointed him his financial agent. After the expulsion of 1492 Abravanel, together with a group of exiles, travelled to Italy and settled in Naples, where he found a protector in its King Ferdinand, who understood how properly to employ his expertise in finance and statecraft. But here again Abravanel was destined not to find rest. The king of France, Charles VIII, conquered Naples, and in 1495 Abravanel was compelled to flee, together with Ferdinand, to Sicily. When the French army occupied Naples, he lost his entire fortune, his books, and also some of his manuscripts. From Sicily Abravanel soon went to Corfu, and from there, at the end of 1496, to southern Italy to the city of Monopoli, where for seven years he dedicated himself exclusively to literary work. In 1503 he moved to Venice, where he died in 1508 at the age of seventy.

Despite the fact that Abravanel was during most of his life a wanderer and devoted much time to financial and political matters, his literary legacy is very considerable.[10] Until the expulsion from Spain he occupied himself relatively little with literary activity,

9. Autobiographical information about Abravanel is to be found in the introductions to his commentaries on Deuteronomy, Joshua, and Kings, as well as in the preface to his *Mayyenei Ha-Yeshuah*. Interesting details are also provided by Baruch Hazketto, who was personally acquainted with Abravanel's son, Joseph, in his introduction to Abravanel's *Mayyenei Ha-Yeshuah*.
10. The list of his works is given by Abravanel himself in his well-known letter to Saul Cohen.

and this only in the realm of Bible exegesis.[11] The most characteristic feature of his Bible commentaries is the fact that in them the statesman, the master of financial problems and questions of politics, is discernible. He is practically the only one among the premodern Bible commentators who explains, along with the text, the social and political conditions of the period in question. He attempts to provide a clear picture of the political order in the period of the Judges, then in the era of the Israelite monarchy and of the prophets. He gives explanations about social circumstances, the significance of various offices, the measures, weights, and coins mentioned in the Bible, and the like. Placed before several of his commentaries are special introductions in which a general overview of the substance of the book in question is given.[12] Abravanel is also virtually the only one among the old Bible exegetes who had a historical sense and understood what historical perspective is—something that both contending parties, the rationalists, on the one hand, and the traditionalists, on the other, completely lacked.

His religious-philosophical works have a significantly lesser value. Abravanel was a philosophically educated theologian of the orthodox right wing, familiar with Jewish, Arabic, and Christian (Latin) authors, but not an original thinker. He does not discuss issues profoundly but only at a superficial level. In his *Mifalot Elohim*, which deals with the problem of the creation of the universe, and *Rosh Amanah*, which is concerned with the principles of Judaism, he merely reiterates the theories of his predecessors and even of his contemporaries, Abraham Bibago and Isaac Arama. Uniquely characteristic is only the great love and devotion with which he speaks in his *Rosh Amanah*[13] of one of the major dogmas that Maimonides set forth in his creed, the belief in the advent of the Messiah and the redemption that will put an end to the terrible exile and its sufferings. Abravanel, for this reason, pours out his anger on Joseph Albo, who permitted himself, in his *Ikkarim*, to assert that the belief in the coming of the Messiah is "not one of the major principles of the religion of Moses our teacher."[14]

11. In the letter to Saul Cohen, Abravanel notes that he wrote his commentaries and other compositions after leaving his native land, for previously he had been occupied in the courts and palaces of the kings and had no leisure to write. He also laments the fact that he spent his days and years in vanity.
12. See the relevant passage in Graetz' *Geschichte der Juden* and S. Dubnow in the *Russian-Jewish Encyclopedia*, I, 136.
13. Chapter 14 *et al.*
14. *Yeshuot Meshiḥo*, p. 25 (we quote according to the Koenigsberg edition of 1861).

After the great tragedy which befell Spanish Jewry Isaac Abravanel focussed his entire attention on the hope for the "end," for speedy redemption. It was the heartfelt cry of the Jewish community as a whole, the expression of the moods which dominated the entire milieu of the physically and spiritually broken children of exile and misery.

Extremely characteristic of these moods is Abravanel's preface to his *Mayyenei Ha-Yeshuah*.[15] The author portrays in fearful colors the troubles and sufferings which the Spanish Jews had to endure in their exile. Of the hundreds of thousands,[16] only one tenth survived. The others perished of hunger and cold, died on the sea and in the deserts, were devoured by wild animals and by men more cruel than the most ferocious beasts. "Wearied, cast down, bowed to the earth," relates the author,

the survivors cried out: "There is no more strength, all hope is gone. Our fate is decreed to fall on the wayside, to perish in the sands of the arid wilderness." I saw that even the best and most pious, with their intense faith in God, also lost hope and complained together with the rest: "God has forsaken the children of Jacob and Joseph. He has determined utterly to destroy the habitation of the daughter of Zion." Then I decided in my heart: One can wait no longer. One must aid the weak and stumbling. One must strengthen despairing hearts and offer consolation to those who languish in homelessness.

In tender, moving words and with great simplicity the author relates how tirelessly he sought and leafed through the pages of sacred scripture in order to solve the great mystery: When will the miraculous redemption come? When will the Messiah appear in his golden splendor? Abravanel felt that he had to discover this secret. He had to give his poor, languishing brethren the joyous tidings: Israel is not orphaned! "Know, my brothers, the day of redemption is at hand. The long-awaited savior comes. Behold, God's grace descends on the mountains of Zion like the blessed dew of Hermon."

But the secret was not so easy to attain. The words of the prophets are obscure and deep; the veil enveloping the mystery of the coming ages is impenetrable. The sufferings of the people, however, became ever more intolerable, their despair constantly greater. The aged Abravanel kept searching with indefatigable

15. The author himself notes that he completed this work in December 1496.
16. Abravanel estimates the number of the Jews expelled from Spain as three hundred thousand. Their total fortune amounted to thirty million golden ducats.

stubbornness, day and night, awake and dreaming. He *must* attain the truth, he *must* bring comfort to his languishing brethren. Finally he solved the mystery. In the obscure Book of Daniel, with its mystic, figurative language, Abravanel at last discovered what he had so laboriously sought—the *mayyenei ha-yeshuah*, the wells of salvation for the suffering people. Systematically he analyzes every verse, every expression, of the Book of Daniel. He considers Daniel not only a righteous and godfearing man, as the sages of the Talmud also portray him, but a true prophet who spoke through the holy spirit.[17] Abravanel was firmly convinced that in Daniel's visions and dreams he had discovered everything that is to happen at the end of days, all the afflictions and punishments which await the Jewish people, as well as the glorious "end" when God's emissary, Messiah the son of David, will arrive and redeem Israel from exile. With moving pathos Abravanel describes the great effort through which he finally succeeded in attaining the truth and uncovering the mystery hidden under allusions and *gematriot* in the Book of Daniel—that in the year 1503 "the times of the Messiah" will commence, and not later than 1535 the full redemption will occur.[18]

Abravanel hastens to announce the glad tidings. He extends "the cup of consolation to the languishing lips of the suffering people" and cries out joyfully: "Happy is he who waits and hopes! Happy is he who courageously endures the afflictions of exile, accepts his trials in love, remains loyal to the faith, and waits for the year 1503 when there will be an end to the troubles and the King Messiah will, with God's help, arrive!"

In tremendous haste Abravanel composes one work after another, all concerned with the same theme, that the Messiah will come speedily and soon. After *Mayyenei Ha-Yeshuah* he writes his *Yeshuot Meshiḥo*. Here are indicated all the passages in the Talmud and Midrashim in which the advent of the Messiah is spoken of. Two and a half months later[19] appears his work *Mashmia Yeshuah*, in which he attempts to show that among the prophets there were seventeen "harbingers" or "proclaimers" who announced that the Messiah will come.

17. In this particular Abravanel adopts the point of view of the Christian Church, which considers Daniel one of the prophets. On the other hand, however, he polemicizes in his *Mayyenei Ha-Yeshuah* against the Christian theologians who wish to show that in Daniel's dreams there are allusions to Jesus and the Catholic Church.
18. See *Mayyenei Ha-Yeshuah*, pp. 8, 11, 12.
19. Abravanel finished his *Yeshuot Meshiḥo* at the end of December 1497, and by the middle of March 1498 his *Mashmia Yeshua* was already completed.

One point is especially interesting in this connection. In all these works dealing with the "problem of redemption" Abravanel always returns to a question which, it seems, greatly agitated not only him but his contemporaries: when the Messiah comes, what will happen to the "forced Christians" or Marranos, those who out of terror outwardly accepted Christianity but remained inwardly loyal to the faith of their fathers? In touching words Abravanel assures them that those who out of compulsion and distress in the time of apostasy and troubles adopted the alien faith will also enjoy redemption; for them, too, the cup of consolation and joy is prepared.[20] Furthermore, Abravanel is firmly convinced that Messiah the son of David will bring redemption not only to the Jewish people but to all mankind. The whole world will be saved, and truth and justice alone will then have dominion over it.[21]

This highly gifted man, with his ardent, loving heart and loyalty to his people, became the *mashmia yeshuah*, the "proclaimer of salvation" to his contemporaries, the preacher of comfort and hope. And later generations remembered his name with gratitude and affection. He was the harbinger of new mystical-redemptive currents whose influence in the following two centuries grew constantly greater in the Jewish quarter as life became ever darker and a solid wall of hatred, cruelty, and deprivation of rights encompassed the ghetto ever more straitly.

The benighted generations of the Middle Ages came to an end. The dawn of a new world appeared. Men began to liberate themselves from the leaden medieval chains, and free speculative thought triumphantly gained its right to independent existence without the tyrannical overseership of theology and the Catholic Church. In the terrible woes of the Reformation Era wars a new way of life with a new world outlook was born. The ascetic ideal of abstinence and self-mortification lost its erstwhile attractiveness. It was replaced by passion and desire for real, earthly life with all its sorrows and joys. But precisely at that time of spiritual and intellectual awakening the Jewish quarter was covered by thick shadows.

The spiritual hegemony of the Jewish people passed from the west to the east, and with this begins the melancholy period of twilight and medieval darkness. As his earthly life became a "vale of weeping," a place of sorrow and lamentation, the Jew sought to

---

20. *Mashmia Yeshua*, 54a (we quote according to the Offenbach edition of 1767).
21. *Ibid.*, 27a.

Conclusion

remove himself from "this world," to isolate himself from the external world and immerse himself in the "upper worlds," in the fantastic realm of mystical concepts and interests which refused to know anything of scientific investigation and free critical thought. Only under the azure sky of Italy, in the land of the Renaissance, did the light of secular Jewish culture still flicker modestly. In the major centers of Jewish spiritual and intellectual life, in German-Polish and Turkish-Palestinian Jewry, however, culture bore a one-sided, theological-rabbinic character. The *Kabbalah Ha-Meshiḥit* (messianic Kabbalah) ruled without restraint over the minds of the ghetto and spun its fantastic web.

Of this twilight period we will speak in the coming volumes of our work.

BIBLIOGRAPHICAL NOTES

The Struggle of Mysticism and Tradition Against Philosophical Rationalism

BOOK ONE

CHAPTER ONE

THE MYSTICS OF PROVENCE

On Shemtov ben Joseph Falaquera, see Israel Efros, "Palquera's *Reshit Hokmah* and Alfarabi's *Ihsa al-Ulum*," *JQR*, XXV (1934-35), 227-35; Henry Malter, "Shem Tob ben Joseph Palquera: A Thinker and Poet of the Thirteenth Century," *JQR*, I, (1910-11), 151-81, 451-501; Solomon Munk, *Mélanges de philosophie juive et arabe* (Paris, 1859), pp. 494-96; and E. Renan, *Averroes et l'averroisme* (Paris, 1866), pp. 183-87.

On Isaac Ibn Latif, see *Encyclopedia Judaica* (Jerusalem, 1971), X, cols. 1446-48.

For discussions of the origins of the Kabbalah, see G. Scholem's superb book-length article "Kabbalah," in the *Encyclopedia Judaica* (Jerusalem, 1971), X, cols. 489-651; idem, *Major Trends in Jewish Mysticism*, rev. ed. (New York, 1946); idem, *Zur Frage der Entstehung der Kabbala* (Berlin, 1928); idem, *Ursprung und Anfänge der Kabbala* (Berlin, 1962); P. Bloch, *Die Geschichte der Entwicklung der Kabbala und der jüdischen Religionsphilosophie* (Trier, 1895); J. Abelson, *Jewish Mysticism* (London, 1913); and A. Franck, *The Kabbalah: The Religious Philosophy of the Hebrews* (New Hyde Park, N. Y., 1967).

A new edition of the *Sefer Ha-Bahir*, prepared by Reuben Margaliyot, was published in Jerusalem in 1950. The work was trans-

Bibliographical Notes

lated, with a commentary, into German under the title *Das Buch Bahir* by G. Scholem (Leipzig, 1923).

Isaac the Blind's commentary on the *Sefer Yetzirah* was published by G. Scholem at the end of *Ha-Kabbalah Be-Provans* (Jerusalem, 1963). On Isaac, see Scholem, *Reshit Ha-Kabbalah* (Jerusalem, 1948) and *Ursprung und Anfänge der Kabbala* (Berlin, 1962).

Azriel's *Perush Ha-Aggadot*, edited by Isaiah Tishby, was published in Jerusalem in 1945. On Ezra and Azriel, see I. Tishby, "Ha-Mekubbalim R. Ezra Ve-R. Azriel," *Tziyyon*, IX (1944), 178–85, and G. Scholem, *Reshit Ha-Kabbalah* (Jerusalem, 1948). See also G. Vajda, *Le Commentaire d'Ezra de Gérone sur le Cantique des Cantiques* (Paris, 1969).

On Isaac ben Jacob Ha-Kohen, see G. Scholem, "Kabbalat R. Yaakov Ve-R. Yitzhak Benei R. Yaakov Ha-Kohen," *Maddaei Ha-Yahadut*, II (1927), 163–293. See also Scholem, *Les Origines de la Kabbale* (Paris, 1966), pp. 310–14, 376–82.

On Jacob bar Sheshet, see G. Vajda, *Recherches sur la philosophie et la Kabbale* (Paris, 1962), pp. 8–113, and G. Scholem, *Ursprung und Anfänge der Kabbala* (Berlin, 1962), pp. 334–39.

CHAPTER TWO

NAHMANIDES AND HIS FOLLOWERS

On Nahmanides, see S. Schechter, *Studies in Judaism*, First Series (Philadelphia, 1896), pp. 99–141; Charles B. Chavel, *Rabbenu Mosheh ben Nahman: Toledot Hayyov Zemano Ve-Hibburov* (Jerusalem, 1967); G. Scholem, *Ha-Kabbalah Be-Gerona*, ed. I. Ben Shlomoh (Jerusalem, 1964); idem, *Ursprung und Anfänge der Kabbala* (Berlin, 1962); and Y. Unna, *Rabbi Mosheh ben Nahman* (Jerusalem, 1954). The writings of Nahmanides, *Kitvei Ha-Ramban*, were edited by Charles B. Chavel (New York, 1963). Chavel is also the translator of *Ramban's Commentary on the Torah: Genesis* (New York, 1971).

On Abraham ben Samuel Abulafia and his "prophetic" Kabbalah, see A. Berger, in *Essays in Honor of Salo W. Baron* (New York, 1959), pp. 55–61; Simon Bernfeld, *Benei Aliyah* (Tel Aviv, 1931), pp. 68–90; I. Guenzig, "Ha-Mekubbal Rabbi Avraham

Abulafia," *Ha-Eshkol*, V (1904), 85–112; G. Scholem, "Eine Kabbalistische Deutung der Prophetie als Selbstbegegnung," *MGWJ*, LXXIV (1930), 285–90; and *idem, Major Trends in Jewish Mysticism*, rev. ed. (New York, 1946), Ch. 4.

On Joseph ben Abraham Gikatilla, see G. Scholem, *Kitvei Yad Ba-Kabbalah* (Jerusalem, 1930), pp. 218–25; *idem, Sefer Ha-Yovel Le-Yaakov Freimann* (Jerusalem, 1937), pp. 163–70; *idem, Major Trends in Jewish Mysticism*, rev. ed. (New York, 1946), pp. 194–95, 405–6; A. Jellinek, *Beiträge zur Geschichte der Kabbala* (Leipzig, 1852), II, 56–64; M. C. Weiler, "Iyyunim Beterminologiyah Ha-Kabbalit Shel R. Yosef Gikatilliah Ve-Yaḥaso Le-Rambam," *Hebrew Union College Annual*, XXXVII (1966), 13–44 (Hebrew section); and Z. Werblowsky in *Zeitschrift fur Religion und Geistesgeschichte*, VIII (1956), 164–69.

CHAPTER THREE

THE *ZOHAR*

An English translation of the *Zohar* by H. Sperling, M. Simon, and P. Levertoff was published in five volumes by the Soncino Press in London, 1931–34. The literature on the *Zohar* is vast. Among the more valuable works dealing in whole or in part with this major work of the Kabbalist tradition are J. Abelson, *Jewish Mysticism* (London, 1931); A. Franck, *The Kabbalah: The Religious Philosophy of the Hebrews* (New Hyde Park, N. Y., 1967); C. D. Ginsburg, *The Kabbalah: Its Doctrines, Development, and Literature* (London, 1865); L. Ginzberg, *The Cabbala in Jewish Law and Lore* (Philadelphia, 1955); A. Jellinek, *Beiträge zur Geschichte der Kabbala* (Leipzig, 1852); *idem, Ginzei Hochmat Ha-Kabbalah (Auswahl Kabbalistischer Mystik)*, I (Leipzig, 1853); *idem, Philosophie und Kabbala* (Leipzig, 1854); D. H. Joel, *Die Religionsphilosophie des Sohar und ihr Verhältnis zur allgemeinen jüdischen Theologie* (third edition, Berlin, 1923); E. Mueller, *A History of Jewish Mysticism* (Oxford, 1946); *idem, Der Sohar und seine Lehre* (third edition, Berlin, 1959); G. Scholem, *Perakim Le-Toledot Ha-Kabbalah* (Jerusalem, 1931); *idem, Zur Frage der Enstehung der Kabbala* (Berlin, 1928); *idem, Ursprung und Anfänge der Kabbala* (Berlin, 1962); *idem, Major Trends in Jewish Mysticism*, rev. ed. (New York, 1946); *idem, On the Kabbalah and Its Symbolism* (New York, 1965); I. Tishby, *Mishnat Ha-Zohar*, 2 vols. (Jerusalem, 1957, 1961); A. E. Waite, *The*

Secret Doctrine in Israel: A Study of the Zohar and Its Connections (London, 1913).

For a bibliography on the Zohar and on Kabbalah in general, see G. Scholem, *Bibliographia Kabbalistica* (Berlin, 1933).

CHAPTER FOUR

THE RENEWAL OF THE STRUGGLE AGAINST RATIONALISM

On the ideological battle centering around Maimonides and rationalist philosophy in the thirteenth century and the beginning of the fourteenth century, see D. J. Silver, *Maimonidean Criticism and the Maimonidean Controversy: 1180–1240* (Leiden, 1965); J. Sarachek, *Faith and Reason: The Conflict over the Rationalism of Maimonides* (Williamsport, Pa., 1935); H. H. Ben-Sasson, *Toledot Am Yisrael*, II (Jerusalem, 1969); Y. Baer, *A History of the Jews in Christian Spain*, 2 vols. (Philadelphia, 1960, 1966); and A. Neuman, *The Jews in Spain*, 2 vols. (Philadelphia, 1942).

Parts of Levi ben Abraham's *Battei Ha-Nefesh Veha-Leḥashim* were published by I. Davidson in *Yediot Ha-Machon Le-Ḥeker Ha-Shirah Ha-Ivrit*, V (1939), 2–42, and in *Scripta Mathematica*, IV (1936), 57–65. See also I. Davidson, "L'Introduction de Lévi ben Abraham à son encyclopédie poétique," *REJ*, CIV (1940), 80–94. On Levi, see L. Baeck, "Zur Charakteristik des Levi ben Abraham ben Chajim," *MGWJ*, XLIV (1900), 24–41, 59–71, 156–67, 337–44, 417–23; A. S. Halkin, "Why Was Levi ben Hayyim Hounded?" *PAAJR*, XXXIV (1966), 65–76; and E. Renan (Adolphe Neubauer), *Les Rabbins français du commencement du quatorzième siècle* (Paris, 1877), pp. 628–701.

CHAPTER FIVE

RABBI MEIR OF ROTHENBURG, RABBI ASHER BEN YEḤIEL, AND RABBI SOLOMON BEN ADRET

For historical background on the Jews of Germany and Spain in the period during which these rabbis flourished, see A. Kohut, *Geschichte der deutschen Juden* (Berlin, 1898); A. Berliner, *Aus dem inneren Leben der deutschen Juden im Mittelalter*, 2nd ed.

Bibliographical Notes

(Berlin, 1900); I. Elbogen, *Geschichte der Juden in Deutschland* (Berlin, 1935); M. Lowenthal, *The Jews of Germany* (Philadelphia, 1936); Y. Baer, *A History of the Jews in Christian Spain*, 2 vols. (Philadelphia, 1960, 1966); and A. Neuman, *The Jews in Spain*, 2 vols. (Philadelphia, 1942). For a discussion of the social and religious life of the Jews in this period, see L. Finkelstein, *Jewish Self-Government in the Middle Ages* (New York, 1924), and I. Abrahams, *Jewish Life in the Middle Ages*, 2nd ed. (London, 1932).

On Meir of Rothenburg, see the exhaustive work of I. A. Agus, *Rabbi Meir of Rothenburg*, 2 vols. (Philadelphia, 1947). See also S. Back, *Rabbi Meir ben Baruch aus Rothenburg* (Frankfurt-am-Main, 1895); E. Urbach, *Baalei Ha-Tosafot* (Jerusalem, 1956), pp. 405–46; and H. J. Zimmels, *Beiträge zur Geschichte der Juden in Deutschland im 13. Jahrhundert* (Vienna, 1926).

Some extracts from Asher ben Yehiel's *Sefer Ha-Hanhagah* are contained in I. Abrahams, ed., *Hebrew Ethical Wills*, I (Philadelphia, 1926), 118–25. On Asher, see A. H. Freimann in *Jahrbuch der jüdisch-literarischen Gesellschaft*, XII (1918), 237–317, XIII (1919), 142–254; and Y. Baer, *A History of the Jews in Christian Spain*, I (Philadelphia, 1960), 297–301, 316–25.

I. Epstein published *The Responsa of R. Solomon ben Adreth of Barcelona (1235–1310) as a Source of the History of Spain* (London, 1925; 2nd ed., 1968). On Solomon, see also J. Perles, *R. Salomo ben Abraham ben Adereth* (Breslau, 1863), and A. Sofer, ed., *Teshuvot Hachmei Provans* (Jerusalem, 1967).

Menahem Meiri's *Bet Ha-Behirah: Bava Metzia* was edited by K. Schlesinger (Jerusalem, 1959). His *Magen Avot* was edited by I. Last (London, 1909), and his *Hibbur Ha-Teshuvah* by A. Sofer and S. K. Mirsky (Jerusalem, 1950). On Meiri, see S. B. Sofer, *Or Ha-Meir* (Jerusalem, 1942).

Yedaiah Ha-Penini's *Behinat Olam* was translated into German by M. E. Stern (Vienna, 1847). An English translation also appeared in London in 1806. On Yedaiah, see J. Chotzner, "Yedaya Bedaresi: A Fourteenth Century Hebrew Poet and Philosopher," *JQR*, VIII (1895–96), 414–25; A. Halkin, "Yedaiah Bedershi's Apology," in A. Altmann, ed., *Jewish Medieval and Renaissance Studies* (Cambridge, 1967), pp. 165–84; and S. Pines, "Ha-Tzurot Ha-Ishiyot Be-Mishnato Shel Yedaya Bedersi," in the *Harry*

Austryn Wolfson Jubilee Volume (New York, 1965), pp. 187–203 (Hebrew section).

CHAPTER SIX

ISAAC ALBALAG AND THE DOCTRINE OF THE "DOUBLE TRUTH"

G. Vajda's *Isaac Albalag: Averroïste Juif* (Paris, 1960) contains a French translation of almost all of Albalag's notes to his translation of Al-Ghazali's *Makazid al-Falasifa* and includes a bibliography of works dealing with Albalag. On Albalag, see also J. Guttmann, *Philosophies of Judaism* (New York, 1964); J. H. Schorr, "Rabbi Yitzhak Albalag," *He-Halutz*, IV (1859), 83 ff., VI (1861), 85 ff., VII (1865), 157 ff.; M. Steinschneider, *Die hebräischen Übersetzungen des Mittelalters und die Juden als Dolmetscher* (Berlin, 1893), pp. 299–306; and C. Touati, "Vérité philosophique et vérité prophétique chez Isaac Albalag," *REJ*, CXXI (1962), 35–47.

CHAPTER SEVEN

ISAAC IBN PULGAR AND JOSEPH IBN KASPI

On Abner of Burgos, see F. (Y.) Baer in *Korrespondenzblatt der Akademie für die Wissenschaft des Judentums* (1929) and in *Tarbitz*, XI (1940), 188–206. See also J. Guttmann, *Philosophies of Judaism* (New York, 1964).

Pulgar's *Ezer Ha-Dat* was edited by G. Belasco (London, 1906). On Pulgar, see G. Belasco, "Isaac Pulgar's 'Support of the Religion,'" *JQR*, XVII (1905), 26–56; I. Loeb, "Polémistes chrétiens et juifs en France et en Espagne," *REJ*, XVIII (1889), 63–70; and J. Guttmann, *Philosophies of Judaism* (New York, 1964), pp. 205–6.

The Hebrew text and an English translation of Joseph Ibn Kaspi's *Sefer Ha-Musar* are included in I. Abrahams, ed., *Hebrew Ethical Wills*, I (Philadelphia, 1926), 127–61. On Ibn Kaspi, see H. Gross, *Gallia judaica* (Paris, 1897); E. Renan (A. Neubauer), *Les Écrivains juifs français du quatorzième siècle* (Paris, 1893), pp. 131–206; W. Bacher, "Josef Ibn Kaspi als Bibelerklärer," in *Judaica: Festschrift zu Hermann Cohen* (Berlin, 1912), pp. 119–35; and M. Steinschneider, *Gesammelte Schriften*, I (Berlin, 1925), 89–137.

Bibliographical Notes

CHAPTER EIGHT

MOSES NARBONI AND GERSONIDES

On Perpignan as a center of Jewish culture, see R. Emery, *The Jews of Perpignan in the Thirteenth Century* (New York, 1959).

On Moses Narboni, see E. Renan (A. Neubauer), *Les Écrivains juifs français du quatorzième siècle* (Paris, 1893), pp. 320–35; S. Munk, *Mélanges de philosophie juive et arabe* (Paris, 1859); J. Guttmann, *Philosophies of Judaism* (New York, 1964), pp. 206–8; and A. Ivry, "Moses of Narbonne's 'Treatise on the Perfection of the Soul,'" *JQR*, LVII (1967), 271–97.

Parts I–IV of Gersonides' *Milḥamot Adonai* were translated into German by B. Kellerman under the title *Die Kämpfe Gottes*, 2 vols. (Berlin, 1914–16), but the translation is not reliable. Parts III and IV were translated into French on the basis of a critical edition by C. Touati and published, with an introduction and notes, under the title *Levi ben Gershom: Les Guerres du Seigneur, Livres III et IV* (Paris, 1968). Gersonides' commentary on the Book of Job was translated into English by A. L. Lassen (New York, 1946). On Gersonides, see N. Adlerblum, *A Study of Gersonides in His Proper Perspective* (New York, 1926); J. Carlebach, *Levi ben Gerson als Mathematiker* (Berlin, 1910); J. Guttmann, "Levi ben Gersons Theorie des Begriffs," *Festschrift zum 75.jährigen Bestehung des Jüdisches Theologisches Seminar*, II (Breslau, 1929), 131–49; idem, *Philosophies of Judaism* (New York, 1964), pp. 208–24; I. Husik, *A History of Medieval Jewish Philosophy* (Philadelphia, 1916), pp. 328–61; M. Joel, *Lewi ben Gerson als Religionsphilosoph* (Breslau, 1862); J. Karo, *Kritische Untersuchungen zu Levi ben Gersons Widerlegung des aristotelischen Zeitbegriffs* (Leipzig, 1935); G. Sarton, *Introduction to the History of Science*, III (New York, 1948), 594–607; M. Steinschneider, *Gesammelte Schriften*, I (Berlin, 1925), 233–70; I. Weil, *La Philosophie religieuse de Lévi ben Gerson* (Paris, 1868); and G. Vajda, *Introduction à la pensée juive du moyen âge* (Paris, 1947), pp. 159–69.

Bibliographical Notes

BOOK TWO: 1348–1492

CHAPTER ONE

THE CULTURAL DECLINE OF SPANISH AND PROVENÇAL JEWRY

On the Black Plague and its effects on the Jews of Europe, see J. Nohl, *Der schwarze Tod* (1924), pp. 239–73; J. Trachtenberg, *The Devil and the Jews* (Philadelphia, 1943), pp. 97–108, and H. H. Ben-Sasson, "Black Death," *Encyclopedia Judaica*, III (Jerusalem, 1971), cols. 1063–67.

On Yomtov Lippmann Mühlhausen, see J. Kaufman, *Rabbi Yom Tov Lipmann Muelhausen* (1927), and I. Sonne, *Studies in Bibliography and Booklore*, I, No. 2 (1953), 60 f. and 68 f.

On Isaac ben Joseph Israeli, see G. Sarton, *An Introduction to the History of Science*, III (1948), 691–92 and the bibliography given there.

On Immanuel ben Jacob Bonfils, see E. Renan (A. Neubauer), *Les Écrivains juifs français du quatorzième siècle* (Paris, 1893), pp. 692–99, and S. Gandz in *Isis*, XXV (1936), 16–45.

On Estori Parḥi, see E. Renan (A. Neubauer), *Les Écrivains juifs français*, pp. 403 ff.; S. Klein, *Toledot Ha-Yishuv Ha-Yehudi Be-Eretz Yisrael* (Jerusalem, 1952), pp. 156–61; and A. Yaari, *Masot Eretz Yisrael* (Jerusalem, 1946), pp. 98–105.

On Jacob ben Asher and his *Arbaah Turim*, see H. Tchernowitz, *Toledot Ha-Posekim*, II (New York, 1947), 199–220; I. H. Weiss, *Dor Dor Ve-Doreshav*, 5th ed. (New York and Berlin, 1924), pp. 118–28; and A. H. Freimann in *Jahrbuch der jüdisch-literarischen Gesellschaft*, XII (1918), 286, 301–8. Extracts from Jacob's testament to his children are given in I. Abrahams, ed., *Hebrew Ethical Wills*, II (Philadelphia, 1926), 202–5.

A critical edition of Baḥya ben Asher's *Kad Ha-Kemaḥ, Shulḥan Shel Arba,* and his commentary to *Pirkei Avot* was published by C. B. Chavel under the title *Kitvei Rabbenu Baḥya* (New York, 1970). On Baḥya, see J. Reifmann in *Alummah*, I (1936), 69–101; B. Bernstein, *Die Schrifterklärung des Bachja ben Asher* (1891);

E. Gottlieb, *Ha-Kabbalah be-Chitvei R. Baḥya ben Asher* (Jerusalem, 1970); and I. Bettan, *Studies in Jewish Preaching* (Cincinnati, 1939).

On David Ibn Bilia, see N. Allony, *Mi-Safrut Yemei Ha-Beinayim* (Jerusalem, 1944); *idem*, in *Aresheth* (1943-44), pp. 377-86; and *idem*, in *Kovetz Al Yad*, VI (1966), 225-44.

On Meir ben Isaac Aldabi, see M. Steinschneider, *Die hebräischen Übersetzungen des Mittelalters und die Juden als Dolmetscher* (Berlin, 1893), pp. 9-27.

CHAPTER TWO

THE CLERICAL REACTION IN SPAIN AND THE LITERATURE OF POLEMICS AGAINST CHRISTIANS

For historical background on the intensification of anti-Jewish attitudes in Spanish Catholicism, see Y. Baer, *A History of the Jews in Christian Spain*, 2 vols. (Philadelphia, 1960, 1966), and A. Neuman, *The Jews in Spain*, 2 vols. (Philadelphia, 1942).

A new edition of Solomon Alami's *Iggeret Ha-Musar* was published by A. M. Habermann (Jerusalem, 1946). On Alami, see Baer, *History*, II, 239-42.

On the public disputations in Spain between Jews and Christians, see J. W. Parkes, *The Conflict of the Church and the Synagogue*, 2nd ed. (New York, 1964), and the bibliography given there.

On Moses Ha-Kohen of Tordesillas, see Baer, *History*, I, 374-75, and I. Loeb, in *REJ*, XVIII (1889), 226-30.

On the massacre at Seville in 1391 and the forced conversion of Jews, see Baer, *History*, Index, *s.v. "conversos"*; C. Roth, *A History of the Marranos* (Philadelphia, 1932); M. Kayserling, "L'Archidiacre Ferrand Martinez et les persecutions de 1391," *REJ*, XXXVIII (1899), 257-67; and B. Netanyahu, *The Marranos of Spain from the Late Fourteenth to the Early Sixteenth Centuries* (Philadelphia, 1966).

CHAPTER THREE

LAMPOONS IN RELIGIOUS DISPUTATIONS; JOSHUA LORKI AND PROFIAT DURAN

Some of Bonafed's poems were published by Schirmann in *Kovetz Al Yad*, XIV (1944), 9–64. See also Schirmann, in *Sefarad*, II (1961), 620–43, 699–700.

On Solomon Ha-Levi of Burgos (Pablo de Santa Maria), see Baer, *A History of the Jews in Christian Spain*, Index; P. L. Serrano, *Los conversos Pablo de Santa Maria y Alfonso de Cartagena* (Madrid, 1942); F. Cantera Burgos, *La conversión del célebre talmudista Salomón Leví* (Santandar, 1933); and I. Abrahams, in *JQR*, XII (1900), 255–63.

On Joshua Lorki (Geronimo de Sante Fé) see Baer, *History*, Index, s.v. "Joshua Halorki"; L. Landau, *Das apologetische Schreiben des Josua Lorki* (1906); A. L. Williams, *Adversus Judaeos* (London, 1935); and A. Pacios López, *La disputa de Tortosa*, 2 vols. (Madrid, 1957).

Profiat Duran's *Al Tehi Ka-Avotecha* and *Kelimmat Ha-Goyyim* are included in J. D. Eisenstein, *Otzar Vikkuḥim* (New York, 1928). On Duran, see Baer, *History*, Index, s.v. "Profet Duran"; E. Renan (A. Neubauer), *Les Écrivains juifs français*, pp. 395–407; and R. W. Emery, in *JQR*, LVIII (1967–68), 328–37.

CHAPTER FOUR

ḤASDAI CRESCAS AND HIS ERA

On Moses ben Isaac Botarel, see A. Jellinek, *Beiträge zur Geschichte der Kabbala*, II (Leipzig, 1852), 1–10, 79; S. Assaf, *Tekufat Ha-Geonim Ve-Safrutah*, edited by M. Margalioth (Jerusalem, 1955), pp. 323–40; and G. Scholem, in *Tarbitz*, XXXII (1962–63), 260–62.

On Abraham ben Isaac of Granada, see G. Scholem, in *Soncino Blätter: Festschrift Aron Freimann* (Berlin, 1935), pp. 54–55.

Most of the secular poems of Solomon Dapiera's *Diwan* were edited and published by S. Bernstein (New York, 1942). Bernstein also published Dapiera's religious poems in *Hebrew Union College Annual*, XIX (1945). On Dapiera, see H. Brody, *Beiträge zu Salomo da Pieras Leben und Wirken* (1893).

On Isaac bar Sheshet, see A. M. Hershman, *Rabbi Isaac Bar Sheshet Perfet and His Times* (New York, 1943).

A photographic edition of Shemtov Ibn Shemtov's *Sefer Ha-Emunot*, printed originally in Ferrara in 1556, was published in Jerusalem in 1969. On Ibn Shemtov, see Baer, *A History of the Jews in Christian Spain*, II, 234-39; G. Scholem, in *Kiryat Sefer*, VIII (1931-32), 398-400; and J. Guttmann, in *MGWJ*, LVII (1913), 177-95, 326-36.

An important segment of Ḥasdai Crescas' *Or Adonai* (Part I of Book One and the first twenty chapters of Part II of Book One) are translated, on the basis of a critical text and with an introduction and notes, by H. A. Wolfson in his *Crescas' Critique of Aristotle* (Cambridge, 1929). Wolfson also includes a bibliography.

On Crescas, see Y. Baer, "Sefer Minhat Kenaot Shel Abner Mi-Burgos Vehashpaato al Ḥasdai Kreskas," *Tarbitz*, XI (1940); P. Bloch, *Die Willensfreiheit von Chasdai Kreskas* (Munich, 1879); J. Guttmann, "Chasdai Creskas als Kritiker der aristotelischen Physik," in *Festschrift zum siebzigsten Geburtstage Jakob Guttmanns* (Leipzig, 1915), pp. 28-54; *idem*, "Das Problem der Willensfreiheit bei Ḥasdai Crescas und den islamischen Aristotelikern," in *Jewish Studies in Memory of George A. Kohut* (New York, 1935), pp. 325-49; *idem*, *Philosophies of Judaism* (Philadelphia, 1964), pp. 225-41; I. Husik, *A History of Medieval Jewish Philosophy* (Philadelphia, 1916), pp. 388-405; M. Joel, *Don Chasdai Creskas religionsphilosophische Lehren in ihrem geschichtlichen Einflusse dargestellt* (Breslau, 1866); D. Neumark, "Crescas and Spinoza," *Yearbook of the Central Conference of American Rabbis*, XVIII (1908), 277-318; S. Pines, *Scholasticism After Thomas Aquinas and the Teachings of Ḥasdai Crescas and His Predecessors* (New York, 1967); M. Waxman, *The Philosophy of Don Ḥasdai Crescas* (New York, 1920); J. Wolfsohn, *Der Einfluss Gazalis auf Chisdai Crescas* (Frankfurt-am-Main, 1905); H. A. Wolfson, "A Note on Crescas' Definition of Time," *JQR*, n.s., X (1919), 1-17; and *idem*, "Crescas on the Problem of Divine Attributes," *JQR*, n.s., VII (1916), 1-44, 175-221.

CHAPTER FIVE

SIMEON DURAN AND JOSEPH ALBO

On Rabbi Simeon ben Tzemaḥ Duran, see E. Atlas, in *Ha-Kerem*, I (1887), 1–26; H. Jaulus, "Simeon ben Zemach Duran," *MGWJ*, XXIII (1874), 241–59, XXIV (1875), 160–78; J. Guttmann, "Die Stellung des Simeon ben Zemach Duran in der jüdischen Religionsphilosophie," *MGWJ*, LII (1908), 641–72, LIII (1909), 46–79; and I. Epstein, *The Responsa of R. Simon ben Zemaḥ Duran as a Source of the History of the Jews in North Africa* (London, 1930).

Joseph Albo's *Sefer Ha-Ikkarim* was translated into English, on the basis of a critical text and with introduction and notes, by I. Husik, 4 vols. (Philadelphia, 1929–30). On Albo, see S. Back, *Josef Albos Bedeutung in der Geschichte der jüdischen Religionsphilosophie* (Breslau, 1869); J. Guttmann, *Philosophies of Judaism* (Philadelphia, 1964), pp. 247–51; I. Husik, *A History of Medieval Jewish Philosophy* (Philadelphia, 1916), pp. 406–27; idem, "Joseph Albo, the Last of the Jewish Medieval Philosophers," *PAAJR* (1930), 61–72; A. Tänzer, *Die Religionsphilosophie Josef Albos nach seinem Werk "Ikkarim" systematisch dargestellt und erläutert* (Frankfurt-am-Main, 1896); and M. Wiener, "Der Dekalog in Josef Albos dogmatischen System," in *Festschrift für Leo Baeck* (Berlin, 1938), pp. 107–18.

CHAPTER SIX

PREACHERS AND DEFENDERS OF THE FAITH

On Ḥayyim Ibn Musa, see D. Kaufmann, in *Bet Talmud*, II (1881), 110 ff.; A. Poznanski, in *Schiloh*, 1904, pp. 251–56; and Y. Baer, *A History of the Jews in Christian Spain*, II (Philadelphia, 1966), 253–54.

On Isaac (or Mordecai) Nathan, see I. S. Reggio, *Iggerot Yashar*, I (1834), 70–76; H. Gross, in *MGWJ*, XXIX (1880), 518–23; S. Mandelkern, *Heichal Ha-Kodesh: Veteris Testamenti Concordantiae Hebraicae atque Chaldaicae*, 2nd ed. (Berlin, 1937), Praefatio, pp. ix–xii; and A. Tauber, in *Kiryat Sefer*, II (1925), 141–44.

Bibliographical Notes

On Joseph ben Shemtov, see Jacob Guttmann, "Die Familie Shemtob in ihren Beziehungen zur Philosophie," *MGWJ*, LVII (1913), 336–40, 418–47; Julius Guttmann, *Philosophies of Judaism* (New York, 1964), pp. 252–53; I. Husik, *A History of Medieval Jewish Philosophy* (Philadelphia, 1916), pp. 429–30; and M. Steinschneider, "Josef ben Shemtobs Kommentar zu Averroës grösserer Abhandlung über die Möglichkeit der Konjunktion," *MGWJ*, XXXII (1883), 459–77.

On Abraham Bibago, see Y. Baer, *History*, Index *s.v.* "Abraham Bivach"; M. Steinschneider, *Die hebräischen Übersetzungen* (Berlin, 1893), p. 89 ff. and *passim; idem*, "Abraham Bibagos Schriften," *MGWJ*, XXXII (1883), 79 ff.; and S. Heller-Wilensky, *Rabbi Yitzḥak Arama U-Mishnato Ha-Filosofit* (Jerusalem-Tel Aviv, 1956), Index.

On Isaac Arama, see I. Bettan, *Studies in Jewish Preaching* (Cincinnati, 1939), pp. 130–91; A. M. Habermann, in *Otzar Yehudei Sefarad* (Jerusalem, 1965), pp. 92–104; C. Pearl, *The Medieval Jewish Mind: The Religious Philosophy of Isaac Arama* (London, 1971); and S. Heller-Wilensky, *Rabbi Yitzḥak Arama U-Mishnato Ha-Filosofit* (Jerusalem-Tel Aviv, 1956).

CHAPTER SEVEN

KABBALISTS AND SATIRISTS

On *Sefer Ha-Kanah* and *Sefer Ha-Peliah*, see G. Scholem, *Major Trends in Jewish Mysticism*, rev. ed. (New York, 1946), p. 211; A. Marcus, *Der Chassidismus* (Berlin, 1901), pp. 244–61; and S. A. Horodetsky, in *Ha-Tekufah*, X (1920), pp. 283–329.

On Shemtov ben Joseph Ibn Shemtov, see H. A. Wolfson, *Crescas' Critique of Aristotle* (Cambridge, 1929), Index; and J. Guttmann, in *MGWJ*, LVII (1913), 447–51.

On Saadiah Ibn Danan, see B. Halper, in *JQR*, n.s., IV (1913–14), 153–224; J. Schirmann, in *Sefarad*, II (1956), 665–66, 700; and N. Slouschz, in *Sura; Sefer Shanah Yisreeli Amerikai*, III (1958), 183–91.

CHAPTER EIGHT

DON ISAAC ABRAVANEL

On the expulsion of the Jews from Spain, see Y. Baer, *A History of the Jews in Christian Spain*, Vol. II (Philadelphia, 1966), and A. Neuman, *The Jews in Spain*, 2 vols. (Philadelphia, 1942).

On Isaac Abravanel, see B. Netanyahu, *Don Isaac Abravanel: Statesman and Philosopher*, 2nd ed. (Philadelphia, 1968); A. J. Heschel, *Don Jizchak Abravanel* (Berlin, 1937); J. Guttmann, *Die religionsphilosophischen Lehren des Isaak Abravanel* (Breslau, 1916); J. S. Minkin, *Abarbanel and the Expulsion of the Jews from Spain* (New York, 1938); J. B. Trend and H. M. J. Loewe, eds., *Isaac Abravanel: Six Lectures* (Cambridge, 1937); J. Sarachek, *Don Isaac Abravanel* (New York, 1938); E. Shmueli, "Don Yitzhak Abravanel," *Kenesset*, III (1938), 295–321; and *idem*, *Don Yitzhak Abravanel Ve-Gerush Sefarad* (Jerusalem, 1963).

Glossary of Hebrew Terms

Aggadah (or **Haggadah**): The non-legal part of the post-Biblical Oral Torah, consisting of narratives, legends, parables, allegories, poems, prayers, theological and philosophical reflections, etc. Much of the Talmud is Aggadic, and the Midrash literature, developed over a period of more than a millennium, consists almost entirely of Aggadah.

Amora (pl. **Amoraim**): The title given to the Jewish scholars of Palestine and especially of Babylonia in the third to the sixth centuries whose work and thought is recorded in the Gemara of the Talmud.

Anusim: Literally, "those forced." A term used to denote Jews who were forcibly baptized in Spain and Portugal. Many of the Anusim became Marranos, crypto-Jews who continued to practice Jewish rites and customs in secret.

efod: The upper garment worn in the Temple by the High Priest, to which the breastplate containing the oracular Urim and Tummim was fastened.

Ein Sof: A Kabbalist term, meaning literally "without end" or "infinite." In the Spanish and later Kabbalah it was used to denote the impersonal aspect of the Godhead, the *deus absconditus,* about whom nothing can be thought or said and with whom men cannot enter into personal relationships.

Gaon (pl. **Geonim**): The spiritual and intellectual leaders of Babylonian Jewry in the post-Talmudic period, from the sixth through the eleventh centuries c.e. The head of the two major academies of Babylonia, at Sura and Pumbeditha, held the title Gaon. The Geonim had considerable secular power as well as religious authority, and their influence extended over virtually all of world Jewry during the larger part of the Geonic age. The title Gaon is occasionally applied, in a general honorific sense, to a very eminent Judaic scholar.

Glossary of Hebrew Terms

Gemara: The second basic strand of the Talmud, consisting of a commentary on, and supplement to, the Mishnah.

gematria: A system of exegesis based on the interpretation of a word or words according to the numerical value of the constituent letters in the Hebrew alphabet.

genizah: A depository for used and damaged sacred books, manuscripts, religious utensils, etc. The most widely known *genizah* was discovered in modern times in the synagogue of Fostat (Old Cairo), which was built in 882.

Haskalah: The movement for disseminating modern European culture among Jews from about 1750 to 1880. It advocated the modernization of Judaism, the westernization of traditional Jewish education, and the revival of the Hebrew language.

ḥoshen: The breastplate that was part of the apparel of the High Priest in the Temple.

Kabbalah: The mystical religious tradition in Judaism. This tradition is described at length in the present *History*.

kelipah (pl. *kelipot*): Literally, "husk" or "shell." A mystical term in Kabbalah, denoting the forces of evil.

kinah: In Biblical and Talmudic times, a dirge over the dead. Later the term came to be applied to a liturgical composition for the Ninth of Av dealing with the destruction of the Temple as well as with contemporary persecutions.

maaseh bereshit: Literally, "work of creation." The term refers to the first chapter of Genesis, the exposition of which was one of the primary concerns of early Jewish mysticism.

maaseh merkavah: Literally, "work of the chariot." The term refers to the first chapter of Ezekiel, the exposition of which constituted the second basic concern of early Jewish mysticism.

makama: An Arabic term referring to the literary form of rhymed prose. The form was employed by a considerable number of medieval Hebrew writers.

Glossary of Hebrew Terms

Maskil (pl. **Maskilim**): An adherent of Haskalah (see above).

mezuzah: A parchment scroll placed in a container and affixed to the doorposts of rooms occupied by Jews, in fulfillment of an injunction in the sixth chapter of Deuteronomy.

Midrash (pl. **Midrashim**): The discovery of new meanings besides literal ones in the Bible. The term is also used to designate collections of such Scriptural exposition. The best-known of the Midrashim are the Midrash Rabbah, Tanhuma, Pesikta De-Rav Kahana, Pesikta Rabbati, and Yalkut Shimeoni.

Mishnah: The legal codification containing the core of the post-Biblical Oral Torah, compiled and edited by Rabbi Judah Ha-Nasi at the beginning of the third century C.E.

nasi: Literally, "prince." In the Talmud, the title of the president of the Sanhedrin and spiritual head of the Jewish people. Later the term was used in certain centers to designate the lay leader of the Jewish community.

notarikon: A method of abbreviating Hebrew words and phrases by writing only single letters, usually the initials.

paytan: A liturgical poet (see *piyyut*).

pilpul: In Talmudic and rabbinic literature a clarification of a difficult point. Later the term came to denote a sharp dialectical distinction or, more generally, a certain type of Talmudic study emphasizing dialectical distinctions and introduced into the Talmudic academies of Poland by Jacob Pollak in the sixteenth century. Pejoratively, the term means hairsplitting.

piyyut (pl. *piyyutim*): A Hebrew liturgical poem. The practice of writing such poems began in Palestine probably around the fifth century C.E. and continued throughout the ages, enriching the Jewish Prayer Book.

sefirah (pl. *sefirot*): A technical term in Kabbalah, employed from the twelfth century on, to denote the ten potencies or emanations through which the Divine manifests itself.

selihah (pl. *selihot*): A special type of *piyyut* begging mercy and pardon for sin.

Glossary of Hebrew Terms

Shechinah: A term used to denote the presence of God in the world, in the midst of Israel, or with individuals. In contrast to the principle of divine transcendence, *Shechinah* represents the principle of divine immanence.

Talmud: The title applied to the two great compilations, distinguished as the Babylonian Talmud and the Palestinian Talmud, in which the records of academic discussion and of judicial administration of post-Biblical Jewish law are assembled. Both Talmuds also contain Aggadah or non-legal material.

Tanna (pl. **Tannaim**): Any of the teachers mentioned in the Mishnah, or in literature contemporaneous with the Mishnah, and living during the first two centuries C.E.

Targum (pl. **Targumim**): The Aramaic translation of the Bible. There are three Targumim to the Pentateuch: Targum Onkelos, Targum Jonathan, and Targum Yerushalmi.

Taryag Mitzvot: A term denoting the 613 commandments traditionally included in the corpus of Jewish law.

tefillin: Two black leather boxes, fastened to leather straps, worn on the arm and head by an adult male Jew, especially during the weekday morning prayer. The boxes contain portions of the Pentateuch written on parchment.

teḥinnah (pl. *teḥinnot*): Private devotions recited by the individual as a supplement to the standard congregational liturgy. Devotional books in Yiddish, intended for women, also came to be known as *teḥinnot*.

Torah: In its narrowest meaning, the Pentateuch. Torah is also known in Judaism as the Written Law. In its broader meaning, Torah comprises as well the Oral Law, the traditional exposition of the Pentateuch and its commandments developed in the late Biblical and post-Biblical ages. In its widest meaning Torah signifies every exposition of both the Written and the Oral Law, including all of Talmudic literature and its commentaries. The term is sometimes used also to designate the scroll of the Pentateuch read in the synagogue service.

Glossary of Hebrew Terms

tzitzit: Threads intertwined with blue cords, the wearing of which on the corners of garments is ordained by Biblical law (Numbers 15:37–41).

yeshivah (pl. ***yeshivot***): A traditional Jewish school devoted primarily to the study of the Talmud and rabbinic literature.

Index

Abba Mari ben Moses Ha-Yarḥi (Don Astruc de Lunel), 66–73, 77, 85n, 86, 88n, 89, 90, 94
Abba Mari Sen Astruc, 118, 151n
Abbahu, Rabbi, 48n, 103n, 225
Abner (Alphonoso) of Burgos, 66, 109–11, 126, 127, 242
Abraham bar Ḥiyya, 12n
Abraham ben David (Ravad II), 11, 117
Abraham ben Isaac of Granada, 196, 197, 200
Abraham ben Solomon of Torrutiel, 282
Abrahams, I., 182n
Abravanel, Isaac, 100n, 117, 128, 162n, 281–89
Abravanel, Joseph, 284n
Abravanel, Samuel, 197n
Abulafia, Abraham, 27–39, 41n, 42n, 43, 44n, 55, 56, 117, 162, 267
Abulafia, Todros, 64n
Aderabah, 87
Adnei Kesef, 116n, 117n
Adret, Solomon ben Abraham, 38, 59, 60n, 61, 62n, 65, 67–77, 85, 86, 88, 89, 90, 93, 94, 95, 98, 99, 151, 154, 155, 162, 254
Agudah, Sefer Ha- (Alexander Ha-Kohen), 146n
Aḥad Ha-Am (Asher Ginzberg), 257
Aharon Ha-Levi, 67n
Akedat Yitzḥak, 57n, 128, 257–58, 260
Akiba, Rabbi, 91n, 122, 196
Akrish, Isaac, 188n
Al Tehi Ka-Avotecha, 188, 245, 251n
Alami, Solomon, 167n, 168–70, 176, 181
Alashkar, Moses, 100n, 200n
Albalag, Isaac, 11n, 99–108, 109, 117, 133n, 157, 192, 201, 208, 225
Albalag und seine Übersetzung des Maḳazid Al-Gazzalis (H. Auerbach), 99n
Albertus Magnus, 158
Albo, Joseph, 233–39, 241, 255, 285
Alconstantini, Solomon, 168n
Aldabi, Meir ben Isaac, 158–62, 169
Alemanno, Yoḥanan, 117, 118
Alexander of Aphrodisias, 134, 243, 248
Alexander of Macedon, 151n, 161
Alexander Ha-Kohen (Zusslein of Frankfurt-am-Main), 146n
Al-Farabi, 7n, 93
Alfasi, 7, 22
Alfonso V, 284
Alfonso X, 166n
Alfonso XI, 171
Al-Ghazali, 6n, 99, 100, 104, 105, 109, 126, 126n, 209n, 229, 250n, 260n
Alguadez, Meir, 182, 188, 247
Alḥarizi, Jehudah, 278
Alilot Devarim, 65n, 271–77, 278, 279
Ammudei Ha-Avodah (Landshuth), 145n
Ammudei Kesef, 116n
Anak (Solomon Ibn Gabirol), 30
Anatoli, Jacob, 60, 61, 63n, 72, 73, 88, 118, 256
Antike Judentum, Das (Max Weber), 31n
Anti-Lipmanniana, 150n
Anusim, 176, 177, 186, 187. See also Marranos
Aquinas, Thomas, 135n, 182, 255n
Arama, Isaac, 57n, 128, 257–60, 261, 270, 285
Arbaah Turim, 154, 155n
Ardutial, Shemtov Ibn Isaac, 153
Aristotle, Aristotelianism, 9, 11, 22, 23, 28, 31, 32, 33, 35, 47, 56, 59, 60, 61, 63, 64, 66, 67n, 69, 100, 103, 104, 105, 107, 110, 115, 116, 117, 119n, 122, 123, 124, 131, 132, 133, 134, 135, 138, 152n, 156, 159,

Index

161, 162, 176, 179, 188, 191, 197, 200, 202, 204, 205, 206, 207, 208, 209, 210, 211, 223, 224, 227, 229, 243, 244, 246, 247, 248, 249, 252, 256, 259, 271
Arlotus de Prato, 244n
Armengaud, Blaise, 152
Ars Poetica (Horace), 180
Asarah Kelei Kesef, 77n, 116n
Asher ben Yeḥiel (Rosh or Asheri), 77, 84, 86, 87, 99, 151, 152, 153, 154, 158, 159, 175, 254
Astruc Raimuch (Francisco Dios Carne), 179, 181
Auerbach, H., 99n
Auswahl Kabbalistischer Mystik, 12n, 34n
Averroes (Ibn Roshd), 5, 63, 67n, 69, 93, 99, 101n, 107n, 114n, 122, 125n, 126, 127, 131, 133, 136, 179, 243, 248, 249, 250n, 251n, 254, 270n
Avicenna (Ibn Sina), 92, 101n, 126
Avkat Rochel, 56n
Avnei Zikkaron, 85n
Avodat Ha-Kodesh (Meir Ibn Gabbai), 162n, 245n
Azriel, 13–16, 21, 24, 46n, 56

Bacher, Wilhelm, 116n
Back, S., 80n, 234
Baeck, Leo, 63n, 64n
Baer, Fritz (Yitzḥak), 26n
Bahir, Sefer Ha-, 11–12, 12n, 19n, 29, 50n, 200, 201, 255
Baḥya ben Asher, 155, 156
Baneth, Eduard B., 82n
Bar Kappara, 122
Baruch She-Amar, 150n
Battei Ha-Nefesh Veha-Leḥashim, 63, 64n, 101n
Bedek Ha-Bayyit, 67n
Bedersi, Abraham, 91
Bedersi, Yedaiah. *See* Yedaiah Ha-Penini
Beḥinat Olam, 96–98
Beiträge zur Geschichte der Kabbala (Jellinek), 13n
Bereshit Rabbah, 48n
Berit Menuḥah, 196, 197n
Bernfeld, Simon, 43n
Bet Ha-Beḥirah, 89, 90
Bet Ha-Midrash, 27n, 29n, 36n

Bibago, Abraham ben Shemtov, 254–57, 285
Biseliches, Mordecai, 4n, 69n
Bittul Ikkerei Ha-Notzerim, 203n, 244n
Blitz, Yekutiel, 139
Bloch, Ph., 206n
Bloch, S., 93n
Boethius, 179, 255n
Bonafed, Solomon ben Reuben, 179–82
Bonafos, Shealtiel, 179
Bonastruc de Porta, 21. *See also* Naḥmanides
Bonfils, Immanuel ben Jacob, 151
Bongoron, David Bonet, 187, 188
Borisov, A., 10n
Botarel, Moses, 195
Brody, Heinrich, 196n, 203n
Broydé, Isaac, 10n
Brüll, Nehemiah, 158n
Bruna, Israel, 147, 148, 148n
Buber, Solomon, 90n

Carmoly, Eliakim, 63n
Caslari, Abraham and Moses, 126
Catalogue des actes de Jaime I, Pedro III, et Alfonso III, rois d'Aragon, concernant les Juifs, 67n, 168n, 170n
Charles VIII, 284
Christiani, Pablo, 26, 173
Claudius, 71
Cohen, Jacob, 190n
Cohen, Samuel, 128n
Cohen, Saul, 284n, 285n
Colon, Joseph, 148
Columbus, Christopher, 281
Copernicus, 71, 226
Cordovero, Moses, 45n, 46n
Crescas' Critique of Aristotle (Wolfson), 206n
Crescas, Ḥasdai, 166n, 168, 175n, 188, 189, 202–26, 227, 228, 231, 233, 234, 235, 237, 245, 246, 252, 271, 283
Crescas Vidal of Marseilles, 65
Crescas Vidal of Perpignan, 69, 70, 71

Daat Elohim (Bernfeld), 43n
Daniel, Book of, 156, 287
Dapiera, Meshullam, 13n

Index

Dapiera, Solomon, 196, 203
David ben Abraham, 59
David ben Daniel, 59
De Anima, 247n
De Arte Cabalistica, 36n
De remediis, 152
De rerum natura, 103n
Delmedigo, Elijah, 128n
Delmedigo, Joseph Solomon, 128, 162n
De Messua Ej usque Adventu Praeterito (Nicholas de Lyra), 242n
Deot Ha-Pilosofim. See *Tikkun Deot Ha-Pilosofim*
Derashot Ha-Torah (Shemtov ben Joseph), 270n
Derech Emunah, 13n, 255
Deuteronomy, Book of, 284n
Devarim Atikkim, 115n
Disputatio contra Lipmanni Nizzachon, 150n
Divrei Ḥefetz, 129n, 180n
Don Chasdai Creskas religionsphilosophische Lehren (Joel), 206n, 234n
Donin, Nicholas, 173
Dor Dor Ve-Doreshav (Weiss), 67n, 80n, 81n, 90n, 146n, 155n, 162n, 168n, 203n, 228n
Dubnow, S., 285n
Dukes, Leopold, 92n
Duns Scotus, 255n
Duran, Profiat (Efodi), 168n, 182n, 185n, 186–93, 195, 203, 230, 245, 251n
Duran, Simeon bar Tzemaḥ, 117, 189n, 228–33, 234, 235, 239, 255
Duran, Simeon ben Joseph An-, 61n, 62n, 88n, 89n, 91n, 94

Ecclesiastes, Book of, 136n
Écrivains juifs français, Les (Renan-Neubauer), 90n, 91n, 92n, 93n, 116n, 119n, 126n, 129n, 152n, 190n, 243n
Edut, Sefer Ha-, 38n
Egers, J., 180n
Eisenstein, J. D., 189n
Eleazar of Worms, 15, 24, 25, 26, 29, 83, 84n, 159, 201
Elements (Euclid), 71
Eliezer, Rabbi, 122
Eliezer of Chinon, 152

Elisha ben Abuyah, 91, 232
Emek Ha-Bacha, 149n
Emunot, Sefer Ha- (Shemtov ben Shemtov), 12n, 100n, 144n, 199–201
En Ha-Kore, 244, 245n
Eppenstein, S., 7n
Ersch und Gruber Lexikon, 244n
Erter, Isaac, 275
Eshkol, Sefer Ha-, 150n
Essenes, 43
Ethics (Aristotle), 116, 119n, 188, 245n, 246, 247, 250, 283
Ethics (Spinoza), 209n, 223n
Euclid, 71, 122
Eusebius, 255n
Even Boḥan (Shemtov Ibn Shaprut), 173
Ezekiel, Book of, 26
Ezer Ha-Dat (Isaac Ibn Pulgar), 110–12
Ezer Ha-Emunah (Moses Ha-Kohen of Tordesillas), 172
Ezra (Kabbalist of Gerona), 13

Falaquera, Shemtov ben Joseph, 4–9, 150n
Farissol, Abraham, 273
Ferdinand (King of Naples), 284
Ferdinand (King of Spain), 277, 281
Ferrer, Vincent, 186n, 189
Filipowski, Herschell, 175n
Flensberg, H., 205n, 234
France israelite, La, 63n
Frances, Joseph, 96n
Franck, Adolphe, 43n
Frank-Kamenetzki, Y. D., 96n
Frederick II, 79
Freimann, Jacob, 146n, 148n
Friedlander, J. T., 190n

Galen, 64, 122
Galippappa, Ḥayyim, 198
Gan Ha-Meshalim Veha-Ḥiddot, 64n
Gans, David ben Solomon, 147n
Gavison, Abraham, 279
Geiger, Abraham, 26n, 63n, 128n, 188n
Gemara, 56, 160
Genesis, Book of, 61, 104, 136n
Gerard de Solo, 151n
Gerondi, Jonah, 67

Index

Gershom, Rabbenu, 80
Gershon ben Solomon of Arles, 129
Gersonides (Levi ben Gershon, Ralbag), 117, 128–39, 143, 144, 156, 157, 198, 200, 210, 211, 212, 213, 214, 217, 218, 219n, 220, 223, 230, 232, 249, 254, 271, 272
Geschichte der Juden (Graetz), 42n, 55n, 59n, 60n, 146n, 170n, 187n, 242n, 245n, 264n, 285n
Geschichte der Juden in Rom (Vogelstein and Rieger), 59n
Geschichte der Philosophie des Mittelalters (Stöckl), 107n
Geschichte des Erziehungswesen und der Kultur der abendländischen Juden während des Mittelalters und der neuern Zeit (Güdemann), 146n
Geschichte des Materialismus (Lange), 33n, 107n
Ghirondi, Mordecai, 156n
Gikatilla, Joseph ben Abraham, 35–36, 42n
Ginnat Egoz, 35n, 36
Ginzei Ḥochmat Ha-Kabbalah, 28n
Ginzei Nistarot, 175n
Gnosticism, Gnostics, 16n, 43, 44n
Gospels (New Testament), 148, 172, 203, 233, 243
Gottesdienstlichen Vorträge der Juden, Die (Zunz), 13n, 162n
Graetz, Heinrich, 11n, 42, 55n, 59, 60, 100, 107, 110, 146n, 170n, 182n, 187n, 203n, 242n, 245, 262, 264, 265, 266, 269, 285n
Graetz Jubelschrift (Ateret Tzevi), 35n, 37n
Gross, Heinrich, 66n, 72n, 129n
Grünhut, L., 153n
Güdemann, Moritz, 7n, 146n
Guide for the Perplexed (*Moreh Nevuchim*), 3, 4, 7, 22, 28, 35n, 41n, 58, 63, 66, 68, 72n, 74, 76, 98, 115, 116, 125n, 126, 127, 128, 143, 156, 158, 162, 190n, 200, 204, 222n, 225n, 246n, 270, 280
Guttmann, A., 10n
Guttmann, J., 228n, 230n, 234, 235n

Ḥadashim Gam Yeshanim, 10n, 47n
Ḥai Ibn Yaktan, 5

Halevi, Jehudah, 24, 30, 81n, 105, 153, 190, 200, 225, 229, 230
Halichot Kedem, 149n
Ha-Maor (Zeraḥyah Ha-Levi), 22
Hanhagah, Sefer Ha- (Sefer Oreḥot Ḥayyim), 84
Hannover, Nathan, 27n
Harkavy, A., 10n, 47n
Haskalah, 42, 252, 275
Hassagot (Abraham ben David), 11, 117
Hassagot (Moses Alashkar), 100n
Ḥatzotzerot Kesef, 65n, 118n, 119n, 121n, 122n
Haviliah, Elijah, 255n
Ḥayyei Ha-Nefesh (Abulafia), 27n, 28n, 33n, 34n, 162
Ḥayyei Olam Ha-Ba (Abulafia), 33n, 34n, 44n
Hayyun, Abraham, 281n
Hazketto, Baruch, 284n
Ḥazut Kashah (Arama), 57n, 257n, 258–60n, 270
Hebräischen Übersetzungen, Die (Steinschneider), 71n, 93n, 100n, 119n, 125n, 126n, 128n, 129n, 131n, 152n, 158n, 241n
Hegel, G. F. W., 32
Heichalot, Sefer, 255
Heller, Yomtov, 96n
Ḥemdah Genuzah, 59n
Hen, Zeraḥyah (Gracian), 22, 30
Henry de Trastamara, 172
Ḥeshev Ha-Efod (Profiat Duran), 189
Hillel of Verona, 22, 28, 58, 159
Hillel II, 231n, 243
Hippocrates, 64, 122
Historia de Prelis, 152n
Ḥochmat Ha-Nefesh (Eleazar of Worms), 25
Horace, 180
Horodetsky, S. A., 269n
Ḥovot Ha-Levavot (Baḥya Ibn Pakuda), 10n, 156
Huss, John, 149

Ibn Aknin, Joseph, 162
Ibn Aknin, Joseph (of Barcelona), 7n
Ibn Bilia, David ben Yom Tov, 157–58

Index

Ibn Danan, Saadiah ben Maimon, 278–79, 281
Ibn Ezra, Abraham, 7n, 29, 30, 93, 94, 115, 128n, 136n
Ibn Ezra, Moses, 12n, 278
Ibn Gabbai, Meir, 13n, 162n, 245n
Ibn Gabirol, Solomon, 4, 10, 11, 30, 44, 46n, 49, 51, 51n, 56, 150n, 180, 223
Ibn Habib, Jacob (Ibn Haviv), 96n, 234
Ibn Hazm, Ahmad, 68n
Ibn Jannah, 116
Ibn Kaspi, Joseph ben Abba Mari, 65n, 115–24, 125
Ibn Latif, Isaac ben Abraham, 8, 9, 19n, 42n, 45n, 56, 64, 65n
Ibn Matkah, Jehudah, 30
Ibn Musa, Hayyim, 241, 242, 243
Ibn Pakuda, Bahya, 10n, 156
Ibn Roshd. *See* Averroes
Ibn Sahulah, Isaac ben Solomon, 7n, 42n
Ibn Shaprut, Hasdai, 166
Ibn Shaprut, Shemtov, 173
Ibn Sina. *See* Avicenna
Ibn Tibbon, Jehudah, 144
Ibn Tibbon, Moses, 63
Ibn Tibbon, Samuel, 4n, 71, 72n, 73n, 144, 256
Ibn Tufail, Abu Bakr, 5
Ibn Yahya, Gedaliah, 95n, 110n, 162n
Ibn Yahya, Joseph ben Solomon, 95
Ibn Zabara, Jehudah, 90
Ibn Zarza, Samuel, 157n, 171
Ibn Zerah, Menahem, 171n
Idealist philosophy, German, 46
Idra Rabba (*Zohar*), 43
Idra Zutta (*Zohar*), 43, 46
Iggeret Hai Ben Mekitz, 5
Iggeret Ha-Gezerah, 110, 126
Iggeret Ha-Harifot, 110
Iggeret Ha-Kodesh, 23, 24n
Iggeret Ha-Musar (Alami), 167n, 168, 169, 170n, 176n
Iggeret Ha-Shemadot, 187
Iggeret Ha-Teshuvah, 8n
Iggeret Ha-Vikkuah, 5
Iggerot Ha-Rambam, 30n, 162n
Iggerot Kenaot, 5n, 58n, 59n, 62n
Iggerot Shadal, 85n, 149n

Ikkarim, Sefer Ha- (Joseph Albo), 233–39, 285
Immanuel of Rome, 30, 119, 152n, 279
Imrei Shefer, 39, 56n
Inquisition, 108, 277
Isaac the Blind, 11–12, 24
Isaac bar Sheshet, 144, 166n, 167–69, 177, 182, 198, 201, 202, 228
Isaac ben Jacob Ha-Kohen, 11n, 12n, 16–17, 30n, 201
Isaac ben Moses of Vienna, 83–84, 153
Isabella (Queen of Spain), 281
Isaiah bar Joseph, 25
Islam und Judenthum, 233n
Israeli, Isaac ben Joseph, 151
Isserlein, Israel ben Petahyah, 146, 147n, 148

Jacob bar Sheshet, 17, 18, 19n, 21
Jacob ben Asher, 85n, 154, 155
Jacob ben Jehudah, 77
Jacob ben Machir, 71, 72, 89, 152
Jacob Ha-Kohen, 30n
James I, 202
Jaré, Guiseppe, 236n
Jaulus, H., 228n, 234
Jeconiah (Jehoiachin) (King of Judah), 161
Jehudah ben Asher, 175, 197n
Jehudah ben Shabbetai, 92
Jehudah ben Yakar, 24
Jehudah Ha-Nasi, 196
Jehudah Hasid, 15, 16, 26, 117, 201
Jellinek, Adolf J., 12n, 27n, 28n, 29n, 30, 34n, 36n, 39n, 43n, 56n, 127n, 228n, 245n, 262n, 267n
Jesus, 287n
Job, Book of, 121, 231
Joel, Manuel, 51n, 56n, 206n, 234, 234n
Joseph ben Meshullam, 273
Joseph ben Moses, 148
Joshua, Book of, 284n
Juan I, 169n
Juan II, 170n, 255
Jüdische Unterrichtswesen während des spanisch-arabischen Periode, Das (Güdemann), 7n

Kabbale, La (A. Franck), 43n
Kad Ha-Kemah, 155–56

Index

Kaftor Va-Feraḥ, 152–53
Kahal Ḥasidim, 269n
Kahana, David, 27n
Kalilah Ve-Dimnah, 173
Kallir, Eleazar, 196, 275
Kallisthenes, 152n
Kalonymos bar Todros (Nasi), 77
Kalonymos ben Kalonymos, 115n, 118
Kaminka, Armand, 180n
Kanah, Sefer Ha-, 261–70
Kara, Avigdor ben Isaac, 149
Karaites, 173, 233
Karo, Joseph, 155
Katzenelbogen, Tzevi, 100n
Kaufmann, David, 91n, 94n, 95n, 225n, 228n, 242n
Kaufmann, J., 148n, 150n
Kayserling, M., 166n
Kehillat Mosheh, 96n
Kelal Katan, 157
Kelalei Ha-Higgayon, 157
Kelimmat Ha-Goyyim, 186n, 189, 203
Kepler, Johannes, 129, 151, 226
Keshet U-Magen, 189n, 233n
Ketav Ha-Hitnatzlut, 93, 98
Keter Malchut (Ibn Gabirol), 51
Kevod Elohim (Joseph ben Shemtov), 245–54, 270
Kevutzat Kesef, 115n
Kibbutz Vikkuḥim, 181n, 188n, 245n
Kings, Book of, 284n
Kinot Le-Tishah Be-Av, 82n
Kobak, J., 59n
Kohn, S., 80n
Kore Ha-Dorot, 24n
Kuntras Ha-Mafteaḥ, 127n, 245n
Kuntras Ha-Rambam, 112n, 114n
Kuntras Taryag, 262n, 267n
Kuzari (Jehudah Halevi), 30, 190, 200, 225n, 226n, 230

Landauer, M. H., 13n, 37n, 43, 55
Landshuth, Eliezer, 145n
Lange, Albert, 33n, 107n
Last, Isaac, 77n, 115n, 116
Lattes, Isaac ben Jacob de, 68n, 90n, 128n
Lehre von der zweifachen Wahrheit, Die (Maywald), 107n
Leket Yosher, 146n, 148
Leon, David Messer, 144n, 167n

Leon, Moses ben Shemtov de, 27, 41, 42, 42n, 43, 56
Leon Joseph of Carcassone, 151n
Levi, Rabbi, 70
Levi ben Abraham ben Ḥayyim, 63, 64, 65, 101n, 110
Likkutim (Falaquera), 150n
Lipschitz, Gedaliah, 234n
Literaturgeschichte der synagogalen Poesie, Die (Zunz), 63n, 81n, 228n
Livyat Ḥen, 64–65, 110
Lorki, Joshua ben Joseph Ibn Vives (Geronimo Lorki), 182–85, 242, 243n
Lucretius, 103n
Luncz, Abraham Moses, 153n
Luzzatto, Joseph, 92n
Luzzatto, Samuel David, 149n

Maamar Al Ha-Atzilut Ha-Semolit, 16
Maamar Be-Segulat Or Ha-Naḥash, 157
Maamar Ha-Beḥirah, 126
Maamar Ha-Yiudim, 243
Ma'ani al-Nafs, 10
Maaseh Efod, 168n, 186n, 190, 191n
Maaseh Nissim, 24n
Machir bar Sheshet, 76, 77
Madda, Sefer Ha- (Maimonides), 3
Magen Avot (Simeon bar Tzemaḥ Duran), 228n, 229n, 230n, 232n, 233, 235n
Magen Va-Romaḥ (Ḥayyim Ibn Musa), 242
Maharil. *See* Mölln, Jacob ben Moses
Maimonides (Moses ben Maimon, Rambam), 3, 4, 5, 7, 11, 21, 22, 23, 24, 25, 28, 30, 35n, 41n, 42n, 50, 57, 58, 59, 60, 61, 63, 64, 66, 68, 72n, 74, 75, 76, 87, 88, 89, 93, 94, 98, 105, 115, 116, 117, 121, 123, 124, 125n, 126, 127, 128, 131, 135n, 136, 137, 138, 143, 150, 153, 154, 156, 157, 158, 159, 162, 190, 191, 198, 200, 204, 205, 206, 207, 208, 210, 212, 217, 219n, 222, 223, 225n, 230, 231, 232, 246, 249, 252, 253n, 255, 270, 271, 272, 274, 277, 278, 279, 285
Makama, 6, 112, 114, 153
Makazid al-Falasifa, 100, 109, 126n

Index

Makrei Dardekei, 244n
Malmad Ha-Talmidim (Jacob Anatoli), 60, 72, 73, 88
Markariah, Jacob, 139n
Marranos, 187, 288. *See also Anusim*
Martinez, Fernando, 174, 175, 189
Martinez, Gonzalo, 165
Martini, Raymund, 68n
Masechet Atzilut, 12n, 19n
Mashmia Yeshuah, 287, 288n
Matzref Le-Ḥochmah, 11n, 162n
Mayyenei Ha-Yeshuah, 284n, 286, 287
Me'ammetz Koaḥ, 243n
Mechilta De-Rabbi Simeon ben Yoḥai, 43n
Megillat Setarim, 162
Meir ben Baruch Ha-Levi, 145–46, 147
Meir ben Baruch of Rothenburg (Maharam), 80–83, 84, 85
Meiri, Menaḥem ben Solomon, 89–91, 94
Mekor Ḥayyim (Samuel Ibn Zarza), 171
Mekor Ḥayyim (Solomon Ibn Gabirol), 4, 11, 49, 150n
Melanges de philosophie juive et arabe (S. Munk), 10n, 47n, 125n, 209n, 234n, 244n, 254n, 270n
Melechet Perek Ha-Shir, 278n
Melo Chofnajim (A. Geiger), 26n, 128n, 188n
Menaḥem ben Abraham ben Zeraḥ, 197
Mendelssohn, Moses, 98n
Menorat Ha-Maor, 24n
Menorat Kesef, 116n, 117n, 118n
Meor Enayim (David Ibn Bilia), 157
Meshal Ha-Kadmoni (Isaac Ibn Sahulah), 7n, 42n
Metaphysics (Aristotle), 248
Mevakkesh, Ha- (Falaquera), 4n, 5–8, 9
Michael, Joseph, 203n
Michlol Yofi (Samuel Ibn Zarza), 171
Midrash Aggadat Bereshit, 12n
Midrash Ha-Ḥochmah (Jehudah Ibn Matkah), 30
Midrash Ha-Ne'elam, 42n
Mifalot Elohim, 285

Migdal Oz (Shemtov ben Abraham Ha-Levi), 162
Mikdash Meat (Moses Rieti), 100, 117
Milḥamot Adonai (Gersonides), 129–39, 143, 144
Milḥamot Adonai (Naḥmanides), 22
Milḥemet Ha-Et Veha-Misparaim, 153
Milḥemet Ḥovah, 26n, 173n, 233n
Milḥemet Mitzvah, 233n
Minhagim (*Minhagei Maharil*), 148
Minḥat Kenaot, 5n, 60n, 62n, 63n, 65n, 66n, 67n, 68n, 69n, 71n, 72n, 73n, 77n, 85n, 86n, 87n, 88n, 89n, 90n
Minḥat Yehudah (Jehudah ben Shabbetai), 92
Minz, Moses, 146
Mishkan Ha-Edut (Moses de Leon), 42n
Mishmeret Ha-Bayyit, 67n
Mishnah, 7, 55, 56, 72, 160, 263
Mishneh Kesef, 116n
Mishneh Torah (Maimonides), 7, 11, 22, 58, 153, 154, 162, 205, 274
Misl I Yazik, 31n, 210n
Mitzvot Gadol, Sefer, 153
Mivtzar Yitzḥak, 243n
Mizrekei Kesef, 117n
Modena, Jehudah Aryeh (Leo) de, 234n
Mölln, Jacob ben Moses (Maharil), 146, 148
Mordechai, Sefer, 80, 153
Mordechai ben Hillel, 80, 153
Moreh Ha-Moreh, 4n, 5n
Moreh Mekom Ha-Moreh, 13n
Moreh Nevuchim. See *Guide for the Perplexed*
Moses of Beaucaire, 118
Moses of Burgos, 201
Moses of Coucy, 153, 155
Moses of Kiev (Ha-Goleh), 162n, 261n
Moses of Marseilles, 102n
Moses Ha-Kohen of Tordesillas, 172
Mühlhausen, Yomtov Lipmann, 148–50
Munk, Solomon, 10n, 47n, 100, 124n, 209n, 234, 234n, 244n, 254n, 270n

Index

Musar, Sefer Ha- (Joseph Ibn Kaspi), 115–16, 123, 125

Naḥalat Avot, 162n
Naḥmanides (Moses ben Naḥman, or Ramban), 21–27, 41, 42n, 43, 67, 68, 110n, 129, 154, 156, 159, 173, 230, 251
Narboni, Moses ben Joshua, 5, 125–28, 156
Nathan, Isaac ben Kalonymos, 243–44
Nathan of Tronquetelle, 152
Nazir, Jacob, 12n
Nefesh Ha-Ḥochmah (Moses de Leon), 56n
Neḥunya ben Ha-Kanah, 262
Neo-Platonism, neo-Platonists, 11, 13, 16n, 56
Neubauer, A., 24n, 69n, 72n, 73n, 76, 85n, 92n, 131n, 278n, 282n
Neumark, D., 206n
New Testament, 173
Nibelungenlied, 274
Nicholas III (pope), 38
Nicholas de Lyra, 242
Nissim ben Reuben, Rabbenu (Ran), 168, 202
Nistarot Rabbi Simeon ben Yoḥai, 43n
Nittai the Arbelite, 122
Nitzaḥon, Sefer Ha- (Yomtov Lippmann Mühlhausen), 148–50, 203
Nominalists, 33n

Occam, William of, 255n
Ohev Mishpat (Simeon bar Tzemaḥ Duran), 229n, 230n, 231n, 232n, 233
Ohev Nashim (*Tziltzal Kenafayim*), 91n, 92, 96
Omer Ha-Shikeḥah, 279n
Orabuena, 183
Or Adonai (Ḥasdai Crescas), 168, 204–26, 231
Or Ha-Ḥayyim (Joseph Yaabetz), 100n, 202n, 259n, 272n, 282n, 283
Or Ha-Ḥayyim (Simeon bar Tzemaḥ Duran), 231
Or Ne'erav (Moses Cordovero), 45n, 46n
Or Zarua (Isaac ben Moses of Vienna), 84, 153

Ot, Sefer Ha- (Abraham Abulafia), 35n, 36, 37, 38n, 39
Otzar Ha-Kavod, 64n
Otzar Ha-Safrut, 63n, 92n, 171n
Otzar Ha-Vikkuḥim, 189n
Otzrot Ḥayyim, 180n, 189n

Pablo de Santa Maria of Burgos. See Solomon Ha-Levi
Palit, Ha-, 157n
Palmon ben Pelet (pseudonym of Joseph ben Meshullam), 271
Pardes, Sefer Ha- (Yedaiah Ha-Penini), 92
Pardes Rimmonim (Moses Cordovero), 45n, 46n
Parḥi, Estori ben Moses, 152–53
Parseeism, 43n
Patai, Joseph, 180n
Paul (Apostle), 203
Pedro de Luna, Cardinal (later Pope Benedict XIII), 173
Pedro the Cruel, 166n
Peliah, Sefer Ha-, 261–70
Pentateuch, 136n, 157, 192, 254n, 258n, 272
Perush Al Ha-Milah Le-Efsharut Ha-Devekut, 248, 249n
Perush Eser Sefirot, 13n, 15, 19n, 24, 46n, 56
Pesakim U-Ketavim (Israel Isserlein), 147n
Petit, Solomon ben Samuel, 5n, 58, 59, 68, 75, 88
Philip de Vitry, 130
Philip the Fair, 94
Philo, 10, 47, 56
Philosophie und Kabbala (Jellinek), 13n, 29n, 30n, 36n, 39n, 56n
Physics (Aristotle), 105, 207, 208, 246, 248, 271
Pichon, Joseph, 169n, 173
Pico della Mirandola, 129
Pinsker, S., 156n
Pirkei Avot, 90, 233n
Pirkei Rabbi Ishmael, 29
Piskei Ha-Rosh, 85n
Plato, 31, 32, 47, 56, 116, 117, 124n, 133, 176, 223, 237, 243
Plotinus, 10
Polemische und apologetische Literatur (Steinschneider), 267n, 270n
Politics (Aristotle), 248

Index

Potebnya, A. A., 31, 210n
Proverbs, Book of, 121
Psalms, Book of, 193
Ptolemy, 9, 243
Pulgar (Polkar), Isaac ben Joseph Ibn, 109–14, 115
Pythagoras, 31

Quellen zur Geschichte der Juden, 80n

Rabbi Meir ben Baruch aus Rothenburg: Sein Leben und sein Wirken, seine Schicksale und Schriften (S. Back), 80n
Rabbi Shelomoh Dapiera (H. Brody), 196n, 203n
Rabbins français du commencement du quatôrzième siècle, Les, 60n, 63n, 67n, 71n, 81n, 89n, 91n, 129n
Ramus, Johann, 129n
Rashi (Rabbi Shelomoh ben Yitzḥak), 75, 76, 77, 80, 84, 272
Ray Santo (Shem Tov), 166n
Raya Mehemna (*Zohar*), 42n
Raziel, 161, 200
Realists, 33n
Recanati, Menaḥem, 11n, 57n
Régné, Jean, 67n, 168n, 170n
Religionsphilosophie des Sohars, Die (Joel), 51n, 56n
Renan, Ernest, 60n, 63n, 67n, 71n, 81n, 89n, 90n, 91n, 107n, 116n, 126n, 129n, 152n, 166n, 190n, 243n
Republic (Plato), 116
Reuchlin, Johannes von, 36n
Reva Yisrael, 71
Rieger, P., 59n
Rieti, Moses, 100, 117
Rimmon, Sefer Ha- (Moses de Leon), 42n
Rindfleisch, 80
Rokeaḥ (Eleazar of Worms), 24, 84, 159, 201
Rosh. *See* Asher ben Yeḥiel
Rosh Amanah (Isaac Abravanel), 285
Rudolph, Emperor, 80

Saadia Gaon, 42n, 94
Sachs, S., 63n, 71n, 92n, 157n
Safah Berurah, 30n
Safrut Yisrael, 24n, 189n

Salaman, Nina, 82n
Sambari, Joseph, 24n
Samson ben Zadok, 83
Samuel bar Benveniste, 76, 77
Samuel ben Daniel Kohen, 59
Samuel ben Kalonymos, 25
Samuel ben Reuben of Béziers, 72
Samuel Ha-Katan, 122
Samuel Ha-Nagid, 166
Schipper, Ignacy, 149n
Scholasticism, Scholastics (Christian), 33, 52n, 107, 132, 135, 255n, 259
Scholem, Gershom, 12n, 13n, 16n, 24n, 41n, 42n, 201n
Schorr, J. H., 100
Seder Ha-Dorot, 278n
Seder Ha-Ḥachamim Ve-Korot Ha-Yamim (Neubauer), 24n, 85n, 282n
Sefer Alfa Beta, 150n
Sefer Ammud Ha-Semoli, 201n
Sefer Ḥasidim, 15
Senior, Abraham, 282
Septuagint, 242
Setirat Emunat Ha-Yishmaelim, 233n
Shaar Ha-Shamayim (Isaac Ibn Latif), 45n
Shaar Ha-Shamayim (Jacob bar Sheshet), 17, 19n
Shaarei Shamayim (Gershon ben Solomon of Arles), 129
Shaarei Tziyyon (Isaac Lattes), 90n, 128n
Shaarei Tziyyon (Nathan Hannover), 27n
Shalshelet Ha-Kabbalah (Gedaliah Ibn Yaḥya), 95n, 110n, 162n
Shem, Sefer Ha- (Abraham Ibn Ezra), 29
Shemtov, Joseph ben, 166n, 182n, 185n, 188n, 189, 203n, 244–54, 256
Shemtov ben Abraham Ha-Levi, 162
Shemtov ben Joseph, 270–71
Shemtov ben Shemtov, 12n, 100n, 144n, 199, 201, 202, 231, 244
Shesh Kenafayim, 151, 152
Shestokriil, 151
Shevet Yehudah, 175, 187n, 202n
Shevilei Emunah (Aldabi), 158–61, 169

Shirim U-Zemirot Ve-Tishbahot, Sefer, 28n, 149n
Shiur Komah, 156, 255
Shivhei Baal Shem Tov, 269n
Shorashim, Sefer Ha- (Saadiah Ibn Danan), 278n
Shoshan Sodot, 162n, 261n
Shulhan Aruch, 155
Shulhan Kesef, 117n, 118n, 121n, 122n
Sifra, 267
Sifra Di-Tzeniuta (Zohar), 43
Sifre, 267
Simeon bar Yohai, 39, 41, 43, 195, 196, 229, 257
Simeon ben Joseph, 151n
Simeon ben Lakish, 122
Socrates, 32, 237
Sod, Sefer Ha- (Joseph Ibn Kaspi), 116n, 118
Sod Darchei Ha-Nikkud Ve-Havarat Ha-Tenuah, 30n
Sokolow, Sefer Ha-Yovel Le-Nahum, 7n
Solomon (king), 161
Solomon bar Isaac of Montpellier, 88n, 89
Solomon ben Abraham, 66
Solomon ben Isaac of Lunel, 60n, 72, 73, 74, 75
Solomon Ha-Levi of Burgos (Pablo de Santa Maria), 182-85, 186, 188, 242
Song of Songs, 13, 138
Spinoza, Baruch, 206, 209n, 221n, 223n, 227
Spinozas Theologisch-Politischer Tractat (M. Joel), 206n
Steinschneider, Moritz, 24n, 71n, 93n, 100, 107, 116n, 125n, 126n, 128n, 129n, 131n, 152n, 158n, 180n, 186n, 189n, 196n, 201n, 233n, 241n, 248n, 254n, 262n, 267n, 269n, 270n
Stern, Z., 90n
Stoics, 44n
Sulami, Solomon, 70
Synagogale Poesie des Mittelalters Die (Zunz), 81n

Taam Ha-Kesef, 116n
Taam Zekenim, 110n, 112n, 113n, 114n, 116n, 124n
Tab al-Nufus, 7n
Tahafut Al Falasifa, 209n, 250n, 260n
Tam, Rabbenu, 75
Tamar ben Menahem, 80n
Tannaim, 265, 267
Tashbetz (Samson ben Zadok), 83n
Tashlich (Isaac Erter), 275
Techunah, Sefer Ha- (Gersonides), 129
Tefillot Rabbi Simeon ben Yohai, 43n
Telunat Sani Ve-Sansani Ve-Samangaluf (Isaac Erter), 275
Teologia, 10, 47, 124n
Terumat Ha-Deshen, 148
Themistius, 122, 243
Theophrastus, 122
Tikkun Deot Ha-Pilosofim (Albalag), 99-108
Tikkun Middot Ha-Nefesh (Ibn Gabirol), 46n
Tikkunei Zohar, 42n, 51, 51n, 55n
Toaliyyot (Gersonides), 139n
Tochahat Mateh (Isaac Nathan), 243n
Toledano, Jacob Moses, 16n
Toledot Aleksander, 152n
Toledot Gedolei Yisrael, 156n
Torat Adonai Temimah (Nahmanides), 26
Torat Ha-Adam (Nahmanides), 22
Torat Ha-Bayyit (Abba Mari ben Moses Ha-Yarhi), 67
Torat Ha-Nefesh, Sefer, 10n
Torquemada, Thomas de, 281
Torricelli, Evangelista, 208
Tosafists, 21, 67, 154, 272
Trabot, Peretz, 244n
Trastamara, Henry de, 171, 197n
Trastamara, Pedro de, 171, 197n
Tratado (Hasdai Crescas), 166n, 203, 213, 245
Triumphator vapulans sive exfulatio, 150n
Tykocinski, H., 83n
Tzedah La-Derech, 171n, 197
Tze'enah U're'enah, 156
Tzemah David, 146n
Tziyyurim (David Ibn Bilia), 157
Tzofeh Le-Bet Yisrael, Ha- (Isaac Erler), 275
Tzofnat Pa'aneah, 228n

Index

Tzurat Ha-Olam (Isaac Ibn Latif), 8n, 19n

Usque, Samuel, 187n

Ve-Zot Le-Yehudah (Blau *Festschrift*), 180n, 181n
Vikkuaḥ (Naḥmanides), 27n
Vikkuaḥ Al Nitzḥiut Ha-Torah, 236n
Vilines, 274
Vogelstein, H., 59n

Waldensians, 149
Weber, Max, 31n
Weil, Jacob, 146
Weiss, I. H., 67n, 80n, 81n, 90n, 146n, 155n, 162n, 168n, 203n, 228n
Wellescz, J., 80n
Wenceslaus (king), 146n
Wiener, M., 146n
Wiener, S., 96n
Willensfreiheit von Chasdai Kreskas, Die (Ph. Bloch), 206n
Wimpfen, Zusskind, 81
Wolfson, H. A., 206n
Wycliffe, John, 149

Xenocrates, 44n

Yaabetz, Joseph ben Ḥayyim, 100n, 117, 202n, 203n, 259n, 272n, 282–83
Yad Ha-Ḥazakah, 162. See also *Mishneh Torah*
Yad Va-Shem Le-Zecher Avraham Zalman Freiduss, 173n
Yareaḥ, Sefer Ha- (Abba Mari ben Moses Ha-Yarḥi), 66n, 67n

Yashar, Sefer Ha- (Abraham Abulafia), 36
Yedaiah Ha-Penini (Yedaiah Bedersi), 91–98
Yeḥiel of Paris, 173
Yellin, D., 64n
Yeshuot Meshiḥo (Isaac Abravanel), 100n, 285n, 287
Yesod Mora (Abraham Ibn Ezra), 7n
Yesod Olam (Isaac Israeli), 151, 152
Yesodot Ha-Maskil (David Ibn Bilia), 157
Yetzirah, Sefer, 10, 11, 19n, 24n, 29, 195
Yishai ben Hezekiah ben Yishai, 58
Yoḥanan, Rabbi, 122
Yomtov Lipmann, Ha-Rav (Kaufmann), 148n, 150n
Yordei Merkavah, 34n
Yuḥasin, Sefer, 129n, 175n

Zacuto, Abraham, 129n
Zanger, M., 189n
Zeh Yenaḥamenu (Bibago), 256
Zeraḥyah Ha-Levi, 22
Zikkuk, Sefer Ha-, 236n
Zohar, 27, 30n, 39, 41–54, 55, 56, 57, 58, 195, 200, 201, 224, 229, 257
Zunz, L., 13n, 63n, 81n, 84n, 162n, 228n
Zunz Jubilee Volume (*Tiferet Sevah*), 61n, 89n, 91n, 92n
Zur Geschichte und Literatur (Zunz), 63n, 84n
Zusslein of Frankfurt-am-Main. See Alexander Ha-Kohen
Zweifel, Eleazar, 173n